John Philip Hore

The History of the Royal Buckhounds

John Philip Hore

The History of the Royal Buckhounds

ISBN/EAN: 9783337039578

Printed in Europe, USA, Canada, Australia, Japan

Cover: Foto ©ninafisch / pixelio.de

More available books at **www.hansebooks.com**

THE HISTORY
OF
THE ROYAL BUCKHOUNDS

Wm Kennedy, Huntsman   King George III   Earl of Sandwich, M B H   Princess of Wales   Prince of Wales.
ROYAL HUNT in WINDSOR PARK.

THE HISTORY

OF

THE ROYAL BUCKHOUNDS

SUBSCRIPTION EDITION.

PART I.
THE HEREDITARY OR MANORIAL PACK.
THE HOUSEHOLD OR PRIVY PACK.

PART II.
THE UNITED PACKS.
ASCOT RACES.

COMPILED BY

J. P. HORE,

AND

ISSUED BY THE COMPILER (HIS PUBLISHERS HAVING "TAKEN
THE KNOCK") AT

HIGH-STREET. NEWMARKET.

MDCCCXCV.

TO
SIR WALTER GILBEY, BART.,
IN APPRECIATION OF
HIS ANTIQUARIAN, SCIENTIFIC, AND ARTISTIC RESEARCHES
RELATING TO THE BRITISH EQUINE RACE,
THIS ASSEMBLAGE OF DOG-LATIN,
FRENCH OF STRATFORD-LE-BOW, AND OLD ENGLISH,
TOGETHER WITH THE
SINGULAR EXEMPLIFICATION OF OFFICIAL DOG-IN-THE-MANGERISM
BY WHICH THE
HISTORY OF THE ROYAL BUCKHOUNDS HAS BEEN CURTAILED,
IS INSCRIBED BY THE

COMPILER.

ERRATA.

Page 1. *For* " 100 centuries " *read* " 10."
,, 25. *For* " 1866 " *read* " 1886."
40-48. *For* " George Boleyne, Viscount Rochester " *read* " Rochford."
,, 80. *For* " August 21, 1520," *read* " April."
390. *For* " Earl of Granville " *read* " Earl Granville."

CONTENTS.

PART I.

THE DUAL PACKS.

CHAPTER I.

THE "HEREDITARY" BRANCH: EDWARD III.—HENRY VIII.

General Introduction.—Hunting "at Force."—England under Edward III.—His Prowess as a Huntsman.—Minimum Establishment of the Buckhounds.—The Huntsmen in Ordinary.—Feudal Services.—The Manor of Little Weldon held by Tenure of keeping the Hounds.—The "Hereditary" Masters and the Hunt-Servants.—Sir Bernard Brocas, First Master.—Annual Tax imposed on the Counties of Surrey and Sussex the Support of the Pack.—The First and Subsequent Payments by the Sheriffs of Sussex to the Hereditary Master of the Buckhounds.—Sir Bernard Brocas, Second Master.—William Brocas, Third Master.—William Brocas, Fourth Master.—John Brocas, Fifth Master.—William Brocas, Sixth Master.—John Brocas, Seventh Master.—George Warham, *jure* Anne Brocas, Eighth Master.—Ralph Pexsall, *jure* Edith Brocas, Ninth Master. 1

CHAPTER II.

THE HOUSEHOLD BRANCH: HENRY VIII.

General Introduction: Social State of England *temp.* Richard II.—Henry VII.—Accession of Henry VIII.—The Household Branch of the Royal Buckhounds instituted.—George Boleyne, Viscount Rochester, First Master.—The Hunt-Servants.—Their Salaries and Emoluments.—Sir Richard Long, Second Master.—Lord Darcy of Chiche, Third Master. 28

CHAPTER III.

THE HOUSEHOLD BRANCH: EDWARD VI.—ELIZABETH.

Celebrity of Hunting in England *temp.* Edward VI.—John Dudley, Earl of Warwick, Fourth Master: April 5 to November 10, 1551.—Sir Robert Dudley, Fifth Master: November 11, 1551, to *c.* August 1553.—The Household Pack *temp.* Philip and Mary.—The Hunt-Servants.—Annual Cost of the Pack.—Accession of Queen Elizabeth.—Annual Cost of the Pack.—The Hunt Servants.—Robert Dudley, Earl of Leicester, Sixth Master: May 28, 1572, to September 4, 1588.—State of the Pack to the End of Queen Elizabeth's Reign.—Dearth of Hunting Intelligence.—The Queen and Ladies in the Hunting Field. . . . 58

CHAPTER IV.

THE "HEREDITARY" BRANCH: HENRY VIII.—CHARLES I.

Sir Richard Pexsall, Tenth Master.—Sir John Savage, Eleventh Master.—Sir Pexsall Brocas, Twelfth Master.—Dispute between James I. and the Master.—Critical Affairs of the Pack.—It is abolished by Royal Warrant.—The Functions of the Office conferred on the Sergeant of the Household Branch.—Order Thereon to the Sheriff of Surrey and Sussex.—Passing Events.—The Hereditary Pack given to Charles, Duke of York.—Sir Pexsall Brocas continues to receive the Emoluments of the Office.—The Hunt-Servants.—Thomas Brocas, Thirteenth Master.—The Manor of Little Weldon, and with it the Nominal Mastership of this Branch of the Royal Buckhounds, sold to Sir Lewis Watson. . . . 80

CHAPTER V.

THE HOUSEHOLD BRANCH: JAMES I. (1603-1624).

Annual Cost of the Pack during the Reign of James I.—The Master and the Hunt-Servants.—Their Annual Salaries, Fees, and Emoluments.—Sir Thomas Tyringham, Eighth Master: July 21, 1604, to March 25, 1625. 95

CHAPTER VI.

THE HOUSEHOLD BRANCH: CHARLES I. (1625-1649).

Annual Expenses of the Pack during the Reign of Charles I., from 1625 to 1640.—The Master and the Hunt-Servants.—Their Salaries, Fees, and Emoluments.—Sir Timothy Tyrell, Ninth Master: March 26, 1625, to May 19, 1633.—Sir Thomas Tyringham (ii), Tenth Master: May 20, 1633, to January 1637.—Robert Tyrwhitt, Esq., Eleventh Master: May 4, 1637, to January 6, 1651.—Reflections on Sport with the Pack from 1603

to 1640.—Hunting Horses.—Hunting Matches.—The Royal Studs.—
Deer- and Hound-Vans.—The Equerries of the Hunting Stables.
—Hunting with the Pack during the Commonwealth.—Poaching.—
Destruction of Deer.—Fate of the Royal Hunt-Servants. . 119

CHAPTER VII.

THE HOUSEHOLD BRANCH: CHARLES II. (1660-1685).

John Cary, Esq., Twelfth Master : July 7, 1661, to February 5, 1685.—
Expenses of the Pack during the Reign of Charles II.—The Master
and the Hunt-Servants.—Their Salaries, Fees, and Emoluments. . 149

CHAPTER VIII.

THE HOUSEHOLD BRANCH: JAMES II. (1685-1688).

Colonel James Graham, Thirteenth Master: March 25, 1685, to September 29,
1688.—Expenses of the Pack during the Reign of James II. . . 177

CHAPTER IX.

THE HOUSEHOLD BRANCH: WILLIAM III. (1689-1702).

James de Gastigny, Fourteenth Master : September 9, 1689, to c. July 1698.—
Reinhard Vincent, Baron Van Hompesch, Fifteenth Master: July 6,
1698, to March 8, 1702.—Annual Cost of the Pack.—Hunting in Holland.
—Hunting in England.—Fatal Accident to the King when hunting
with the Pack.—Various Accounts of the Spill, and a Poor Record
of the Runs towards the End of his Reign. 184

CHAPTER X.

THE "HEREDITARY" BRANCH: CHARLES I.—ANNE.

Sir Lewis Watson, first Baron Rockingham, Fourteenth Master.—Edward
Watson, second Baron Rockingham, Fifteenth Master.—Lewis Watson,
first Earl of Rockingham, Sixteenth, and Last, " Hereditary " Master. 203

PART II.

THE UNITED PACKS.

CHAPTER XI.

ANNE (1702-1714).

The Hereditary and Household Branches amalgamated.—The United Packs placed on the Establishment of the Prince Consort.—Death of H.R.H.—The Buckhounds Re-established and Re-organised.—Appertains to the Lord Chamberlain's Department.—Annual Expenses of the Pack.—The Huntsmen and the Hunt-Servants.—The Hounds.—The Buckhunting Season.—The Sport.—Ladies' Costume in the Hunting Field.—Sir Charles Shuckburgh, Thirtieth Master: June 6, 1703, to September 2, 1705.—Walter Chetwynd (Lord Rathdown and First Viscount Chetwynd), Thirty-first Master: October 4, 1705, to June 7, 1711.—Sir William Wyndham, Thirty-Second Master: June 8, 1711, to June 27, 1712.—George, Third Earl of Cardigan, Thirty-third Master: June 28. 1712, to June 11, 1715.—Ascot Races instituted in connection with the Royal Buckhounds.—Reflections on Sport with the Pack during the Reign of Queen Anne.—Deer.—Officers of Windsor Forest.—Ascot Races.—"Queen Anne is Dead." 216

CHAPTER XII.

GEORGE I. (1714-1727).

The Earl of Cardigan re-appointed Master of the Royal Buckhounds. November 6, 1714.—Resigns Office July 11, 1715.—No Official Master onward during the Reign of George I.—Mr. William Lowen, Senior, appointed Huntsman to the Pack.—The Hounds.—The Hunt-Servants.—The Pack re-organised.—Annual Expenses of the Establishment during the Reign of George I.—Some Records of the Runs.—Popularity of the Hunt.—Is in great Favour with the Fair Sex.—Dearth of Hunting Intelligence during the Reign of George I.—Alderman Humphrey Parsons.—Ascot Races 252

CHAPTER XIII.

GEORGE II. (1727-1732).

Colonel Francis Negus, Thirty-sixth Master, July 11, 1727, to September 9, 1732.—Annual Cost of the Pack.—Records of the Runs from 1728 to 1732.—Ascot Races. 268

CHAPTER XIV.

GEORGE II. (continued). (1733-1736).

Charles, Earl of Tankerville, Thirty-seventh Master: June 21, 1733, to June 1736.—Records of the Runs from 1733 to 1736.—Ascot Races. . 292

CHAPTER XV.

GEORGE II. (*continued*) (1737-1744).

Ralph Jenison, Esq., Thirty-eighth Master: July 7, 1737, to December 25, 1744. 317

CHAPTER XVI.

GEORGE II. (*concluded*) (1715-1760).

The Earl of Halifax, Thirty-ninth Master: December 31, 1744, to June 25, 1746.—Ralph Jenison, Esq. (ii), Fortieth Master: July 2, 1746, to February 5, 1757.—Viscount Bateman, Forty-first Master: July 1, 1757, to October 25, 1760.—Records of the Runs.—Annual Expenses of the Pack during the Reign of George II.—The Huntsmen and the Hunt-Servants.—Their Salaries and Emoluments.—Ascot Races. . . 336

CHAPTER XVII.

GEORGE III.—VICTORIA.

The History of the Royal Buckhounds stopped by Her Majesty's Ministers.—Official Dog-in-the-Mangerism.—Red Tape.—No more Official Information permitted.—Conjectures and Speculations.—No Official Information of the Buckhounds during the Reigns of George IV., William IV., and Victoria.—The Masters and the Hunt-Servants.——And " God Save the Queen ! " 372

CHAPTER XVIII.

SWINLEY LODGE . 382

CHRONOLOGICAL INDEX TO THE MASTERS, HUNTSMEN, AND HUNT-SERVANTS OF THE ROYAL BUCKHOUNDS FROM THE REIGN OF KING EDWARD III. TO THE REIGN OF H.I.M. QUEEN VICTORIA . . . 388

POSTSCRIPT . . . 391

PART I.
THE DUAL PACKS.

CHAPTER I.

"*HEREDITARY BRANCH*"—*EDWARD III. TO HENRY VIII.*

General Introduction.—Hunting "at Force."—England under Edward III.—His Prowess as a Huntsman.—Minimum Establishment of the Buckhounds.—The Ordinary Hunt Servants.—Feudal Services.—The Manor of Little Weldon held by Tenure of keeping the Hounds.—Sir Bernard Brocas, First Master.—Annual Tax imposed on Surrey and Sussex towards supporting the Pack.—The First and Subsequent Payments by the Sheriff of Sussex to the Masters of the Buckhounds.—Sir Bernard Brocas, Second Master.—Sir Rustin Villenove, Intervenient Master.—William Brocas, Third Master.—William Brocas, Fourth Master.—John Brocas, Fifth Master.—William Brocas, Sixth Master.—John Brocas, Seventh Master.—George Warham *jure* Anne Brocas, Eighth Master.—Ralph Pexsall *jure* Edith Brocas, Ninth Master.

THE hunting establishments of the kings, queens, and princes of Great Britain from the earliest to the present times form a subject so abstruse that no one has ever attempted their investigation in connection with the history of the chase. The ramifications of those establishments are so varied and complicated, that if a sporting writer were to attempt to follow up the "scent" in this historical hunt—extending, as it would do, to over a hundred centuries—he would doubtless come to grief in the progress of the "run," leaving only his ghost to be in at the death to tell the tale. In our prosaic days ghosts and dead men tell no tales, consequently the subject is a covert which, we fear, will be "drawn blank" for evermore. The days of chivalry passed away without producing a champion who essayed such a task, and lived to record the result of his researches. It may be, however, that some of those "spectre-hunters," whom so many of the mediæval chroniclers testify as having been seen in the witching hours of night pursuing the pleasures of the chase with hound and horn, set out on a historical hunt of this description. If so, it is evident the poor enthusiast came to grief, and met his fate in the pursuit of such a quarry. Truly an appalling conjecture! This infatuation must have claimed many victims, for, seek where we will, there is no important forest mentioned by the superstitious writers of old without its "spectre hunter." Yet this ghost was a popular ghost. Even Shakespeare pays homage to the venatic spirit that held its nocturnal sway in Windsor Forest. With such dire conjurations before us we must at once close our eyes, and exclude from sight the multifarious sections of the chase connected with royalty, and confine our investigations to one portion only of the hunting establishment of the reigning sovereigns of these realms, so far as it relates to the "Royal Buckhounds."

Even in this single department we find several distinct and separate elements. In the first place, there are the Buckhounds and the officers of the hunt, as officially recognised by the Lord High Chamberlain's department, the annual cost of which was defrayed by the Treasurer of the Chamber of the Royal Household. Secondly, the royal prerogative in the chase continually occurred by which the sovereign frequently augments the pack by seizing any hounds he liked belonging to his subjects, consequently we find the royal kennels "well replenished" from time to time with drafts obtained from this source. Thirdly, when a bishop or an abbot departed this world for other happy hunting grounds, the contents of the ecclesiastical kennel immediately reverted to the reigning sovereign. Fourthly, the sergeanties, that is, those estates held of the Crown by tenure of providing and keeping a certain number of Buckhounds and other sorts of dogs for the king's "disport." Fifthly, the obligations of the sheriffs of Surrey and Sussex, who were obliged to furnish certain contributions towards the cost of the pack out of the issue of those counties yearly. And sixthly, the somewhat complicated functions and privileges of the Hereditary Masters and the Household Masters of the pack, of whom the latter were nominated by the sovereign when feudal services gradually became obsolete in the sixteenth and eventually lapsed in desuetude early in the eighteenth century. Under each of these distinct sections were many subsidiary ones, as we shall see from time to time; the whole surroundings and the associations of the pack constituting a quaint picture in the history of the chase from the time when the Royal Buckhounds, *per se*, were first instituted in the reign of Edward III. down to comparatively modern times.

There is no doubt that buckhunting was a branch of the royal chase long before the time of Edward III. It seems special importance was imparted to the Royal Buckhounds in the reign of Edward III., when the pack is first specifically mentioned: "Canum nostrarum damorum vocatum buckhoundis," with a Master and other officers appointed by the king to manage it, the Mastership being a hereditary office, and exercised by the Brocas family through many generations. About this period a manifest change took place in buckhunting. Before this time the sport was a mixture of coursing and stalking the fallow deer with bow and arrow. The change referred to altered from that method to hunting the buck with hound and horn "at force"—that is to say, by rousing the quarry from his lair, laying on the hounds, and riding to them in pursuit, somewhat after the manner followed at the present time. It would be interesting to give a report of such a run with this pack in the days of the third Edward; but, alas! the fraternity of the quill, who so graphically depict such scenes in our days, did not exist until the nineteenth century was out of its teens. And are we not now referring to sporting events occurring more than five hundred years ago, during a period when pen, ink, and parchment gave way to the sword, blood, and mail armour?

Dean Hook, in his "Lives of the Archbishops of Canterbury," very truly remarks that " the domestic history of Edward III. can scarcely be said to exist, all modern historians having directed attention to the warlike splendours of his reign." Under such circumstances our task, though a labour of love, becomes a very difficult one. The game is abundant, but so wild, that we frequently find ourselves fields behind the quarry, and, alas! the scent is far from holding. The glory of this era militates and obscures the detailed records of the chase, so much so that the "imitation of war" had to give place to the genuine article—Mars, not Diana, monopolising for a great part of the time the attention of kings, princes, nobles, knights, squires, and clerics.

Merry England in the days of Edward III. was not unlike ancient Rome in her greatest prosperity—successful wars, glorious conquests, splendid spoils, brilliant triumphs; in short, our ancestors at this period might be justified in adopting the imperial motto, and place over their triumphal arches, "Antique, sublime, and alone!" Hence it happens that ordinary every-day events in England are rarely mentioned by the chroniclers of the time; local incidents of a pastoral nature were lost sight of, or eclipsed by the martial glory of the era. Notwithstanding these drawbacks we must don our hunting tabard, mount our horse, wind our horn, and seek for some information relating to the Royal Buckhounds, as the facts may happen to be occasionally inscribed "on time's backward roll."

King Edward III. was every inch a sportsman. He usually took his hounds and hawks with him wherever he went, whether at home or abroad, in time of peace or in time of war. There is little doubt that his hunting establishment was spacious, well furnished with all the accessories of the chase, and kept upon a proper footing. With one portion of it only we are now concerned—namely, the Royal Buckhounds, as reorganised and dignified by this magnificent Plantagenet monarch. For reasons given above, it is impossible to say precisely the number of hounds usually uncoupled at a meet of this pack. According to the conditions of the sergeanty, the minimum number of hounds in the pack was fifteen couples. These were probably supplemented from other sources when required. The same may be said of the hunt servants. Strictly speaking, the Hereditary branch of this pack only comprised the Master, the huntsman, the two "berners," whose duties were probably somewhat similar to the yeomen prickers of after times and the whippers-in of our own period. It is also impossible to give the nominal or the actual yearly cost of the pack. We know nothing of these expenses beyond the fact of the manor of Little Weldon, Northamptonshire, having been held by tenure of keeping the hounds, with a supplementary tax imposed on the counties of Surrey and Sussex, amounting to 63*l*. 17*s*. 6*d*. from the 36th year of the reign of Edward III. (A.D. 1362); and afterwards 50*l*. a year down to the year 1707, when those annual payments terminated. Bearing these circumstances in mind, it is safe to assume a glorious cavalcade assembled at a meet of the Royal Buckhounds in the vicinity of Windsor, when Edward III. and his illustrious Court attended there to enjoy the pleasures of the chase.

At the headquarters of this Royal Hunt yclept Windsor Forest, we find Edward III.—Dei gratia Rex Franciæ, et Angliæ, et Domnius Hiberniæ, et Dux Aquitaniæ—about this time making considerable extensions to those happy hunting-grounds. Thus we find Sir William Trussel granting to his sovereign lord and master, in exchange of other lands, certain assarts from the soil of the Forest of Windsor, Old Windsor, New Windsor, Wynkefield and Ascot, which appertained to the Castle and Manor of Windsor, in times before the said lands were brought into cultivation, with the obvious intention (sad to say) that they should be re-afforested for the benefit of the game. In like manner Sir John Brocas gave the King (for a *quid pro quo*) all his lands in Clewer, Bray, Dyneworth, and Windsor. And so on in various similar cases, which are unnecessary to recapitulate in detail. These transactions are adduced merely to show that Windsor Forest, spacious as it was in those days, was not deemed large enough for the venatic requirements of this great and mighty monarch.

Almost contemporaneous and co-existent with the institution of the Order of the Garter, the Mastership of the Royal Buckhounds partook of, and participated in, the splendour and magnificence of the age. The first Master was a grand sportsman, a distinguished statesman, and an intimate and trusted friend of the king. Apart from his official connection with the pack, he was in receipt of a grant of 50*l*. a year for good service rendered to the Crown. He was also Master of the Horse, a post of great distinction and profit; and as a soldier he was pre-eminent among the many valiant and brave men who flourished under the all-conquering sway of the triumphant Edward. Now let us picture to ourselves the brilliant scene presented at a meet of the Royal Buckhounds in those days. In our mind's eye we see King Edward in his pride of place, accompanied by the Black Prince and his wife,—who has achieved such celebrity as "The Fair Maid of Kent," through whom the Order of the Garter is said to have originated,— "time-honoured Lancaster," Lineol of Clarence, and a brilliant troop of lords and ladies, knights galore, and doubtless many a squire of low degree, who had but recently won his spurs on numerous hard-fought fields—all well mounted and eager for the chase. Besides the natives, let us glance at the foreigners of distinction who are present at the meet. The French king, a prisoner of war on parole, the Duke of Orleans, with their suites, the flower of the nobility of conquered France, are there, trying to forget their misfortune in the pleasures of the chase. How the heart of the peasant who came to see the meet must throb with national pride as he looked upon the royalty of humbled France! What pleasure he must feel as he tells his sweetheart by his side that yonder sorrel carries Ralph Earl of Eu and Guisnes, High Constable of France, and on either side she sees Charles Lord of Blois, and the Earl of Tancarville. David King of Scotland and his queen are likewise present, and likewise prisoners of war. There are other great personages at the meet among King Edward's guests upon whom fortune has not frowned, whom the fame of England attracts to visit her hospitable shores. From the East we see the King of Cyprus, from the North the Sovereign of Denmark. The reigning Duke of Bavaria, the Duke of Brabant, Sir Frank van Hall, Sir Henry Eam of Flanders, "and many great lords and knights of Almain, Gascoigne, and other countries," are also to the fore. A highly-coloured picture perchance, yet withal a faithful one without exaggeration. Such a scene was doubtless witnessed in the vicinity of Windsor in those (then rare) piping days of peace, preparatory to the Master throwing off the hounds to seek the "antlered monarch of the glen" within the confines of the Forest "full of wilde dere," with "hornes hie," the greatest that "were ever seen with eie," as old Chaucer hath it. These "grand huntings" were of frequent occurrence, upon which the king expended, says Barnes, in his "History of Edward III.," "extraordinary sums, 100*l.* one day and 100 marks the other, and so on, while the sport continued, which was both long and very diverting."

Leaving the hunting field for the present, we must now hark back, and briefly follow the fortunes of the Hereditary Masters of the Royal Buckhounds from the reign of Edward III. to the 7th year of the reign of Charles I. (1633), when the Brocas family ceased to hold the official horn of the pack.

According to a popular tradition, in the year 1066 Sir Bernard Brocas, a knight of high renown, came into England with William the Conqueror, under whom he was a great commander, and had, in requital for his military services, the selection of lands to the then value of 400*l.* per annum given him by that king. This estate he chose in Hampshire, and upon a part of it built his mansion house, calling it Beaurepaire, from a place of the appellation in France, of which his immediate ancestors were lords, encompassing it with a large moat, dug by his soldiers, which cost a mark (13*s.* 4*d.*) or two of silver. In his progeny this estate continued until the twenty-first year of Henry VII. (A.D. 1506), when William Brocas, Esq., having only two daughters,—Anne, who died without issue, and Edith, who married Sir Ralph Pexsall,—

with these two ladies the *direct* line terminated; yet from a younger branch, having their chief residence at Horton Hall, in Buckinghamshire, and who were owners of many fair lordships in that county, the succession, through Bernard Brocas, Esq., of Horton Hall, the lineal heir, was continued until the male line finally became extinct on the death of Bernard Brocas, Esq., Lieutenant-Colonel of the Hants Militia, the last of the family, November 8th, 1777.

Passing from the founder of the family above mentioned, and the three succeeding knights of the same name, we get down to the time of Sir John Brocas, of Beaurepaire, co. Hants, who served with distinction under Edward III. at the siege of Calais, in 1346. This martial knight died in 1372, and had issue three sons: (1) Sir John, who obtained in the eighteenth year of Edward III. (A.D. 1344) a grant from the King of the Keepership of Nottingham Castle for life, and died, without heirs, on the battle-field, fighting against the French, in 1349; (2) Sir Oliver,* who was Grand Seneschal of the Duchies of Guienne and Aquitaine, and Governor of Bordeaux, under Edward III., as alleged in an old MS. in French, of the laws and customs by which he governed that province, then pertaining to the English Crown. This Sir Oliver Brocas married Margaret, daughter and heiress of Sir Thomas Hever, Knight, by whom he had an only son, John Brocas, who survived his father only sixteen years, and died without heirs in 1377. (3) SIR BERNARD BROCAS, Knight, the first Hereditary Master of the Royal Buckhounds, who married, first, Agnes Vavasour, divorced in 1360; secondly, Mary, daughter and heir of Sir John de Roches, Knight, and widow of Sir John de Borhunte; and, thirdly, Catherine, widow of Sir H. Tyrrell. On the death of his nephew, John Brocas above mentioned, this Sir Bernard succeeded to the family patrimony; and, as

* He held the Manor of Apse, in Surrey, by the service of rendering fifteen bushels of malt, oats, barley, and wheat to make ale, and two bushels and a half of wheat and barley to make bread, together with a hog, or in lieu thereof 12*d*., to be distributed in alms annually on All Souls' Day, in the Manor of Apse, for the repose of the souls of the Kings of England for ever. (Ing. P. M., 37 Edw. III., No. 7.)

previously described, he was appointed by Edward III. to the office of Master of the Royal Buckhounds. About this time Sir Bernard Brocas acquired the manor of Little Weldon, Northamptonshire, which had been held of the Crown, from the earliest times, as a sporting sergeanty, under the following circumstances :—

There is no doubt that some portion of the Manor of Little Weldon, Northamptonshire, was held by the tenure of keeping the King's Buckhounds prior to this illustrious monarch's reign. Here, however, we must distinguish the difference between the tenure of *Keeping* these hounds and *Mastership* of the pack. Prior to the 36th year of the reign of Edward III. (A.D. 1362) we cannot find any authentic mention of the Master of the Royal Buckhounds in any of the various official deeds relating to the custody of the pack appertaining to the holders of the Manor of Little Weldon. This essential distinction appears to have been overlooked by Professor Montagu Burrowes in his very interesting history of " The Family of Brocas of Beaurepaire and Roche Court, Hereditary Masters of the Royal Buckhounds." In that volume (p. 264) the gallant and erudite author gives the following " List of the Hereditary Masters of the Royal Buckhounds by tenure *in capite* of Hunter's Manor, in Little Weldon, Northamptonshire :—

" 1. [?] Osborne Lovel, Chamberlain to Henry II.
" 2. [?] William Lovel.
" 3. Hamon le Venour, by grant from Henry III. in 1216. (?) Resumed and regranted to Lovel.
" 4. William Lovel.
" 5. John Lovel, ob. 1316.
" 6. Thomas de Borhunte, ob. 1340, *jure* Margaret Lovel.
" 7. William Danvers, ob. *jure* Margaret Lovel.
" 8. Sir Bernard Brocas (1363), ob. 1395, *jure* Mary de Borhunte."

Now, with reference to the first seven individuals mentioned in the above list, as having been Hereditary Masters of the Royal Buckhounds, we are unable to accept them in that capacity. We can find no confirmation or allusion to any of those persons ever having held the office of Master, although they were undoubtedly the *custodians* of a portion of the King's Buckhounds and other dogs for the time being.

In some instances they are styled huntsmen. In no instance are they called Masters. Even the number of buckhounds in the custody of the holders of the Manor varied from time to time. In the 10th year of the reign of Edward II. (A.D. 1316) the Manor of Little Weldon was held by tenure of keeping seven and a half couples of the King's Buckhounds every year in Lent. The same number is mentioned in the original Inquisition taken in the 14th Edward III. (A.D. 1340);* and in a similar document of the 40th Edward III. there are only seven couples mentioned.

It is unnecessary for us to dwell on the peculiarities of the tenure or sergeanty attached to the Manor of Little Weldon during the period it was held solely by keeping certain drafts of the King's Buckhounds and the contingent services thereof, as this part of the subject is gone into by Professor Burrows. It will be sufficient for our purpose to begin with the manor when it passed to Sir Bernard Brocas on his marriage with Mary de Borhunte. Here we are somewhat at fault in not being able to ascertain the exact date of this alliance. Sir Bernard Brocas is said to have been divorced from his first wife, Agnes Vavasour, in 1360. When he married his second wife, Mary de Borhunte, the relict of Sir John de Borhunte, is not stated in the family pedigree, as set out in Professor Burrows' volume. If the divorce did not take place before 1360 the marriage with Mary de Borhunte must have been subsequent to that date. On June 6th, 1366, in consideration of a payment of 4*l.*, Sir Bernard Brocas obtained the King's licence to permit Matilda Lovel to make a grant of the Manor

* Professor Burrows gives a copy of an undated document written in French, preserved among the Brocas family muniments, relating to Thomas de Borhunte, the holder of the tenure at this time, in which the number of buckhounds in his custody is set down as twenty-four, and six greyhounds. This does not correspond with the original Inquisition above mentioned; and it appears to refer to a later period when the tenure was altered after Sir Bernard Brocas became the first Master (*per se*) of the Royal Buckhounds.

THE MANOR OF LITTLE WELDON.

of Little Weldon, and the bailiwick of keeping the Royal Buckhounds, with the appurtenances, to the said Sir Bernard and Mary his wife for the natural term of her life; should she survive Matilda and her heirs, the manor, etc., was to revert to the said Mary; and after her death it was to go to Sir Bernard and his heirs.* She having died about the year 1381, and no claimant appearing, the manor and bailiwick, with the

---

* P. BERNARDO ⎱ R/ omnibȝ ad quos &c. salt͂m Sciatis qd̄ de g͂ra n͂ra
   BROCAS   ⎰ spali & p̄ quatuor libris quas dilcus & fidelis n͂r
Bernardus Brocas Chiualer nob̄s soluit concessione & licenciam dedim̄ȝ p̄ nob̄s & heredib̄s n͂ris quantū in nob̄ est Matiƚƚ Louel qd̄ ip̄a concedere possit qd̄ mañiū de parua Weldon ac ballinā custodiendi canes n͂ros damaricios cum p̄tui que de nob̄ tenent in capite & que p̄fatus Bernardus & Maria ux. cius tenen͂t ad t͂minū vite ipsius Marie que eciam post mortem eiusdem Marie ad p̄fatam Matiƚƚ & heredes suos reūti deberent post decessum eiusdem Marie remaneant p̄fato Bernardo & heredib̄ȝ suis tenend̄ de nob̄ & heredib̄ȝ n͂ris p̄ suicia inde debita & consueta imp̄pm et eidem Bernardo qd̄ ip̄e mañiū & ballinam p̄dc̄ā cum ptiñ post mortem ipsius Marie retinere possit sibi & heredib̄ȝ suis tenend̄ de nob̄ & heredib̄ȝ n͂ris p̄ suicia sup̄dc̄ā imp̄p̄m tenore p̄senciū similit͂ licencia dedim̄ȝ spalem̄ nolentes qd̄ p̄dc̄ā Matiƚƚ vel heredes sui aut p̄fatus Bernardus vel heredes sui ronē p̄missor p̄ nos vel heredes n͂ros Justic̄ Escactores vicecomites aut alios ballinos seu Ministros n͂ros quoscunȝ occonentȝ molestentȝ in aliquo seu g͂ᵃuentʳ. In cuiȝ &c., T. R. apud Westm̄, vj die Junii.

                et p̄dc̄ā quatuor libre solūt sunt in hañ.

Vide Patent Roll, 40 Edward III., Part I., m. 19. See also Originalia Roll (Exch. L. T. R.), 40 Edward III., Ro. 27, under "Grossi Fines." In the I. P. M., 40 Edward III. (2nd numbers, No. 40b), the tenure was for the custody of fourteen of the King's buckhounds with one man to keep them, amounting to £4 a year. This document is very faded.

custody of the King's Buckhounds, and the appurtenance, henceforth belonged to Sir Bernard and his heirs. Down to the time this deed was executed, in June 1366, we believe we are correct in saying that there is no direct evidence of the Mastership (in contradistinction to the custodianship) of the Royal Buckhounds having appertained to the holders of this manor. The details of the tenure, so far as it relates only to the custody of so many couples of the Royal Buckhounds, etc., do not directly affect the Hereditary Office of the Master of the Pack, as we shall find it hereafter established and fulfilled. Therefore the marriage settlement of June 1366 is of paramount importance, provided we may take it as fixing the date of Sir Bernard's second marriage; for if he did not acquire the Manor of Little Weldon by right of his second spouse, before the year 1366, he must have held the Office of Master of the Royal Buckhounds independently and apart from the tenure incident to the custody of the Buckhounds appertaining to that property.

Professor Burrows commits a singular mistake when he asserts that "We first hear of the salary [*i.e.*, of the Hereditary Master] being first assigned on the revenues of the Sheriff of Surrey in 1421, a memorandum of which date we find in the Brocas chest concerning a payment of part of the salary due to William Brocas from John Halle, Sheriff of Surrey."* The year 1421 was the 9th regnal year of the reign of Henry V.; and, instead of this having been the first payment to the Hereditary Master of the Royal Buckhounds, the stipend had been received by the holders of the office from the 36th year of the reign of Edward III. (A.D. 1362-63). This would be nearly five years anterior to the execution of the deed of settlement between Matilda Lovel and Mary de Borhunte, the second wife of Sir Bernard Brocas; consequently he could have no legal right to the Manor of Little Weldon and the bailiwick of the custody of the King's Buckhounds thereunto belonging, until after his

* "The Family of Brocas," p. 256.

FIRST PAYMENT BY THE SHERIFF OF SUSSEX. 13

marriage with that lady, upon whom the manor shortly after devolved.*

This brings us face to face with the first payment recorded in the Pipe Rolls of the counties of Surrey and Sussex to the Hereditary Masters of the Royal Buckhounds, which is as follows :—

(Reduced facsimile, vide Pipe Roll 36th Edward III., item "Sussex.")

This facsimile, with the contractions extended, reads as follows :—

Et Bernardo Brocas Custodi canum Regis pro Damis cui Rex concessit duodecim denarios per diem pro vadiis suis, et Waltero SuthWyke Roger Popham et Johanni Hayne quibus Rex concessit videlicet cuilibet eorum pro vadiis suis duos denarios per diem, et Johanni de Benham garcioni pro vadiis suis unum denarium et unum obolum per diem, et pro putura xxiiij canum currencium et sex leporariorum in custodia predicto [*for* predicti] Bernardi existencium videlicet pro quolibet eorum unum obolum et ferlingum per diem videlicet pro hujusmodi vadiis et putura a festo sancti Michaelis anno xxxv finiente usque idem festum proximo sequens per ccclxv dies—lxiij$^{li.}$ xvij$^{s.}$ vj$^{d.}$ per breve Regis irrotulatum in Memorandis predictis termino predicto et unam partem indenture inter prefatum vicecomitem et predictum Bernardum de receptis.

Translation.—And to Bernard Brocas, keeper of the King's buckhounds, to whom the King granted twelve pence a day for his wages;

---

* The Manor of Little Weldon, with the tenure of the custody of the King's Buckhounds, passed by marriage through the female heirs from the Lovels to the de Borhuntes, and then to Sir Bernard Brocas, subject to the settlement above.

and to Walter Suthwyke, Roger Popham, and John Hayne, to whom the king granted, namely, to each of them for his wages, twopence a day; and to John de Benham, groom, for his wages, a penny half-penny per day; and for meat of 24 running dogs and 6 greyhounds being in the keeping of the said Bernard—namely, for each of them a halfpenny farthing per day; that is to say, for such wages and meat from the feast day of Saint Michael in the 35th year ending up to the same feast day next ensuing for 365 days—63*l*. 17*s*. 6*d*.—by the king's writ inrolled in the said Remembrances in the term aforesaid, and by one part of the Indenture [made] between the said sheriff and the said Bernard concerning receipts.

In this entry it will be seen (Sir) Bernard Brocas is styled custodian of the King's dogs—viz., 24 running dogs and 6 greyhounds. The word " custodian " here was altered in 1400 to " Master," and in nearly all subsequent entries on the Pipe Rolls the latter designation prevailed.

The original word employed in the documents reciting the tenure of the bailiwick appertaining to the custody of the hounds is " damaricois," but it is never used in the same sense in the Pipe Rolls. This distinction is important, and probably indicates the change which now took place in the method of Buck-hunting "at force " with " running dogs," called Buck-hounds, in contradistinction to the method formerly employed in Buck-hunting with the " damaricois," which was a slow work.

In the following year, ended at Michaelmas 1363, Sir Bernard Brocas was paid a like sum of 63*l*. 17*s*. 6*d*. by the Sheriff of Sussex ; but for the year 1364 he only received 38*l*. 0*s*. 3*d*. The payment to him in the 39th year of this reign (1365) was increased to 85*l*. 10*s*. 11*d*., at which sum his stipend continued until the 42nd year (1368)—viz., for his wages at 12*d*. per day, the wages of Walter de Suchwyke, John Hayn, and Roger de Popham, huntsmen, at 2*d*. per day each; the wages of John Parker, groom, at 1½*d*. per day, and the keep of 40 dogs and 9 greyhounds at ½*d*. each per day for 365 days, altogether amounting to 85*l*. 10*s*. 11*d*. This increase in the hunt servants and the hounds was only temporary, for in the ensuing year (1369) the cost only amounted to 45*l*. 7*s*. 4*d*. —viz., for Sir Bernard's wages, the wages of Suchwyke and Popham, the "berners," and Hayn the huntsman, the food of 24 running dogs and 6 greyhounds, less the food of 15 running dogs and the wages of one huntsman during the 40 days of Lent, etc. Without going into full details, we may take it generally that from the year 1370 to 1373 these payments to Sir Bernard Brocas by the Sheriffs of Sussex amounted, on an average, to about 50*l*. a year, at which the charge of the pack may be said to have been established henceforward, until it was finally discontinued in the reign of Queen Anne.

During the remainder of the reign of Edward III., it is to be presumed, Sir Bernard performed the duties appertaining to the office of Master of the Royal Buckhounds, and on the accession of Richard II. he obtained from that king the confirmation of the appointment, which he held until his death, which took place in 1395, when he was succeeded by his son and heir,

SIR BERNARD BROCAS, Knight, who married Joan, daughter and heiress of Gilbert Banbury, Esq. He was the second Hereditary Master of the Royal Buckhounds, Lord Chamberlain to Anne, Queen-Consort of Richard II., and a faithful adherent to the deposed sovereign, which allegiance cost him his life; for, being concerned in a conspiracy with the Lord John Holland and others, at Reading, he took up arms with them and sought to raise forces. He was, with others, arrested by the people of Reading (partisans of Bolingbroke), and confined in the Abbey there. From this restraint the loyal prisoners attempted to escape by setting fire to some of the houses in that town; but this expedient failed, and the discovery so enraged the townspeople, "that they drew out and executed several of them instantly." But Sir Bernard Brocas was reserved for a more public execution; he was brought to London, and, as William of Worcester records in his "Annals," was hung and beheaded at Westminster (*suspensus et decapitatus apud Westmonasterium*), in January 1400. His mangled corpse was buried in the chapel of St. Edmund, in Westminster

Abbey, where the following epitaph remains round the verge of a curious tomb, adorned with his effigy, etc. :—

"Hic jacet Bernardus Brocas, Miles, T. T. quonda' camare Anne Regine Anglie, cuj' aie p. pr'cietur Deus : Amen."

The back of this tomb was filled in with the following modern inscription, which is inaccurate in some respects :—

"Here lieth buried SIR BERNARD BROCAS, third son of Sir John Brocas, who had a considerable command of Archers at the siege of Calais, in 1347, and was a lineal descendant from Sir Bernard Brocas, youngest son of the Earl of Foix, in France, who came into England with the Norman King William; and in requital for his services, had a grant of lands in Hampshire to the then value of 400*l.* a year, which he chose near Basingstoke, and thereon he built a mansion house and called it Beaurepaire. This Sir Bernard served in the French Wars, and being afterwards sent against the Moors, overcame the King of Morocco in battle, and was allowed to wear, for his crest, a Moor's head crowned with an old Eastern crown. His elder brother, Sir John, being slain in an engagement with the French, near Southampton, and his second son, Sir Oliver (who was Captain Seneschal of Guienne and Aquitaine, and Governor of Bordeaux, under King Edward III.), dying without issue, Sir Bernard Brocas succeeded to the parental inheritance both in England and France: and having married Mary, daughter and heiress of Sir John de Roche, had a large estate with her, and the hereditary post of Master of the Buckhounds; which was confirmed to him by King Edward III., and held by the family until sold in James I.'s reign. He was Chamberlain to Queen Anne, Richard II.'s Queen, and his son, a knight of the same christian name, was carver to his said Majesty. The son was one of the conspirators against King Henry IV. at Oxford, and was afterwards taken and executed at Cirencester, in Gloucestershire ; and he himself, having raised a considerable force on the same side, advanced to Reading, in Berkshire, which place refusing him admittance, he burnt a part of it, and made the rest his quarters, till on the retreat of the conspirator's forces into Oxfordshire, Sir Bernard's dispersing, he, with many of his adherents, became an easy prey to the townsmen of Reading, who executed several upon the spot, but sent Sir

Bernard to London, where he was beheaded on Tower Hill in January 1400."

During the four years in which the second Hereditary Master of the Royal Buckhounds officiated, he received from 49*l*. 19*s*. 0½*d*. to 50*l*. and 16*d*. per annum from the Sheriff of the county Sussex by right of his office towards the cost of the pack. John Napper was the huntsman; and the other two hunt servants were William and Richard Hunte.

The allegiance of this Sir Bernard Brocas to Richard II. not only cost him his life, but likewise imperilled the continuancy of the office of custodian or mastership of the Buckhounds in the family of his heirs and successors. Immediately after his execution, "jauncing Bolingbroke" appointed Sir Rustin Villenove Master of the Buckhounds, and Sir Rustin received the emoluments of the office, amounting to 41*l*. 9*s*. 3½*d*., from the Sheriff of Sussex in the 1st year of the reign of Henry IV., at which time John Napper was still the huntsman, and John Backhous and John Hunt were the two yeomen berners. And, it is a singular circumstance that Sir Rustin Villenove is specifically styled Master (*Magistro canū Regis*) —the earliest instance on record where the term Master (*per se*) occurs in any official document relating to this subject. Down to this time the two preceding Brocas were styled custodian. In some instances their office was not even mentioned; the abbreviation "cap" (= taking) certain sums of money, only being used. Who this Sir Rustin Villenove may have been we are unable to say. His appointment must have been a temporary one, as we hear no more of him after this year. It is evident he had no interest in or connection with the Manor of Little Weldon, to which the office of custodian of the Royal Buckhounds appertained, consequently the inference that the office of Master of this pack was created, and did not exist prior to the year 1362 (when the counties of Surrey and Sussex were first obliged to defray the annual cost of the Master, the hunt-servants, and the hounds), is thereby reduced to a moral certainty.

The second Sir Bernard Brocas had issue five sons, of whom the eldest, WILLIAM BROCAS, ESQ., of Denton, Yorkshire, and Beaurepaire, Hampshire, inherited the honours and estates of his ancestors, and in the 2nd year of the reign of Henry IV. (September 30, 1400 to September 29, 1401) became the third Master of the Royal Buckhounds, when he received 50*l*. 0*s*. 7*d*. from the Sheriff of Sussex by virtue of his office. He is officially styled Master of the King's dogs (*Magr̃o canū Regis*), as all the succeeding Hereditary Masters are invariably designated in the Pipe Rolls from this time onward. It seems, however, some hitch or dispute occurred concerning this office in the 27th year of Henry VI. (A.D. 1449), whereupon the Master presented the following petition to the King, in which he set forth his claims, and had his claims allowed :—

"To the Kyng and Sovain Lorde.

"Bisecheth mekely your humble servaunt William Brocas Squyer, Maister of your Bukhounds. Forasmuche that he holdith of you, and alle his Auncestres of tyme that no mynde is have holden to your noble pgenitours, the Manior of Lityll Weldon in the Counte of North', by Graunte Sergeaunte, that is to witte, to be Maister of your Bukhoundes, and to kepe xxiiij reunyug houndes, and vj grehoundes, and to fynde a yeoman Veantrer, and two yomen Berners; which Office was of olde tyme ordeyned for the pleasir and disporte of your noble pgenitours, and their successours; to the which Office soo to mayntene and susteyne, been accustumed and due certeyn wages and fees, by Statute and Ordñaunce of the Housholde of your noble pgenitours and yours of alde tyme purveyed, as hit apperith in a Cedule to this bille annexed. Of which wages and fees, the said Bisecher and his Auncestres have been paid of the issues and p'fits of the Countees of Surr' and Sussex, by the Shirriff for the tyme therbeyng, by vertue of a Warante under your Pryve Seal yearly to him made and direct, fro the tyme of your noble p'genitour Kyng Edward the Thirde, unto thre yeres last past, that the Shirref of the said Countees for the tyme beyng, seth that tyme is soo charged of othir wages and annuytees graunted by your fres patentes to othir divers psonys, that the issues and pfites of the said Countees wolle not suffice to contente the wages and fees of your said Bisecher, over the wages anunytee soo graunted to othir p'sonys; and soo your said Bisecher cannot be paid of the Shirrefez of the said Shirez for the tyme beyng, because that the said wages and fees were assigned yerely to be paid by waraunte of your Pryve Seal, and not by warant of your lres patentes: And thus he is like to lose his wages and fees aforsaid, withoute that your moost habundaunt grace be shewed unto him in this partye. Wherefore please hit unto your Highnesse, as wele tenderly to consider these pinisses, as the trewe contynuell service that your said Bisecher hath doon unto your noble p'genitours, as to your Highnesse, by th'advys of your Lordes Spirituell and Temporell beyng in this psente Parlement, to graunte unto your seid Bisecher the said wages and fees, by your lres patentes to be made in fourme, after the tenure of a Cedule to this Bille annexed; and he shal pray God for you.

"Responsio.
"Soit fait come il est desire, juxst le continue d'un Cedule a ycest Peticion annexe."*

The schedule, which is in Latin and of very considerable length, recites much of the foregoing, and says that Brocas and his ancestors, as Masters of the King's dogs, called "Bukhundes," received 12*d*. a day, a huntsman 2*d*. a day, and two whippers-in each 1½*d*. a day for their wages; and to feed the said 24 running dogs and 6 greyhounds each day ½*d*. a day from the Feast of St. Michael to the 24th day of June. But from the 25th day of June to the Feast of St. Michael following, Brocas received 7½*d*. a day in the King's household for his salary, whilst his men had their above-mentioned rates of pay, and the dogs the same allowance.

There was given, in addition, to Brocas, 40*s*. for his livery, and 13*s*. 4*d*. to each of the three hunt servants for his livery, and for their shoes 4*s*. 8*d*. each annually. These salaries, liveries, shoes, and the food of the hounds amounted, it is said, to 50*l*. a year; and the King, with the advice of the Lords Spiritual and Temporal in Parliament, and at the request of the county representatives, by the authority of Parliament, granted the same to Brocas and his heirs male out of the

* Rot. Parl., *sub anno*.

revenues of Surrey and Sussex, by the hands of the Sheriff, in equal proportions at Easter and Michaelmas. Besides the foregoing, and not included, was the wages of a "berner," for the keep of 15 running dogs during the 40 days of Lent.

From the year 1401, this William Brocas, the third Hereditary Master of the Royal Buckhounds, received 50*l.* and 16*d.* out of the issues of the county Sussex towards the expenses of his office. From the year 1400 to the year 1405 John Napper was the huntsman, and John Backhous and John Hunte were the two other hunt-servants of the pack. But in the last regnal year of Henry V.'s reign (A.D. 1422) the huntsman was Roger Kent. The stipend to the Master and his hunt-servants, 50*l.* and 8*d.*, was paid to them by the Sheriff of the county Sussex for the time being.

During the reign of Henry V. (March 21, 1413—August 31, 1422) there was no material change in the Master, hunt servants, or the cost of the pack, which was supported, as heretofore, out of the issues of the county Sussex.

From the 1st to the 17th year of the reign of Henry VI. (September 1, 1422—August 31, 1439) the same state of affairs prevailed, except that we find the names of the hunt servants recited with the Masters in the acquittances given to the Sheriff of Sussex when the payments were made. This Hereditary Master of the Buckhounds obtained a patent of the office of Master of the King's dogs, called Buckhounds, from Henry VI., in 1449, which is the earliest document of the sort we have met with, in which the Mastership of the pack is conferred in express words. By virtue of this document the Master was entitled to 50*l.* per annum from the Sheriffs of Surrey and Sussex, towards the expenses of the pack (*Pat.* 27, *Henry VI.*, *Part ii.*, *m.* 28). He died in 1456, for which year he received 49*l.* 17*s.* 4*d.* out of the issues of the county of Sussex for his salary, including the usual allowances of the huntsman, Thomas Childe, and the two hunt-servants, Richard and Peter Hunte.

This William Brocas, Esq., third Hereditary Master of the

Royal Buckhounds, was succeeded by his eldest son (by his first wife), WILLIAM BROCAS, Esq., of Beaurepaire, etc., the fourth Hereditary Master of the Royal Buckhounds.

We cannot find any payment to him recorded on the Pipe Rolls before the 12th year of the reign of Edward IV. (March 4, 1472—March 3, 1473), when he received 50*l*. out of the issues of the county Sussex for himself, his huntsman, Thomas Parker, and his two hunt servants, Peter Hunte and John Donne. Five years later the huntsman is designated as Thomas Parker, senior, of Windsor, and one of the hunt servants as Thomas Parker, junior, of Bromley. Down to the 22nd year of Edward IV.'s reign we find the same huntsman, but the other two hunt servants then were William Ingelfield and Richard Brown. The last payment to this Hereditary Master of the Buckhounds and his subordinates occurs on the Pipe Roll for the county Sussex for the 1st year of the reign of Richard III., when he received the usual stipend from the Sheriff of that county by virtue of his office. This William Brocas, the fourth Hereditary Master, died on April 22, 1484. He married, first, Agnes, daughter of Thomas Berkingham, Esq., by whom he had issue, JOHN BROCAS, his son and heir, the fifth of his family who officiated as Hereditary Master of the Royal Buckhounds. It appears from the subjoined inquisition that, owing to certain formalities not having been complied with on the demise of his father in the 1st Richard III. (A.D. 1484), the family honours and estates were in abeyance for some time; however, these legal technicalities were soon after adjusted, to the satisfaction of all concerned.

Whereas by a certain inquisition taken at Bulwek, 20 Oct 2 Ric. iij., late King of England " de facto et non de jure," before Richard Burton, the said King's escheator co. Northampton, and returned unto the said King's chancery, it was found among other things that William Brocas esq., deceased, held in the said county on the day of his death, in his demesne as of fee, the manor of Parva Weldon called " Hunters Maner," with its appurtanances in the said co. : And that the said manor was held of the said King by fealty and the service of "keeping the King's dogs called bukhoundis": And that the said William Brocas died on 22 April, 1 Ric. III., and John Brocas was son and heir of the said William, and was forty years of age : And whereas it has been made known to the present King (that though the said manor, through the death of the said William, was taken into the said King's hands by pretext of the aforesaid inquisition, and still remains in the present King's hands), the said John without due licence, presentation, or livery, &c., &c., &c., has held the said manor, with its appurtananees, from the aforesaid William, and still holds it, &c., &c. Writ to the Sheriff of Northampton to summons the aforesaid John Brocas to appear before the King in the Chancery on the morrow of St. Martin next to come, to show reason why he should not answer to the King for the issues and profits of the said manor from the time of the said William's death, &c., &c., and render homage and fealty to the King in respect of the premises.

In the 2nd year of the reign of Richard III. the fifth Hereditary Master of the Royal Buckhounds was paid 50*l*. out of the issues of the county Sussex for his own salary and allowances, and those of his huntsman, John Parker, and the two hunt-servants, R. Brown and W. Ingelfield, before mentioned. He does not appear to have received his annual stipend for the 3rd and last regnal year of Richard III.; but during the first three years of the reign of Henry VII. he was paid 50*l*. per annum by the Sheriffs of the county of Sussex. Down to 1485 Jacob Henton was the huntsman, and Richard Brown and William Ingelfield were the two berners. But in the following year (3 Henry VII., A.D. 1488) Henry Uvedale was the huntsman, and Henry Towers and John Stevens were the berners of the pack. During the ensuing two years the payments were again in abeyance; they were resumed and paid in the 6th and 7th regnal years of the reign of Henry VII., in which latter year (1492) this Master died.

Following the example of his father and grandfather, John Brocas, Esq., the fifth Master of the Royal Buckhounds, married twice. By his first wife Anne, daughter of Edward Longford, Esq., he had two sons: Edward, who died young, and WILLIAM BROCAS, his successor, the sixth Master of the Royal Buckhounds.* He married Mary, daughter of John Griffin, Esq., of Braybrooke, by whom he had issue two daughters, Anne and Edith, of whom the latter eventually became his sole heiress. This William Brocas, Esq., the sixth Master of the Royal Buckhounds, dying in the twenty-first year of Henry VII. (A.D. 1506), was succeeded by his daughters, Anne and Edith Brocas.

On the Pipe Rolls for the 9th regnal year of Henry VII. William Brocas, the sixth Master, was paid 50*l*. by the Sheriffs of the county Sussex, but we can find no payments to him for the 10th and 11th years of this reign. The stipend of his office was resumed on the 12th, and continued to be paid to him regularly and in full until the 22nd Henry VII. (A.D. 1506), in the course of which year he died. During this period Henry Uvedale was the huntsman, and Henry Towers and John Stevens were the other hunt servants to the pack.

On the Pipe Roll of the county Sussex for the 23rd (and last) regnal year of the reign of Henry VII. (A.D. Aug. 22, 1508—April 21, 1509) JOHN BROCAS, ESQ., the seventh Hereditary Master of the Royal Buckhounds, was paid the usual stipend of 50*l*. by virtue of his office by the Sheriff of that county in that year. Who this John Brocas was we cannot tell, as he is not mentioned as having ever held the office in Professor Burrows' work. At any rate, he also officiated as the Hereditary Master during the 1st, 2nd, and 3rd years of Henry VIII.'s reign (April 22, 1509—April 21, 1512), receiving 50*l*. a year out of the issues of the county Sussex by the hands of the Sheriff of that county for the time being. The hunt servants under him were the same as in the time of William Brocas, the sixth Master. We do not find any payment on account of this portion of the Royal pack inscribed on

---

* On June 16th, 1492, licence of entry without proof of age was granted to William Brocas, Esq., son and heir of John Brocas, Esq., and grandson and heir of William Brocas, and great-grandson and heir of William Brocas, all deceased. (Pat. Roll, *sub dato*.)

the Pipe Rolls of Surrey or Sussex for the following year; therefore the assumption is that the office was in abeyance until the ensuing year (5 Henry VIII.), when we ascertain that pursuant to an inquisition taken before Lambert Langtry, the King's escheator, at Rowell,* Northamptonshire, on November 3, 1506, it was proved that Anne and Edith, daughters of William Brocas, Esq., deceased, held the Manor of Little Weldon *in capite* by tenure of keeping † the King's Buckhounds, and that those ladies and their husbands were paid the usual stipend of the office amounting to 50*l*. a year, by the Sheriffs of Surrey and Sussex for the time being.‡

This inquisition was avowedly entered on the Pipe Roll in order to show the authority for the payments to be made by the Sheriffs of Surrey and Sussex to ANNE and EDITH BROCAS and their husbands. However, the only payment we have found in their joint names occurs in the Pipe Roll of the county Sussex for the 5th year of the reign of Henry VIII. (A.D. April 22, 1513—April 21, 1514), when George Warham and Rudulpho Pexsall, Masters of the King's dogs—*Magris canū Regs.*—received the usual stipend of 50*l*. by right of their office. The money was paid to them jointly. Thomas Carnevill was the huntsman; John Love and John Stevens the two berners, each of whom received the same remunerations as heretofore allowed to their predecessors in the same employment. Anne Brocas, the wife of George Warham, eighth Hereditary Master, having died childless in 1514, the Manor of Little Weldon, with the bailiwick appertaining to the King's Buckhounds, passed to her sister Edith Brocas, the wife of Ralph Pexsall, ninth Hereditary Master, who held the tenure

---

* Rothwell (pronounced as spelt above), a celebrated racecourse in the seventeenth century. See "History of Newmarket and the Annals of the Turf," vol. iii., *v.*, Index.

† In this, as in all other documents relating to the tenure of the Manor of Little Weldon, the word used is *custody* (*costod. canis damr.*) of the King's Buckhounds. It is only in the Pipe Rolls that the word "Master" is employed. This seems to confirm the assumption that the Mastership did not merge into the tenure before the first payment through the Sheriff of Sussex in 1363.

‡ Pipe Roll, 5 Henry VIII. *Item. Adhuc Sussex, dorso.*

appertaining to that manor and the Hereditary Mastership of the Royal Buckhounds by right of his wife's inheritance. He received the usual stipend of the office out of the issues of the county Sussex in the 7th and 11th, and from the 12th to the 18th years of the reign of Henry VIII. in full;* but from the 19th to 25th ensuing years his payments were intermittent—a portion on account varying from 22*l*. 4*s*. 10*d*., to 27*l*. 0*s*. 2*d*. per annum, and in addition the arrears overdue in some cases—and from the 26th to the 29th years following he does not appear to have obtained any payment whatever from the Sheriffs of the counties of Surrey or Sussex. However, in the 30th regnal year of the reign of Henry VIII. (A.D. April 22, 1539—April 21, 1639) he was paid 50*l*. in full by the Sheriff of the county of Sussex, which is the last payment recorded to him as Master of the Royal Buckhounds that is entered on the Pipe Rolls. At this time Reginald Hannington was the huntsman; Hugh Carter and Thomas Jordan were the berners, each of whom were in receipt of the same fees and emoluments as their predecessors in office—viz., George Hunt, John Bland, and John Chenry.

Apparently Miss Anne Brocas carried the official insignia of the Royal Buckhounds about the time Henry VIII. ascended

---

* Referring to the joint Mastership about this time Professor Burrows remarks: "From the joint petitions of the two husbands of the two wards we were able to obtain some clue to an obscure portion of the family history. But not only were the arrears petitioned for never paid, but in the ninth, tenth, and eleventh years of Henry VIII. the Sheriff still continued to refuse payment, and Pexsall appears to have obtained no redress. We may, however, suppose that these difficulties now came to an end, for we hear no more of them." ("Family of Brocas," p. 258.) This deduction does not correspond with the Pipe Rolls, which Professor Burrows has apparently not consulted, and consequently he missed the best official information on the point. We do not advert to this in any way reflecting on the learned author's lack of investigation, as it would be preposterous to expect the Chichele Professor of Modern History at the University of Oxford to waste the time and put up with the indignities which the search would now (1866) involve at the Public Record Office. Upon this search alone the writer was occupied for six months. If the documents had been in the British Museum it could have been accomplished in six days.

the throne.* On the death of her father, which appears to have taken place in 1506, she and her sister Edith were given in wardship to John Audley, Thomas Cobham, and Anthony Wingfield. We hear nothing of her family again until July 16, 1512, when Anne Brocas, Ralph Pexsall, and Edith, his wife, obtained licence to enter upon the Manor of Little Weldon, Northampton, and on the office of keeping the King's Buckhounds—*ac in offic'm custodiend' canes n'str's damarum*—as held by William Brocas, deceased, *temp.* Henry VII. Miss Anne Brocas married George Warham, Esq.; but she appears to have died in 1514, as on December 16 of that year Ralph Pexsall and Edith, his wife, who had become her sister's heir, and Hereditary Master (or Mistress) of the Buckhounds, obtained livery of the Manor of Parva Weldon, otherwise "hunter's manor," Northampton, and the property of the said Anne; of the manor and other premises in Weldon; of the office of keeper of the King's Buckhounds, and the profits thereof; and of all possessions held to the use of them and their heirs. This Miss Edith Brocas having married Ralph Pexsall, Esq., he, by virtue of his wife's inheritance, became jointly with her the nominal Master of the Buckhounds to Henry VIII. at this portion of his reign. Pexsall seems to have found favour with the king and the cardinal; was a J.P. for several counties, and was appointed, with others, at various times, a commissioner to collect the subsidy in Hampshire. He was likewise appointed a teller of the royal wardrobe, and had an appointment in Wolsey's train, when the suite of his Eminence almost excelled that of the king. He was Sheriff of Hants in 1527, 1529, and 1530. On March 6, 1522, he was appointed Clerk of the Crown in Chancery, with a salary of 20*l.* a year and a livery similar to Richard Sturgeon and Thomas Ive, his predecessors in office, *temp.* Henry VII. The following year he obtained a "corrody" in St. Mary's monastery, Thetford. On January 26,

---

* At the present time there are two ladies in France who own and hunt their own packs of staghounds—viz., the Duchesse d'Uzès, in the vicinity of Rambouillet forest, and Mme. Quimet, from her château in the Saône-et-Loire.

1532, he was among the witnesses present when Henry VIII. took the Great Seal from the custody of Thomas Audley, and, after holding it for a quarter of an hour, " returned it to the custody of the said Thomas Audley, appointing him Chancellor of England." About this time Ralph Pexsall seems to have disposed of the reversion of his office of Clerk of the Crown to Thomas Pope, including his livery of a fur robe of office, which he obtained annually from the Great Wardrobe. This is the last reference we have found of this joint Hereditary Master of the Royal Buckhounds. He died c. 1540. By Edith, his wife, who died in 1517, he had issue two sons, John Pexsall, Esq., who died without heirs, and Sir Richard Pexsall, knight, the tenth Hereditary Master of the Buckhounds, whose demise occurred in the 13th year of Queen Elizabeth's reign, A.D. 1571.

CHAPTER II.

HOUSEHOLD BRANCH—HENRY VIII.

General Introduction.—Social State of England *temp*. Richard II.—Henry VII.
—Accession of Henry VIII.—The Household Branch of the Royal Buckhounds instituted.—George Boleyne, Viscount Rochester, First Master.—
The Hunt Servants : their Salaries and Allowances.—Sir Richard Long,
Second Master.—Lord Darcy, of Chiche, Third Master.

THE rural history of England during the fifteenth century is almost unknown. From the deposition of Richard II., in 1399, until a few years before the accession of Henry VIII., in 1509, we find a sanguinary era, one of the saddest to be found in the annals of any civilised country. Yet in those rare and short intervals of peace and prosperity that intervened, the rural sports so characteristic of our country are occasionally mentioned incidentally by contemporary chroniclers.* We may, therefore, deduce that the innate love for field sports,

* It is recorded by Holinshed that Richard II., his Queen, John, Duke of Lancaster, the Duke of York, Thomas Woodstock, Duke of Gloucester, the Archbishop of York, the Earl of Arundel, the Earl of Huntingdon, "with other bishops, lords and ladies a great many," assembled at Leicester, about the Feast of St. Peter and Vincent, 1389, to hunt in the forest and all the parks appertaining to the said Duke of Lancaster. Holinshed also attests that Edward IV. indulged in the pleasures of the chase whenever a favourable opportunity presented ; and he further specifically mentions that "in the summer the last he ever saw [A.D. 1483], his highnesse, being at Windsore in hunting, sent for the maior and aldermen of London to him, for none other errand but to have them hunt and be merry with him ; when he made them not so stately, but so friendly and so familliar cheare, and sent venison from thence so freely into the city, that no one thing in many dayes before gat him either more hearts or more hearty favor among the common people, which ofentimes more esteeme and take for the greater kindness a little courtesie than a great benefit."

which has at all times been prominently associated with the inhabitants of this country, though latent in those days of civil strife, was not extinguished. Unfortunately, the field of battle in a great measure supplanted the pleasures of the hunting-field; consequently it is impossible to give any succinct account of the progress of the chase in a general way, or of the Royal Buckhounds and their Masters during the fifteenth century. We are unaware of any records or similar documents to which we can apply for information relating to details of the hunting establishments of the fourth, fifth, and sixth Henrys, of the fourth and fifth Edwards, of Richard III., or of Henry VII.; nevertheless, there is little doubt that those royal venatic establishments were sustained as efficiently as the disjointed times and adverse circumstances permitted. It is to be presumed the Hereditary Masters of the Buckhounds continued to fulfil their normal duties, provided always the holder of horn was loyal to the reigning sovereign. But to act thus he must have been a partisan of the House of York or of the House of Lancaster in turn, as the White or the Red Rose faction ruled the realm. To do so he would have to adopt the policy of the Vicar of Bray, which would be repugnant to the hot Norman blood of the lords of Beaurepaire. Bearing in mind these discordant circumstances, and in the absence of any precise information on the point, it can only be assumed, with all reserve, that the succeeding Hereditary Masters of the Buckhounds, who are mentioned in the preceding chapter, continued to exercise their functions until that time, when George Boleyne, Viscount Rochester, was appointed Master of that portion of the Royal Buckhounds appertaining to the Household, by his brother-in-law, in December 1528.

But, as previously mentioned, sport with the Royal Buckhounds in those unsettled times must have been very intermittent. The same may be said with regard to the numerous packs that were found to be dispersed throughout the country. The great feudal barons and the lord abbots emulated kings and princes in the extent and efficiency of the hunting establishments which they kept up. The appalling consequences of the civil war frequently spoiled the sport, and often rendered hunting altogether out of the question. The history of those dark days is too well known to require much notice at our hands; but, in order to show how difficult it was to enjoy the pleasure of the chase, a brief allusion to the fate of some of the prominent sportsmen of this period, who kept vast hunting establishments at their feudal seats, may not be out of place.

In the course of that long and terrible contest thirteen pitched battles were fought, three kings met with untimely ends, eighty princes of the blood had fallen, and twenty-six Knights of the Garter perished either by the sword or by the hand of the executioner. The ancient nobility of England was almost entirely annihilated. Of the royal house of Plantagenet, Richard, Duke of York, and his son, the Earl of Rutland, were slain at the battle of Wakefield; the Duke of Clarence died the death of a traitor; Edward V. and his brother, the Duke of York, were murdered in the Tower of London; and, lastly, their uncle, Richard III., was killed at Bosworth. Of the House of Lancaster, King Henry VI. perished mysteriously in prison; his son Edward, Prince of Wales, was slain at Tewkesbury. Of the kindred of Queen Elizabeth Woodville, the consort of Edward IV., her father, Richard, Earl Rivers, and her brother, Sir John Woodville, were beheaded at Northampton; her husband, John, Lord Grey of Groby, fell at the second battle of St. Albans; her son, Sir Richard Grey, was beheaded at Pomfret; and on the same scaffold perished her brother, the accomplished Anthony Woodville, Earl Rivers. Of the royal house of Beaufort, Edmund, Duke of Somerset, formerly Regent of France, was slain at the first battle of St. Albans; Henry, the second duke, was beheaded after the battle of Hexham; Edmund, the third duke, was beheaded after the battle of Tewkesbury; and in the same battle was slain Sir John Beaufort, son of the first duke. Of the great house of Stafford, Humphrey, Earl of Stafford, fell at the first battle of St. Albans; his father, Humphrey, Duke of Buckingham, fell at the battle of

Northampton; Henry, the second duke, was beheaded at Salisbury; and of another branch of the Staffords, Humphrey, Earl of Devon, perished on the scaffold at Bridgewater. Of the house of Neville, Richard, Earl of Salisbury, was beheaded after the battle of Wakefield; his sons, Richard, Earl of Warwick, the "Kingmaker," and John, Marquis of Montagu, fell at Barnet; a third son, Sir Thomas Neville, fell at Wakefield; Sir John Neville was killed at the battle of Towton; Sir Henry Neville, son and heir of Ralph, Lord Latimer, was beheaded after the battle of Banbury; and Sir Humphrey Neville and his brother Charles, after the battle of Hexham. Of the Percys, Henry, second Earl of Northumberland, one of the heroes of Agincourt, fell at the first battle of St. Albans; two of his gallant sons, Henry, the third earl, and Sir Richard Percy, were slain at Towton; a third son, Thomas, Lord Egremont, perished at the battle of Northampton; and a fourth son, Sir Ralph Percy, at Hedgerley Moor. Of the house of Talbot, John, second Earl of Shrewsbury, and his brother, Sir Christopher Talbot, were slain at Northampton; their kinsman, Thomas Talbot, Lord Lisle, fell in a skirmish at Wotton-under-Edge. Of the Courtnays, Thomas, sixth Earl of Devon, was beheaded after the battle of Towton; Henry, the seventh earl, was beheaded at Sarum; and at Tewkesbury was slain their only remaining brother, the eighth earl. Of the De Veres, John, twelfth Earl of Oxford, and his eldest son, Sir Aubrey de Vere, perished together on the scaffold on Tower Hill. Of the Cliffords, Thomas, the eighth lord, was slain at the first battle of St. Albans; and his son John, the ninth lord, at the battle of Towton. Of the house of Hungerford, Robert, third Baron Hungerford, was beheaded after the battle of Hexham; and his heir, Sir Thomas Hungerford, was beheaded at Salisbury. Of the Bourchiers, Humphrey, Lord Cromwell, was slain at the battle of Barnet; and Sir Edward Bourchier, brother of Henry, Earl of Essex, at Wakefield. Lastly, of the house of Welles, there perished the representatives of three generations: Leo, Lord Welles, was slain at the battle of Towton; his son Richard, Lord Welles and Willoughby, and his grandson, Sir Robert Welles, severally perished by the axe of the executioner. Long as is this catalogue of slaughtered heroes, there might be appended many other and no less illustrious names. At the battle of Blorcheath was slain James Touchet, Lord Audley; at the battle of Northampton, John, Viscount de Beaumont; at Wakefield, William Bonville, Lord Harrington; at Tewkesbury, John, Lord Wenlock; at Towton, Ranulph, Lord Dacre of Gillesland; and at Bosworth, John Howard, Duke of Norfolk, and Walter Devereux, Lord Ferriers of Chartley. Lastly, on the scaffold perished William Herbert, Earl of Pembroke; John Tiptoft, Earl of Worcester; James Butler, Earl of Wiltshire; William Bonville, Lord Bonville; William, Lord Hastings; Sir Owen Tudor, grandfather of Henry VII.; and Sir Bernard Brocas, second Hereditary Master of the Royal Buckhounds, under the circumstances mentioned in the preceding chapter. The ancient nobility had been almost entirely annihilated; and in the renowned and powerful Earl of Warwick, who is said to have feasted at his board, in the different manors and castles he possessed, upward of thirty thousand persons, there had fallen the greatest and the last of those mighty barons by whom the Crown had in former times been checked and overawed. Such, indeed, had been this deluge of noble blood in the field or on the scaffold that Henry VII. could find only twenty-eight temporal peers to summon to his first Parliament; and such the change effected by it, in a political sense, on the management of public affairs, that the accession of the first Tudor is considered the origin of the modern system, and from it the constitutional historian of England, notwithstanding all the charters and acts to be found in the statute-book prior to this time, has dated the commencement of his history.

This fearful picture of the state of the country in those days supplies a sufficient excuse for the barrenness of our subject during this unhappy period. With the union of the Houses of York and Lancaster by the marriage of Henry VII. with Elizabeth of York a happier state of affairs ensued.

The king now inaugurated a new policy, and a wise one, by abolishing, as far as possible, all feudal services. Such of the great baronial houses as survived the Civil War were curtailed of those armed retainers that had formerly constituted the power of the nobility for good or for evil. As an illustration of the effect of the king's new policy and the way it was carried out, the following instance may be mentioned. When the Earl of Oxford, Lord High Admiral and Great Chamberlain to the king, entertained Henry VII. at one of his castles in 1498, with all the splendour and hospitable display of the old *régime*, the king, when taking his departure, said, "By my faith, I thank you for your good cheer; but at the same time I cannot have my laws broken before my face by you, my lord; my Attorney-General must have some serious talk with you"; and soon after the earl was fined fifteen hundred marks for thus having violated the law. Now, with this instance before us, we must be very circumspect in attaching too much importance to the actual effect of the feudal service appertaining to the Royal Buckhounds and the Hereditary Mastership, held by the Brocas family in those days. Consequently, we can only assume that those gentlemen exercised the functions of the office as their ancestors from the time of Edward III. may have done. The privy purse expenses of Henry VII. contain no reference to the pack. There are no accounts or ordinance of this king's household extant. The entire surroundings are so shrouded in obscurity that it would be a bootless task to indulge in speculations which cannot be supported by any genuine evidence.

It is, nevertheless, apparent that even at this time there was a Royal Pack of Buckhounds other than the Hereditary one. Unfortunately, all we know about it consists in the fact that on October 16, 1485, Henry VII. appointed John Wydor yeoman (*valectorum*) of his dogs called Buckhounds, under the Master thereof, to have and hold the said office with the usual wages and fees thereunto belonging (Pat. 1, Henry VII., Part 1, m. 24). The name of this Master is not mentioned. It could hardly have been John Brocas, the seventh Hereditary Master; and, moreover, John Wydor was not connected with the Hereditary branch of the pack at, prior, or subsequent to, this time. It would, therefore, appear that Henry VII. contemplated the formation of some supplementary pack of Buckhounds immediately after his accession to the Crown. But it seems the intention was abandoned, as we can find no further official reference to it during the rest of his reign.

Henry VII. was very partial to rural sports. He filled up every office appertaining to the chase from the Chief Justice of the Forests on this side and beyond the Trent to the very subordinate official whom he appointed to be his swanherd on the river Thames. So far as concerned the royal prerogative the Forest Laws were strictly enforced. All his liege subjects were enjoined to observe the statutes and ordinances touching the preservation of the game. Deer, of all species, birds and beasts of venery, were vested only in the king and in those to whom he had granted, or confirmed existing grants, of free chase and free warren.

Apart from the Buckhounds, *per se*, his hunting establishments were speedily restored to their pristine status. Thus we find on October 12, 1485, Henry VII. made a grant for life to Sir Giles Daubeney of the office of Master of the Royal Harthounds, and of the emoluments heretofore enjoyed therewith by his predecessor in the said office, Henry, late Earl of Essex. Three days later a similar grant was conferred upon Sir William (afterwards Lord) Willoughby of the office of Master of the King's Harriers, with the wages out of the issues of Bedford and Bucks, and of the alnage of cloths in the counties of Somerset and Dorset, with the emoluments heretofore enjoyed by John Worth, Esq., with that office. There was also a Royal Pack of Otter Hounds, besides various accessories of the chase in connection with the Crown, which it is unnecessary to recapitulate here. Under the circumstances, we will proceed at once to investigate the "Privy" or Household branch of our pack in the reign of Henry VIII.

We must view the character of bluff King Hal as a sportsman only. He excelled in all manly sports and pastimes. As a huntsman he had few equals and no superior. He seems to have introduced the use of led horses in a run to hounds when hunting "at force"—a practice generally supposed to be a comparatively modern innovation. He tired out several led horses in the course of a single day's hunting. As to the extent and the cost of his hunting establishment very little is known. Later on in his reign there are, however, somewhat fuller details; but the information is not sufficiently ample to warrant any general conclusion.

So far as the facts can be gathered from the fragmentary historical data available for consultation relating to the hunting establishments of Henry VIII., it appears that during the period now under consideration—*i.e.*, 1528-1536—the officers of what we may style the Household branch (in contradistinction to the Hereditary portion) of the Royal Buckhounds consisted of the Master and four subordinate servants. The then Master, George Boleyne, afterwards styled Viscount Rochester, is mentioned as being in receipt of certain fees for "feeding the hounds," or for "finding meat" for them, as recorded from time to time in our biographical memoir of that unfortunate nobleman. The State papers and cognate historical documents of the period throw no light on the number of hounds belonging to this branch of the pack, nor can we find any ordinance by which all the departments of the Royal household were usually established and regulated. As to the subordinate officials of the household branch of the pack, we find, in the year 1528, that the three sergeants—viz., Humphrey Raynsford, Richard Pery, and George Node—were each entitled to receive for wages *and board wages* 15d. a day. Of this stipend they appear to have only received about 3¼d. *per diem* out of the king's privy purse; from what fund the balance was obtainable we are unable to ascertain. They occasionally obtained supplementary gifts in money and grants from the king by way of "reward." * It

---

* *E.g.*, on March 29, 1542, George Nodes obtained from the king a grant of Shephall for himself, his heirs, and assigns for ever, of the site of the chief

seems they also provided the hounds meat, "chippings"—now known as "dog biscuits"—for which they received from 9s. to 9s. 4d. a month. They were likewise entitled to a livery coat yearly, which cost 1l. 2s. 6d., and on occasion a donation of 11s. or 12s. wherewith to buy a jerkin of Kendal green. Richard Pery died in 1529, from which date onwards we find some changes in the hunt servants. A hound-van is mentioned, and some miscellaneous disjointed particulars so far as it came within the scope of the privy purse expenses of Henry VIII., from 1529 to 1532 :—

		£	s.	d.
1528.				
Dec. 30.	Paid to Humphrey of the privy hounds for meat by the space of one month	0	9	0
1529.				
June 30.	Paid to Humphrey Raynezford* for chippings for the king's privy buckhounds for two months the which be ended the last day of June	0	18	8
Nov. 29.	Paid to him for chippings for a month	0	9	0
1530.				
Jan. 25.	Paid to him for chippings for the king's privy buckhounds for one month	0	12	4
Feb. 26.	Paid to him for chippings	0	9	4
March 12.	Paid to him for a month's wages now ended	0	9	4
„ 28.	Paid to him for one month now ended (sic)	0	9	4

messuage of the Manor of Shephall and of divers lands there. which belonged to the Monastery of St. Albans, Herts. On October 20, 1537, Henry Sell, yeoman pricker (*valet prykker*) of the Buckhounds, obtained a grant for life of the site of the manor and lordship of Cherton, Herts, with all houses, barns, edifices, orchards, and gardens thereunto belonging by the payment of a red rose (*unam rubram rosam*) per annum upon St. John the Baptist's Day. Also twenty-four acres of meadow in "Le Frethe" in the said lordship, from the death of Henry, late Duke of Richmond and Somerset, at the annual rent of 3l. Also to be keeper of the wood called "Lee Old Park," in the said lordship, with fees of 13s. 4d. per year, and one "holowe oke" yearly out of the same wood.

* The names of these gentlemen are spelt in all sorts and manner of ways. Dodsworth's descendants were connected with the royal hunting establishment until nearly the close of the Stuart dynasty. A member of this family owned and probably bred the famous stallion of that name which forms the foundation of Weatherby's Stud Book.

THE HUNT-SERVANTS: SALARIES AND ALLOWANCES.

1530.			£	s.	d.
April 8.	Paid to him for his livery		1	5	0
June 6.	Paid to him for chippings for the king's privy buckhounds for one month		0	9	0
„ 26.	Paid to him for one month's wages		0	9	0
July 15.	Paid to him for one month's wages		0	9	0
	And to him in reward to buy a jerkin . . .		0	12	4
Aug. 16.	Paid to him for a month's wages ended August 12th		0	9	0
„ 18.	Paid to him by way of reward		0	6	8
Sept. 13.	Paid to him for a month's wages ended the 3rd day of this month		0	9	0
Oct. 2.	Paid to him for his wages ended for one month		0	9	0
„ 15.	Paid to him for his coat by the king's commands		1	2	6
Nov. 9.	Paid to him for his month's wages now ended		0	9	0
Dec. 25.	Paid to him for his month's wages now ended		0	9	0
1531.					
Jan. 19.	Paid to him for a month's wages then ended		0	9	0
Feb. 24.	Paid to him for his wages, due for one month, now ended		0	9	0
March 16.	Paid to him and Lawrence Lee for their wages due for one month this present day		0	18	0
May —.	Paid to him for his wages due for one month		0	9	0
June 2.	Paid to him for a month's wages now ended .		0	9	0
„ 10.	Paid to him and Lawrence Lee to buy them a Kendal coat		1	2	0
„ 28.	Paid to him, Thomas of London, Hugh Harris, Ralph Mundy, and Christopher Fausconer, for their livery coats, every man at . . .		1	2	6
July 9.	Paid to him and Ralph Mundy, by the king's commands, in reward		0	9	4
Aug. 12.	Paid to him for canvas to cover the cart [hound-van] to carry the same hounds . .		0	7	6
„ 23.	Paid to him for [two] months' wages ended this day		0	18	0
Sept. 7.	Paid to him, Cox the footman, and Watt, by the king's commands.		1	0	0

		£	s.	d.

1531.

Sept. 14. Paid to him, Watt, and Ralph, by the king's commands 0 15 0

„ 30. Paid to him, Ralph Mundy, and Walter Dodsworth 3 7 6

Oct. 1. Paid to him, Ralph Mundy, and Dodsworth, for meat for the privy [buck]hounds for the space of one month, at 9s. a-piece . . . 1 7 0

Nov. 20. Paid to him, Ralph Mundy, and Walter Dodsworth, for their hounds' meat for a month 1 7 0

Dec. 17. Paid to him, Ralph Mundy, and Walter Dodsworth, for their hounds' meat for a month now ended 1 7 0

„ 28. Paid to him, Walter Dodsworth, and Ralph Mundy, for their livery coats, each of them 1l. 2s. 6d. 3 7 6

1532.

Jan. 9. Paid to him, Ralph Mundy, and Walter Dodsworth, for their hounds' meat for one month now ended 1 7 0

Feb. 12. Paid to him, Walter Dodsworth, and Ralph Mundy, for one month's wages, every man 9s. 1 7 0

March 9. Paid to him, Dodsworth, and Ralph Mundy, for their hounds' meat for a month now ended 1 7 0

April 8. Paid to him, Ralph Mundy, and Walter Dodsworth, for their hounds' meat for one month ended the last day of March 1 7 0

„ 16. Paid to him in reward towards his marriage by the king's command 2 0 0

„ 25. Paid to him, Ralph Mundy, and Walter Dodsworth, for their hounds' meat for a month now ended 1 7 0

May 20. Paid to him, Ralph Mundy, and Walter Dodsworth, for their hounds' meat for one month now ended 1 7 0

1532.

		£	s.	d.
June 16.	Paid to him, Ralph Mundy, and Walter Dodsworth, for their hounds' meat by the space of one month	1	7	0
,, 28.	Paid to him, Ralph Mundy, and Walter Dodsworth, for their liveries	3	0	0
July 2.	Paid to him, Walter Dodsworth, and Ralph Mundy, for the meat of their hounds for one month now ended	1	7	0
,, 20.	Paid to him for ten ells of canvas to cover the cart with the king's hounds	0	5	0
	Paid to him for [the hire of?] the said cart	0	1	0
	Paid to him for 300 nails for the said cart .	0	0	6
	Paid to him for boards to make a chest within the said cart and for carpenter's labour .	0	3	4
,, 24.	Paid to him, Walter Dodsworth, and Ralph Mundy, for their hounds' meat for one month ended the 23rd day of July, at 9s. each	1	7	0
,, 29.	Paid to him for removing with the cart with hounds from Ampthill to Grafton . . .	0	2	4
Aug. 6.	Paid to him for bringing the cart with the hounds from Grafton to Woodstock . . .	0	3	6
	Paid to him, Walter Dodsworth, and Ralph Mundy, in reward	0	15	0
,, 16.	Paid to him for carrying the cart with the hounds from Woodstock to Langley . . .	0	1	2
	Paid to him, Walter Dodsworth, and Ralph Mundy, for their hounds' meat for one month ended the 21st day of August . .	1	7	0
,, 22.	Paid to him for the cart with the hounds from Langley to Abingdon	0	2	4
,, 23.	Paid to him, Walter Dodsworth, and Ralph Mundy, by way of reward	0	15	0
,, 29.	Paid to him for carrying the cart with hounds from Abingdon to Newlem Park	0	1	4
	Paid to him for carrying the said cart from Newlem to Reading	0	2	0

1532.   £   s.   d.
Sept. 12. Paid to him, Dodsworth, and Mundy, for
           their hounds' meat for one month   . . .   1   7   0
  „   19. Paid to him for the cart with hounds from
           Windsor to Chertsey.   0   2   0
  „   30. Paid to him for his cart with hounds from
           Hampton Court to Greenwich   0   2   6
Oct.   7. Paid to him, Dodsworth, and Mundy, for their
           month's wages.   1   7   0
Nov. 28. Paid to him, Walter Dodsworth, and Ralph
           Mundy, for their wages for two months
           now ended 2 14   0
Dec. 24. Paid to him, Ralph [Mundy], and Walter
           [Dodsworth], to every of them 22s. 6d. for
           their coats   3   7   6
  „   25. Paid to him and Walter [Dodsworth], "the
           houts" for their hounds' meat for one
           month   1   7   0

GEORGE BOLEYNE, VISCOUNT ROCHESTER, the First Master of the "Privy" or Household branch of the Buckhounds to Henry VIII. from 1528 to 1536, was the third son and heir of Sir Thomas Boleyne, Viscount Rochford, Earl of Wiltshire and Ormonde, K.G., by Elizabeth, eldest daughter of Thomas Howard, second Duke of Norfolk, E.M., K.G. He was born at Hever Castle, Kent, about the year 1509. It is a somewhat singular circumstance that this castle, in which the young viscount was born and in which he chiefly resided during his youth, belonged to Sir Oliver Brocas when the Royal Buckhounds were first instituted in the reign of Edward III. "Hever," says Mr. William Hepworth Dixon, in his "History of Two Queens," "was poetic and retired. Beyond the moat and garden lay an orchard and a bowling-green. Not many paces off the river Eden brawled and chafed among the stones. Grassland and woodland stretched on every side; here swelling into mound and ridge, there dropping into flat and marsh. Some rare and famous nooks lay screened amidst these depths of wood. Seven miles north stood Knole, where Warham dwelt among his books and papers. Seven miles east rose Tunbridge, where Buckingham used to keep his state. Nearer still lay Penshurst Park, of which young Boleyne's father was the ranger. To the south, beyond the level grounds, rose Ashdown Forest. In and out among these woodlands becks and rivulets sang their pilgrimage towards the sea. Sweetbriars grew in every hedge, and linnets built in every copse. The pools were rich with lilies, and the air, though laden with the scent of many herbs, was freshened by the salt of neighbouring seas." In this charming residence young George Boleyne and his sister Anne dwelt for many happy years, and there they doubtless were " well entered" to the mysteries of the chase, in which they afterwards excelled and continued to enjoy, until they were both sacrificed by ruthless bluff King Hal.

The earliest notice of George Boleyne, afterwards Viscount Rochester and Master of the Buckhounds, etc., occurs in a patent dated April 29, 1522, in which his name appears, joined with that of his father, as the holder of various offices about Tunbridge. On July 2, 1524, he received a grant to himself of the manor of Grimston, in Norfolk. On September 26, 1528, he received an annuity from the Crown of fifty marks, payable by the Chief Butler of England out of the issues of the prizes of wines. On November 15 of the same year, by another grant, in which he is styled "Squire of the Body," he obtained the keepership of the Palace of Beaulieu, *alias* the manor and mansion of Newhall, Essex; gardener or keeper of the garden and orchard of Newhall; warrener or keeper of the warren in the said manor and lordship; keeper of the wardrobe in the said palace or manor in Newhall, Dorchame, Walkfare Hall, and Powers, in Essex; with certain fees in each office, and the power of leasing the said lands, etc., for his lifetime. During the following month (December 1528) he appears to have been appointed Master of the Buckhounds, and to have received a fee of 4*l*. 10*s*. for feeding or providing food for the hounds. We have been unable to find the original patent, the only information relating to it being a brief entry of enrolment of the grant. This and some subsequent payments to him of a similar nature do not correspond to the sums received by the subordinate officers of the pack under this head. On February 1, 1529, George Boleyne, Master of the Buckhounds, obtained a grant of the office of Chief Steward of the Palace of Beaulieu, and of all possessions annexed thereto by authority of Parliament or otherwise, and Keeper of New Park, with a fee of 10l. a year for the former and 3d. a day for the latter.

About this time his sister Anne had become the avowed object of the king's attentions, and there can be no doubt to what influence these honours were due. The fair sister of the Master of the Buckhounds was a famous equestrian, remarkable among the hard riders of the royal pack. The king frequently encountered her in the hunting-field, admired her prowess in the saddle, and her skill in the mysteries of the chase. When she was out with the hounds he accompanied her in the first flight, and if she were absent his thoughts were with her; the first *billet doux* she received from her royal lover is closely associated with our subject, having been indited in the hunting-field on the termination of a run with the pack. "That you may think of me the oftener as I am," wrote Henry, "I send you a buck killed with my own hand, hoping when you eat of it you will remember the hunter." From these flirtations in the hunting-field momentous events occurred. Henry created "his entirely beloved Anne Boleyne" Marchioness of Pembroke, divorced Catherine of Arragon, and soon after married and murdered the accomplished sister of the Master of the Royal Buckhounds. In June 1529 George Boleyne, "Master of the King's Buckhounds," received 60s. for finding the said hounds meat. On July 27 he was appointed Governor of Bethlehem Hospital, and in the ensuing month of September he obtained from the king 65l. 6s. 8d. for one year's allowance, in advance, apparently in connection with his post of "Esquire of the Body." Towards the end of that year he was sent on an embassy to France with Dr. Stokesley, who was shortly after made Bishop of London, to consult with Francis I. and the Duke of Albany on various modes of counteracting the projected treaty between the Emperor Charles V. and James V., King of Scotland, and to prevent the assembling of a general council, with an allowance as ambassador of 40s. a day. As yet his designation was only Squire of the Body, or Gentleman of the Privy Chamber; but just about this time he appears to have been knighted, and, on the elevation of his father to the Earldom of Wiltshire and Ormonde, to have acquired the courtesy title of Viscount Rochester, by which name the fallen Cardinal Wolsey granted him, by Cromwell's recommendation, an annuity of 200 marks out of the revenues of his bishopric of Winchester to secure his favour. By this name also he signed, along with the rest of the nobility, a memorial to Pope Clement VII., urging him to consent without delay to the king's wishes on the subject of his divorce from Catherine of Arragon. During the year 1531 he was usually styled Lord Rochester, and was in constant attendance at the court and on intimate terms with the king. Thus in April he received 6l. for bets won from the king at tennis, three angles a game; August 24, 3s. 6d. to give to the officers of the hunt; September 25, 5l. 6s. 8d. won in a shooting match from the king at Hunsdon; and 3l. 15s. "for his charges carrying the [buck]hounds from St. Thomas's day after midsummer to Holy Rood day, as appears by a bill signed by the said Lord Rochester." These friendly relations between the king and his Master of the Buckhounds evidently continued throughout the ensuing and for some subsequent years. On July 7, 1531, Viscount Rochester received 58l. which he won from the king in a shooting match at Hampton Court, and on August 26 there was a payment to him of 3l. 8s. 6d. under the same head. About this time he was joined by his father in a grant of the office of Steward of the honour of Raylegh, keeper of Raylegh Park, Master of the hunt of deer in that park and Thundersley Park, and bailiff of the hundred of Rochford, Essex, with 10l. a year for the office of bailiff, and 4d. a day for the keepership of Raylegh Park, payable out of the issues of the manor and honour of

Raylegh, and of the lordships and manors of East Woodbury, Thundersley, and Lonedon, Essex, and the herbage and pannage of Raylegh Park, in as full manner as they had been held by Thomas, Marquis of Dorset, then lately deceased.

This Master of the Buckhounds' new year's gift to the king in 1532 was two "hyngers gilt, with velvet girdles," which were probably intended to hold the *couteau de chase* with which the buck was gralloched when he was pulled down by the hounds at the termination of a run. In the privy purse expenses the following payments were made to Viscount Rochester by the king's commands in 1532:—

Jan. 23. 45*l*. won from the king at shovelboard,* and by betting on the same game.
Feb. 18. 36*l*. ditto.
„ 22. 5*l*. 12*s*. 6*d*., ditto.
March 16. 40*l*. 10*s*., ditto.
„ 18. 9*l*. won at bowls.
„ 20. 7*s*. 6*d*. won at tennis.
April 20. 2*l*. 5*s*. won at bowls.
„ 22. 30*l*. won ditto.
June 28. 18*l*. won at archery.
July 19. 6*l*. 13*s*. 4*d*. for the king's huntsmen for their charges going to Sussex.
Oct. 6. 55*l*. won from the king on a coursing match in Moat Park.

The following year Viscount Rochester was summoned by the king to be present in the Parliament at Westminster on February 5, 1533; and on the 25th of the following month he witnessed the marriage of his sister to the king in the private chapel of Westminster Palace, where Dr. Lee, the learned Bishop of Lichfield, tied the nuptial knot. Shortly after the ceremony that proved so fatal to him and his sister he was again sent on an embassy to France. In connection with this mission he received (March 11) 106*l*. 13*s*. 4*d*. for diets for fourteen days, beginning on that day. The primary

---

* This game is minutely described in Strutt's "Sports and Pastimes," p. 267.

object of his embassy was to convey to Francis I. the intelligence that his sister, the Marchioness of Pembroke, was married to King Henry, and that they trusted his Catholic Majesty would support them in resisting any papal excommunication. Lord Rochester was also enjoined to invite Francis to visit England, to enjoy the pleasures of the chase with King Henry, who, in anticipation of the visit, issued orders to put the royal parks, etc., in order, and revoked all licences which had been given to hunt in those preserves, so as to ensure plenty of game in case the invitation was accepted. This, however, Francis was obliged to decline; and Lord Rochester returned to England early in the following month, where for some time he was in constant attendance upon the court, and apparently getting the best of his royal brother-in-law in those rural sports in which they were so expert. In June he was again sent abroad, in company with the Duke of Norfolk and others, to dissuade Francis from his proposed meeting with the Pope at Marseilles, which, however, actually took place later in the year. During the absence of the Master of the Buckhounds on this diplomatic mission his duties in connection with the pack were doubtless well administered by a competent deputy, as Eustace Chapuys, the ambassador of Charles V. at the English court, in a despatch dated July 30, informs the emperor that Thomas Cromwell, the reigning minister (who was an enthusiastic sportsman), had offered him a licence from the king to hunt in any of his parks, etc., and that he (Cromwell) would accompany him with the hounds as often as he pleased, and mount him also on one of the finest hunters in England. Although this offer was then declined, his Excellency subsequently participated in some runs with the Royal Pack in the vicinity of London. In the interval Lord Rochester went back to England, probably to render an account of the progress of the embassy to Henry, but he soon after rejoined Norfolk and the other diplomats in France. He was home again in September, and was present at the christening of his niece, the infant Princess Elizabeth, at Greenwich, when, assisted by Lord Hussey, Lord William and Lord Thomas Howard, he bore the canopy over the future good Queen Bess at that interesting ceremony. Early in October we find the Master of the Buckhounds coursing with his royal brother-in-law, and winning a large sum from him at that sport; and ten days later he set up his household in the royal Manor of Beaulieu, Essex, which the king ordered his eldest daughter, the Princess Mary, to quit to make room for him.

On January 15, 1534, Viscount Rochester was summoned with other peers to attend at the opening of Parliament at Westminster. He continued in attendance at the court until the end of March, occasionally taking an active part in parliamentary and cognate affairs of State. Early in April he obtained the reversion of the lieutenancy of Guisnes Castle, then held by Lord Sandes; and on the 12th of this month he was appointed, with Sir William Fitzwilliam junior, Envoy Extraordinary to Francis I., concerning certain proceedings of Charles V. and other potentates which were deemed prejudicial to British interests. The ambassadors arrived at Boulogne on the 17th of that month, and soon after reached the *locale* of the French court at Coucy, where they had an immediate audience with Francis. The negotiations that then and there took place resulted in Henry and Francis being united by closer ties "as friends to friends and enemies to enemies." Having thus accomplished their mission, the ambassadors immediately returned to England. They arrived at Dover on May 5th, where they spent a short interval in fowling dotterels,* and with the contents of the bag proceeded to London, where the young envoys presented nine brace of the silly (but savoury) birds to the queen, who ordered three brace to be served for her dinner, three for her supper, and the other three brace for breakfast on the following morning. Lord Rochester now resumed his ordinary duties, and we find him in attendance on the king and queen at Hampton Court during the leafy month of June. On or about the 11th of that month

---

* The novel method pursued in fowling dotterels in those days is described in " The History of Newmarket and the Annals of the Turf," vol. ii., p. 281.

he was appointed Constable of Dover Castle and Warden of the Cinque Ports, though his patent did not pass the Great Seal until June 23rd. Honours and emoluments continued to pour on this apparently fortunate Master of the Buckhounds. The following month he was again sent to France as Envoy Extraordinary, touching an interview which Henry was eager to have with his "Right Excellent, Right High, and Mightie Prince, his eldest brother, and perpetuall allie, the French King," but which it became necessary in the end to put off. In the "hunter's month" we find Lord Rochester once more located at Hampton Court, surrounded by sporting attributes, whence he sent one of his servants to Flanders to purchase hawks. Later in this year his duties as Lord Warden necessitated occasional visits to and sojourns at Dover. The reception given by Lord Rochester to the French Admiral Brion, who was sent to Henry VIII. in embassy, on his landing at Dover, was a memorable affair. The entertainment having lasted four days, the envoy and his train were conducted to Blackheath with semi-regal splendour.

In the spring of 1535 Lord Rochester obtained from the king a grant of the Manor of Oetham, a parcel of Begham Abbey lately suppressed; also the manor of South, in Kent, with the advowson, etc., thereunto belonging. In May his services were once more employed in a diplomatic mission to France, to negotiate a marriage contract between his niece, the Princess Elizabeth, and Charles, Duke of Angoulême. The duke wanted to wed the Princess Mary, but Henry refused to give him her hand, and wished to substitute that of the Princess Elizabeth instead, which offer the duke rejected. Curiously enough, many years after, the duke became a suitor for the hand of the Virgin Queen, but she in her turn rejected his offer. Lord Rochester returned to England in June. By this time he had attained the meridian of his power. His influence was all-powerful, his favour with the king appeared to be unshakable and permanent. Despite these outward appearances, he was fast approaching his fall. He little thought, as he sat on the jury which found Fisher guilty,

that he would soon be arraigned, and his life left to the
mercy of a similar tribunal. But, as he soon discovered, trial
by jury in those days was a judicial farce. Meanwhile we
find him during the autumn of this year conducting with
great ability and tact many intricate affairs relating to the
Cinque Ports, and he appears to have resided chiefly at
Dover Castle, where he was well plied with suitors soliciting
his patronage in the dispensation of the many posts which he
controlled, through his close relationship with the king. But,
unfortunately for Lord Rochester and his sister, the king now
became enamoured of Lady Jane Seymour, and in order to
wed her, Queen Anne and all her family were fated to perish.
The breach between Henry and Anne is a matter of history
to which we need not now allude. With the rise of Anne
her brother George rose; with her fall he likewise fell. On
May 1, 1536, he was one of the challengers in that tourna-
ment at Greenwich from which the king abruptly departed;
the next day he rode up from Greenwich to his London house
without the least suspicion of his danger until he was informed
of his sister's commitment to the Tower. Three or four hours
after her arrest he also was immured in the same fortress.
The two were arraigned together on May 15 for acts of
incest and high treason; the jury found them guilty, and
judgment of death was pronounced upon each. Lord Rochester
defended himself, and so ably, that the betting in court was
ten to one that he would be acquitted. Nevertheless, he was
found guilty, sentenced to be drawn to Tyburn, hung by the
neck, cut down alive, ripped open, quartered, and beheaded.
The king so far commuted the sentence by ordering that his
ex-Master of the Buckhounds should be done to death by the
axe of the headsman only. Thus died George Boleyne, Viscount
Rochester, on Tower Hill, May 17, 1536. He married Jane,
daughter of Sir Henry Parker (eldest son and heir of Henry,
Lord Morley), a bad woman, who continued Lady of the Bedchamber to the three succeeding queens, but eventually shared
the fate of Katherine Howard. Lord Rochester had no issue.
He was attainted soon after his execution, when, of course, all

the honours and emoluments which had been conferred upon him by his royal brother-in-law and the vast estates to which he was heir-presumptive reverted to the king.*

Before concluding our biography of this Master of the Buckhounds, it may perhaps be excusable if we pause for a moment to glance at the end of his unfortunate sister. She was not to die, as her brother died, by the stroke of an old English axe. In France they had a method of executing criminals by the sword, and Henry, wishing to introduce that method into England, chose to have the first experiment tried on his own wife! No man in London was accustomed to do the work, and Cromwell had to send to Calais for an expert in this novel craft. Anne shrank in horror from such novelties; but the Lieutenant of the Tower, meaning to be kind, assured her in his burly way that "her head would be off in no time," as indeed the sequel proved. Two days after her brother's execution, on the morning of May 19, the king, attired for the chase, with his huntsmen and buckhounds around him, was at a meet of the pack at Pleshet, near East Ham, in Epping Forest, breathlessly waiting the signal-gun from the Tower which was to announce that the sword had fallen on the neck of his once "entirely beloved Anne Boleyne." At last, towards noon, the sullen sound of the death salute boomed along the windings of the Thames. Henry started with ferocious joy. "Ha, ha!" he cried with satisfaction, "the deed is done. Uncouple the hounds, and let us follow the sport." The chase that day bent towards the west, whether the quarry led it in that direction or not, for at nightfall the king was at Wolfhall, in Wiltshire, telling the news to his elected bride, whom he next morning married.

* The terrible severity of this attainder extended even to his lordship's debts and obligations. All moneys due to him became forfeited to the Crown, his debts could not be recovered by those to whom they were owing, although the unfortunate Master of the Buckhounds had ample means and was willing to satisfy such claims. For instance, he owed to George Brown, Archbishop of Dublin, 400*l.*, who lent him this sum for "the redempcion of a cuppe of golde," upon the security of his house; yet the mortgage was invalid, as the whole of his lordship's effects went into the clutches of the king.

SIR RICHARD LONG and LORD DARCY, of Chiche, Masters of the Royal Buckhounds, are recited in the patent granted to Sir Thomas Tyringham in 1603, as being among others his predecessors in the branch of this pack under the Lord Chamberlain of the Household; but we are unable to say when those masters were appointed or how long they filled this office. Sir Richard Long died in 1545, and Lord Darcy in 1558. It is, therefore, evident that Sir Richard Long became the second Master of the Household branch of the Royal Buckhounds some time subsequent to the execution of George Boleyne, Viscount Rochester. As previously noticed, the accounts of the Treasurer of the Chamber, which would contain the payments to these Masters of this portion of the royal pack, amounting to 33*l*. 6*s*. 8*d*. a year, are lost or missing. If those interesting documents were available for consultation, we could then ascertain when and for what period Sir Richard Long filled the post. No enrolment of any patent or privy seal conferring or relating to his appointment to the Buckhounds can be found, consequently we are quite in the dark as to the principal incidents of his career relating to our subject. This is particularly disappointing, as he seems to have been the first Master of the Household part of the royal pack who enjoyed during his tenure of office the annual fee of 33*l*. 6*s*. 8*d*. —a figure at which the remuneration of those Masters remained until the accession of Charles II. This Sir Richard Long, of Shengay and Hardwicke, co. Cambridge, was the second son of Sir Thomas Long, of Draycot-Cerne, co. Wilts. He was knighted on October 18, 1537, when his arms were quartered 1st and 4th sable, crusily a lion rampant argent; 2nd, argent on a chief gules a bezant between two stags' heads cabossed or; 3rd, gules, two wings conjoined or, and for his crest a demi-lion rampant argent, holding in the mouth a human arm, couped proper. Possibly the two stags' heads, which he then bore in the second quarter of his coat, may have reference to his office as Master of the Buckhounds, and he may have obtained the appointment in succession to Lord Rochester at or about this time. The valiant knight was "an esquire of

the King's stable," and was evidently a favourite with
Henry VIII., from whom he obtained many valuable grants
and offices from time to time, including the custody of Eltham
Park, a portion of the Forest of Deane, keeper of the Manor
and Pleasaunce of Greenwich, lease to farm the royal Manor of
Eltham, with custody thereof, grant of the Priory of Kington
with the temporalities thereof in various parts, grant of the
Manor of Coggeshall, seneschal of the Manor of Deptford, grant
of the Manor of Great Saxham and elsewhere in co. Suffolk,
grant of the site of the Hospital of St. Thomas, within the
Borough of Southwark, with the endowment of the same in
various counties; annuities to the amount of 120$l.$ a year, and
a house in London; and Governor of the Channel Islands,
which appointment he held at the time of his death. Marillac,
the French Ambassador, in a despatch to Francis I., dated
London, June 25, 1541, announced to the King, his master, that
Sir Richard Long, whom His Excellency designates "a personage
of a certain authority and experience in military affairs," had
been lately sent to Calais in great haste, for the purpose of
inspecting the fortifications of that and other places in France
belonging to England, and to report thereon. Sir Richard
Long, the second Master of the Household Branch of the Royal
Buckhounds, died on September 29, 1545.

Very likely Thomas, Lord Darcy, K.G., succeeded Sir Richard
Long, and became the third Master of this portion of the Royal
Buckhounds about the year 1546, and probably retained the
office until it was conferred upon John Dudley, Earl of Warwick,
temp. Edward VI. But, as in the preceding instance, we are
equally in the dark as to the particulars relating to this
Master's tenure of office. All we can find about him is that
he was the only son of Roger Darcy, Esquire of the Body to
Henry VII., and Elizabeth, daughter of Sir Henry Wentworth
and widow of John Bourchier, Earl of Bath. He was born in
1506. In course of time he became a prominent personage
at the Court of Henry VIII. He was knighted at Calais,
on November 1, 1532. In 1545 he was constituted Master
of Ordinances within the Tower of London, and in the next

year made a Gentleman of the King's Privy Chamber. He obtained large grants of Church lands for Essex from Henry VIII., with whom he was a great favourite. On May 24, 1550, he obtained from Edward VI. the keepership of the King's "Turkey-cocks and Cocks of the Game" at Greenwich Palace. The turkey must have then been a *rara avis* in the land: the game chanticleer was (until lately) emblematical of British pluck and endurance. On April 5, 1551, Sir Thomas Darcy was created Baron Darcy of Chiche, co. Essex, at which time he was Vice-Chamberlain of the Household, Captain of the Royal Guard, and one of the Knights of the Privy Chamber to King Edward VI. He was soon after installed Knight of the Garter. His Lordship died at Wyvenhoo Hall on June 28, 1558.

CHAPTER III.

HOUSEHOLD BRANCH.—EDWARD VI.—ELIZABETH.
1547—1602.

Celebrity of Hunting in England *temp.* Edward VI.—John Dudley, Earl of Warwick, Fourth Master: April 5 to November 10, 1551.—Sir Robert Dudley, Fifth Master: November 11, 1551 to *c* August, 1553.—The Household Pack *temp.* Philip and Mary.—The Hunt Servants.—Annual Cost of the Pack.—Accession of Queen Elizabeth.—Annual Cost of the Pack.— The Hunt Servants.—Robert Dudley, Earl of Leicester, Sixth Master: May 28, 1572 to September 4, 1588.—State of the Pack to the End of Elizabeth's Reign.—Dearth of Hunting Intelligence.—The Queen and Ladies in the Hunting Field.

As the accounts of the Treasurer of the Chamber are not extant, we are unable to give any particulars of the cost of the "Privy," or Household portion of the Royal Buckhounds in the reign of Edward VI. Beyond the fact that John Dudley, Earl of Warwick, and his son, Sir Robert Dudley (afterwards Earl of Leicester), held the office of Master of this branch of the pack in Edward VI.'s reign, there is nothing further known of the hunt servants or the cost of this establishment for the time being. Nevertheless, we may safely assume that it was maintained as in the preceding reign. The fame acquired by the Royal packs was well known in continental Courts. For instance, it is recorded that Marshal Jacques d'Albon St. André, Ambassador of Henry II. at the Court of Edward VI., brought in his suite, in May 1551, "a great number of the young gentlemen of the French Court" who were "desirous to have some experience in the English hunting, wherein they (the English) do excel other nations." In the sixteenth and seventeenth centuries it was one of the duties of the Masters of the Buckhounds to contribute, to the best of their ability, to the venatic predilections of the foreign Ambassadors and the Corps Diplomatique generally, whenever they would "a hunting go."

JOHN DUDLEY, EARL OF WARWICK, Duke of Northumberland, etc., fourth Master of the Household branch of the Royal Buckhounds (*temp.* Edward VI.), from April 5 to November 10, 1551, was eldest son of Edmund Dudley, Viscount Lisle, the celebrated lawyer and statesman of the reign of Henry VII. He was born in 1502, and afterwards became one of the most powerful subjects this kingdom ever saw. At the time his father was beheaded he was about eight years old; and, it being known that the severity exercised in that act was rather to satisfy popular clamour than justice, his friends found no great difficulty in obtaining an Act of Parliament, in 1512, to reverse his father's attainder and to restore in blood and degrees his heir, so that he might inherit all his deceased father's lands. After an education suitable to his quality, he was introduced at the brilliant Court of Henry VIII. about the year 1523, where, having a fine person and great accomplishments, he soon became admired. He attended Charles Brandon, Duke of Suffolk, in the expedition to France against the Duke of Bourbon, and distinguished himself so much by his gallant behaviour that he obtained the honour of knighthood. In 1528 he attached himself to the suite of Cardinal Wolsey, whom he accompanied in his embassy to France, and in eight years afterwards he was made Master of the Armoury in the Tower of London, for life, with the wages of 12$d.$ a day for himself, and 3$d.$ a day for his groom in the office. In 1540 he was appointed Master of the Horse to Anne of Cleves, and the next year, in the jousts held at Westminster, he was one of the principal challengers, his horse being accoutred with white velvet. On March 12, 1542, he was elevated to the peerage, in the ancient dignity enjoyed by his mother's family, that of Viscount Lisle, and was appointed Warden of the Marches of Scotland in that year.

On January 26, 1543, he received the high preferment of Lord High Admiral for life. In this capacity his lordship displayed great gallantry, and did good service for his country against France and Scotland. He became a Privy Councillor on April 23, 1543, and on the concurring festival of St. George was elected a Knight of the Garter. In 1544–45 his lordship was appointed Captain of Boulogne. Up to this period he owed all his honours and fortunes to Henry VIII., from whom he received very large grants of Church lands; which, however, created him many enemies. He was also named by Henry VIII. in his will to be one of his sixteen executors; and received from him a legacy of 500*l*. which was the highest he left to any of them.

After the death of Henry VIII., which occurred on January 28, 1547, the Earl of Hertford, afterwards Duke of Somerset, who was the young king's uncle, without having any regard to Henry's will, got himself proclaimed Protector of the Kingdom, and set on foot many projects. Among the first, one was to get his brother, Sir Thomas Seymour, made Lord High Admiral, in whose favour Lord Viscount Lisle was obliged to resign; but in recompense for the loss of that office he was created Earl of Warwick, with a grant of Warwick Castle, by patent dated February 17, 1547. But in 1550 he was again made Lord High Admiral. His lordship was appointed Master of the Buckhounds to Edward VI. on April 15, 1551, with an annual fee of 33*l*. 6*s*. 8*d*., payable half yearly, by even proportions, at Easter and Michaelmas, in as full and ample a manner as enjoyed by his predecessors in that office. However, after holding the horn for a short time, he resigned the appointment, apparently in favour of his son, Lord Robert Dudley (afterwards Earl of Leicester). In the following year the Earl of Warwick was constituted Lord Steward of the Household. Henceforward his lordship's ambition appears to have known no bounds, and to have hurried him into acts of great baseness and atrocity. Through his intrigues the quarrel arose between the Protector Somerset and his brother Thomas, Lord Seymour, which terminated in the public execution of the latter; and he was at this period accused of acquiring considerable wealth by the plunder of the Church. On October 11, 1551, he was advanced to the dignity of Duke of Northumberland, a peerage, which, by the death of the last Earl of Northumberland, without heirs, and the attainder and execution of his brother, Sir Thomas Percy, the Percy estate became vested in the Crown. His grace had previously been constituted Earl Marshal of England.

Having now attained the highest honour in the peerage, and power the most unlimited, the Duke proceeded, with scarcely the semblance of restraint, in his ambitious projects; and the Protector Somerset, one of his earliest and steadiest patrons, soon fell a victim to their advancement. That distinguished personage was arraigned, through the intrigue of Northumberland, before his peers, and, though acquitted of high treason, was condemned for felony, and sentenced to be hanged. The eventual fate of the Lord Protector Somerset is well known, and, considering his own conduct to his brother, not deplored. He was executed by decapitation on Tower Hill, on February 22, 1552, upon which day the Duke of Northumberland succeeded him as Chancellor of Cambridge. From the death of Somerset the Duke of Northumberland became so unremitting in his attentions upon Edward VI., and had so much influence over him, that he prevailed upon the King to sign and seal a patent, conferring the succession upon Lady Jane Grey (grand-niece to King Henry VIII.), the wife of his third son Lord Guildeford Dudley. His subsequent efforts, after the decease of Edward VI., to establish this patent by force of arms proved abortive. On the accession of Mary a proclamation was issued by the new Queen, offering land to the value of 1,000*l.* to any nobleman, 500*l.* to any knight, 500 marks to any gentleman, or 100*l.* to any yeoman that might be so fortunate as to arrest the ex-Master of this branch of the Royal Buckhounds, and deliver him up to the Queen. He was soon after arrested upon the charge of high treason at Cambridge, and being condemned thereof, was beheaded on Tower Hill on August 22, 1553, when all his honours became forfeited under the attainder. This John Dudley, Viscount Lisle, Earl of Warwick, and Duke of Northumberland, K.G., E.M., married Jane, daughter of Sir Edward Guildeford, Knt., and had issue seven sons and two daughters. His fourth son, Robert Dudley, afterwards Earl of Leicester, was appointed Master of the "Privy" or Household branch of the Royal Buckhounds on November 11, 1551, and to the same office again on May 28, 1572.

The few days Lady Jane Grey reigned preclude any information of the Household branch of the Royal Buckhounds in her time, consequently we find ourselves harboured in the reign of Mary (July 6/19, 1553—November 17, 1558) before one can say "Tally-ho!" Neither Mary nor her royal consort, Philip of Spain, seem to have been imbued with that love for field sports usually so characteristic of the English sovereigns. During her father's lifetime Mary was persecuted for her religious opinions, and when she succeeded to the throne she became an easy prey to the fanatics, by whom she was driven to sanction alleged atrocities which rendered her "sanguinary reign" notorious. Philip was morose; he had no sympathy with the habits and customs of the people of this country; yet on one occasion, as recorded in Machyn's "Diary," he "rode hunting in the Forest [of Waltham], and killed a great stag with guns." This is the only allusion we have found of King Philip participating in the chase during his residence in England; nevertheless, we must not dogmatise upon the apparent dearth of the Royal sport, as it may, for all we know to the contrary, have flourished, though no details of it have been preserved. Such a hypothesis is not too far-fetched, inasmuch as the Royal hunting establishment was sustained as in the days of yore. Fortunately the accounts of the Treasurer of the Chamber of the Household of Philip and Mary are extant, and from the facts and figures therein set forth, we ascertain the following particulars relating to this branch of the Royal Buckhounds for the year ending December 31, 1557, from which it appears that some of the hunt servants who officiated in the reign of Henry VIII. were still to the fore, and that the pack cost the Royal Exchequer, in the year mentioned, the sum of 95*l*. 10*s*. 1*d*.

Officers of the Huntes.

George Nodes, S^{r}iauntc of the Buckhoundes at xxij^{li}. xvj^s. p annm' for his wage for iij q^{u}rters of a yere ended at Cristmas annis iiij^{to} and v^{to} in full payment of his wage then due amounting to . . . xvij^{li}. ij^s.

Will'm Howell, a hunte at vj^{li}. xiij^s. iiij^d. for his wage for iij q^{u}rters ended at Cristmas dict° ann' in full payment then as in the saide booke appearith amounting to . . . v^{li}.

James Mapley at vj^d. p diem for his wage for lyke tyme in full payment then due amounting to . . . vj^{li}. xvj^s. x^d. ob.

Henry Sell for lyke wage and tyme in full payment then due amounting to . . . vj^{li}. xvj^s. x^d. ob.

Humfrey Rainsforthe at C^s. p ann. for his wage due for lyke tyme in full payment amountinge to lxj^s. vj^d.

Walter Doddesworthe at vj^{li}. xiij^s. iiij^d. P ann. for his wage due for one hole yere endyd at Easter dict annis iiij^{to} et v^{to} in full payment then as in the saide booke appearithe . . . vj^{li}. xiij^s. iiij^d.

Thomas Doddesworthe for the like wage and tyme endyd at Easter aforesaide in full payment due to hym at that tyme amountinge to . . . vj^{li}. xiij^s. iiij^d.

Walter Godsome for lyke wage and tyme endyd at Easter aforesaide in full payment due to hym at the tyme amountinge to . . . vj^{li}. xiij^s. iiij^d.

Christopher Duck for lyke wage and tyme in full payment then due amountinge to . . . vj^{li}. xiij^s. iiij^d.

Ralfe Mundaye at xv^{li}. per ann. for his wage for one hole yere endyd at Easter dict. ann. iiij^{to} et v^{to} in full payment of his [wages] due at tyme amountinge as in the saide pticler booke appearethe . . . xv^{li}.

John Lynde at vj^{li}. xiij^s. iiij^d. p ann. for his for iij. q'rters of a yere ended at Cristmas the yere aforesaide in full payment then amountinge to as in the saide booke appearethe . . . C^s.

The Gromes of the Buckhoundes for their houndes meate at xiiij^{li}. vj^s. p ann. in full paymente endyd at Cristmas dict. ann. iiij^{to} et v^{to} as in the saide pticler booke appearith amountinge to . . . ix^{li}. xiv^s. vj^d.

Total . . . iiij^{xx} xv^{li}. x^s. j^d.

It is evident that the hunting establishment of the king and queen was fairly well kept up, as we find the following additional facts relating to it in the accounts of the Treasurer and Chamberlain of the Exchequer of the Household above mentioned—viz., seventeen officers of the hawks and falcons, and one keeper of the spaniels, received 172*l*. 11*s*. 8¾*d*. Three takers and keepers of pheasants and partridges received 23*l*. 8*s*. 9*d*.; six officers of the leach received 10*l*. 8*s*. 4*d*.; two officers of the toils received 15*l*. 7*s*. 6*d*.; eight keepers of Waltham Forest received 94*l*. 15*s*.; the officer of the crossbows, Randolph Churchill, Esq., received 9*l*. 2*s*. 6*d*.; three keepers of the beares and mastives received 35*l*. 15*s*., and John Pierce, "keeper of the warren of hares at Everley," obtained for his wages, for one year and nine months, ended in September 1557, 6*l*. 14*s*. It will thus be seen that the entire cost of the Royal hunting establishment for the year 1557 amounted to 463*l*. 12*s*. 10¾*d*. This is the first account extant of the Treasurer of the Chamber of the Household in the Audit Office series. The account of Sir John Mason, Knight, "one of the Queen's Majesty's most honourable Privy Council, Treasurer of the Chamber, and Master of the Posts," from Michaelmas 5 and 6 Philip and Mary (A.D. 1558) to 2 Elizabeth (A.D. 1560), is somewhat similar to the preceding. With the exception of Walter Godson, then deceased, all the officers of the Buckhounds were in receipt of the same salaries beforementioned, except the grooms, who received for their hounds' meat "after the rate of 13*l*. 6*s*. 8*d*. per annum."

The account for the year ended at Michaelmas 1561, is the first clear annual audit of the Treasurer of the Chamber of Queen Elizabeth's Household. The entire cost of the Queen's "Hunts" is set down at 100*l*. 1*s*., comprising the following payments—viz., to George Nodes, Sergeant of the Buckhounds, for his wages at 22*l*. 16*s*. a year; James Mapley and Henry Sell at 6*d*. each per day; Humphrey Rainesford at 5*l*. a year; Ralph Mundy at 15*l*. a year; John Lynde, Thomas Dodsworth, and Christopher Duck, each at 6*l*. 13*s*. 4*d*. a year; and the Grooms of the Buckhounds, for hounds' meat 13*l*. 6*s*. 8*d*.

Besides the "Hunt" proper, we find a pack of harriers now mentioned, with a yeoman pricker, two yeomen barrenters, two yeomen fewterers, and two grooms. These officials received only 1*l*. 2*s*. 6*d*. each at Easter for their several liveries, amounting altogether to 7*l*. 17*s*. 6*d*. per annum. The Sheriffs of Somerset and Dorset, however, were obliged to contribute certain fees* yearly towards the maintenance of this pack. It may be also noted that the Queen's falconers cost the Royal Exchequer 119*l*. 2*s*. 8*d*., the leach 10*l*., the crossbows 22*l*. 13*s*. 2*d*., the toils 117*l*. 1*s*. 6*d*., the keepers of Waltham Forest 89*l*. 14*s*. 10*d*., the takers and keepers of pheasants and partridges 24*l*. 6*s*. 8*d*., and the keepers of beares and mastives 48*l*. 12*s*. 8½*d*.

From 1562 to 1567 we find no material alteration in the annual cost of the Royal "Hunts," which were sustained at an expenditure of about 86*l*. a year. In 1565 Henry Harvey succeeded George Nodes as Sergeant of the Buckhounds; and in 1567 Thomas Brown succeeded Ralph Mundy as a yeoman pricker of the pack, with a salary of 15*l*. a year, payable quarterly during his life, and 20*s*. yearly for his livery coat. In the account for the half year ended at Michaelmas 1567, John Lynde, Thomas Dodsworth, Walter Dodsworth, and Christopher Duck are specifically mentioned as "Grooms of the Buckhounds," and were in receipt of 13*l*. 6*s*. 8*d*. per annum for hounds' meat. We notice no change in the yearly cost or the *personnel* of the pack until the year 1571, except that John Grambold succeeded James Maperley, yeoman pricker, who it appears died on December 21, 1567, and Walter Godsone, one of the grooms of the Buckhounds, deceased, was succeeded by Thomas Forest. Henry Sell, another yeoman pricker, who died on February 21, 1565–6, was succeeded by Henry Woop, with a fee of 6*d*. a day during life, "and vj^{li}. iij^s. x^d. p ann. for his Lyveryes before tyme payed

* Henry, Earl of Huntingdon, the Master, 1*s*.; Richard Lovelace, the Sergeant, 7¼*d*.; two prickers of horses, 4*d*. each; two kennel servants and two ground keepers, 2*d*. each; two boys, 1¼*d*.; food for two horses, 3¼*d*.; forty dogs and twelve greyhounds, each ¾*d*.; and three bloodhounds, 1*d*. each per day.

in the greate Wardrobe dewe to him, viz., for fyve hole yeares and thre q"rters endyd at Mic^{h}as anno xiij^{mo} D'D' Re^{gn}, accompting from the daye of the death of the said Henrye Sell, wch was the xxjth of Februarye 1565 [–6] vntill M^{ch} aforesaid 1572, as by Certificate thereof remayning apperythe and the saide Henrye Sell payed vntil x'pās anno viij^{mo} D'D' Regine."

In the account of (Sir) Thomas Henneage, Treasurer of the Chamber of the Houschold from Michaelmas (13 and 14 Eliz.) 1571, to Michaelmas 1572, the name of the Earl of Leicester as Master of the Buckhounds heads the audit list of the officials of the Royal Pack :—

Also allowed for money paid to the righte honnorable Roberte, Erle of Leicester, m^r of the quenes ma^{ts} Buckhoundes for his fee at xxxiij^{li}. vj^s. viij^d. p ann' paiable everie half yere at thannun'ciacon' of o^r Ladie and S^t. Michell tharchaungell' by even porcoñs, viz., Paid to hym for half a yere Due at m^{as} last A^o xiiij R. R. Elizabethe, by vertue of her ma^{ties} libate' Dormaunte vnder the greate Seale of England. Dated at Westm' xxviij^o die maij anno antedeo' . . . xvj^{li} xiij^s. iiij^d.

Each of the acting hunt servants above mentioned were in receipt of the same salaries and allowances, except Henry Wood, one of the yeomen prickers, who died on June 6, up to which date his wages were paid in full; the whole cost of the pack for this year being set down at 125l. 15s. 10d. The following year it amounted to 161l. 4s. 6d., and continued at about that sum until the end of Elizabeth's reign, so far as relates to the annual accounts given in this series. Thomas Dodsworth, one of the grooms of the Buckhounds, died on January 10, 1574, "as appeareth by cirtificate subscribed wth the hands of the Curate and Church Wardens of Lewesham, in the Countie of Kent." About the same time Henry Crockeson succeeded Henry Wood, yeoman pricker, deceased. During the following six or seven years no change had taken place in the officials or the cost of the pack, according to the accounts of the Treasurer of Chamber, save a trifling difference made to three of the hunt-servants in their annual allowance for their summer and winter liveries.

SIR ROBERT DUDLEY, Baron Denbigh, EARL OF LEICESTER, etc., fifth and sixth Master of the Household branch of the Royal Buckhounds, *temp.* Edward VI. (appointed November 11, 1551) and, secondly, *temp.* Elizabeth (May 28, 1572—September 4, 1588), fourth son of John Dudley, Duke of Northumberland, and Jane, daughter of Sir Edward Guildeford, knight, was born about the year 1532. Having been introduced at the Court of Edward VI., where his father at the time was in high favour, young Dudley met with a cordial reception, and a brilliant career lay before him. On August 15, 1551, he was sworn one of the six Gentlemen of the Bedchamber to the King. In about three months afterwards, when his father resigned his post of Master of the Buckhounds, Robert, his son, obtained the honour of knighthood, and on November 11 he became fifth Master of this branch of the Royal pack which his father apparently relinquished in the young courtier's favour. How long he held the Mastership under Edward VI. we have not been able to ascertain. It is, however, safe to conclude that in consequence of his father's treason, attainder, and execution, his son's connection with the Buckhounds had, for the present, terminated on the accession of Queen Mary. Immediately after Queen Mary's accession, in July 1553, Sir Robert Dudley was committed to the Tower, and on January 15 following he was arraigned of High Treason, confessed the indictment, and was sentenced to be hanged, drawn, and quartered. But he was soon after pardoned; the Queen restored him in blood, received him into favour, and made him Master of Ordnance, at the siege of St. Quintain. In this service he remained abroad for some time. On his return to England he seems to have lived in comparative retirement with his first wife, the unfortunate Amy Robsart, and to have given himself up, in a great measure, to the enjoyment of those rural sports in which he was so proficient. On the death of Queen Mary, in November 1558, Sir Robert Dudley rode to Hatfield, "mounted on a snow-white steed, being well skilled in riding a managed horse," and paid

his homage to the Princess Elizabeth on his knees. At this
time he is said to have been furnished with all possible
advantages both of mind and body. His person was comely,
and well proportioned, his countenance open and liberal, his
bearing affable and engaging; and to these were added a
graceful action and delivery, and such an absolute command
of temper, that he could naturally adapt himself to every one's
humour or designs, as he saw occasion. Thus when he presented himself so opportunely before Elizabeth, his beauty,
stature, and florid youth were such powerful recommendations,
that she then and there nominated him Master of the Horse,
and confirmed the appointment by patent under the Great
Seal, dated Westminster, January 11, 1559, by virtue of which
he obtained a fee of 100 marks (66*l.* 13*s.* 4*d.*) per annum,
payable out of the Exchequer half yearly, at Easter and
Michaelmas, by equal proportions, in as full and ample manner
as enjoyed by his predecessors in that office. It may, however,
be mentioned that he held this appointment subject to the
Queen's pleasure, in contradistinction to the various other
grants and offices that had been showered on him, from time
to time, during the reign of his Royal Mistress, which were
usually given to him for life, or to him and his heirs for ever.
From this time the gay young knight (who bore the courtesy
title of Lord Robert Dudley until he was advanced to the
Earldom of Leicester in 1554) became a star of the first
magnitude at the Court of good Queen Bess, with whom he
was a prime favourite. It would fill volumes to recount the
many parts he played during the twenty-nine years of his
sway at the Court of Queen Elizabeth, as he had not only a
finger, but a whole hand, in every pie from which a plum
could be extracted. From the highest honours, the richest
emoluments, the greatest grants, and the best monopolies, to
the most trivial things imaginable, over which the Crown had
any dispensation, were grasped by this avaricious courtier.
In commerce he was the leading merchant of the era. His
speculations in mines and minerals savoured of insanity. He
adventured largely " beyond the seas," while, as a manufacturer

at home, his mills were to be found at work in all parts of the kingdom. Yet he was every inch a gentleman; a dashing horseman, an expert sportsman, a good scholar, a fine linguist, a patron of literature, science, and art, and kept a company of "poor players." With such a variety of discordant elements before us, it is necessary to confine our brief memoir of this Master of the Buckhounds to some of the leading incidents of his remarkable career.

No important preferment was conferred on Lord Robert Dudley from the date of his appointment as Master of the Horse until June 3, 1559, when, "to the admiration of all men," he was installed a Knight of the Garter with great solemnity. Up to this time he was by no means well off in a pecuniary sense, consequently he kept a sharp look-out for wardships, monopolies, and similar accessories whereby he could put money in his purse. His all-powerful influence with the Queen was sufficient to secure him those advantages, and as such pickings cropped up, his lordship carefully gathered them together without exciting that jealousy which was certain to follow if he had flown at higher game. Little by little this profitable mode of acquiring wealth and influence went on, gradually increasing in magnitude, so much so, that shortly after he was appointed Constable of Windsor Castle for life (February 23, 1562), he obtained the exclusive monopoly of exporting all sorts of wool and woollen cloths, wood, corn, and minerals. His comparative poverty was apparently well known to the Queen, as in the autumn of this year (October 22, 1562) she gave him an annuity of 1,000*l*. for life. The following year (June 9, 1563) he obtained a grant of the manor and castle of Kenilworth, with other vast estates in Derbyshire, Lancashire, Surrey, Rutland, Carmarthen, Yorkshire, Cardiganshire, and Salop. About this time the projected marriage between Mary Queen of Scots and the Archduke Charles was opposed on political grounds by Elizabeth, who did not wish the alliance to take place. Deeming that the bearing and the accomplishments of Dudley would not fail to make a favourable impression on her Royal cousin, she despatched him in the following year on a pilgrimage of love, with instructions to cut out the Archduke. If he was successful in his suit, Elizabeth promised him that she would, with the authority of Parliament, declare Mary heir to the Crown of England, in case she died herself without issue. Owing, however, to the influence of France, the project was marred, and in the end Mary was married to Lord Darnley. On September 9th, 1564, Lord Robert Dudley was created Baron Denbigh and Earl of Leicester. The ceremony was performed in St. James' Palace in the presence of the Queen and all the high officers of State; and during the solemnity Her Majesty put on the Earl's robe of State, girded him with his sword of sway, and placed the coronet of dignity on his head, with her own right Royal hands. He was the last earl that was thus invested by the sovereign, the ceremony of investiture being abolished in 1615, when it was declared to be unnecessary; and though the form of creation was thenceforth disused, it continued to be recited as the manner of creation until the reign of Queen Anne, shortly after which period a clause was inserted in all patents of earldoms, dispensing with the ceremony of investiture by express words. During this year the Earl of Leicester attended the Queen in her progress to Cambridge, where the Royal party were entertained by the heads of the University with great splendour, and during the Royal visit, the Earl (who had been elected High Steward in 1563) received the degree of M.A. The notoriety of these proceedings appears to have excited jealousy among the dons of the sister University; and towards the end of this year (December 31, 1564) they appointed Leicester Chancellor of their *alma mater*—a proceeding they repented of at leisure, as his lordship ordered great reforms in the statutes of the institution, and enforced a discipline repugnant to them, but to which they were obliged to conform.

From about this period the Earl of Leicester became one of the greatest magnates in the land. On August 3, 1565, he obtained licence to have a hundred persons in his retinue. He lorded it like a feudal baron of the old *régime*, yet he found it difficult to make both ends meet; and in order to defray the heavy charges of his almost regal establishments he was obliged to part with many a fat manor. Thus within this year he alienated Hamsby, a splendid estate in Norfolk, to Sir Thomas Gresham, his great rival in commercial pursuits. However, Court favours continued to pour upon him. In June 1556 he obtained vast grants of lands in Warwick, Somerset, Herts, York, Denby, Lincoln, Beds, etc., and on July 2 he was appointed Chamberlain of the County Palatine of Cheshire for life. During this year he received the Order of St. Michael from Charles IX., King of France, and was invested with it in the Chapel Royal at Whitehall with all the magnificence worthy of the occasion. No Englishman had ever been admitted before into this order, except King Henry VIII., King Edward VI., and Charles Brandon, Duke of Suffolk. Leicester, in his capacity of Chancellor, received the Queen on the occasion of her first visit to Oxford, in 1566. The royal sojourn extended over seven days, during which time Her Majesty was magnificently entertained, all the entertainments having been excellently carried out under the earl's supervision. He received great praise for his pains from his royal mistress, with whom he was then held in the highest favour. However, on the return of the Court to London, he indiscreetly advocated certain measures in Parliament relating to the Royal succession, whereby he incurred the Queen's displeasure, and for some time he was excluded from the Presence Chamber, and prohibited access to her person. But this hitch was soon adjusted, and the Earl again became the Queen's prime favourite. On November 28, 1567, he obtained a licence for twenty-two years for transporting all sorts of wood and timber growing in Shropshire. In 1571 he secured the reversion of the chief stewardship of Northamptonshire and Buckinghamshire for life.

He was appointed Master of the Royal Buckhounds on May 28, 1572, with a yearly fee of 33*l*. 6s. 8*d*. for life, which office he held to the day of his death. About this time some serious disputes took place between the Archbishop of Canterbury and the Earl of Leicester relating to the goods of the Church. The Archbishop got the best of the arguments, but the Master of the Buckhounds got the temporalities in question, which he appropriated for his own personal uses. The following year (April 20, 1574) he obtained another vast grant of Crown lands in various counties in sundry parts of the kingdom; and on July 19 ensuing he received a grant of the old palace of Maidstone, with other estates in the county Kent and various other localities. Some of these manors were soon after sold to different persons, and on February 13, 1575, he got licence to alienate the manor of Cumnor, county Bucks, to Henry Lord Norries, where his first wife, the Countess Amy, was done to death. The Queen gave him another annuity of 1,000$l.$ a year for life by patent, dated Westminster, July 17 of this year, and two days afterwards he obtained a very considerable grant of lands in Monmouthshire. He was appointed Chancellor and Chamberlain (*camerar*) of North Wales, where he had large mineral works and plenary mining monopolies, by patent dated September 26, 1575. It was in the summer of this year that he entertained the Queen at Kenilworth. Admitting the Royal visit entailed the heavy expense attributed to it, the magnitude of the grants the Earl received from the Queen during this year alone must have been ample recompense, and well repaid the cost of the festivities at Kenilworth. At this period the Earl of Leicester had many avowed enemies, and some rivals who aspired to supplant him in the mighty Court favour which he so absolutely controlled, having met with a sudden and unexpected death, were said to have been poisoned by his means. But to the impartial investigator of those intriguing times, little, if any, justification will be found in support of such charges, which most likely were the outcome of envy and disappointment. At any rate, the Master of the Buckhounds continued in the favour of his sovereign until the arrival of the Duke of Anjou's ambassador in October, 1578, to negotiate a marriage contract between the Duke and Elizabeth. This envoy excelled in the accomplishments of a courtier—his manners, his wit, and his gallantry made an irresistible impression. Aware that his chief obstacle was the influence which Leicester possessed over the Queen, he made it his first object to wean her from her affection for that nobleman, by disclosing to her the secrets of his amours, and informing her of his recent marriage with the relict of the late Earl of Essex, a marriage hitherto concealed from her knowledge. The Queen was mortified and irritated. Leicester added to her displeasure by his indiscretion and impatience. He attributed the influence of the envoy to philters and witchcraft, and occasionally let fall threats of personal vengeance. But the Queen ordered him to be confined at Greenwich, and by proclamation took under her special protection all the members of the Duke of Anjou's embassy, and subsequently invited Anjou to plead his own case, which he promptly accepted. He was favourably received, apparently prospered in his suit, but eventually, in deference to the wishes of her subjects and her council, Elizabeth declined his offer, in the determination to sacrifice her own happiness to the tranquillity and welfare of her kingdom.

Before the Duke of Anjou returned to Antwerp the Earl of Leicester was restored to favour. In the meantime he acquired the manor of Wanstead and other large tracts of land in Woodford, Walthamstowe, Leyton, and Ilford, in the county of Essex. These properties were soon after augmented by further grants of land in Stafford, Wilts, and Herts, besides several rich wardships that had fallen to the Crown during this interval. He was appointed custodian of the New Forest and all the Crown lands in the county Southampton for life, by patent dated June 25, 1580. The following year he obtained various grants in England and Wales, including a lease for twenty-one years of the demesne lands of Grafton, county Northampton. At the same time he alienated some portion of his estates, including the manor of Gravesend, county Kent. This will not cause surprise, for the establishments he kept up were various and vast, and everything he did necessitated an enormous expenditure of money; and with this Master of the Royal Buckhounds it was "easy come, easy go."

When the Duke of Anjou definitely decided to return to Antwerp, the Queen, to make up for having jilted him, resolved to see him off with befitting dignity. He had been elected King of the Netherlands, and his subjects were clamouring for the presence of their new sovereign. On February 1, 1582, the Duke, accompanied by the Queen and a splendid retinue, departed from Greenwich *en route* to Sandwich, from which port he was to embark to Flushing. At Canterbury Elizabeth parted from him in tears. As he pursued his journey he received from her repeated messages of inquiry after his health; and for greater distinction she ordered the Earl of Leicester, with six lords and as many knights, and a numerous train of gentlemen, to accompany him, not only to the seaside, but as far as the city of Antwerp. On his arrival there he was solemnly invested with the ducal mantle as Duke of Brabant, and afterwards at Ghent was crowned as Earl of Flanders. During the summer, aided by England and France, he opposed with chequered success the attempts of the Prince of Parma; but observing that the States were jealous of his followers, and that the real authority was possessed not by himself but by the Prince of Orange, he conceived the idea of giving the law to his inferiors, by seizing most of the principal towns in the country. However, the attempt failed in almost every instance, many thousands of his followers were slain, and he escaped, disheartened and ashamed, into France. His death on June 10, 1584, freed Queen Elizabeth from a passion which might have led her into a repetition of her amour in that quarter, and removed the greatest rival in her affections that Leicester had ever encountered.

On his return to England, the Earl of Leicester was graciously received at Court, where he resumed his normal duties, and continued to be the recipient of remunerative emoluments which still flowed upon him with a prosperous tide. Thus, during the year 1582, he obtained, jointly with John Morley, Esq., a grant of every cloth-mill that could be appropriated, for their sole use and benefit throughout the country ; and on December 16, the former obtained an acquittance from the

Exchequer of 5,000*l*. touching the purchase of the lordship and manor of Denbigh; for which he obtained a clear grant on January 15, 1584. In political projects he took some active steps, as in the course of the last-mentioned year he prevailed upon the nobility and gentry to subscribe an association to pursue unto death whomsoever should attempt anything against Queen Elizabeth. This association was subsequently approved by Parliament, and a law was passed to carry it into execution. This enactment proved the ruin of Mary Queen of Scots, and the heads of the Roman Catholic party in England. On October 2, 1585, the Earl of Leicester was appointed Captain-General in Holland and Zealand in the English expedition to the Netherlands; and on the 22nd of the same month he was further nominated Lieutenant and Commander-in-Chief of the forces in Belgium. He embarked on December 8, and on the 10th arrived at Flushing, where he was received with extraordinary and long-continued rejoicings. The Queen, too, herself, absolutely refused the sovereignty of the United Provinces; but Leicester was induced, without consulting her, to accept the office of Governor and Captain-General of the country. On January 25, 1586, he was solemnly installed at the Hague, taking an oath to preserve their religion and maintain their ancient rights and privileges, whilst the States-General and other persons in authority bound themselves by an oath of fidelity to him. On the same day proclamation was made consummating those proceedings, and declaring that the Earl, over and above the authority given him by the Queen, had the highest and supreme command, and absolute authority above and in all matters of warfare, with the administration and use of policy and justice over the United Provinces; with all such powers as any former governor of the Low Countries had possessed, and with authority to receive and administer all contributions towards the maintenance of the war. This high-handed conduct aroused the Queen's indignation, nor could Burghley, Walsingham, and Hatton mitigate her fury. She despatched Sir Thomas Heneage to the Low Countries with instructions, the subject of which was that Leicester was to resign his authority with the same publicity with which he had received it. Heneage's instructions being subsequently somewhat modified, Leicester continued to retain his office for some time; but the States became uneasy and discontented. Having formally surrendered his authority, he embarked for England, arriving at Richmond on November 23, 1586. Notwithstanding all that had passed, His Excellency (who was the first Englishman that was so styled, this appellation of dignity having been conferred upon him by the Flemings), was well received by the Queen, who soon after constituted him chief justice in eyre of all the forests south of Trent. During the following year he received a royal warrant upon the Exchequer for 26,000l. on account of Her Majesty's service, for his second expedition in the Low Countries. He also, by virtue of a like warrant, obtained 5,000l. due to him for furnishing 250 horses in that expedition, "after the rate of 2,000l. for every hundred horses." This would be at the rate of 20l. a horse—a sum, in all probability, equivalent to about 200l. a horse in modern currency—an exorbitant price to pay for cavalry remounts, provided the expenditure had been incurred by any other person than the reigning favourite; but he could silence any audit or expostulation in the Exchequer under this head, as the account was duly passed by the Master of the Horse—*i.e.*, himself.

In the meantime the Earl of Leicester had resumed his former sway at the Court, and exercised the authority invested in him as the Master of the Buckhounds, and in the multifarious offices he held under the Crown. Nor was he content with those sweets of office. No vacancy was too large or too small for his avarice. For instance, we find him securing a Crown lease to farm the manor of Great Soukey, county Lancaster, in reversion for thirty-one years from March 1, 1587; and on June 21, following, by another grant he secured all the fines on alienations "paid into the Court of Chancery for three years from March 25, last past." And here it may be noted as a singular circumstance that this, the most limited emolument which he ever had from the Crown, outlived him. However, he had no thought of death, as five days after he had secured the rich chancery fees, he was made Lord-Steward of the Household for life. About the end of the same month he was sent to Zealand with a considerable force for the relief of Gluys. The loss of that important town revived the misunderstanding between him and the States, who refused to re-establish him in the absolute authority he had formerly enjoyed, and the Queen recalled him by an instrument dated November 9, 1587, at the same time appointing Lord Willoughby Captain-General of her forces in those parts. On Leicester's return to England the Queen again admitted him into her former grace and favour, and Lord Buckhurst, who had accused him of misconduct in the management of affairs in the Low Countries, was censured, and confined to his house for some months.

On the apprehension of the Spanish invasion, the Earl of Leicester was appointed Lieutenant-General of the forces which assembled at Tilbury. He also solicited the office of Lieutenant of England and Ireland, which the Queen consented to grant him; but his patent was stayed in consequence of remonstrances from Sir Christopher Hatton, the Lord Chancellor, and Lord Burleigh, the Lord Treasurer, who represented to Her Majesty the hazard she would incur by entrusting such large and unheard-of powers to a single person. Apart from this disappointment, his various other posts kept him fully occupied, particularly the onerous duties and responsibilities attached to conducting the defence of the country during the then imminent invasion. In a quaint epistle from Leicester to the Queen, which unites in a remarkable manner the character of a love-letter with a Privy Council minute of instructions, he completely directed Her Majesty's movements, under the veil of flattering anxiety for her safety. By this means he endeavoured to induce the Queen to make Havering her head-quarters. This was fourteen miles from Tilbury, where the advanced lines of the defensive forces were encamped, and from this basis of operations he could control the whole army without the interference of the Queen, who was generalissimo in command. Although he sought to keep her in the rear, and thus gratify his inordinate ambition, she proceeded in martial pomp to Tilbury, and there reviewed the royal forces, by whom she was received with sincere manifestations of loyalty and reverence. This event has been considered the most interesting in her life. Never, certainly, did she perform her part, as the leader of a heroic nation, with such imposing effect as on that occasion. She was then fifty-five years old, and had borne the sceptre and the sword of the Empire for thirty years. The destruction of the Armada delivered England from all immediate apprehension; the camp at Tilbury became a sylvan court; the Royal Buckhounds were brought upon the scene to contribute to the pleasures of the gallant defenders, but, sad to say, the grand old style of hunting at force had then given place to the indolent method of driving the deer to "stands," from which the Queen and her courtiers fired as the quarry fled by. The records of the Court of attachment, which was held at Chigwell in those days (when Waltham Forest extended over immense tracts of Essex now disafforested), circumstantially record what bucks were shot by the Queen and the ladies and gentlemen of her suite on these occasions; and, alas! the fee bucks that were given to the Sergeant of the Buckhounds "in consideration that he hunted not," is an indelible satire of the venatic predilections of the Court.

About the end of August the Earl of Leicester set out from London to Kenilworth, but on his way stopped at his house at Cornbury, in Oxfordshire, where he was taken ill, and there breathed his last on September 4, 1588. Up to the day of his death he carried the official horn of the Royal Buckhounds; and although all the high offices of State which he had held during his career devolved on his demise upon other nobles and magnates of the Court, the Queen declined to appoint any one to succeed him in the Mastership of this branch of the pack, which remained vacant until Sir Thomas Tyringham obtained it from James I., soon after that monarch ascended the throne of England.

The Earl of Leicester was married three times: firstly, to Amy, daughter of Sir John Robsart, June 4, 1550, when the nuptials were honoured with the presence of King Edward VI., who has recorded that after the ceremony certain gentlemen strove who should first transfix with a sword on horseback the head of a goose hung alive across two posts. It is said that the Earl married, secondly, Lady Douglas Howard, widow of John, Lord Sheffield. The fact of this marriage is not free from doubt, and occasioned great controversy. By this lady he had a son (who was titular Earl of Warwick and Duke of Northumberland, a notable sportsman, and said to be the first person "that taught a dog to sit in order to catch partridges") and a daughter. He married, thirdly, Lettice, daughter of Sir Francis Knollys, K.G., and widow of Walter Devereux, Earl of Essex. By her he had a son, Robert, called Lord Denbigh, who died July 19, 1584. By his will, made at Middleburgh, August 1, 1587, he appointed his widow sole executrix; and expressed in strong terms his fidelity and duty to the Queen, to whom he bequeathed three great emeralds, several diamonds, and a rope of fair white pearls to the number of six hundred.

This Master of the Buckhounds enjoyed extraordinary power for nearly thirty years. There was no part of the kingdom in which he had not extraordinary influence, and in the counties around Kenilworth almost everything was dependent upon him either through hope or fear. It is almost impossible to enumerate all the local and subordinate offices which he held. They must have greatly strengthened his parliamentary influence, and he seems to have been a perfect master of those arts to which a subsequent age gave the appellation of boroughmongering. He had the sagacity to perceive the growing importance of the House of Commons, and took care to fill it with his dependants, and persons devoted to his interest. He was a patron of literature, the drama, and the arts, and, being well aware of the advantages of trade and commerce, warmly encouraged those voyages of discovery which redounded so greatly, if not to the honour, to the advantage of the kingdom. Of his mining operations, cloth and woollen manufactures, and his monopolies, we have already given ample evidence. In short, there was no opportunity for the acquisition of wealth or influence that fell to his dispensation as minister of the Crown which he did not embrace for his personal use and benefit. Yet he was looked upon as a finished courtier in every respect. Elegant in his dress; liberal in his way of living; bountiful to soldiers and men of letters; very adroit in choosing his time and carrying his point; complaisant in his temper, but insidious towards rivals; amorous in the former part of his life, but in the latter uxorious to a strange degree. As for the rest, as he preferred an envied height of power to solid virtue, he furnished matter for a multitude of malicious detractors to descant upon, who, even in the zenith of his glory, failed not to prosecute him with their libels, which were mixed with abundance of untruths. To sum up all, the Earl was a statesman for his own ends, and what was said of him in public had the air of praise and panegyric; "but in private, and where people durst be free," he was represented in quite a different light. Thanks to the author of "Kenilworth," the Earl of Leicester has become one of the most familiar personages of the sixteenth century; nevertheless, there is hardly a circumstance in his career which the distinguished novelist has not misrepresented, either in chronological or historical accuracy.

Although no one was appointed to fill the office of Master of the Royal Buckhounds, appertaining to the Lord Chamberlain's department of the Household—which became vacant on the death of the Earl of Leicester on September 4, 1588—until (Sir) Thomas Tyringham obtained it from James I. on June 21, 1603, there is no doubt that this branch of the pack, and the subordinate officers attached to it, continued to be sustained as usual during the remainder of Queen Elizabeth's reign. The annual accounts of the Treasurer of the Chamber from 1589 to 1602 contain every detail relating to the officials, their several salaries, allowances for uniform, etc., as heretobefore recorded; the total cost of the pack amounting, on an average, to about 140*l.* a year. During those fourteen years the

Master's annual fee of 33*l.* 6*s.* 8*d.* is conspicuous by its absence. In all probability the duties of the Master partly devolved on the Sergeant of the pack for the time being: Henry Harvey, Esq. (*ob.* 1596), James Bond, Esq. (*circa* 1598), and Francis Joye, Esq., successively. Without going into details it may be noted, *en passant*, that Walter Dodsworth, one of the grooms to the pack from the time of Henry VIII., died in 1588, and was succeeded by " William Sale *alias* Dilly." Every particular bearing on the *personnel* of this branch of the Royal Buckhounds is thus circumstantially recorded. The fame acquired by those hounds, at the time now under notice, must have been notorious, as the following incident shows: When Sir Edward Wotton was sent on a special embassy to James VI., King of Scotland, in 1585, his best credentials to that sporting monarch were a draft of buckhounds from the royal kennels, and two race horses and four hunters from the royal stud. Unfortunately they were forgotten by the ambassador. On his arrival at Edinburgh, James anxiously inquired for the hounds and horses. Wotton was obliged to pretend that they were on the road; and, to remedy the blunder, he had to despatch a special messenger in hot haste to Sir Francis Walsingham, with a missive directing him to forward the hounds and horses without delay to the King. " Since his mynd doth so runn vpon them & he put in head of some in coming, the want of them might breed conceiptes which the adverse partis would work vpon." Wotton adds that he had also written to the Earl of Leicester as earnestly as he could to send six or seven couples of buckhounds, and urged Sir Francis to take order for their transmission " with all convenient speed." These hounds and horses soon after arrived in Edinburgh, and were formally presented on June 12 to the King, who declared them to be " the rediest hounds and horses that ever he had seen." This novel stroke of diplomacy had the desired effect; the ambassador's object was instantly attained; and, it is said, the King immediately after left his capital, the cares of State, and his own mother's fate to the tender mercies of her avowed enemies, for the hunting fields of the Fife of Falkland, there to practically test the Elizabethan present " in hunting of the buck."

In all probability there were many similar requisitions made on the Royal kennels from time to time, as draughts of those hounds were frequently presented to foreign potentates and other distinguished personages at home and abroad. And in order to keep the Royal kennels " well replenished " in such essential accessories of the chase, the Sergeant of the Buckhounds had a warrant authorising him to seize any hounds he chose " for Her Majesty's disport," as well as " horses, mares, and draughts for the carriage of the said hounds from place to place." It is therefore evident that this branch of the Royal Buckhounds was kept up to its normal efficiency, *sans* the Master; and there is no reason to suppose there was any diminution in the number of meets, or any falling off in the sport the pack gave to its followers during the last years of the reign of good Queen Bess. Unfortunately the records of such meets and runs are few and far between; little or no notice was taken of such common-place events by the chroniclers of those times. Nevertheless we ascertain that the Queen continued to patronise the hunt with her presence. Marshal de Bassompierre, happening to be at Calais in 1601, his friend, the Duke de Biron, " debauched " him into an excursion to England. Bassompierre got no further than London. Queen Elizabeth being then at the Vine in Hampshire, Biron followed her thither, and had the pleasure of seeing Her Majesty " hunt, attended by more than fifty ladies, all mounted on hackneys." *

* Stowe gives a different account of the Duke de Biron's visit to Hampshire, to the following effect : "The fourth day [September 9] after the Queen's coming to Basing, the Sheriff was commanded to attend the Duke of Biron at his coming into that county. Whereupon, the next day being the 10th of September, he went towards Blackwater, being the uttermost confines of that shire towards London, and there he met the said Duke, accompanied with above twenty of the nobilitie of France, and attended with about four hundred Frenchmen. The said Duke was that night brought to the Vyne, a fair large house of the Lord Sonds, which was furnished with hangings and plate from the Tower and Hampton Court; and with seven score beds and furniture, which the willing and obedient people of the county of Southampton, upon two days' warning, had brought thither, to lend the Queen. The Duke abode there four or five days, all at the Queen's charges, and spent her more at the Vyne than her own

A few days after he returned to rejoin his friend in London, and after a further sojourn of three days the travellers returned to France—Biron to lose his life on the scaffold, and Bassompierre to risk his in the field, and hardly less often in the intrigues of the Court. However, after many vicissitudes, he lived to represent his country at the Court of Charles I. This incident is important, as it establishes an irrefutable authority that the chase was patronised by the fair sex nearly three hundred years ago, and, as we shall have occasion to record hereafter, many ladies, fair and famous, continued to follow the Royal Buckhounds in the days of yore as they do in our own times.

On March 23, 1603, Queen Elizabeth died at Richmond,

Court for that time spent at Basing. And one day he attended her at Basing Park at hunting, where the Duke stayed her coming, and did there see her in such Royalty, and so attended by the nobility, so costly furnished and mounted, as the like had seldom been seen." However, we get the official account of this royal hunting progress in the subjoined extracts from the returns of the Lord Chamberlain for the time being: "To Richard Conningesby for the allow'nce of himselfe, one yeoman vsher, three yeomen, and twoo gromes of the chamber, twoo gromes of the wardrobe, and one grome porter, viz., for makeinge readie a standinge in the little P'ke at Windsor against ye huntinge there, for two daies, mense Augusti 1601, xxxix^s. iiij^d. For makinge readie M^r. Meredithe's house at old Wyndsor for her Matie to dyne at when she hunted in the foreste, by like tyme eod. mense, xxix^s. iiij^d. . . . For makinge readie Sir Robert Kennington's house at Barraper for a dynninge place by the space of twoo daies, mense Septembris 1601, xxix^s. iiij^d. For makinge ready Sr Humphrey Foster's house at Aldermanton by the space of x^{en} dayes, mense Augusti 1601, ix^{li}. xvj^s. viij^d. For makinge readie the Lord Marques [of Winchester] his house at Basynge by the space of xiiij^{en} dayes mense Septembris 1601, xiij^{li}. x^s. iiij^d. *For mukeinge ready the Lorde Sandes' house at the Vyne for the frensh Ambassado^{rs} by like tyme mense pred', ⟨xiij^{li}. xv^s. iiij^d.* For makinge readie a standinge in Basynge P'ke for two dayes dčo mense ⟨xxiv^s. iiij^d. For makinge readie a chamber ouer the gate there for her highnes to dyne wth the Frenchmen by the space of iiij^{or} dayes, mense Septemberis 1601, ⟨ lxxviij^s. viij^d. For alteraçons at Basynge in the presence and p'vie chambe^{rs} to retyre into after dinner by like tyme and in the same moneth, ⟨xxxix^s. iiij^d. For makinge readye the Ladye Marquesse, her house at Basynge for the Frenchmen to dyne by the space of twoo dayes, mense Septembris, ⟨1601 xxxix^s. iiij^d. For makinge readie the Chapple at Basynge by the like time, ⟨ xxxix^s. iiij^d. For makinge readie Sr George More's house at Losley by the space of x^{en} days, mense Septembris, ⟨1601, ix^{li}. xxvj^s. viij^d."—Accounts of the Treasurer of the Chamber of the Household. E. L. T. R. Series 1, Box F, Bundle 3, m. 67d. MS. P.R.O.

where she had frequently patronised the meets of the Royal Buckhounds during the last year of her glorious reign. Windsor, Richmond, and Eltham were the favourite localities where she hunted in that year. But beyond the formal entries of payments made to the apparellers for her accommodation during those royal venatic excursions, there is little known about the sport. Doubtless the sport was worthy of the splendour by which it was surrounded. The grand old Queen delighted to mingle with her subjects; they reciprocated that feeling on all occasions, and in no place did she more amply experience their loving homage and sterling loyalty than in the hunting-field or on the racecourse. The public at large were the Queen's body-guards, and to them she trusted her royal person with implicit faith. It is a well-known historical fact that when Vitelli was employed to assassinate her in the hunting-field, where, as he was truly instructed, she was to be always found without the yeomen of the guard or police of any denomination, that, on observing the silent homage and unmistakable loyalty of what we would now technically call the field, he relinquished his intention in despair, and so forfeited all hope of earning the pension and title of nobility which were guaranteed to him by his vile employers, as well as the immortality which he was told awaited him in the world to come. Elizabeth survived her death in the affection of her people; they continued to keep up her birthday as if she still occupied that throne which many held to have been usurped by "an alien race." In course of time her successor became a most popular monarch with his sporting subjects, though, unlike Elizabeth, he objected to a crowded meet or a large field riding to his hounds. His predilection for the chase, and for field sports of all sorts, is well known to all who are acquainted with the rural annals of his reign. We have already had an example of the high esteem he had for the hounds and horses of the Elizabethan sporting establishment, and we may well conclude that he anxiously looked forward to the day when he would become the proud possessor of the royal studs, kennels, and mews, of "the Land of Promise."

CHAPTER IV.

HEREDITARY BRANCH.—HENRY VIII.—CHARLES I.

Sir Richard Pexsall, Tenth Master—Sir John Savage, Eleventh Master—Sir Pexsall Brocas, Twelfth Master. Dispute between James I. and the Master.—Critical Affairs of the Pack.—It is abolished by Royal Warrant. —The Functions of the Office conferred on the Sergeant of the Household Branch.—Order thereon for the Sheriff of Surrey and Sussex.—Passing Events.—The Hereditary Pack given to Charles, Duke of York.—Sir Pexsall Brocas continues to receive the Emoluments of their Office.—The Hunt-Servants.—Thomas Brocas, Thirteenth Master.—The Manor of Little Weldon, and with it the nominal Mastership of this Branch of the Royal Buckhounds, sold to Sir Lewis Watson.

THE first payment to SIR RICHARD PEXSALL, tenth Hereditary Master of the Buckhounds, occurs on the Pipe Roll of the county Sussex, for the 11th year of the reign of Henry VIII. (April 22, 1519—August 21, 1520), when he received 50*l*. from the Sheriff of that county, due since the 4th Henry VIII. (April 22, 1512—April 21, 1513), the payments on account of this portion of the pack having been often in arrears during the reign of Bluff King Hal. About this time George Hunte was the huntsman, and John Bland and Hugh Carter the yeomen berners. This Master obtained part payments on account of the usual stipend allocated out of the issues of the county Sussex, in support of his office, pretty regularly to the end of the reign of Henry VIII. Lapses sometimes occur where the rolls are imperfect; and as it is hardly necessary to go into these details year by year, it only remains to mention that Reginald Harrington was the huntsman, and John Massey and Thomas Cook were the subordinate officers of this pack for some years before and for some years after the end of Henry VIII.'s reign. However, from the 34th regnal year of the reign of Henry VIII. (1542–43) to the time of Sir Richard's death in the 13th of Elizabeth (1570–71), he received the stipend of his office, amounting to 50*l.* per annum; those payments having been derived from the issues of the county Sussex during the reigns of Henry VIII., Philip and Mary, Edward VI., and Elizabeth, except from the 9th to the 12th of Elizabeth, when the payments to him came out of the issues of county Surrey.

Sir Richard Pexsall obtained a patent from Queen Mary, dated May 23, 1554, by virtue of which the office of Custodian or Master of the Royal Buckhounds, with the Manor of Little Weldon, etc., was confirmed to him, and also the office of "Custodian or Master" of the Queen's "Privy Buckhounds." This document contains some very strong expressions reflecting on the institution of the Privy or Household branch of the pack by Henry VIII., which, if uttered during his reign, would, inevitably, have brought the tenth Hereditary Master to the block. His status as "Custodian or Master" of the Household branch, pursuant to this patent, seems equivocal, as he was not recognised or recompensed in the same manner as were his predecessors and successors holding the office of Master of the "Privy" or Household branch of the pack.

On the death of Sir Ralph Pexsall, in 1540, his second and only surviving son, Sir Richard Pexsall, claimed all the family honours, etc., including the Hereditary Mastership of the Royal Buckhounds. This claim, however, was disputed by Bernard Brocas, Esq., of Alton, county Hants, the lineal heir, on the plea that when the *direct* male line failed on the demise of William Brocas, Esq., of Beaurepaire, in 1509, the Hereditary Mastership reverted to him as the lineal representative of the family, through Bernard Brocas, Esq., of Alton, second son of Sir Bernard Brocas, the second Master of the Royal Buckhounds. Upon this plea Bernard Brocas, the lineal heir, sued the Pexsalls, the heirs general, for Beaurepaire, and sixteen manors in the county of Southampton, besides other estates in Wiltshire, Northampton, etc.; and for ending all contentions espoused Anne, the eldest of Sir Richard Pexsall's four daughters and co-heirs, who (by will, dated October 19, 1571), having all bequeathed to her, brought the ancient seat and hereditaments into the name again, after it had for sixty-five years been possessed by that of Pexsall. But Sir Richard Pexsall's widow, Lady Eleanor, having married, secondly, Sir John Savage, he began a suit to upset the family settlements—a subject which we need not go into here, as it is detailed in Professor Burrows' volume, the upshot being that from the death of Sir Richard Pexsall, in 1571, to the year 1573 no payment was made by the Sheriff of Surrey and Sussex to any Hereditary Master of the Buckhounds. During those three years the post seems to have been in abeyance. In the interval Sir John Savage married Sir Richard Pexsall's widow, and by the subjoined deed of settlement, he, as the holder of the fourth part of the Manor of Little Weldon, became, by the family arrangement, the "Hereditary" Master of the Buckhounds:—

"THIS INDENTURE, made the three and twentithe daie of Maie in the fifteenthe yeare of the reign of our sov'igne ladie Elizabeth by the grace of God, of Englande, Fraunce, and Ireland, defendor of the faith, &c., Whereas Sr John Savage of Clifton in the countie of Chester knighte vpon the one P'tie : And the righte honorable Edward Earle of Rutlande, John Manners of Haddon in the countie of Derbie esquire, Roger Manners esquire, one of the Queene's Maties esquires of the bodie, and Richard Buckley of Chednell in citie of Chester esquire vpon the other P'ortie WITNESSITHE that whereas John Jobson late of the citie of London esquire, and Elizabeth Jobson wife of the said John, one of the daughters and coheirs of Sr Richarde Pexall late of Barow per al^s Bewre per in the countie of Southampton knighte lawfullie conveyed and assured as well by fyne as otherwise the fourthe P'tes of the mannors of Bawrep al^s Bewreper &c. . . . with their appurtenances &c. . . . And also the forth p'tes of the mannor of Little Weldon with thapp'tn'ces, and tenne toftes, ten gardens, two hundred acres of land, floure and twentie of medowe, two hundreth acres y^t pasture, and tenne acres of woode with th'app'tence's in Little Weldon : And the fourth p'tes of the Bailiewicke of the custodie or keepinge of the kinges Buckehoundes, and fee of fyftie Poundes by the yeare for the keepinge of the same Buckhoundes to be paid yearlie by the hands of the Sheriffe of Surr' and Sussex in the countie of Northampton. . . ."

From 1574 to 1584 Sir John Savage apparently exercised his functions as the Hereditary Master of the Buckhounds, as he received 50*l.* per annum during those years from the Sheriff of Surrey and Sussex, by virtue of this office. From 1585 to 1593 this post was again in abeyance, as no payment was made to any Hereditary Master until 1594, when Pexsall Brocas, Esq., succeeded to the office, the profits of which he held during the remainder of Queen Elizabeth's reign and in the reign of James I.

SIR JOHN SAVAGE, knight, eleventh "Hereditary" Master of the Royal Buckhounds, the eldest son and heir of Sir John Savage, of Clifton, Cheshire, and Lady Elizabeth Somerset, daughter of Charles, first Earl of Worcester, enjoyed this office, *temp.* Elizabeth, from 1574—1584, by virtue of the deed of settlement dated May 23, 1573, as above set forth. During those ten years he received the sum of 50*l.* per annum from the Sheriffs of Surrey and Sussex for his fee, and supplying the hunt-servants with their wages and liveries according to the customary regulations appertaining to this branch of the royal pack, as set forth (for instance) in the subjoined writ of Privy Seal and the entry of the payment on the Pipe Roll:—

POUR LEZ BUCKHOUNDS.

Treshonor' Seigneur' violes faire tres de guarrante de sonbz' le privie seau de ñre soveraigñe dame la Royne Derect a le Vicecount de Surr' et Sussex pour faire payment dez issues de sa bailaye po[r] lez gages des vennres et puture de chiens en manier de sonbz escrit. Conftafavoir A John Savage mil. M[r] dez Buckehoundes a Royne xij[d] le io[r]. A John Withers vealterer ÿ[d] le io[r]. A Allano Bowet et Guillam Gardin' valect barners chascn' de eulx j[d] ob'. le io[r] pour leur gagies et pour le puture de vj lemryers et xxiiij[or] chiens currants pour chascū de eulx ob' le io[r]. Comenceantz a la feast de sainct Michaell larchange dernivement passe Inques a xxiiij[or] io[r] de Jugne lors prochaine ensuiuant lung et lautre io[r] accomptz pour prinst le puture de xv chiens cuffants pour chascū de eulx ob le io^r. Et lez gages pour ang varlect barner pour xl io^r en quarismo que anly seront au lez Coñstages du dict John Savage pour lez Statuts dull' ostiell mesme nr̃e Dame. Et anxi quitts faire paiement a dict John pour lez gages en la Cote vij^d ob le io^r. Le susdict John Withers vealterer ij^d le io^r et a dict Guillam Gardin' et Allano Bowett pour chascū de eulx j^d ob le io^r pour leur gage, vj lenryers et xxiiij^{or} chiens currants chascū de eulx ob le io^r de xxv^{mo} io^r de Jugne debant dict, tanq^r a xxix^{mo} io^r de Septemb^r adunq^r prochaine ensuivant lung et lautre io^r accomptz. Et Veltre plus quil faire payment a dict John Savage pour cez deulx Robes, pour la xl^s. Et a lez vealterers et Barn's pour lure Robes chascū de eulx xiij^s iiij^d. Et pour chamicz pour chascū de eulx iiij^s. iiij^d. pour lan. Don' a la maneir de Grenwiche le xxv^{mo} io^r de Septembris lan le Reign' de ñre soverigñc Dame Elizabeth 𝔓 la grace de dien Royne dangliterr' ffrañc et direlands defendo^r de la foye xxme.

Ex^m p Gregor' Lovell, Clerc, Compt.

A Treshono^r Seignr̃e gardian du privie Seau de nre Dame la Royne.

The French of Stratford-le-Bow, which had been immortalised by Chaucer about the time when the Royal Buckhounds were instituted under the first Hereditary Master in the reign of Edward III., compares favourably with the language of diplomacy " as she was writ " by the scribe attached to the Court of Queen Elizabeth, when he indited the royal commands to the Keeper of the Privy Seal, directing him to issue a writ to the Sheriff of Surrey and Sussex to pay Sir John Savage and his staff the several sums due to them on account of the cost of this branch of the pack for the year 1578, as transcribed *verbatim et literatim* above. The Lord Privy Seal acted promptly on his instructions, as we learn from an entry on the Memoranda Roll of that year, as also from the following extract in the Pipe Roll, showing that the Sheriff, by virtue of the Privy Seal in question, paid out of the issues of the county of Sussex the sum of 50*l*. to Sir John Savage for the purposes therein set forth :—

" Di Johi' Savage militi magr̃o canū dnē Regine nūc 𝔓 damis capiendi xij^d 𝔓 diem 𝔓 vadii' suis extra cur' ac Johi' Wether veantr' ijᵈ Pᵉ diem Alano Bowett & Wiłłmo Gardiner valect Barūs' utriq' eoū' jᵈ ob Pᵉ diem Pᵉ vadiis suis & Pᵉ putur' sex leporar' & xxiiij ᵒʳ canū curren' Pᵉ quoits' ob Pᵉ diem affesto Sci Michīs Arche' anno xxᵐᵒ Regine huius usqʳ xxiiijᵗⁱᵒ diem Junij tunc Pᵉx sequen ultroq¹ die computato except putur' xv canū currene' Et Pᵉ vadiis unius valect barñs' Pᵉ xl diebȝ in quadragesima qui erunt ad custodi dci Johi' Pᵉ statut hospicij dñc Regne & eidem Johi' Pᵉ vadiis suis in cur' vijᵈ ob'. Pᵉ diem Et Pʳfat' Johi' Wether veante' ijᵈ Pᵉ diem. Et Pʳfat' Alana Bowett & Wiłłmo Gardiner valect' barns' utriqʳ eoū' jᵈ ob Pᵉ diem Pᵉ vadiis suis & Pᵉ putur' sex leporar' & xxiiijᵒʳ canū curren Pᵉ quoit' eoū' ob Pᵉ diem a xxv die Junii anno xxjᵐᵒ usqʳ xxix diem Septembʳ tunc Pᵉx sequen ultraqʳ die computato & Pʳfat' Johi' Pᵉ duabȝ Robis suis xlˢ & Pᵉ Robis dict veantr' & Barns' euilt' eoū' xiijˢ nyᵈ & Pᵉ calcułłar suis iiijᵈ Pᵉ diem viz de hoīnoi vadiis fleodi & Robis Pᵉ uno anno funt's ad ffestū Sci' Miches Arche' anno xxjᵐᵒ Regine huius ~ L¹. Pᵉ Pᵉ'cessu uide & Cons' Baronū in cons casū hit' & annotat' in memor'ᵈ ex Pᵉte Remem Thes' de anno xvᵐᵒ Regine nūc Elizabeth viz int' precepta de termīo sci Hiłł Rotlo. In quodm̄ Pᵉ cessū tangen' Johem Pelham. Ac nup vic' com' Pᵉdcor' de anno xiijᵐᵒ Regine Pᵉdc̄c̄. Ac Pᵉ b're dñc Regine nūc de priuato Sigillo suo Pᵉfat' vic direct' ac łrās acquietañc Roberti Creswell ar' attornat' Pᵉ'dcc' Johi' de Recepcōne."*

Although we have not yet met with the actual—which was probably retained by the Sheriffs—Privy Seal (without the production of which the Hereditary Master could not recover his annual stipend, or the wages and other allowances of the hunt-servants under him, from the Sheriff of Surrey and Sussex), we obtain all necessary details bearing on this branch of the Royal Buckhounds, in the instructions here recited, the recapitulation of the missing document in the Memoranda Roll, and the full statement above quoted from the Pipe Roll. It will thus

---

* Pipe Roll, 20 Eliz., membrane, *sub. tit.* "Item, Sussex." As above explained, this is the earliest reference we have met with, in the sixteenth century, to the Privy Seal, by which the Sheriff of Surrey and Sussex was warranted to pay the Hereditary Master of the Buckhounds, for the time being, the fees, etc., appertaining to the office, amounting altogether to 50*l.* a year. It is obvious, however, that privy seals were issued to and received by the said Sheriffs for this purpose, as they are recited every time the payment was made, the first to Sir John Savage having occurred in the year 1574.

be seen that there was very little alteration in the constitution of this part of the pack from the time of Edward III. to Elizabeth. As heretofore, the Master's fee was 1s. a day and 2l. a year for his official uniform, and 7½d. per day additional when he was in attendance upon the Court. The same number of hunt-servants were employed, their wages, liveries, and allowances being substantially similar to those enjoyed by their predecessors in office. The cost of the hounds' meat is set down at the same figure as given in the original ordinance. The total expense of this department of the Buckhounds amounted to 50l. a year.

In 1565 Sir John Savage built "a fair new house" at Clifton (afterwards called Rock-Savage), which his posterity have ever since retained. Sir John was a very prominent personage in Cheshire during many years in Elizabeth's reign. He was Sheriff of the county in 1560, 1570, 1574, 1579, and 1591, and Mayor of the City of Chester in 1569, 1574, and 1597. In 1567 he was appointed, in conjunction with Sir Hugh Cholmondeley and Sir Lawrence Smith, to view and make all the levies for the expedition then fitting out and subsequently despatched from Chester for service in Ireland. For this purpose the Commissioners had to borrow certain sums of money from merchants and other persons in Chester; but it is doubtful if they ever recovered the amount thus obtained from the Treasury. In 1569 he and his brother magistrates of the county Palatine formally made declaration to the Council of having conformed to and accepted the Act of Parliament for the uniformity of Common Prayer, out of duty to the Queen, by whom was opened up to them "the plain path of virtue to their eternal salvation." Sir John continued to take an active part in similar local transactions relating to the county Palatine until his death, which took place on December 5, 1597, when he was, for the third time, Mayor of Chester. His descendants ascended, step by step, from knighthood, baronetcy, viscountcy, earldom, to the dignity of Marquis of Cholmondeley. This Sir John Savage married, first, Elizabeth, daughter of Thomas Manners, Earl of Rutland, by whom he had five sons and five daughters. She dying on August 8, 1570, he married, secondly, Elinor, relict of Sir Richard Pexsall, but had no children by her, and in consequence of this alliance he became the eleventh Hereditary Master of the Royal Buckhounds from 1574 to 1584, during which time he received 50*l*. a year from the Sheriff of Surrey and Sussex in support of the office, as above mentioned.

SIR PEXSALL BROCAS, the twelfth Hereditary Master of the Royal Buckhounds, *temps*. Elizabeth, James I., and Charles I.—from 1584 to 1630—was the eldest surviving son of Bernard Brocas, Esq., of Horton, county Buckingham, and Anne, eldest daughter of Sir Richard Pexsall, of Beaurepaire, county Hants. Professor Montagu Burrows, in his work on "The Family of Brocas, of Beaurepaire," tells us that young Pexsall Brocas was brought up with his father and mother at Ickenham, near London, from whence he was sent to Gray's Inn, of which he became a member. Before he came of age it seems he indulged rather freely in the dissipations of the Metropolis; and, even after attaining his majority, he preferred life in London to hunting, home, and duty. Whether he claimed his right to the Hereditary office of Master of the Buckhounds or not when he came of age in 1584 we are unable to say; but it is evident that no payment was made to him, by right of that post, by the Sheriffs of Surrey and Sussex, before the 36th year of Elizabeth's reign—*i.e.*, in 1594. It consequently follows, so far as relates to the stipend usually allocated towards the support of this department of the Royal Buckhounds, that it was financially in abeyance during those ten years. But in 1594 he received his first payment as the Hereditary Master of the Buckhounds—viz., 50*l*. This sum comprised the Master's fee of 1*s*. a day for his wages, 2*l*. a year for his livery, and the usual dole of 7½*d*. a day for his attendance in court. His huntsman, Thomas Browne, the two principal hunt-servants, Richard Mercer and Thomas Duke, received the usual remuneration, with allowances for uniforms, and for feeding and keeping the fifteen couples of hounds which constituted this portion of the pack. During the remainder of Queen Elizabeth's reign Pexsall Brocas continued to be paid 50*l*. a year by the Sheriff of the county Sussex, as above recorded.

In the meantime Pexsall Brocas married Margaret, daughter of Sir Thomas Sherley, of Wiston, county Sussex; and was soon after elected M.P. for Steyning. These new responsibilities did not act as a curb on his wayward disposition, as he continued to indulge in excesses, which got him into some serious scrapes. These transactions are related by Professor Burrows, and call for no recapitulation here.* However, some other events in connection with the office of this Hereditary Master of the Buckhounds, which are not given in Professor Burrows' volume, cannot be passed over. Thus, on January 27, 1590, we find he obtained a commission to take up hounds for her Majesty's service, "as heretofore hath been accustomed"; the Sergeant of the Household branch of the pack and their several deputies being included in the commission. Doubtless those gentlemen continued to exercise the authority by which they were invested until the end of Elizabeth's reign, as shortly after the accession of James I. Sir Pexsall Brocas obtained a similar commission from the new King, by whom he was knighted at the Charter House, London, and in all probability the latter commission was given to him on that occasion, as it is dated May 11, 1603, the very day he was dubbed. At any rate, Sir Pexsall Brocas seems to have been on good terms with the King and the court favourites at this time, as his claim of the Hereditary Master of the Buckhounds was unquestioned, although his claim to officiate by virtue of his office at the King's coronation was not allowed.† At any rate, he invari-

* Professor Burrows, in a letter to the Editor of the *Times*, dated November 8, 1892, says: "When Pexall Brocas came of age in 1584 he entered on the hereditary mastership without licence; but Elizabeth established him in his rights in 1589. In 1598 and 1599 he deputed Sir John Stanhope to do his duties." We can find no official verification or confirmation of these allegations. Are we to infer that they are based on the "forged deeds" mentioned on p. 90?

† He received a dole of scarlet cloth, value 5*l*., out of the King's great wardrobe for his livery on the occasion of the state entry of James I. into London.

ably received 50*l.* a year, by virtue of the sergeanty appertaining to the Manor of Little Weldon, from the Sheriffs of Sussex, from this time until the end of the King's reign. On the Pipe Roll of the 2nd James I. he is described as Pexsall Brocas, "late Esquire, now Knight," "magister canes regis"; Thomas Browne, the huntsman, and Richard Mercer and Robert Duke, yeomen berners, being still the hunt-servants under him.

Nevertheless, the affairs of the Hereditary branch of the Royal Buckhounds did not run smoothly. The ripple of dissatisfaction which appeared on the surface of the establishment of this important adjunct of the Royal chase early in the reign of Henry VII. developed energy during the reign of Bluff King Hal, producing, as we have seen, the Privy, or Household, branch—first as an auxiliary, soon afterward independent, and now, in the time of James I., in actual antagonism to the old, so-called, hereditary establishment. "Tempora mutantur!" This branch of the Royal Buckhounds exhibited symptoms of decay early in the sixteenth century. Like the White Hart in the fable, although it was doomed to death early in the seventeenth century, it was not destined to die at least for another hundred years to come. Throughout its history we find, from time to time, radical changes. Thus, under Edward III., when hunting "at force" became customary, and infused new life into the pleasures of the chase, the method then observed failed to meet the exigencies of the dashing horseman of the Tudor era, when led horses were introduced by Henry VIII., and those who rode to the Royal Buckhounds. It is apparent the Hereditary pack did not meet the demands made upon it in those days. It may have suffered through the practical abolition of feudal service; it must have been out of touch with a court whose headquarters were at Westminster and Windsor, where its Master was only obliged to appear in person during the forty days of Lent. These and other circumstances brought about a crisis in its fate soon after the accession of James I.

We now find antagonism openly manifested between the two branches. Whether the Trojan Master of the Hereditary, or the Tyrian Master of the Household branch hath his quarrel right is a complicated question, and one for the jurist rather than the sportsman to determine. But the King took the part of the Household branch, and who durst gainsay the wisdom of the British Solomon?

According to the accounts of the Treasurer of the Chamber of the Royal Household and contemporary warrants, it is evident that James I., as early as Midsummer 1603, was desirous to annex the Hereditary Kennel, so as to have those hounds under his direct control, with a view, probably, of amalgamating the two branches. At this time the King was not on bad terms with Sir Pexsall Brocas. For instance, in April 1604, he obtained a pardon for all riots and unlawful assemblies in which he had been implicated before the 20th of March last past, and for forging and publishing forged deeds, and of all forfeitures, due and depending, concerning the same; but, soon after, affairs between them became invidious, and then ensued the rupture. It is possible that, at this time, Brocas was riding for a fall. At any rate, he offered no impediment when the administration of the Hereditary branch of the pack was practically taken out of his hands, and conferred upon Silvester Dodsworth, by a warrant under the signet, in August 1603. It is evident the Hereditary Kennel was not kept up to the maximum pursuant to the terms of the sergeanty, as certain drafts of buckhounds were requisitioned in the North of England, in order to "replenish" it. Moreover, the King had to find the money required to pay for the food of those hounds. This unsatisfactory state of affairs went on for five years. Then came a climax. On January 26, 1608-9, a royal sign-manual, by the King's command, was issued to the officers of the Household, " to forbear to make any warrant for a Privy Seal, to be directed to the Sheriffs of Surrey and Sussex, for the time being, for the payment of any sums and entertainment to Sir Pexsall Brocas, for himself and the keeping of a kennel of hounds, with offices appertaining, which, His Majesty's pleasure is, shall from henceforth cease." This was a strong manifestation of royal wrath; yet it was as mild as the note of a hunting-horn compared with the ultimatum at the end of the King's letter: "And to insert in the said warrant instead of him (Sir Pexsall Brocas) the name of Robert Rayne, now Sergeant of the Buckhounds for that Kennel, requiring in the same, the said Sheriff to make all payments, mentioned in the said Privy Seal, to the said Robert Rayne, until His Majesty's pleasure be signified to them to the contrary." To conform with the King's arbitrary behest would be illegal, as, pursuant to the Patent of the 27th Henry VI., no one, other than the holder of the Manor of Little Weldon, was entitled to receive the stipend appertaining to the Hereditary Master of the Royal Buckhounds, and payable to him in that capacity by the Sheriffs of Surrey and Sussex, for the time being. Without going to such an extreme, the King had the power of effectually stopping the Hereditary Master's annual stipend by simply withholding the Writ of Privy Seal. Without that warrant the Sheriff would not be authorised to pay the stipend levied on the issues of those counties. On the other hand, the fact of Robert Rayne having been foisted into the office held by Brocas, clearly indicates that the Hereditary Mastership was, at this time, practically considered obsolete. This opinion, however, did not invalidate the financial obligations incidental to the office, nor did it affect the sergeanty of the custody of the hounds appertaining to the Manor of Little Weldon; for, so long as the writ of Privy Seal could be obtained, the stipend could not be withheld, provided the Sheriff could raise sufficient money to meet the claim. That this view of the case was ultimately adopted (when calmer councils prevailed, after the storm had subsided) is manifested by the fact that Sir Pexsall Brocas obtained his Privy Seal, and the Sheriff of Sussex paid him 50*l*. by right of his office in 1610. At this time Thomas Brown was still the huntsman, and Richard Ailiff and Robert Duck the yeomen berners of this branch of the pack.

Robert Rayne continued to officiate as sergeant of the

Hereditary branch of the pack; but whether his control extended to the whole or to only a portion of it is uncertain. He enjoyed the same privilege and power as Silvester Dodsworth and Sir Pexsall Brocas previously exercised, with free ingress and egress to hunt in any grounds, parks, forests, and chases belonging to the King or his subjects, in order to train hounds. And he obtained an annuity of 50l. a year for life, over and above his salary, emoluments, and allowances, as set forth in the accounts of the Treasurer of the Chamber. This arrangement continued, without any material alteration, down to Lady-Day 1613, when the whole, or some portion, of the Hereditary pack and a draft from the Privy or Household pack was formed into a separate kennel for Charles, Duke of York. Timothy Tyrrell, Esq., was appointed Master of it; Robert Rayne still continued to act as the sergeant. The other hunt-servants and some particulars of this pack are given in our Memoir of Sir Timothy Tyrrell, therefore it is unnecessary to further allude to it here. It reappears again when it was incorporated in the Household branch on the accession of Charles I. in 1625.

The annual stipend of 50l., which had been paid by the Sheriffs of Sussex to Sir Pexsall Brocas, without intermission, from 1594 to 1625, terminated with the end of the reign of James I. No further payment was made to this Hereditary Master of the Buckhounds until the 3rd year of Charles I.'s reign (1627-8), when he received the sum of 50l. out of the issues of the county Sussex, which is the final payment to him recorded on the Pipe Rolls. At this date Edward Remington was the huntsman, and Thomas Chaddock and John Mancell or Morrell were the two yeomen prickers appertaining to this branch of the Royal Buckhounds. Thus, during the thirty-six years that Sir Pexsall Brocas held the Hereditary office of Master of the Buckhounds, we find the annual fees allocated towards the support of this branch of the royal pack were in abeyance for fourteen years—viz., from the 26th to the 36th Elizabeth, and the 1st and 2nd and the 4th and 5th of Charles I. It is impossible to satisfactorily account for the nonpayment of the money in the years above-mentioned. If the Master's title was good in the 3rd year of Charles I. it must have been equally valid in the two preceding and the two subsequent years. It is an obstacle we cannot negotiate, and the only way to clear it is by assuming that the Master was refused the writ of Privy Seal to the Sheriffs of Surrey and Sussex, and without the production of that warrant they were not bound to pay up. This document could be withheld by the King, and the Lord Privy Seal for the time being could fall back on many excuses, and refuse to stamp it, which would render it invalid. It is also possible in the latter years that the sheriffs may not have had funds to spare for these payments, as many new claims were then being made upon their resources by the Crown, and the impending civil war had already cast its shadow on the land, to the great detriment of the chase and all its concomitants. We shall have many sad proofs of this presently, and it only remains to mention here that Sir Pexsall Brocas died in the 5th year of the reign of Charles I. (1630), leaving an only son, Thomas Brocas, the last of his family who bore the Hereditary insignia of the Royal Buckhounds.

THOMAS BROCAS, Esq., thirteenth Hereditary Master of the Royal Buckhounds, from 1630–1633, the son and heir of Sir Pexsall Brocas, of Horton and Beaurepaire, county Hants, succeeded to the diminished estates and hereditaments of his family on the death of his father in 1630. His career was very uneventful, and calls for little notice at our hands. The vast estates once held by his ancestors had been gradually diminishing, and when he assumed the horn of this branch of the royal pack his territorial possessions were sadly curtailed. He sold the Manor of Little Weldon in June 1633, and with it the so-called Hereditary Mastership of the Buckhounds, which was held by the Brocas family for 270 years, passed by purchase to the Watsons of Rockingham Castle. In the meantime, Mr. Brocas, following the lead of other courtiers of the period, endeavoured to improve the shining hour in adding to his income by means of the monopolies which were a considerable source of revenue to Charles I., and to the favoured few who participated in the spoil. Thus, on October 27, 1625, Thomas Brocas and Abraham Chamberlain obtained from the king a lease for twenty-one years of all mines of gold and silver in the county Kerry, Ireland, without rent to his Majesty for the two first years, and afterwards during the residue of the term rendering to the Crown only the tenth part of the clear gains of gold and silver derived therefrom; and on February 6, 1626, Thomas Brocas obtained another grant of all the mines-royal in the said county for a further term of twenty-one years. It seems certain that this Hereditary Master of the Buckhounds did not realise a colossal fortune out of those gold and silver mines, as after he inherited his estates he was chiefly occupied in selling the remnants of the property left to him by his improvident father. With the exception of the Manor of Little Weldon those transactions are irrelevant to our subject, consequently it only remains to record that, during the three years which Thomas Brocas held the Hereditary horn of the Royal pack, he received the fees appertaining to the office from the Sheriffs of Surrey and Sussex for one year only —viz., in the 7th of Charles I. (1633), when he obtained the sum of 50l. out of the issues of the county Sussex; Edward Remington being at the time the huntsman, and Thomas Chaddock and George Chase the other hunt-servants under him. As above mentioned, with the sale of the Manor of Little Weldon to Sir Lewis Watson, the Mastership of this branch of the Royal Buckhounds went to the new owners of that property, by virtue of the terms of the patent of the 27th Henry VI. This Thomas Brocas, Esq., married Elizabeth, daughter of Sir R. Wingfield, by whom he had seven sons and two daughters. He died in 1663.

CHAPTER V.

HOUSEHOLD BRANCH.—JAMES I.

1603—1624.

Annual Cost of the Pack during the Reign of James I.—The Master and the Hunt Servants.—Their Annual Salaries, Fees, and Emoluments.—Sir Thomas Tyringham, Eighth Master: July 21, 1604, to March 25, 1625.

QUEEN ELIZABETH died March 24, 1602-3,* when James VI., King of Scotland, became the reigning sovereign of England, Scotland and Ireland, under the style of King James I. On his accession to the dominions of England and Ireland, the Privy or Household branch of the Royal Buckhounds reverted to him, by whom it was probably esteemed as the greatest jewel in his diadem.

Reverting, for a moment, to the state of this pack, as we find it constituted in the last complete account of the Treasurer of the Chamber, for the last whole year of Elizabeth's reign, ended at Michaelmas 1602, we ascertain that it cost the Royal Exchequer 164*l*. 6*s*. 7*d*. In this year, ended at Michaelmas 1602, Francis Joye, the Sergeant, was in the receipt of 22*l*. 16*s*. a year for his wages, and 13*l*. 6*s*. 8*d*. per annum for his livery and other allowances—for lymes, chains, collars, etc. He also

---

* It is necessary to bear in mind that the dates of the regnal years are calculated from the accession of James I. to the English crown. Previous to September 1752, the Civil or Legal Year in this country commenced on March 25 (Lady-Day), whilst the Historical Year began on January 1. Consequently, according to the former computation, the reign of James I. commenced on March 24, 1602, and, according to the Historical computation, on March 24, 1603; nevertheless the second day of his reign, according to both systems, was March 25, 1603.

received 13*l*. 6*s*. 8*d*. a year "for hounds meat for the said hounds." Thomas Forest, groom, obtained 6*l*. 13*s*. 4*d*. a year. He had no livery. Robert Ducke, yeoman pricker, at 6*d*. a day for his wages, and 6*l*. 3*s*. 10*d*. per annum for his summer and winter liveries, was paid 15*l*. 6*s*. 4*d*. Richard Mercer and John Broughton, yeomen prickers, had 15*l*. a year each for their wages, and 1*l*. per annum each for their liveries. Four grooms in livery—viz., William Sale, *alias* Dilly, Richard Monday, Thomas Murralde, and Anthony Duck received 6*l*. 13*s*. 4*d*. each, a year, for their wages, and 8*l*. 3*s*. 10*d*. per annum, each, for their summer and winter liveries. All these several sums were payable quarterly, and, as before mentioned, amounted in the aggregate to 164*l*. 6*s*. 7*d*. Thus we find that the Household branch of the Royal Buckhounds, during the last whole year of Queen Elizabeth's reign, ended at Michaelmas 1602, consisted of the Sergeant, three yeomen prickers, and five grooms.

1602-3. The next account of the Treasurer of the Chamber, from Michaelmas 1602 to Michaelmas 1603, only embraced the last half-year, minus two days (from Michaelmas 1602 to Lady-Day 1602-3), down to the death of Queen Elizabeth; and the half-year of the first regnal year of James I. *plus* two days (from Lady-Day 1602-3 to Michaelmas 1603). In this account we therefore obtain the staff and the cost of the pack as it ran down to the death of Queen Elizabeth, and the changes which ensued from Lady-Day 1602-3 to Michaelmas 1603—the latter half-year being in the first regnal year of King James I.'s reign. Consequently the last half-year of Elizabeth's reign and the first half-year of the reign of James I. (to September 29, 1603) constituted together, in these accounts, one whole year, from September 29, 1602, to September 29, 1603. A brief analysis shows that all the old staff under the late Queen were now in the same service under James I., and that their remuneration and allowances remained substantially, for the present, as heretofore.

Apart from this standing arrangement an increase in the officials of the pack immediately ensued. First, Anthony

Duck, one of the grooms under good Queen Bess, who had predeceased his royal mistress, was replaced by Richard Rea, with wages at 6*l*. 13*s*. 4*d*. a year, and 8*l*. 4*s*. 10*d*. per annum for his winter and summer livery. Five "newlie erected" yeomen prickers were added to the staff—viz., Francis Dodsworth, Robert Rayne, Edward Dodsworth, John Broughton, and William Cocker, at 20*d*. each a day for wages, and 20*s*. each per annum for liveries, by virtue of H.M. warrant, dated at Woodstock, September 17 in the first year of his reign.* Richard Kilbourne was appointed (an additional) groom with 13*d*. a day for his wages, payable quarterly, and 20*s*. per annum for his livery, payable at Christmas. And Thomas Atkinson, "one other of the yeomen prickers," was appointed at 20*d*. a day for his wages, by virtue of the King's warrant dated "at Winchester the last day of September, in the first year of H.M. reign." It therefore appears that during this first half-year of the reign of James I. (ended September 29, 1603), this branch of the Privy or Household branch of the Royal Buckhounds was augmented by six yeomen prickers and one groom, each of whom was paid his several salary and allowance down to date. But we must not omit to mention that Robert Walker was appointed to keep and feed sixteen couples of Buckhounds, at the yearly allowance of 100 marks, from Midsummer 1603, during His Majesty's pleasure, and a further allowance "unto him for his own maintenance, and keeping one horse or gelding to serve with the said hounds," the sum of 3*l*. 12*s*. monthly, by virtue of H.M. warrant under the signet dated at Winchester September 30, 1603. This charge does not appear, wholly or in part, in the Account of the Treasurer of the Chamber above mentioned; nevertheless it comes out, as we shall presently see, in that for the year ended on September 29, 1604, when Mr. Walker was paid in full for one year and a quarter, amounting to 137*l*. 7*s*. 8*d*.

* By a warrant dormant to the Treasurer of the Chamber, subscribed by the Lord Treasurer and the Chancellor of the Exchequer, dated at Woodstock, Sept. 17, 1603, the additional names of Robert Walker and Thomas Holland, yeomen prickers, are also mentioned.

In the next account we obtain the expenses of the pack for the first whole year in the reign of James I.—viz., from September 29, 1603, to September 29, 1604. It amounts to 642*l*. 16s. 5¼*d*. The officials consisted of the Master, two sergeants, eleven yeomen prickers, six grooms, and one waggoner or keeper of the hound-van. The pack numbered sixteen couples of hounds, and a subsidiary draft of the Hereditary branch under the control of Silvester Dodsworth and Sir Pexsall Brocas. The technicalities and the various wages and emoluments of these gentlemen may be ascertained by any reader of sufficient courage to follow the subjoined *verbatim et literatim* copy of this account:—

Alsoe allowed for money payde to Thomas Tyrringham esq^r M^r of his Maties Buckhoundes at xxxiij^{li}. vj^s. viij^d. P ann. for his fee or wages due to him for one whole yere and Cxxj dayes begon the first day of June Anno Regni Regis Jacobi primo by vertue of his Ma^{ts} tres pattents vnder the greate Seale bearing date at Westm̃ the firste day of June Anno primo—xliij^{li}. ix. ij^d.

Alsoe allowed for money payde to ffrauncis Joye esq^r S^{r}giaunt of his highnes Buckhounds at xxij^{li} xvj^s. P ann. for his wages & xiiij^{li}. xj^s. vij^d. P ann. for his lyverie and the other allowaunces for loames, Cheanes, &c. all payable quarterlye due to him for one quarter of a yere ended at X'pm̃as anno Regni Regis Jacobi primo—ix^{li}. vj^s. x^d. ob. qr.

Also allowed for money payde to Thomas fforest groome of his Maties saide Buckhoundes at vj^{li}. xiij^s. iiij^d. P ann. for his wages due to him for one whole yere ended at Michās Anno Regni Regis Jacobi sc̃do—vj^{li}. xiij^s. iiij^d.

Alsoe allowed for money payde to Willm Sale als Dillie grome of his Maties sayde Buckhoundes at vj^{li}. xiij^s. iiij^d. P ann. for his wages and viiij^{li}. iiij^s. x^d. P ann. for his wynter and somer lyveries all payable quarterlie due to him for halfe a yere ended at o^r Ladie daye anno p'd—vij^{li}. ix^s. i^d.

Alsoe allowed for money payde to Robert Duck yeoman pricker of his Maties sayde Buckhoundes at vj^d. P diem for his wages and vj^{li}. iij^s. x^d. P ann. for his wynter and somer lyveries all payable quarterlie due to him for the lyke tyme—xv^{li}. vj^s. x^d.

Alsoe allowed for money payde to Thomas Murrall groome of

his Maties sayde Buckhoundes at vj^li. xiij^s. iiij^d. for his wages and viij^li. iiij^s. x^d. ℔ ann. for his wynter and somer lyveries all payable quarterlye due to him for three quarters of a yere ended at mydsomer Anno Regni Regis Jacobi sĉdo—xj^li. iij^s. vij^d. ob.

Also allowed for money payed to ffrauncis Dodsworth, Walter Rayne, Edward Dodsworth, John Broughton, Thomas Holland, William Cocker and Thomas Atkinson, yeoman prickers of his Maties pryvie Buckhoundes, everie of them at xx^d. ℔ diem for theire wages payable quarterlye due to them for one whole yere ended at Miĉhas Anno, p'd—CCxiij^li. x^s.

Alsoe allowed for money payde to the said ffrauncis Dodsworth, Robt. Rayne, Edward Dodsworth, John Broughton, Thomas Holland and William Cocker, everie of them at xx^s. ℔ ann. the peece for their lyveries payable at Xpm̃as due to them w^thin the fore sayde yere—vj^li.

Alsoe allowed for money payde to Richard Kilborne grome of his Maties pryvie Buckhoundes at xiij^d. ℔ diem for his wages payable quarterlye and xx^s. ℔ ann. for his lyverie payable at Xpm̃as all due to him for one whole yere ended at Myĉhas Anno Regni Regis Jacobi sĉdo—xx^li. xvj^s. vj^d.

Alsoe allowed for money payde to Robte Walker at C M'ke ℔ ann. for the keepinge and feedinge of xvj couple of Buckhoundes for his Matie payable quarterly and lxxij^s. everye month for his mayntenance and entertaynement and for keepinge a geldinge or horse all due to him for one whole yere and a quarter begon at the ffeaste of St. John Baptiste Anno Regni Regis Jacobi primo and ended at Michãs Anno Regni Regis Jacobi sĉdo by virtue of his Maties warraunt dormant vnder the Signett bearing date at Wilton the xj^th daye of November Anno Regni Regis Jacobi primo w^thin the tyme of this Accompte—Cxxxvij^li. vj^s. viij^d.

Alsoe allowed for money payde to Richard Brassie one of his Ma^ts yeoman prickers of the pryvie Buckhoundes at ij^s. ℔ diem for his wages payable quarterlie due to him for the like tyme by vertue of the foresayde warrante—xlv^li. xiiij^s. vj^d.

Alsoe allowed for money payde to George Howme Keeper of the waggon for his Maties pryvie Buckhoundes in the Som̃er season and for the Harriers in the wynter tyme at xx^d. ℔ diem for his chardges and allowaunces payable quarterlie due to him for one whole yere ended at Michãs Anno Regni Regis Jacobi sĉdo by vertue of his highnes warrant dormant vnder the Signet bearing date at Westm̃ the xx^th daye of ffebruarie Anno Regni Regis Jacobi primo—xxx^li. x^s.

Alsoe allowed for money payde to Silvester Dodsworth S^rgiant of his Maties Buckhoundes appertayninge to thoffice of Sr Pexell Brokas at xxij^li. xvj^s. ℔ ann. for his wages and xiiij^li. xj^s. vij^d. ℔ ann. for his wynter and somer lyveries and for other allowaunces or other executinge the same before him had all payable quarterlie due to him for three quarters of a yere begon at X^pm̃as Anno Regni Regis Jacobi primo and ended at Michãs then next followinge by virtue of his Maties l'res patents bearing the date at Harfeld the xxvj^th daye of August Anno p'ed.—xxviij^li. viij^d a/qr.

Alsoe allowed for money payde to Willm̃ Sale als Dillie one of the yeoman prickers of his Maties privie Buckhoundes at xx^d ℔ diem for his wages payable quarterlie and xx^s. ℔ ann. for his liverie payable at X'pm̃as due to him for his sayde wages for halfe a yere begon at o^r Ladie Day Anno Regni Regis Jacobi sc̃do and ended at Michãs followinge by virtue of his Maties warrant dormant vnder the Signet bearinge date at Greenewich the last day of June Anno p'd—xv^li. iiij^s. ij^d.

Alsoe allowed for money payde to Thomas Murrall one of the yeoman prickers of his Maties pryvie Buckhoundes at xx^d ℔ diem for his wages payable quarterlie and xx^s. ℔ ann. for his lyverie payable at X'pm̃as due to him for his sayde wages for one quarter of a yere begon at Midsomer Anno Regni Regis Jacobi sc̃do and ended at Michãs Anno p'd by vertue of his Maties warrant dormant vnder the Signet bearing date at Hamptoncourte the xx^th day of September Anno p'd—vij^li. xij^s. j^d.

Alsoe allowed for money payde to Edward Willyams and Thomas Wyer gromes of his Maties pryvie Buckhoundes everie of them at xiij^d. ℔ diem the peece for theire wages payable quarterlie and xx^s. ℔ ann. for theire lyveries payable at Xpm̃as due to them for theire wages for one quarter of a yere begon at Midsomer Anno Regis Jacobi Regis Jacobi sc̃do and ended at Michãs followinge by virtue of his Maties fore sayde warrant dormant vnder the Signet bearinge date at Hamptoncourte the xx^th daye of September Anno p'd—xiiij^li. xvj^s. vj^d. ob. qr.

Alsoe allowed for money payde to Richard Mondaye and Richard Rea, groomes of his Maties sayde Buckhoundes eyther of them at

ANNUAL SALARIES, FEES, AND EMOLUMENTS.   101

vj^{li}. xiij^s. iiij^d. ℔ ann. for theire wages and viij^{li}. iiij^s. x^d. ℔ ann. the peece for theire wynter and somer lyveries payable quarterlie due to them for one whole yere ended at Michās Anno Regni Regis Jacobi sc̄do—xxix^{li}. xvj^s iiij^d.

Sum total—vj^{c}xlij^{li}. xvj^s. v^d $\frac{a}{q}$.

1604-5. In the Account for the following year, amounting to 895l. 15s. 10$\frac{3}{4}d$., we find the Master now styled Sir Thomas Tyrringham, Knight, in the receipt of 33l. 6s. 8d. "for his fee or wages paiable q^{a}rterlye and due to him for one whole yeare ended at Mchās anno tercio Jacobi regis." No material change is noticeable in the *personnel* of the officials of the hunt, each of whom was paid as on the establishment recited in the preceding account. It appears, however, that Richard Little had succeeded "in the roome and place" of George Howme as Keeper of the hound-van with the same salary and emoluments as enjoyed by his predecessor in that capacity. We also find that Francis Joy, the Sergeant, with his fee or wages set down in full at 51l. 3s. 3d., and due to him for one whole year and three-quarters, "begon at X'pm̄as anno primo regni regis Jacobi and ended at Michās anno regni dc̄i dn̄i regis tercio by vertue of his Maties tres pattents bearing date at Westminster the xixth daye of October anno regni cnise. D'm. regis sc'do," and now amounting to the sum of four score nine pounds, ten shillings and eight pence. The yeomen prickers received in addition twelve pence each a day "by way of his highnes rewarde over and above their wages, from the feaste of St. John Baptiste anno tercio vntill Mychās nexte followinge." Four grooms and Richard Little, the waggoner, likewise received six pence a-day each for the same time "in regarde of their painfull servyce and attendaunce on his highnes the somer laste paste anno tercio by vertue of his Maties warraunte vnder the Signett bearinge date at Hamptoncourt the laste daye of September anno regni Jacobi regis tercio, am^{m}ountinge to the some of 65l. 9s. 6d. Sir Pexsall Brocas received 30l. (at the rate of 13l. 6s. 8d. per annum) "for the feedinge of certen of his Maties Buckhoundes in his chardge and keepinge, dewe to him for two whole yeares and a q^{u}rter begone at Midsōmer anno regni regis Jacobi primo and ended at Mychās anno regis tercio, by vertue of his highnes warraunte vnder the Signett bearing date at Greenw[ch] the xxij[th] day of June pred. anno tercio." It seems some addition was made to the yeomen prickers enumerated in the first and in this account, as we now find the names of Thomas Dodsworth, Richard Vincent, Anthony Dodsworth, Francis Beckham, Thomas Pickney, Augustine Grigg, and George Harwell, in the receipt of sixpence per day, each, for their wages and 6*l*. 3*s*. 10*d*. for their several liveries, all payable quarterly and due to them for a year ended at Michaelmas, 1605, by vertue of H.M. warrant under the signet, dated at Westminster 8th October, 1605. Likewise, with regard to the grooms: Anthony Dodsworth, Jerome Medcalf and Robert Goulding were now on the establishment of the pack in that capacity, each of whom received 6*l*. 13*s*. 4*d*. per annum, for wages, and 8*l*. 4*s*. 10*d*. for their several liveries, "by vertue of the said warrant."

1605-6. The expences of this branch of the Royal Buckhounds during the fourth year of James I., from Sept. 29, 1605, to Sept. 29, 1606, as recorded in the Accounts of the Treasurer of the Chamber of the Household, is set down at 925*l*. 7*s*. 5*d*. We find the Master and the hunt servants in the receipt of their several salaries and emoluments as previously enjoyed by them. A new entry occurs "for money payde to Thomas Tyllesley, gent. of his Ma[ties] pryvie Buckhoundes vnder the Chardge of S[r] Thomas Tirringham, Knight, at ij[s] ᵽ diem for his enterteynement and chardges payable q[a]rterly due to him for one q[a]rter of a yeare ended at Michās anno Regni Regis Jacobi quarto by vertue of his Ma[s] warr[unte] vnder the Signet bearinge date at Greenew[ch] the xiiij[th] day of Julie Anno quarto," 9*l*. 2*s*. 6*d*. Silvester Dodsworth, "S[r]giaunte of his Ma[s] Buckhoundes apperteyning to S[r] Pexsall Brockas" at 22*l*. 16*s*. per annum for his wages and 14*l*. 11*s*. 7*d*. per annum for his living due to him for one whole year ended at Michaelmas, 1606, received 37*l*. 7*s*. 7*d*. Sir Pexsall Brocas was likewise paid 13*l*. 7*s*. 8*d*. "for the feeding of his

Ma^{ts} Buckhoundes in his Chardge and Keeping," within the period of this account.

1606-7. During the period comprised in this account, this branch of the Royal Buckhounds entailed an expenditure, from September 29, 1606, to the same date 1607, of 948l. 5s. 9½d. But as many of these payments to the officials of the pack were for the half-year ended at Lady Day 1607; others for three-quarters, and some for a quarter only, the total amount paid must be considered as incomplete and falling short of what the actual cost would have been if the incidental liabilities had been paid in full down to date. And, moreover, other changes had taken place in the remuneration of and in the staff of the pack. Thus we notice that Robert Walker (the successor of Francis Joy) was paid for the feeding and keeping of sixteen couples of Buckhounds at the rate of 66l. 13s. 4d. (*i.e.* 100 marks) yearly, and 3l. 12s. a month for himself and the keep of a horse or gelding down to Midsummer 1607 "And thenceforth for his fee or wages at 51l. 3s. 3d. $\mathbb{P}$ annum in the room and place of Francis Joy deceased, and 100l. $\mathbb{P}$ annum for the keeping and feeding of sixteen couples of Buckhounds, due to him for a quarter of a year ended at Michaelmas, 1607, by H.M. warrant under the signet dated at Westminster the 17th day of January in the 7th year of his highness reign." Richard Brassy, one of the yeomen prickers, likewise received his salary at the rate of 2s. a a day for three-quarters of a year ended at Midsummer 1607; and thenceforth in the place of Robert Walker at 72s. per month "for his maintenance and the keeping of a gelding, and 20s. for his livery, payable at Christmas, and due to him for one quarter of a year ended at Michaelmas, 1607, by H. M. warrant under the signet, dated at Hampton Court, Sept. 6, 1607." William Sale, yeoman pricker, was promoted to the office relinquished by Brassy, and obtained an increase in his salary from 20d. to 2s. a day and 20s. for his livery, payable at Christmas. Richard Kylbourne, one of the grooms, was promoted to the place vacated by Sale, with an increase in his wages from 1s. a day to 1s. 8d. a day. William Kellsy stepped into the place Kylbourne filled heretofore, and a few immaterial changes which are unnecessary to follow in detail occurred among the subordinate servants of the pack. We must not omit to notice that Sylvester Dodsworth was still in evidence in connection with the hounds appertaining to Sir Pexsall Brocas, and received his salary and livery for the whole year ended at Michaelmas 1607, amounting to 37*l*. 7*s*. 7*d*.; and that Sir Pexsall, "for keeping and feeding the Buckhounds in his charge and custody," received, for one whole year ended Michaelmas 1607, 13*l*. 6*s*. 8*d*.

1607-8. The accounts for this year show an expenditure of 1045*l*. 5*s*. 5¾*d*. As it is a fairly full and clear audit from Michaelmas 1607 to Michaelmas 1608, a brief recapitulation may be admissible here. First, in his pride of place, comes the Master, Sir Thomas Tyringham, for his not extravagant annual salary of 33*l*. 6*s*. 8*d*., Robert Walker, the Sergeant, at 51*l*. 3*s*. 3*d*., and 100*l*. per annum for feeding and keeping 16 couples of hounds. Nine yeomen prickers, at 1*s*. 8*d*. a day for their wages each, and 1*l*. a year for their several liveries, payable at Christmas yearly: viz., F. Dodsworth, E. Dodsworth, J. Broughton, T. Holland, W. Cocker, T. Atkinson, T. Murall, R. Kilbourne, J. Owen. This is minus one yeoman pricker—viz., Robert Rayne, who was now made Sergeant of the Hereditary branch of the Royal pack. William Lampard was appointed a yeoman pricker *vice* Rayne promoted. Another yeoman pricker, Richard Brassy, for his maintenance and the keep of a horse, received 3*l*. 2*s*. a month, and 1*l*. a year for his livery. The "gentleman" of the pack, Thomas Tillesley, Esq., under the Master, received 2*s*. a day for his entertainment, and for "chardges due to him for the aforesaid tyme," amounting altogether to 36*l*. 12*s*. Another yeoman pricker, William Sale, received 2*s*. a day wages and 1*l*. for his livery. Four groomes obtained 1*s*. a day each for wages, and 1*l*. each a year for liveries. Richard Little, waggoner for the Buckhounds in the summer season and for the Harriers in the winter time, was paid at the rate of 20*d*. a day. Silvester Dodsworth, Sergeant of H.M. Buckhounds appertaining to Sir Pexsall Brocas at

22*l*. 16*s*. per annum for his wages and 14*l*. 11*s*. 7*d*. per annum for his livery, received, in both, for this year ended at Michaelmas 1608, 37*l*. 7*s*. 7*d*. Thomas Forest, groom, 6*l*. per annum sans livery. Five other grooms were rated at 6*l*. 13*s*. 4*d*. each for wages and 8*l*. 4*s*. 10*d*. per annum each for liveries. Seven other yeomen prickers, viz., R. Duke, R. Vincent, A. Dodsworth, F. Beecham, T. Pinckney, A. Gregges, and G. Harwell, at 6*d*. each per day for their wages, and 6*l*. 3*s*. 10*d*. each per annum for their liveries, received within the period of this account 107*l*. 7*s*. 10*d*. Thomas Dodsworth, yeoman pricker, was paid at the same rate for three-quarters of a year, ended at the Feast of St. John the Baptist 1608, " at which time he departed this life"; on and after that festival he was succeeded by Richard Dodsworth in the same capacity. Sir Pexsall Brocas, " at 20 marks per annum for the feeding and keeping of certain of H.M. Buckhounds in his charge and custody, payable quarterly, due to him for one quarter of a year ended at Christmas 1607," received 3*l*. 6*s*. 8*d*., and George Howme, the waggoner, received, down to date, 6*l*. 13*s*. 4*d*. for his wages and 8*l*. 4*s*. 10*d*. for his livery.

1608-9. The cost of the pack for this year, as recorded in this account, amounted to 1136*l*. 17*s*. 7½*d*. The hunt servants appear in their several capacities and emoluments as we find them in the preceding year. One important change must be noted, with regard to Sir Pexsall Brocas' connection with this pack, as exhibited in the preceding accounts. In the last one we find him paid down to Christmas 1607. Now we find, by the two following entries, that the affinity hitherto subsisting between the Hereditary Master and a certain draft connected with the Privy or Household branch of the pack is brought to an end:—

To Roberte Rayne Sergeaunte of his Ma^{ts} buckhowndes apperteyninge to Sr Pexall Brocas Knight, in the place of Silvester Doddesworthe at xxij^{li}. xvj^s. ℞ ann. for his wages and xiiij^{li}. xj^s. vij^d. ℞ ann. for his winter and somer liveries all paiable q^{rt}erlie and due to him for one whole yeare ended at Mich̄s 1609, anno septimo Jacobi regis by vertue of a warraunte vnder the Signett dated the xxixth of Auguste 1608 anno sexto Jacobi regis pred., xxxvij^{li}. vij^{s}. vij^{d}.

To Roberte Rayne aforesaid Sergeaunte of his Ma^{ts} saide Buckhoundes at twenty markes ℔ ann. for the feedinge and keepinge of the saide Buckhoundes, as S^{r}. Pexall Brokas latelie hadd, payable q^{r}terly and due to him for one whole yeare and a halfe ended at Michās 1609 anno septimo Jacobi regis, by vertue of his highnes warraunte vnder the Signett dated the xxth of January in the sixth yeare of his Ma^{ts} raigne . . . xx^{li}.

As the various phases bearing upon this incident are recapitulated in our memoir of Sir Pexsall Brocas, it is unnecessary further to refer to it here. It seems the salary of the "lymmerman" on the staff of this branch of the pack (yclept Richard Crockford) had been in arrears for "twoo whole yeares": 20d. per day for wages and 20s. a year for livery, he was now paid in full 62l. 16s. 8d. down to Michaelmas 1609; and William Lampard was appointed a yeoman pricker *vice* Robert Rayne, promoted under the circumstances above mentioned.*

1609-10. In the account now under review we find the Privy or Household branch of the Royal Buckhounds classified under two separate heads : viz., "The Huntes for his Ma^{ts}. Privy Buckhounds," and "The Huntes for His Ma^{ts}. Old Buckhounds." The cost of the first-mentioned portion, from Michaelmas 1609 to Michaelmas 1610, is set down at 760l. 15s. 7d.; the latter at 309l. 7s. 3d.; consequently the new subdivisions of this pack amounted altogether to 1070l. 2s. 10d. A brief analysis of this account shows that, under the first division, the following held office : viz., the Master, Sir Thomas Tyrringham ; the Sergeant, Robert Walker, salary 51l. 3s. 3d. a year, and 100l. a year for keeping and feeding sixteen couple of buckhounds ; Richard Brassy, yeoman pricker, salary

---

* By virtue of a warrant under the signet dated at Westminster, January 12, 1608-9. Robert Rayne, "Sergeant of the Buckhounds whereof Sir Pexsall Brocas, Knight, is master." obtained a grant of 40l. a year during his life, "as Silvester Dodsworth lately had." As we will presently see, this sum of 40l. a year previously had been paid out of the King's privy purse.

3*l*. 2*s*. per month, including his maintenance and the keep of a horse; ten yeomen prickers, 20*d*. a day each for wages and 20*s*. a year each for their liveries; Thomas Tillesley, the "gentleman" (huntsman?), salary 2*s*. a day, including his entertainment and charges; William Sawle, another yeoman pricker, at 2*s*. a day for his wages and 1*l*. per annum for his livery; four groomes at 20*d*. a day each for wages and 20*s*. per annum for their several liveries; John Hawke, waggoner for the privy Buckhounds in the summer season and for the Harriers in the winter time, 20*d*. a day for his wages and nothing per annum for his livery. Richard Crockford, lymmerman, received 20*d*. a day for his wages and 20*s*. per annum for his livery. It thus appears that the Privy or Household branch of the Royal Buckhounds, *per se*, under the new arrangement, consisted of the Master, the Sergeant, one yeoman pricker keeping his own horse, eleven yeomen prickers, the "gentleman" huntsman, four groomes, a waggoner, and a lymmerman.

Now, as to the "Huntes for his Maties old Buckhounds" —evidently a draft if not actually the whole of the Hereditary branch of the pack—we find the Sergeant of this division of the pack, Robert Rayne, in the receipt of 22*l*. 16*s*. a year for his wages, and 14*l*. 11*s*. 7*d*. for a winter and summer livery, as also 13*l*. 6*s*. 8*d*. "for feeding the said Buckhounds," and 40*l*. per annum "formerly paid by the Keeper of the Privy Purse," all of which sums were payable quarterly and due to him for one whole year ended at Michaelmas 1610, amounting to 90*l*. 14*s*. 3*d*. Eight yeomen prickers received 6*d*. each a day for their wages at 6*l*. 3*s*. 10*d*. per annum each, for their winter and summer liveries. Six grooms received 6*l*. 13*s*. 4*d*. each per annum for their wages and 8*l*. 4*s*. 10*d*. each for their liveries. The waggoner, George Howme, had 6*l*. 13*s*. 4*d*. for his wages, and 8*l*. 4*s*. 10*d*. for his livery, per annum. It therefore appears that the "old" division of this pack now consisted of a sergeant, eight yeomen prickers, six groomes and a waggoner. According to evidence, apart from and not alluded to in this series, Timothy Tyrell, Esq., was the acting master of this appendage of the pack, which finally disappeared from the purview of these accounts after Christmas 1610. As we shall presently see, it was, soon after, given over to Charles, Duke of York (Prince of Wales).

1610-11. The account for the year from Michaelmas 1610 to Michaelmas 1611 is carried on with the distinction observed in the preceding one, so far as regards the division of this branch of the pack under the classification of the "Privy" and the "Old" rearrangement. The first part relating to the "Privy" division is calculated in full for the whole year ended at Michaelmas 1611. It amounts to 640*l.* 15*s.* 7*d.* The cost of the "old" portion is only made up for one quarter ended at Christmas 1610; therefore it does not tally with the full period comprehended in the other part of this now divided pack. The latter, for one quarter of the year ended at Christmas 1610, only totals the small sum of 77*l.* 6*s.* 9½*d.* As this precludes any full analysis, it is unnecessary to dwell upon the financial affairs of the two sections collectively within the periods under review. It may be observed, however, that no material change had taken place in the officials of the "Privy" section, except that William Smith had succeeded William Lampbard as one of the yeomen prickers. And as the "Old" division does not reappear in those accounts after the quarter of the year ended at Christmas 1610, we may conclude some new arrangement was provided for sustenance of that portion of the pack. The nature of this arrangement did not transpire until July 10, 1613, when we find, by a warrant under the signet, that the Treasurer of the Chamber was ordered to pay to certain yeomen and grooms of his Majesty's Old Buckhounds, "being dismissed from their attendance," the following pensions, to be paid unto them quarterly from Christmas 1612, during their lives—viz., to Richard Vincent, Thomas Pickney, and Henry Sams, yeomen, to each of them 19*l.* 2*s.* 4*d.*; to Richard Monday, groom, 14*l.* 18*s.* 2*d.*; and to Thomas Forrest, groom, 6*l.* 13*s.* 4*d.* per annum.

It further appears, by virtue of a similar warrant, "subscribed and procured by Sir Thomas Lake," dated at Greenwich June 10, 1613, and addressed to the Treasurer of the Chamber, that that official was ordered to pay Timothy Tyrell, "Master of his Ma^{ts} Old Buckhounds," the sum of 20*l.* per annum; Robert Rayne, sergeant of the same hounds, 19*l.* 14*s.* 3*d.*; Anthony Dodsworth, yeoman, 40*l.* 6*s.*; Augustine Griggs, Nathan Jackson, and Anthony Brakenbury, yeomen, each 26*l.* 13*s.* 4*d.*; to Edward Staunton, yeoman, 36*l.* 16*s.* 8*d.*; to William Reading, yeoman, 26*l.* 13*s.* 4*d.*; to William Rawson, waggoner, 26*l.* 5*s.* 2*d.*; to Jerome Metcalf, Anthony Dodsworth, William Gwilliams, and Francis Beachamp, groomes, each 20*l.* per annum. Most of these former servants of the "Old" wing of the King's Privy or Household pack were reinstated when that division was revived as a separate pack on the establishment of Charles, Duke of York (Prince of Wales).

1611-12. The account for this year, ended at Michaelmas 1612, solely relates to the Privy or Household branch of the pack, under the entire sway of Sir Thomas Tyringham, the Master thereof, the cost of which amounted to 762*l.* 3*s.* 6*d.* The sergeant, Thomas Walker, is in receipt of the same salary and emoluments as heretofore; Brassy, the yeoman pricker, and the keep of his horse; the ten yeomen prickers, received the same wages and emoluments as they previously enjoyed; Swale, another yeoman pricker, still obtained 4*d.* a day more than the others; four groomes as before; and Thomas Lee in the place of William Kelsey, deceased. Crockford the lymmerman and Hawke the waggoner are still to the fore with the fees and liveries as previously enjoyed by them. As previously observed, the whole staff of the "Old" portion of this pack have entirely vanished from the purview of this account.

1612-13. The account for the year ended at Michaelmas 1613, amounts to 760*l.* 15*s.* 7*d.* There is no change in the officials or in their several fees and emoluments as we have found them set forth in the two previous accounts.

In place of the "Old" branch of this pack, which was discontinued on and after Christmas 1610, we now find a new and separate pack instituted for "the Prince"—Charles, Duke of York. But, strictly speaking, it had no connection with the King's privy or Household branch of the Royal Buckhounds *per se*, except that all the hunt servants formerly attached to it (save those who were pensioned), were re-employed in the separate service of the Prince. It does not, therefore, come within the province of this history here to go into its affairs. Some particulars relating to it will be found in our memoir of Sir Tymothy Tyrell (p. 130). So, wishing it every prosperity and success, we respectfully bow-wow it out.

1613-14. The account for the year ended at Michaelmas, 1614, amounts to 758*l*. 15*s*. 7*d*. Thomas Tissley (the "gentleman" to the pack, as heretofore, paid at the rate of 2*s*. a day) is now degraded or promoted to the office of yeoman pricker, and in receipt of 3*s*. 8*d*. a day for his wages, by virtue of his Majesty's letters patents, dated at Westminster January 3, 1613-14. Richard Hunt was likewise appointed one of the yeomen prickers at 3*s*. 4*d*. a day by virtue of the same patent.

1614-15. The account for year ended at Michaelmas 1615 amounts to 758*l*. 10*s*. 9*d*. All the hunt officials are still to the fore and in the receipt of their several salaries and emoluments save Thomas Wyer, one of the grooms, who died on January 14, 1615, when he was succeeded by George Fowler, with the wages of 20*d*. per day and 20*s*. for his livery payable at Christmas.

1615-16. The account for this year amounts to 769*l*. 6*s*. 5*d*. One of the yeomen prickers, Thomas Murrall, died about Christmas 1615. He was succeeded by William Connock, with remuneration at 20*d*. a day and 20*s*. a year for his livery "by virtue of H.M. warrant under the Signet, dated at Newmarket the 28th day of February," 1615-16; and Edward Walworth, one of the grooms, who died some time before Lady Day 1616, when he was succeeded by Thomas Stevens, "at 20*d*. a day for his wages and 20*s*. per annum for his livery, during his natural life, the first payment thereof to begin at the Feast of the Annunciation of the Blessed Virgin Mary,

1616." Anthony Holland was appointed yeoman pricker on July 14, 1616.

1616-17. The account for the year ended at Michaelmas 1617 amounts to 668*l.* 19*s.* 5*d.* Except the Master, Sir Thomas Tyringham, who is missing, there is no material matter to notice in this as compared with the officials, etc., mentioned in the preceding accounts. It appears, John, Lord Stanhope, surrendered his office of Treasurer of the Chamber to Sir William Uvedale on October 6, 1617. It seems this change of office occasioned some temporary omissions in the payment to certain officials who derived their salaries and emoluments through this department. In order to adjust the account and reimburse those who were accidentally or otherwise omitted, a supplementary account was made out by Sir W. Uvedale, in which such arrears were duly set forth, and those persons were eventually paid. Among those we find Sir Thomas Tyringham received 33*l.* 6*s.* 8*d.* "for his wages due to him for one whole year ended at Michaelmas 1617." In like manner Richard Brassy, for his wages and the keep of a horse, was paid 10*l.* 16*s.* for a quarter of a year ended at Michaelmas 1617. Three yeomen prickers were paid for the half-year; and Anthony Holland, another yeoman pricker, received at 2*s.* a day, for his wages, and 20*s.* per annum for his livery, due to him for one whole year ended at Michaelmas 1617.

1717-18. The account for this year amounts to 796*l.* 4*s.* 8*d.* Sir Thomas Tyringham, the Master, reappears in the full enjoyment of his salary as heretofore—viz., 100 marks or 33*l.* 6*s.* 8*d.* per annum, under whom all the subordinate officials appear in the receipt of their respective salaries and emoluments as previously mentioned.

1618-19. The account for this year amounts to 796*l.* 5*s.* 7*d.* John Cocker succeeded William Smith, yeoman pricker, on September 15, 1619. That was the only change in the *personnel* of the pack during this year.

1619-20. The account for this year amounts to 797*l.* 16*s.* John Holland, one of the yeomen prickers, deceased, was succeeded by Robert Hancock, on November 2, 1620. The rest of the staff as heretofore.

1620-21. The account for this year amounts to 814*l*. 10*s*. 8*d*. It was on the usual line. Robert Patterson was now appointed yeoman harbinger with the wages of 12*d*. per day, payable quarterly, "by H.M. warrant under the Signet, dated the 17th day of November, 1620." That is the only change in this and the preceding audit.

1621-22. The account for this year amounts to precisely the same total as the foregoing one. On February 26, 1621-22, Roger Williams (ex-groom) succeeded William Connock as yeoman pricker, with 20*d*. a day for his wages and 20*s*. per annum for his livery. John Williams succeeded to the vacancy vice Connock promoted, while Connock stepped into the shoes of Thomas Tilsely, "yeoman pricker, at 3*s*. 8*d*. per day" (*sans* livery), "by virtue of H.M. letters under the Signet, dated Feb. 6, 1621-22." Another of the grooms, Thomas Stevens, went out at Christmas 1621. His office was filled by Ralph Read, with an allowance of 20*d*. a day for his wages and 20*s*. per annum for his livery, "by virtue of H.M. letters under the Signet dated at Westminster, 4th Feb., 1621-22."

1622-23. The account for this year amounts to 815*l*. 5*s*. 7½*d*. There is no change to record, save that by the death of Richard Brassy, Robert Hancock was appointed in his place, "by letters patents under the great seal of England, dated the 29th day of September anno xxj, as well for his wages at ij^s. vj^d. q$_r$ di. q^{a}r. ℞ diem payable quarterlie, and xx^s. ℞ ann. for his liverie at Christmas, as also the wages of 20*d*. per diem in somer season as yeoman pricker & 20*s*. ℞ ann. for his liverie payable at Christmas, due to him for one quarter ended at Michãs 1623"; or in other words, 46*l*. 6*s*. 4¾*d*. a year for his wages, *plus* allowances for his liveries.

1623-24. The account for this year amounts to 818*l*. 4*s*. 4¾*d*. Thomas Lee succeeded John Owen, yeoman pricker, deceased, " by virtue of H.M. letters under the Signet, dated Westminster, November 28, 1623," with wages at 20*d*. a day and 20*s*. per annum for his livery; and William Hopkins was made groom to the pack *vice* Lee promoted.

1623-24. The account for this year is the last one (for a whole year calculated from Michaelmas 1623 to Michaelmas 1624) of the reign of James I. It amounts to exactly the same sum (818*l*. 4*s*. 4¾*d*.) as in the preceding year. There is absolutely no change in the officials of the pack, nor in their respective salaries and emoluments, as we find it on the establishment down to date. On the accession of Charles I., in the following year, many changes necessarily ensued. As these changes are investigated in detail in Chapter VI., it is only necessary here to make a brief recapitulation of the Privy or Household branch of the Royal Buckhounds as we find it down to Michaelmas 1624. The Master, Sir Thomas Tyringham, wages 33*l*. 6*s*. 8*d*. per annum; the Sergeant, Robert Walker, fee 51*l*. 3*s*. 4*d*. per annum, and 100*l*. a year for feeding and keeping 16 couples of hounds; Robert Hancock, head yeoman pricker (probably the huntsman), at 2*s*. 6¾*d*. a day and no livery; eight yeomen prickers at 20*d*. each a day for wages and 20*s*. per annum each for liveries—viz., E. Dodsworth, F. Dodsworth, J. Cocker, W. Cocker, R. Crockford, Rt. Hancock, Roger Williams, and William Lee; two yeomen prickers— Wm. Sale and Anthony Holland—at 2*s*. a day each wages and 20*s*. each for liveries; one yeoman pricker, Wm. Connock, 3*s*. 8*d*. a day for wages and no livery; one yeoman pricker, Wm. Hunte, at 3*s*. 4*d*. a day wages and no livery; one waggoner, John Hake, wages 20*d*. a day and no livery; one yeoman harbinger, Robert Pattison, wages 12*d*. a day and no livery.

Apart from these payments charged on the establishment of this branch of the pack, the Treasurer of the Chamber of the Household distributed an additional sum of 101*l*. 17*s*. to F. Dodsworth, E. Dodsworth, T. Lee, H. Dodsworth, W. Sale, W. Cocker, J. Cocker, J. Hake, Roger Williams, A. Holland, R. Pattison, R. Crockford, and R. Walker, "yeomen of H.M. Buckhounds, each of them at 12*d*. per diem"; to Richard Hunter, Wm. Connock, and Robert Hancock, "each of them at 2*s*. per diem"; and to G. Fowler, Ralph Read, William Hopkins, and John Williams, grooms, "each of them at 6d. per diem," as H.M. "free gift' from the feast of St. John the Baptist, 1624, to Michaelmas following, "by virtue of H.M. Letters under the signet" dated September 28, 1624. These supplementary royal gifts to the hunt servants were apparently begun by James I. in the year 1605, and were continued annually to the time of his death.* In some instances these free gifts to the hunt servants "for their pains and[travel" were granted to them for the natural term of their lives.†

SIR THOMAS TYRINGHAM, eighth Master of the Household branch of the Royal Buckhounds, eldest son of Sir Anthony Tyringham, by his wife Elizabeth, eldest daughter of Sir Thomas Throckmorton, Master of the Hawks to Queen Elizabeth, was born on September 28, 1580, at Tyringham, county Bucks, which manor was held by his family from the time of Henry II. The earliest mention that we can find of him occurs in the subjoined patent of his appointment of Master of the Buckhounds to James I., dated at Westminster, June 21, 1603.‡ In this interesting document he is described as Thomas Tyringham Esquire, "one of the gentlemen pensioners." However, he was knighted at Syon, with four other gentlemen, during this

* To H.M. Huntsmen of the Privy Buckhounds, by vertue of H.M. warrant under the signet bearing date at Hampton Court. October 6, 1610—viz., to R. Brassy, F. Dodsworth, E. Dodsworth, W. Sale, J. Broughton, T. Holland, W. Cocker, T. Murrall, R. Kilbourne, J. Owen, W. Lampard, T. Atkinson, and T. Tyllesley, yeomen, and to R. Crockford, lymmerman, at 10d. each per day, and to E. Walworth, and to R. Williams, G. Fowler, and W. Kelsey and J. Hawke, waggoner, each at 2d. per day, by way of H.M. free gift and reward in regard of their attendance on His Highness this summer—viz., from Midsummer Day, 1610, until Michaelmas following, being 97 days—80l. 0s. 6d.

† In some instances the hunt servants obtained farther payments under this head. Thus, Robert Hancock, yeoman pricker, received a warrant under the signet dated November, 1620, authorising the Treasurer of the Chamber to pay him for his allowance for attending the said hounds in the summer season the fee of 20d. per diem during his natural life, and 20s. for his winter livery yearly. Robert Pattison, yeoman harbinger, was similarly favoured with a fee of 12d. "of lawful money of England," by the day, for like services.

‡ By a Privy Seal warrant dated Westminster, June 1, 1603, he was nominated to hold this office during his life "as Sir Robert Dudley had the same by Letters Patents of King Edward the Sixth."

month, evidently on some day after June 21, when he first received the official insignia of the Royal pack, which he carried until he resigned it to his successor in October 1625. His patent is one of the earliest (*per se*) that we have met with relating to this branch of the Royal Buckhounds; and as will be seen by it that Sir Thomas obtained the appointment for the natural term of his life, with an annual fee of 33*l*. 6*s*. 8*d*., payable half yearly, in equal proportions, by the hands of the Treasurer of the Chamber of the Household. A further interest is attached to this patent, because it recites that he was entitled to hold the office in as full and ample manner as enjoyed by his predecessors, amongst whom are mentioned Sir Richard Long, Thomas Lord Darcy of Chiche, John Earl of Warwick, and Sir Robert Dudley (afterwards Earl of Leicester), or any other.

The enrolment of his patent reads briefly thus :—

"Rex om'ibuȝ ad quos, &c., sal'tm. Sciatis qu nos de grā nrā spiāli ac ex ēta daencil & mero motu nris dedimuȝ & concessimȝ, Ac p' p'sentes p' nob' hered' & successoribȝ n'ris damu⁸ & concedimȝ dil'co & fideli suien' nro' Thome Tyringham ar' uni generos Pencionar' nrōȝ offic'm magri Canum nrōr vocat Buckhoundes. h'end ex'tend tenend occupand & gaudend idem offic p'fat Thome Tyringham p' de vel p' sufficien deputat sun' sine deputat suos sufficien ad tminū & p' tmino vite ip'ms Thome Tyringham recipiend' leband & an'uatim p'cipiend p' vad & feod suis in & p' eodem offic ex'ceend et occupand triginta tres libras sex solid & octo denar' p' manus Thesaurar nr camere nr p' tempore existen ad tminos sn' Michīs archi' et Pasche equis porc'oibȝ una cum om'bȝ al' vad feod p'sic allocat regard com'oditat et emolument de'o offico quoquo modo spectan seu p'tinen in tam amplis modo & forma p'ut Ricūs Longe miles vel Thomas d'nus Darcye de Chiche, aut Johes Comes Warwic aut Roburts Dudley mil aut aliquis alius dim aliqui alij offic illud antehac occupans h'uit & p'cepit h'uer & p'ceptr seu here & p'cip'e dehuer aut debuit in & p' eodem absq' compō seu aliquo alio nob' hered & successoribȝ nris p'inde reddend soluend seu faciend. In qo' expressa mencio, &c. In cuius rei, &c., &c. R. apud Westm' vi'esimo primo die Junij."

On September 17 Sir Thomas received a royal commission, by which he was empowered "to take up, by himself or his assignes, hounds and greyhounds for His Majesty's disport." In August 1604 he received another commission from the King for the preservation of the red deer in the Manor of Knotting. By a warrant dormant, dated July 18, 1607, the Keeper of the Royal Wardrobe was commanded to supply this Master of the Buckhounds with "stuff for his livery." Unfortunately, as in the case of all warrants dormant in the accounts of the Great Wardrobe in those days, no description is given of the materials from which the official uniforms of the Master or the subordinate officers of the pack were made; nothing save the entry of the cost of the "livery" is given, consequently we are unable to tell at present (although we hope to do so later on) how those individuals were attired for the Royal chase. Early in the following year the King wrote to Sir Thomas Oxenbridge, to permit Sir Thomas Tyringham to follow the Buckhounds into his grounds, which were probably protected by a grant of free warren or free chase. On July 4, 1613, Sir Thomas obtained a grant in reversion, after Sir Charles Howard, of the Keepership of the Great Park of Windsor. In July 1614 a warrant was issued under the Great Seal to furnish him with sixteen beds and provision for thirty horses, and for the King's hounds, in all places adjacent to the Court, "at reasonable prices"; and in April 1621 he received a similar warrant, empowering him to take up, in places adjacent to the Court, beds, stable room, etc., on his own terms, which must have been a questionable blessing to those who had such valuable places to let. In July 1623 the King wrote to the Earl of Nottingham, Chief Justice in Eyre, south of Trent, expressing a desire that Sir Thomas Tyringham should succeed Mr. Creswell, lately deceased, as the Keeper of one of the walks in Windsor Great Park, "his office rendering him the fittest man for it," a royal recommendation that had the desired effect. Some curious circumstances occurred at Windsor Park during this Master of the Buckhounds' term of office upon which he had to adjudicate. A keeper there, who committed an assault on a man, was condemned in a fine of 7*l*. or imprisonment; while another keeper, who killed a poacher "in the execution of the duty of his place," the case was referred to the King, who decreed that the assassin should be held harmless in the matter, as the offence (if any) occurred within the precincts of the Royal park, therefore it came under the Royal prerogative, and consequently the common law could take no cognisance of it. The most curious part of this case was that, when it was submitted to the law officers of the Crown, they concurred with the judgment of the British Solomon. On another occasion, Henry Sawyer, of Holme, Huntingdonshire, a professional mole-catcher, while exercising his vocation in a field near Windsor, was overheard to remark that the King would be assassinated during his progress in Scotland. Sawyer was therefore arrested and arraigned before Sir Thomas Tyringham, who carefully investigated the alleged "plot"; but he, finding there was neither high nor low treason in the matter, let the indiscreet mole-catcher off scot-free. Sir Thomas Tyringham, by virtue of his keepership of Windsor Park, apparently made free with the King's deer; but he did not forget absent friends, as frequent mention of a "huntsman's token," *i.e.*, two venison pasties, "a brace of buck's shoulders and ambles," and occasionally a haunch or two, are mentioned as presents sent to his friends and patrons, by whom such gifts were thankfully received and gratefully acknowledged.

These were not mere expressions of ordinary courtesy; they meant very much more than the words conveyed. In those days the sale of venison was prohibited, and the savoury viand could only be obtained from the King, or surreptitiously, through the officials of the royal forests, parks, and chases—hence the proverb: *Non est inquirendum unde venit* VENISON. This probably indirectly led to subsequent abuses, as we find Sir Thomas Tyringham was ordered by warrant, dated November 1633, not to kill any deer in Windsor Park without he had special directions under the Royal sign manual to do so. Keepers of ordinaries, hotels, etc., were prohibited to buy any venison; nor were they allowed to buy any pheasants, partridges, or grouse to sell again.

Sir Thomas Tyringham resigned his office of Master of the Buckhounds in 1625. His successor, Sir Timothy Tyrell, had been Master of the privy Buckhounds to Charles, Prince of Wales, from 1611 to the death of James I.; and on the accession of Charles I., Sir Timothy obtained the horn of the Royal pack from the new monarch by Privy Seal, dated October 12, 1625, which he held till his death in 1632.

On May 20, 1633, Sir Thomas Tyringham was re-appointed to the office, and consequently became the tenth Master of the Household branch of the pack, which he filled to the satisfaction of all concerned until the day of his death. He died in 1637, and was buried at Tyringham on January 24 of that year, in the fifty-sixth year of his age.

CHAPTER VI.

HOUSEHOLD BRANCH.—CHARLES I.

1625—1649.

Annual Expenses of the Pack during the Reign of Charles I., from 1625—1640.
—The Masters and the Hunt-Servants.—Their Salaries, Fees, and Emoluments. Sir Timothy Tyrell, Ninth Master : March 26, 1625 to May 19, 1633.
—Sir Thomas Tyringham (ii.), Tenth Master : May 20, 1633 to January 1637.
—Robert Tyrwhitt, Esq., Eleventh Master : May 4, 1637 to January 6, 1651.
—Reflections on Sport with the Pack from 1603 to 1640.—Hunting-Horses.
—Hunting Matches.—The Royal Studs.— Deer and Hound-Vans.—The Equerries of the Hunting Stables.—Hunting with the Pack during the Commonwealth.—Poaching.—Destruction of the Deer.—Fate of the Royal Hunt-Servants.

1624-25.—The first Account of the Treasurer of the Chamber of the Household, in the reign of Charles I., from September 29, 1624, to September 29, 1625, includes the expenses of the "Privy," or Household branch of the Royal Buckhounds for the last half year (plus two days) of the reign of James I. (who died on March 27, 1625), and for the half year of the first regnal year of Charles I. (minus two days), ended on September 29, 1625. In this audit we therefore ascertain the cost and the *personnel* of this pack as it was on the establishment down to the death of James I., and as it was reorganised during the first half year of the reign of Charles I. It will serve our purpose here to briefly mention that no material change had taken place in the state of its affairs down to the death of James I.; but on the accession of Charles I. many changes supervened, as we shall have occasion presently to notice. However, as this account of the Treasurer of the Chamber is carried on from September 29, 1624, to September 29, 1625, we ascertain that the cost of the pack, as chargeable on this Department, within this year amounted to 965*l*. 8*s*. 5½*d*. This was an increase—compared with the last half and the two preceding whole years of the reign of James I.—of 147*l*. 4*s*. 0¾*d*., chiefly incurred during the first half year of the reign of Charles I.

From a brief investigation of the facts and figures now before us we find that Sir Thomas Tyringham, the Master, under James I. was paid his fee at the rate of 33*l*. 6*s*. 8*d*. per annum, for the half year, ended at Lady Day 1625, when "Sir Timothy Tirell, Knight, Master of H.M. Privy Buckhounds, succeeding Sir Thomas Tyringham," received for his fee, payable quarterly, "by vertue of H.M. letters under the signet, dated October 13, 1625, due to him, began at Lady Day 1625 and ended at Michaelmas next following," the sum of 16*l*. 13*s*. 4*d*. Robert Walker, the Sergeant, received, as heretofore, 51*l*. 13*s*. 4*d*. for his fee, and 100*l*. per annum for feeding and keeping sixteen couples of buckhounds. The eight yeomen prickers, mentioned in the last account, at 20*d*. each a day for wages and 20*s*. each per annum for livery, were paid as usual, except Francis Dodsworth, who died at Christmas 1624, when he was succeeded by Henry Dodsworth, and paid at the same rate down to date. Robert Hancock, another yeoman pricker, *sans* livery, was still in receipt of 2*s*. 6¾*d*. per diem. Sale-Dilly and Holland also received 2*s*. a day each and 20*s*. each per annum for livery. Connock and Hunt, yeomen prickers, obtained 3*s*. 4*d*. a day each for their wages. Hake, the waggoner, had 20*d*. a day as heretofore. And Robert Pattison, the harbinger, received his usual remuneration at the rate of 12*d*. a day for the time being. Thus far we find the old staff as in the last years of the reign of James I.

But we are now introduced to George Fowler, John Williams, Ralph Reade, and William Hopkins, "grooms of the said buckhounds," each of whom were paid 12*d*. a day for their wages and 20*s*. per annum for their several liveries. Thomas Lee, an additional yeoman pricker, obtained 20d. a day for his wages and 20s. per annum for livery. Robert Jackson and William Rawson, " twoe of his Maties Huntesmen [yeomen prickers] for the said Buckhounds at xxvj^{li}. xiij^{s}. iiij^{d}. per ann. to either of them for theire wages payable quart'ly; and xx^{s}. the peece for theire Lyveryes payable at Xpmas, By vertue of his Ma^{ts} Lres. vnder the Signett, dated the said xij^{th} of October 1625, due to them for halfe a yeare ended at Michas 1625, Aō. RR. Caroli primo —26l. 13s. 4d." Richard Ray, Paul Story, and Thomas White, " three other Huntsmen [yeomen prickers] for the said Buckhounds at xxvj^{li}. xiij^{s}. iiij^{d}. the peece ℙ ann. for theire wages, and xx^{s}. the peece ℙ ann. for theire Lyveryes, due to them for the same tyme and payable as aforesaid by vertue of the warraunte beforemcōned "—40l. Anthony Dodsworth, " one other of the said Huntesmen [yeomen prickers] at iiij^{s}. ij^{d}. per diem for his wages payable quarterly, and xx^{s}. ℙ ann. for his Lyvery payable at Xpmas, due to him for the like tyme "— 38l. 0s. 5d. William Gwilliams, James Medcalfe, and James Kipling, " Huntesmen [grooms] likewyse, at xx^{li}. the peece ℙ ann. for theire wages payable quarterly, and xx^{s}. ℙ ann. for their Lyveryes payable at Xpmas, due to them by the same warr^{te}, for thaforsayd tyme "—30l. And to Robert Walker, junior, yeoman of the said Buckhounds, 20d. a day for his wages and 20s. ℙ ann. for his livery, by vertue of the said letters under the Signet, dated October 12, 1625, received 15l. 4s. 2d.

1625-26.—The account for this year, ended at September 29, 1626, amounts to 919l. 5s. 6¾d. All the officials, as in the preceding year, being in the enjoyment of their posts and emoluments, the subject calls for no comment. However, apart from this, and not included in the above, some of the staff were allowed an additional honorarium, " being H.M. free guift to them for one quarter of a year ended at Michaelmas 1626," amounting to 157l. 12s. 6d., " by vertue of H.M. Signet dated 25th of September, 1626 "—viz., R. Hunt, W. Connock, R. Hancock, A. Dodsworth, and R. Raye, yeomen of the Buckhounds, to each of them 2s. a day ; R. Jackson, W. Reading,

P. Stacy, W. Rawson, W. Cocker, T. White, A. Holland, T. Lee, H. Dodsworth, R. Walker, junr., E. Stanton, R. Norman, J. Cocker, E. Dodsworth, W. Beale, J. Hake, R. Crockford, and R. Pattison, yeomen of the said Buckhounds, to each of them 12*d*. a day; R. Eldridge, J. Kipling, G. Fowler, R. Read, J. Williams, W. Hopkins, W. Gwilliams, F. Becham, and J. Metcalfe, grooms of the said Buckhounds, 6*d*. a day each. This was a considerable increase under this head compared with the amount distributed in the time of James I.

1627-28.—The account for this year amounts to 1,214*l*. 14*s*. 6¾*d*. We find all the hunt-servants as before paid at the usual rates down to date; and in addition the names of Ralph Reade, John Williams, William Hopkins, and George Fowler—in what capacity not stated—engaged at 12*d*. each for their wages, and 20*s*. each for their several liveries. Henry Dover was appointed a yeoman pricker in the place of Richard Hunt "at xx^d. $\cancel{p}$ diem being the one halfe pay to be paid quarterly, By virtue of his Ma^{ts}. ires vnder the Signett dated the xxvijth of Septemb^r Anno Tertio Regis Caroli due to him for the like tyme." An increase in the wages and emoluments of some of the staff is noticeable in this audit. Thus, Richard Eldridge, yeoman pricker, received for his wages 40*l*. per annum and 40*s*. for his livery. The other instances recorded, being of less significance, call for no minute notice here. The King's "free guift" to the yeomen prickers, the waggoner, and the grooms of the Privy Buckhounds, for their attendance from the Feast of the Nativity of St. John the Baptist (June 24), until Michaelmas 1628, in addition to the above total, amounted to 158*l*. 5*s*. 6*d*.

1628-29. — The account for this year amounts to 1,338*l*. 18*s*. 6¾*d*. The only change that had taken place within this year was the appointment of Thomas Oxley "groom of H.M. Buckhounds in the room and place of John Williams, deceased, at 13*d*. per day for his wages payable quarterly, and 20*s*. for his livery payable at Midsummer, by vertue of H.M. letters under the signet dated the 11th of September in the 5th year of H.M. reign, the first payment to begin from the death of the said John Williams, due to him in full at Michaelmas quarter 1629, 4*l*. 9*s*. 1¼*d*." The King's "free guift" to the yeomen prickers, the yeoman of the waggon, and the grooms, from Midsummer to Michaelmas 1629, was 158*l*.

1629–30.—The account for this year exhibits a nominal decrease, in consequence of some of the hunt-servants having been "put to pension." It amounts to 986*l*. 18*s*. 8¾*d*. for the acting staff; but if we include the payments to the other individuals affiliated therewith who were now pensioned at a charge of 296*l*. 3*s*. 1*d*. per annum, the total cost of the pack for this year, ended on September 29, 1630, would be 1,283*l*. 1*s*. 9¾*d*. Apart from the hunt-servants "put to pension," there is very little alteration in the *personnel* or the remuneration of the staff as we find it heretofore on the establishment. It may be noted, however, that William Connock, a yeoman pricker, at 3*s*. 8*d*. a day for his wages and 40*s*. per annum for his livery, was awarded an increase of 20*s*. per annum for his uniform, "by vertue of H.M. letters under the signet, dated the 20th of September anno regis Caroli decimo [*sic*], due to him for a year—together with the arrears of the said 20*s*. per annum, formerly disallowed, and due for six years ended at Michaelmas 1630," was now paid down to date, in full, the sum of 73*l*. 18*s*. 4*d*. Thomas White, another yeoman pricker, obtained an increase in his wages (which had been at the rate of 26*l*. 13*s*. 4*d*. a year, and 20*s*. per annum for his livery down to Midsummer 1630). He now received 3*s*. 1½*d*. a day for his wages and 40*s*. per annum for his livery, "payable quarterly during his life, by vertue of H.M. letters patents under the great seal of England bearing date the 13th day of July anno sexto regis Caroli, the first payment to begin from the 20th day of June then last past and due to him for a quarter of a year and ten days ended at Michaelmas 1630."

The officials now pensioned were Edward Stanton and William Sale, yeomen prickers, at 2*s*. a day each for wages and 20*s*. per annum each for liveries; William Reading, yeoman pricker, at 8d. a day for wages and 20s. per annum for livery; William Norman, yeoman pricker, at 26l. 13s. 4d. a year for wages and 20s. per annum for livery; Robert Pattison, yeoman harbinger, at 12d. a day for wages and no livery; Edward Dodsworth, yeoman pricker, at 20d. a day for wages and 20s. per annum for livery; Richard Crockford and John Hake, yeomen prickers, at the same rate; William Darrant, yeoman pricker, at 14l. 18s. a year for wages, sans livery. George Fowler, groom, at 13d. a day for wages and 20s. per annum for his livery; Henry Sams, at 19l. 2s. 4d. for his wages per annum. And though last, not least, among those venatic "pensioners" is Edward Kingesley, "in the Roome and place of Richard Vincent, Bonesetter, at xix^{li}. ij^s. iiij^d. $\tilde{p}$ ann. by virtue of his Ma^{ts} lres vnder the Signett dated the xxth of November Anno quinto Regis Caroli. The first payment to begin from Midsomer then last past, and due to him for a yeare ended at Mich$\tilde{a}$s aforesaid—xix^{li}. ij^s. iiij^d." The King's free gift to the hunt officials, from Midsummer to Michaelmas, amounted to 157l. 11s. 2d.

1630–31.—The account for this year ended on September 29, 1631, amounts to 1,290l. 3s. 7½¼⅛d. There is no change in the staff of sufficient importance to particularly notice, consequently we pass on to the next account, comprehending an apparent lapse, as this audit only embraces a period from September 29, 1632, to September 29, 1633, during which the pack cost the Royal Treasury 1,266l. and 15½¼⅛d. A brief analysis shows that Sir Thomas Tyringham was re-appointed to his former office of "Master of H.M. Privy Buckhounds in the room and place of Sir Timothy Tirell, deceased, for his wages at 33l. 6s. 8d. per annum, payable half yearly, by equal portions, by vertue of H.M. letters patents under the Great Seal of England, bearing date the 20th day of May, anno 9 regni Caroli, and due to him for half a year ended at Michealmas 1633." Robert Walker, senior, the Sergeant, at 51l. 3s. 4d. a year for his wages and 100l. per annum for keeping the hounds, received, as heretofore, 151l. 3s. 4d. Eight yeomen prickers—viz., R. Hancock at 4s. $2\frac{1}{2}\frac{1}{4}\frac{1}{8}d.$ per day for wages and 40s. per annum for livery; Anthony Dodsworth, at 4s. 2d. a day for wages and 20s. per annum for livery; W. Connock and R. Walker, junr., at 3s. 8d. a day for wages and 40s. per annum for livery ; Thomas White, at 3s. 1d. a day for wages and 40s. per annum for livery; A. Holland and E. Stanton, at 2s. a day for wages and 20s. for livery; Paul Stacey, at 2s. 11d. a day for wages and 40s. per annum for livery. Eight grooms—viz., R. Ray, W. Rawson, R. Norman, at 26l. 13s. 4d. a year for wages and 20s. per annum for liveries ; R. Reade, T. Ockley, W. Hopkins, G. Fowler, at 13d. a day for wages and 20s. per annum for liveries. Then we have the following (but in what capacity not mentioned)—viz., W.Cocker, J. Cocker, T. Lee, H. Dodsworth, H. Dover, F. Dodsworth, R. Crockford, J. Wake, at 20d. a day wages and 20s. per annum for liveries; J. Metcalfe, W. Gwilliams, J. Kipling, at 20l. a year for wages and 20s. per annum for liveries; R. Eldridge at 40l. a year for wages and 40s. per annum for liveries; W. Reading, at 18d. a day for wages and 20s. per annum for livery; R. Pattison, at 12d. for wages, *sans* livery; H. Sames and Edward Kingesley, at 19l. 2s. 4d. a year; and, lastly, to William Darrant, at 14l. 18s. a year, payable quarterly, and due to him for one quarter of a year ended at Christmas 1632, and to Edward Lambert, succeeding him, at 6l. 13s. 4d. a year for his wages, and 8l. 4s. 10d. per annum for his summer livery, both payable quarterly, by virtue of H.M. letters under the Signet, dated September 27, anno 9, Charles I., and now due to him for one quarter ended at Michaelmas 1633, 74s. 6d.

1633–34.—The account for this year, ended on September 29, 1634, amounts to 1,290l. 3s. $9\frac{1}{2}\frac{1}{4}\frac{1}{8}d.$ There is no change in the staff nor in their several remunerations and allowances. The King's free gifts to "huntsmen of the Privy Buckhounds" for their attendance in the summer season, amounted to 157l. 17s.

1634–35.—The account for this year amounts to 1,325l. 2s. $4\frac{1}{2}\frac{1}{4}\frac{1}{8}d.$ Robert Walker, the Sergeant, died some time prior to Christmas 1634, when he was succeeded by

Anthony Dodsworth, who was accorded 50*l.* a year for his wages, and "a new fee" of 50*l.* more per annum, besides the usual allowance of 100*l.* yearly "for the keeping of sixteen couple of hounds for His Majesty's service," in all 200*l.* per annum, payable quarterly, by virtue of H.M. letters under the Signet bearing date February 12, anno regis 10th Charles I., to hold and enjoy the said several wages, fees, and allowances to him or to his assignees during his natural life, the first payment to begin at the Feast of the Annunciation of the Blessed Virgin Mary (March 25) then next following, due for three-quarters of a year, ended at Michaelmas 1635, amounting to 150*l.**

Anthony Holland was promoted to the place of yeoman pricker, now vacated by the elevation of Anthony Dodsworth to the Sergeantship of the pack. But whereas Dodsworth's wages had been at the rate of 4*s.* 3*d.* a day, the wages of his successor was 3*d.* a day less, and an annual allowance of 20*s.* per annum for his livery. Thomas Lee, yeoman pricker, died in November 1634. He was succeeded by William Reading, at 20*d.* a day for his wages and 20*s.* per annum for his livery. Robert Norman, groom, died at Midsummer 1635. He was succeeded by William Goodwyn, with the wages of 26*l.* 14*s.* 4*d.* and 20*s.* per annum for livery. These changes occasioned some further promotion among the subordinate hunt-servants, which it is hardly necessary to detail.

1635–36.—The account for this year amounts to 1,335*l.* 4*s.* 5¾*d.* Anthony Dodsworth, the Sergeant, is set down as having received 100*l.* for his wages and 100*l.* for "keeping of xvj couple of hounds." He also received 50*l.* (not included under this heading), under the classification of annuity or pension; consequently he was paid altogether at the rate of 250*l.* a year.

* Apart from the direct expenses under this head, the following entry occurs under "Annuities and Pensions": "To Anthony Dodsworth sergeant of the privy Buckhounds, in consideration of keeping the hounds at 50*l.* per annum payable quarterly by virtue of H.M. letters under the signet, dated the last of August anno regis Caroli 11mo.—the first payment to begin at the Feast of the Nativity of St. John the Baptist last past, and to continue during his life due for half a year ended at Michaelmas 1635, 25*l.*"

Paul Stacey, yeoman pricker, who was succeeded by Francis Dodsworth (December 11, 1635), was paid at the rate of 2s. 6d. a day for wages and 40s. per annum for livery. William Wetherall was thereupon appointed to fill the vacant post. William Basse obtained Wetherall's place; and John Crockford became lymberman vice Richard Crockford, dead or retired, by virtue of H.M. letters under the signet, dated June 23, 1636. The King's free gifts to the hunt-servants for their attendance during the summer season amounted, in addition, to 154l. 7s.

1637–38.—The account for this year, from September 29, 1637, to September 29, 1638, amounts to 1,338l. 0s. 0$\frac{1}{2}\frac{1}{4}\frac{1}{3}$d. There is no change in the *personnel* of the staff, except the appointment of George Fryer, groom, *vice* William Rawson; Robert Bedborough, *vice* R. Pattison and W. Pitman, *vice* William Connock, deceased. The King's free gifts to the hunt-servants were 157l. 10s. The Master is called Sir Thomas Tyrwhitt, knight—clearly a mistake by the engrosser, who should have written "Robert Tyrwhitt, Esq."

1638–39.—The account for this year, ended at September 29 1639, amounts to exactly the same sum as the preceding one. The Master is here styled "Robert Terwhitt, Esq." He received 33l. 6s. 8d. "for his wages per annum, payable quarterly and due for one whole year ended at Michaelmas 1639."

1639–40.—The account for this year, ended on September 29, 1640, amounts to 1,340l. 6s. 5¼d. It is the penultimate, and, moreover, the last complete one preserved in this series during the reign of Charles I. It is consequently replete with the establishment of this branch of the Royal Buckhounds. A brief analysis of the interesting facts and figures contained therein must be especially welcome here, particularly as we shall find no further details during the ensuing dark and dismal twenty years.

First and foremost comes Robert Tyrwhitt, Esq., the Master, at the head of the hunt-servants of this branch of the pack, whom we find in the receipt of his salary in full, for one whole year ended at Michaelmas 1640, amounting to the usual sum of 33l. 6s. 8d.

Anthony Dodsworth, the Sergeant, received 200*l*. "for his fee and wages due and payable as before"; and apart from, and not included under this head, 50*l*. additional in the form of an annuity or pension "for an increase of allowance towards the feeding and keeping of new hounds, payable quarterly and due to him for the aforesaid time," amounting altogether to 250*l*. per annum.

The following yeomen prickers were paid at the undermentioned rates—viz., Robert Hancock, wages 4*s*. $2\frac{1}{4}\frac{1}{2}\frac{1}{8}d$. a day and 40*s*. per annum for livery; Anthony Holland, 4*s*. a day wages and 20*s*. per annum for livery; Robert Walker, 3*s*. 8*d*. a day wages and 40*s*. per annum for livery; W. Cocker, W. Reading, J. Hake ("waggoner"), J. Cocker, H. Dodsworth, J. Crockford, and W. Pitman ("yeomen"), each at 20*d*. a day wages and 20*s*. each per annum for livery; E. Staunton, W. Wetherall, and W. Ledman, "yeomen prickers," 2*s*. a day each wages and 20*s*. each per annum for livery; Francis Dodsworth, "another yeoman pricker," at 2*s*. 11*d*. a day wages and 40*s*. per annum for livery; Thomas White, yeoman pricker, at 3*s*. 1½*d*. a day wages and 40*s*. per annum for livery; James Kipling, at 22*d*. a day wages ("as yeoman pricker") and no livery; W. Basse, "yeoman," 18*d*. a day wages and 20*s*. per annum for livery.

The following grooms are specifically mentioned—viz., R. Ray, W. Goodwin, and George Fryer ("waggoner"), at 26*l*. 13*s*. 4*d*. a year each wages and 20*s*. each per annum for livery; G. Fowler, W. Hopkins, and T. Ockley, at 13*d*. a day each wages, and 20*s*. per annum each for livery; W. Gwilliams, J. Metcalfe, and T. Fowkles, 20*l*. a year each wages and 20*s*. per annum each for livery. "And to Ralph Read one of the grooms of the said Buckhounds for his wages at 13*d*. a day and 20*s*. per annum for his livery (the wages payable quarterly and the livery at Christmas) and due to him for one quarter and sixteen days in part of this year, 6*l*. 18*s*. 3¼*d*., and to Bartholomew Dixon, succeeding him in the said place, by virtue of H.M. letters under the signet, dated the 10th of March, anno regis Caroli præd. 15to, the first payment to begin from the death of said Ralph Read, and to continue during his life, and due to him for the residue of this year, 13*l*. 18*s*. 1¾*d*.; in all, 20*l*. 16*s*. 6*d*."

Redward Roe, "Harbinger for the Huntsmen, in the place of Robert Bedborough at 12*d*. a day for his wages, payable quarterly, and due to him for the like time, by vertue of H.M. warrant under the Signet, dated the 26th of October, 1639, the first payment to begin from the Feast of St. Michael the Archangel last past and to continue during his life."

Henry Sames and Edward Kinsley, "bonesetters," "to each of them 19*l*. 2*s*. 4*d*. per annum for their wages, and due to them, for the aforesaid time," received 38*l*. 4*s*. 8*d*.

In what capacity, not stated, Richard Eldridge received at the rate of 40*l*. a year for wages and 40*s*. per annum for his livery. Edward Lambert was in the receipt of 6*l*. 13*s*. 4*d*. a year wages and 8*l*. 4*s*. 10*d*. for his livery.

1642.—The final account preserved in this series, so far as our subject is concerned, only relates to the payment made to this branch of the Royal Buckhounds for one half year ended on Lady Day 1642. It only amounts to 710*l*. 10*s*. 4*d*. Nearly all of the officials appear to have been paid at the established allowance as indicated in the preceding audit for the year ended at Michaelmas 1640. As previously observed, we shall not hear anything further relating to the expenses, or of the individuals who constituted the executive, until the Accounts of the Treasurer of the Chamber of the Royal Exchequer were again resumed soon after the Restoration.

SIR TIMOTHY TYRELL, or Tirell (as the name is generally written in the official documents), the ninth Master of the Privy or Household branch of the Royal Buckhounds—from March 26, 1625, to May 19, 1633—was the second son of Sir Edward Tyrell, Knight, M.P. for Oakley, county Bucks, and Margaret, daughter of Thomas Aston, Esq., of Aston. The family is reputed to have descended from Sir Walter Tyrell, who killed William Rufus accidentally with an arrow when hunting in the New Forest, county Hants, on August 2, 1100. The date of the birth of this Master of the Royal Buckhounds has not been recorded; and the first mention of him to be found in official documents occurs in the year 1610, when he was appointed by James I. Master of the "Old" pack, on the occasion of the annexation of the Hereditary branch, and its amalgamation with the Household kennel, at that time, under the circumstances already recorded. It appears his salary, in this capacity, was at the rate of 20l. per annum, and that this stipend and the concurrent cost of this "Old" branch of the pack was defrayed out of the King's Privy Purse from Christmas 1610 onward to Christmas 1612. However, in the ensuing year, when it was formed into a separate pack for Charles, Duke of York, we find the whole cost and particulars included in the Accounts of the Treasurer of the Chamber, and payable out of the Royal Exchequer for three-quarters of a year ended at Michaelmas 1613, viz.:—

HUNTESMEN FOR THE PRINCES BUCKHOUNDES: To Tymothie Tirrell Esquire Master of the Princes buckhoundes at xx^{li} $\mathcal{P}$ ann. for his wages payable quarterlie due to him for three quarters of a yeare ended at Mychās, 1613, by his Ma^{ts} war^{a}unte vnder the signett dated at Grenewiche the xth day of June 1613—xv^{li}.

To Roberte Rayne Sergeaunte of the saide buckhoundes by the same warraunte at iiij^{li}. xiij^s. iij^d. $\mathcal{P}$ ann. for his wages payable quarterlie, due to him for the same tyme—lxviij^{li}. viij^d. qr.

To Anthonie Dodesworthe yeoman by the same warraunte at xl^{li}. vj^d. $\mathcal{P}$ ann. for his wages due to him for three quarters of a yeare ended at Michās 1613—xxx^{li}. iiij^s. vj^d.

To Augustyne Crigges, Nathan Jackson, Anthonie Brackenburye, Will^{a}m Readinge and Richarde Raye yeomen of the buckhoundes by the foresaide warraunte at xxvj^{li}. xiij^s. iiij^d. $\mathcal{P}$ ann. for theire wages payable & due for the same tyme—C^{li}.

To Edwarde Stanton yeoman at xxxvj^{li}. xvj^s. viij^d. $\mathcal{P}$ ann. & Will^{a}m Rawson yeoman waggoner at xxvj^{li}. v^s. ij^d. $\mathcal{P}$ ann. for theire wages by the same warr both payable quarterlie, and due to them for three quarters of a yeare ended at Michās 1613 —xlvij^{li}. vj^s. iiij^d. ob.

SIR TIMOTHY TYRELL, NINTH MASTER. 131

To Jerome Metcalfe, Anthonie Dodesworth, Will'm Gwillams, & Francis Beawchampe groomes of the said buckhoundes by the said warr'^t at xx^{li}. the pece P ann. for theire wages payable quarterlie, and due to them for the aforesaid tyme—lx^{li.}
Total CCCxx^{li}. vj^s. vj^d. ob. ¦.

During the year ended at Michaelmas 1614 the Duke of York's pack of Buckhounds was sustained by the Royal Exchequer at a cost of 427*l*. 8*s*. 9*d*. In 1615 and 1616 similar sums were allocated for its support. Mr. Tyrell was still the Master, nor was any change made in the hunt-servants, except that Sergeant Rayne surrendered his office to Edward Hart,* by virtue of H.M. letters under the Signet, dated at Newmarket, February 30, 1615–6. When the Duke of York was created Prince of Wales, on November 4, 1616, he entered upon an establishment appertaining solely to himself and sustained by himself, consequently we lose all trace of this tail, or appendage, of the Royal Buckhounds, its Master, and its staff, from Michaelmas 1616 until Michaelmas 1625. On the Prince's accession to the throne this tail of the Royal Buckhounds again reverted to the parent kennel, and was again amalgamated with the Household branch, under the Mastership of Sir Timothy Tyrell, *vice* Sir Thomas Tyringham, resigned.

In the meantime, we must hark back, and record in proper chronological sequence that Mr. Tyrell, in 1614, married Eleanor, daughter of Sir William Kingsmill, of Sidmanton, county Hants, by whom he had issue four sons and three daughters. He was knighted at his "Lodge in Oxfordshire" by James I., when that sporting monarch was his guest there during a hunting expedition on August 29, 1624.

As previously mentioned, Sir Timothy retained his post of Master of the Buckhounds to the Prince of Wales until the death of James I., and on the accession of Charles I. he was doubtless promoted to carry the horn of the regal hunting establishment, and became *pro formâ* Master of the Buck-

---

* He obtained a pension of 90*l*. 14*s*. 3*d*. a year on the accession of Charles I., and was paid at that rate down to Michaelmas 1640.

hounds to the new King, with whom he was evidently a prime favourite and a faithful servant. We have been unable to find any patent* of his appointment of Master of the Buckhounds to Charles I., but he is specifically mentioned as the holder of that high office in the grant of a pension of 100*l.* a year for life given to him by the King, dated October 6, 1625. Burke asserts that Sir Timothy Tyrell was Master of the Buckhounds to Henry, Prince of Wales, and an officer of the bedchamber to Charles I. ("Dormant and Extinct Baronetage"), but both of these assertions are probably inaccurate. At all events, this Master of the Buckhounds was in high favour at the court of Charles I., and that he knew how to play his cards to his own advantage we have ample evidence. Thus, in October 1628, Sir Timothy Tyrell and Timothy Tyrell, his son, obtained a grant from the King during their lives successively, of the custody and stewardship of the Forest of Shotover and Stoe Wood, county Oxford, and the herbage and pannage thereof, with all fees, liberties, and commodities thereunto pertaining. Practically this amounted to the disafforestation of those forests, and it soon afterwards led to great disputes between the Admiralty and the grantees concerning the timber required by the former for the wooden

* In the patent of Master of the Buckhounds, which is transcribed in the preceding chapter, it will be seen that James I. granted Sir Thomas Tyringham the office for the natural term of his life. There is also a clause by virtue of which he could transfer the office to a sufficient deputy, hence it is obvious that on the accession of Charles I. some mutual arrangement was made between the King, Sir Thomas, and Sir Timothy, whereby the last-mentioned knight continued to act as Master of the amalgamated packs —the Privy Buckhounds of the new King and the regal pack of the late monarch. Sir Thomas Tyringham received his salary, amounting to 16*l.* 8*s.* 4*d.* for the half year ended at Lady Day 1625 ; and the first payment to Sir Timothy Tyrrel, succeeding Sir Thomas Tyringham as Master of the Buckhounds to Charles I., occurs in the accounts of the Treasurer of the Chamber for 1625—"due to him for half a year began at Lady Day [March 25, 1625] and ended at Michaelmas next following, 16*l.* 8*s.* 4*d.*" The authority given for the latter payment is "H.M. letters under the signet, dated at Westminster, Oct. 12, 1625." Unfortunately we have not been able to find that warrant; it would likely recapitulate the particulars of the transaction, and probably confirm our conjectures upon that point.

walls of Old England. About the same time this Master of the Buckhounds obtained a similar grant of Hickshill in Barneswood Forest, county Bucks, at the fine of 1,650$l.$, and a yearly rent of 2$l.$ 4$s.$ 3$d.$ reserved to the Crown for ever with a tenure of socage. By virtue of this grant, Sir Timothy, his heirs and successors, acquired waifs, strays, felons' goods, and free warren within the same, and freedom from tithes, with licence to construct woodlands into arable or pasture.

As the Shotover Forest grant gave rise to some curious complications between this Master of the Buckhounds, the Admiralty, and the royal prerogative (in connection with the forest laws), and as the proceedings exhibit some quaint phrases in rural economy at this period, perhaps a brief account of these bickerings may be admissible here. It seems, according to a survey made by the Admiralty, that about this time there were 32,366 trees suitable for shipbuilding, in Shotover Forest, which were valued at 11,321$l.$ 1$s.$ 8$d.$ Most of this timber was claimed by the Admiralty, but whenever that Board sent any of their officials to take view of the trees they proposed to fell, the Master of the Buckhounds and his keepers came to loggerheads with them, and prevented them executing their commissions. As a natural consequence, complaints were made on both sides, but it seems that the influence of the Master of the Buckhounds with the King, to ward off the Admiralty, eventually prevailed, and the disafforestation of the forest proceeded slowly but surely until it was, by the grantees, denuded of all its best timber. Among those who participated in the spoil was Archbishop Laud, who obtained a great quantity of timber from the forest to complete St. John's College, Oxford. When all of the best trees were cut down and disposed of, Sir Timothy Tyrell was summoned to attend at the chambers of the Attorney-General, in Lincoln's Inn, for the purpose of having the validity of his grant investigated. And when the dispute was formally submitted to Charles I., he decided in favour of his Master of the Buckhounds, and so the matter ended. A rather remarkable feature (but not an uncommon one in cognate circumstances) in the dispute was that Sir Timothy's keepers were, at this time (1632), ten years in arrear of their salaries.

In conclusion of our brief memoir of this Master of the Buckhounds it only remains to be stated that he, and Sir Thomas Badger, and Thomas Potts, enjoyed a royal licence to transport to any parts beyond the seas all manner of hounds, beagles, and sporting dogs, with a special command to the officers of ports not to admit any other person to transport any kind of sporting dogs without their permission first obtained in that behalf. Sir Timothy Tyrell died in December 1632, to the great regret of the King, who continued to extend his favours to Lady Tyrell and her children, as we find a warrant under the Privy Seal was issued, in April 1633, to the Master and other officers of the Court of Wards and Liveries authorising them to discharge Lady Tyrell of the sum of 300*l*. payable to the Crown by way of composition of a fine for the custody, wardship, and marriage of the son and heir, and also the yearly composition and rent of 30*l*. payable during his minority. Sir Timothy's eldest son was knighted by Charles I. September 24, 1643.

As above mentioned, Sir Thomas Tyringham was reappointed on May 20, 1633, and thus became the tenth Master of this branch of the Royal Buckhounds, and that he held the office until his death, in January 1637.

ROBERT TYRWHITT, Esquire, eleventh Master of the Household branch of the Royal Buckhounds, *temp.* Charles I., from May 4, 1637, to January 6, 1651, was the second son of Robert Tyrwhitt, Esquire, of Scrotter, county Lincoln, and Anne, daughter of Edward Bassett, Esquire, of Fledborough, county Notts. He was placed in the household of Thomas Howard, first Earl of Suffolk, Lord High Treasurer, *temp.* James I., and about this time he unfortunately added to the troubles of the famous Sir Walter Raleigh, by fighting a duel with Walter, his eldest son. A few years after Robert Tyrwhitt was introduced by Lord Suffolk to the service of Charles, Prince of Wales, and remained in it thirty-two years. He was a dashing horseman, and seems to have inherited all the predilection for the chase for which his ancestors were so notorious in ancient times. As to his early prowess in horsemanship, Sir John Finett records that when the Princess Henrietta Maria landed at Dover, he rode thence with the news of her safe arrival, "within half an hour and six minutes," to the King at Canterbury, a distance of fifteen miles. Considering the state of the roads in those days this was considered to be a remarkably expeditious journey. On the accession of Charles I. Robert Tyrwhitt was appointed Eldest Esquire of the Horse, or what we would now term Senior Equerry to the King, from whom he received a pension of 100*l.* a year for life, by writ of Privy Seal dated November 25, 1625. In conjunction with Sir Francis Clarke, he was appointed joint Lieutenant of the Forests of Aylesholt and Wolmer, county Hants, for life, by a similar writ, dated June 19, 1629. About this time he became one of the largest butter-merchants in England; probably in this line he had no equal in the whole world. As we have already seen, some of the Masters of the Buckhounds largely participated in the monopolies of the era. This growing evil assumed great dimensions in the reign of Charles I., by whom monopolies were granted indiscriminately to court favourites, and eventually led to flagrant abuses, which soon became a potent factor in the dissensions that culminated in the Civil War. In the case in point Robert Tyrwhitt, Esquire, "His Majesty's servant," on November 25, 1625, obtained a grant for twenty-one years for the yearly transporting five thousand barrels of butter out of England, for which he had to pay the King 100*l.* per annum, over and above all commissions and duties payable on the same.* In the following year (September 1629) this grant was amended and renewed to him for a

---

* This grant is also entered under date of July 1628—"by order of the Earl of Marlborough, late Lord High Treasurer of England, subscribed by Mr. Attorney-General and procured by Mr. Cary of the Bedchamber." The last mentioned became Mr. Tyrwhitt's successor in 1660.

further term of twenty-one years, by virtue of which he obtained a monopoly to transport beyond the seas into any kingdom or country in amity with the King three thousand two hundred barrels of butter yearly to be bought in the counties of Norfolk, Lincoln, and York, and other counties north of the county of York; he paying to the King 2s. 6d. for every barrel of butter so transported, in lieu of all customs and duties for the same. He was not to buy any butter to be sent to any places where the price thereof exceeded 4d. per lb. The grant was to be void in case the Lord High Treasurer, or the Lords of the Privy Council, for the time being, declared it to be inconvenient. Remonstrances and protests having been afterwards made relating to the hardships and inconveniences arising therefrom, the grantee got over the difficulty by paying a further rent of 100l. to the King, and so the matter rested in May 1631. In the meantime this gallant cavalier obtained a grant for issuing billets upon all suits commenced in His Majesty's Courts of Justice in Wales, and the marshes of the same, with a fee of 2d. for every billet so issued. The Lord President, the Chief Justice, and justices within the Principality of Wales were commanded to take notice thereof; but the principal notice they took of this new-fangled monopoly was to protest against it left and right; and the Attorney-General went so far as to draft a document declaring the grant illegal. The King, however, was true to his trusty servant, and quashed the Attorney-General's proceeding, consequently the grant remained in force. Subsequently a new difficulty arose between the grantee and his deputy, who, in 1640, obtained an order in Chancery to fill the office and perform the duties of it during his life. Thereupon the Master of the Buckhounds presented a formal petition to the King, in which he set forth that "his daily attendance on His Majesty" in various parts of the country prevented him opposing the motion made by his deputy in the Court of Chancery; that he had not time to instruct counsel, and that as he dare not trust the management of his cause to a solicitor, he prayed that the Lord Keeper be requested to stay further proceedings until the next term, when he would be prepared to show cause that the said order should not stand. Before the next term came round the Roundheads gave the King and the cavaliers other work to do, and in the troubles that ensued billets of another sort put the 2d. billets of the Master of the Buckhounds quite out of court, consequently the final issue of this curious legal tempest in a teacup is lost to posterity.

In following the windings of these monopolies we have got somewhat ahead of other and more important incidents in the course of Robert Tyrwhitt's eventful life. In May 1632 he obtained a grant of the manor and park of Hendley, county Surrey, at an annual rent of 10l. and a fine of 850l. to the Exchequer. In December 1634 he had licence to travel beyond the seas with three servants, 50l. in money, and all his necessary carriages. On April 12, 1636, a despatch was sent by the King to the Lord Deputy of Ireland, with a petition enclosed in favour of Robert Tyrwhitt, Esq., "His Majesty's servant." This is the last time he is so styled in the contemporary State papers. Afterwards he appears as the Master of the Buckhounds, having been appointed to that post, in succession to Sir Thomas Tyringham, by patent, dated at Westminster, May 4, 1637.* This document is substantially the same (*mutatis mutandis*) as that granted to his predecessor by James I. in 1603, except that the new Master's salary was payable quarterly instead of half yearly, as in the previous cases. Practically his tenure of office must have been a brief and sorrowful one. The times were sadly out of joint. Hunting, racing, and all our national field sports were almost abandoned during this appalling interval. As we have seen, Robert Tyrwhitt received his annual salary of 33l. 6s. 8d. down to the year ended at Michaelmas 1640, and the last payment to him was for half a year ended at Michaelmas 1642. With that year the accounts of the Treasurer of the

* He was appointed Master of the Buckhounds by writ of Privy Seal, dated April 16, 1637, but the patent was not enrolled until May 4, 1637, which probably accounts for the difference in the dates of the two documents.

Chamber came to an abrupt end. Nor are they again resumed until the Restoration. Hence we lose sight of all details relating to this branch of the Royal Buckhounds for nearly twenty-one years. Very little remains to be told of this Master of the Buckhounds. He followed his unhappy sovereign throughout the Civil War, and, to use his own words, was in "daily" attendance upon him, from 1640, until the flight of Charles I. from Oxford, on the night of April 27, 1646, severed the intimacy which had prevailed for many years between the King and this Master of the Buckhounds. Tyrwhitt remained in the besieged city for nearly two months; and when the royal garrison surrendered to the Parliamentary forces, he obtained from General Sir Thomas Fairfax a pass, dated June 22, 1646, to go forth with his servants, horses, arms, and all other necessaries, and to repair, without molestation, to London, or elsewhere, upon his necessary occasions, and with protection to his person, goods, and estate, and to have liberty at any time within six months to go with his servants, etc., beyond the seas. However, we find he remained at home, as on June 28 he presented "his humble petition" to the Committee for Compounding with Delinquents, at Goldsmith Hall, London, in which he describes himself as one of His Majesty's Equerries and Master of the Buckhounds. He stoutly declared his loyalty to the King, confessed that he attended on His Majesty's person "ever since the begininge of theis troubles, but was never in armes or had any martiall imployment whatsoever." Unlike many of the cavaliers, he neither took the negative oath nor conformed to the National Covenant; and for his delinquencies he submitted to the Sequestrators his poor estate, which at the time only consisted of a rent-charge of 200*l.* per annum out of the manors of Butterswick and Freeston, in the county of Lincoln, and Kirkdighton, in the county of York. He adds that he held, by letters patent, the office of Lieutenant of the Forests of Alice Holt and Wolmer, in the county of Southampton, during the term of his life, the fees of which amounted to 31*l.* 11*s.* 10*d.* From his statement of his income we may safely conclude that no payment or fees were received by him from his office of Master of the Buckhounds in 1646; in all probability his salary was in arrear from Michaelmas 1642. His rent-charge, above mentioned, was also in arrear from 1643, so that he must have been in very embarrassed circumstances; nevertheless, the Parliamentary Sequestrators imposed upon him a fine of 200*l*., as appears in the subjoined transcripts of the transaction:—

> To the hon^{ble} the Comittee' for Compoundinge with Delinquents at Goldsmithes hall.
> The humble peticōn of Robert Terwhitt one of his Maties Equeries & Master of the Buckhounds.
>
> Sheweth,—
> That the pet^r did (as hee humbly conceiueth he was bound by Oath & ye duty of his place)* attend on his Maties p'son ever since the begininge of theis troubles; but was neuer in Armes or had any martiall Imployment whatsoer. Only he humbly confeseth that he adhered to his Matie in this warre against the Parliament and for his delinquency therein his Estate is vnder or liable to sequestration.
>
> The pet^r humbly praieth hee may bee admitted to a fauorable composicōn for his delinquency according to the Articles of Oxford he being comp^{r}hended within the same. And hee shall pray &c.
> 28th Jui. 1646.
>
> (*Signed*)   R. TERWHIT.

> Robert Terwhitt of London, one of his Mat^s Equerries, and Master of his Buckhounds.
> His Delinquency, that he deserted his dwellinge and went to Oxford and lined there whiles it was a Garrison holden for the Kinge against the Parliam^{te} and was theire at the tyme of the Surrender, and is to haue the benefit of those Articles as by Sr Thomas Fairfax Certificate of the 28th of June 1646 doth appeare.
> he hath neither taken the negative oath, nor Natoñall Couvnant but prayes to be therein spared, vpon the Articles of Oxford and vote of the house of Coñons pursuant.

* The words in the brackets are cancelled.

> he compounds vpon a perticuler deliuered vnder his hand by which he doth submit to such Fine &c. and by which it doth appeare,
>
> That he is seized of an Annuity or rent charge duringe tearme of this life issueinge out of the manno^{rs} of Butterwicke and Freeston in the County of Lincoln, and Kirkdighton in the County of Yorke of the yeerely value of 200^{li}.
>
> Whereof there is foure yeers arreare, for which he also desires to compound.
>
> That he is Leiutenant by lres Patents of the Forrests of Alice Holt and Wolmer in the County of Southampton duringe tearme of his life, the fee thereof is 31l. 11s. 10d.
>
> 19 December 1646.
>
> Fine 200l.

His occupation gone, his estate sequestrated, and without hope for the future, Robert Tyrwhitt lingered unmolested at Hampton Court for a few years. He died on January 6, 1651, aged sixty-one, and was buried in Hampton Church, where a monument is erected to his memory.

Now, in bringing this chapter to a conclusion, and in taking a retrospective view of the affairs of the Royal Buckhounds during the reigns of the first and second sovereigns of the House of Stuart, one is naturally struck by the absence of any full and reliable account of the "runs" with the pack, particularly as ample and authentic details abound relating to the annual expenses and the entire staff from 1603 to 1640. Unfortunately we have no means to enable us to supply an omission so important and so interesting. It is the old story, and one that shall endure in these pages until we approach the reign of George II., when the chroniclers of that time devoted some attention in recording some of the passing events of the "Sport of Kings." There is, notwithstanding, no lack of inferential evidence by which we can, to some extent, picture to ourselves the pleasures of the chase as it was then enjoyed by the followers of the Royal Buckhounds. But no scribe or "intellenger" of that era ever dreamt that an ordinary "run" with this, or with any other pack of hounds, would be worth the trouble to record or describe. Such common-place occurrences were enjoyed day by day "in the season of the year," perhaps talked of at the moment, and then emphatically forgotten. But, if happily some untoward incident occurred, and if some kind gossip happened to be writing, on the occasion, to some friend afar, in lieu of more important news, the untoward incident, in that emergency, might serve as a stopgap, and be unearthed in after ages, if not to point a moral and adorn a tale, it would prove to future generations that in hunting, at any rate, there is nothing new under the sun. Thus we find Mr. Chamberlain writing to Sir Dudley Carleton, September 4, 1624, that there was "great sport at Windsor at the hunting of Cropear, a noted and notorious stag, whose death was solemnised with so much joy and triumph as if it had been some great conquest, there wanting nothing but bells and bonfires." In this accidental bit of gossip we ascertain the fact that in those days, as in these, a quarry which had given rare runs, perhaps for many successive seasons, became popular with the followers of the hunt and identified by a specific patronymic. And, when "the King had a dangerous fall when hunting," or when His Majesty was thrown "into the river and nearly drowned" whilst enjoying the chase, these royal "spills" were occasionally noticed by the chroniclers of the times. But we seek in vain for further particulars. All the rural annals of the era, so far as a descriptive run with the Royal Buckhounds in those days, will, we fear, be drawn blank.

In the absence of actual contemporary information giving the vicissitudes of a run with the Royal pack, during the period now under review, there is, nevertheless, ample evidence from which we may deduce that the riding was not only fast and furious, but that at the same time it was conducted under the rules and customs of the art of venery then in vogue. Then, as now, the horse was the primary element in the chase. Speed and endurance were the essential qualifications of the hunter. He had to be proficient in all his paces and to take his fences without a blunder. There was a great demand for hunters of that class, and, apparently, hunters of that class were obtainable to meet that demand. Of course in this class there were degrees of quality. The choice and select hunter of the early Stuart period in England was tended and trained with all the care bestowed on the racehorse of our own times. The hunting match of those days corresponded with the steeplechase of our days, save that under the early seventeenth-century rules of racing and 'chasing the horse and horsemanship of the "tryer" was paramount, for the result and the honour of the "hunting-match" depended on the "tryer," and not upon the jockey and the horse by which he was represented in the match. These sporting events were ridden over many miles, intersected with such natural obstacles and fences as were peculiar to the course selected for the race, and the race had to be ridden under the complicated rules and regulations alluded to as above, which have long been obsolete and now are almost forgotten.

These circumstances appropriately lead us on to the subject of hunting "at force" which prevailed in those days. In the Accounts of the Treasurer of the Chamber we find hardly any reference to the horses used in hunting the Royal Buckhounds. The hunters ridden to the hounds by the King, the Master, and hunt-servants nominally came under the cognisance and supervision of the Master of the Horse. But it further appears that, for this purpose, the Sovereign depended more on his own private studs for these mounts than upon the official studs under the control of the Master of the Horse. Thus, in treating this important element, we lose sight of the Sovereign's private and particular stud of hunters; and the only information available on these points appertains to the lesser and more insignificant official studs under the Master of the Horse. It is therefore almost impossible to get the actual number of hunting horses annually allocated to this particular service with the Royal Buckhounds. We find commissions issued from time to time, "according to the ancient form," to Sir Thomas Tyringham and to Robert Tyrwhitt, Esq., to obtain, wherever they attended the King in his royal disport, provisions for horses, the number of horses varying from forty-eight to eighty.* Snape, the marshal farrier, invariably presented a heavy bill for extras on account of the Royal Stud, but independent of this, Woodcock, "yeoman farrier for His Majesty's hunting horses," made a separate claim, and had his claim allowed.†

Horses were also required for the deer-van and the hound-van. These were ponderous four-wheel waggons. One mentioned in the Accounts of the Great Wardrobe for 1630 cost 236*l.*; repairing an old one cost 94*l.* 14*s.* 4*d.*; the total cost for incidentals, under this head alone, having amounted to 511*l.* 11*s.* 3*d.* And from another source we find all Mayors, Sheriffs, Justices, etc., were to see that due provision was made, when required, for a sufficient team of horses or oxen, with harness to draw the waggons to such place as the King shall appoint.‡

---

* The Master and the hunt-servants also enjoyed a preëmption to obtain hay, oats, and straw "at easy rates," which was "a great benefit" to them. This privilege, however, terminated with the reign of Charles I. In a MS. Book of Stable Warrants, dated 1630, we find there were, at this time, "20 of the King's hunting horses maintained on the establishment of the Master of the Horse. Each of those animals was provided annually with a wattering head-stall and reins of red leather, a pair of pastrons, trammels, a double collar, a double reins, a white and green cloth, horse-howses lined with canvas and bordered with white and green cloth, a canvas hood, a leading reins, a sursingle of brown web, a horse-combe, a main-comb, a sponge, a round hair brush, 48 ells of canvas for a bag, a dusting cloath, a hunting snaffle, a girth, and a stirrup leather. The King was furnished through this Department with 10 hunting saddles a year, which were covered with coloured velvet, garnished with gold and silver lace and fringe. To each saddle there were 4 silver-gilt nails and silver fringe. Each saddle had an undercloath garnished with silver and gold lace, stirrup leathers, girths, stirrup irons, etc. All the principal officials of the Household are mentioned as being entitled to certain provision of horses and accoutrements for the same."—*Lord Chamberlain's Records*, G.W., vol. i., R.L. 829, etc.

† "Henry Woodcock yeoman farrier for H.M. hunting horses for divers drenches, oyntments and other medicines by him employed for H.M. service for a year ended at Michaelmas 1640, 26*l.* 4*s.* 2*d.*"

‡ "Thomas Jones, Esq., Master of H.M. Toyles by warrant dated the 18th April 1640 for his own, with John Wood and Asa Scandover, yeomen of the Toyles, their allowances for taking red deer in eight walks in Windsor Forest, and for

Apart from the Master and the hunt-servants, it would appear that the "Equerries of the hunting stable," affiliated with the Royal Hunt, were a corps of gentlemen in the enjoyment of good appetites. By a writ of Privy Seal, dated February 10, 1626-7, the Treasurers of the Exchequer were ordered to pay the Cofferers of the Household "the sum of five hundred, three score, and nineteen pounds, for a diet of six dishes of meat every meal with *bouche* of Court and all other allowances incident to the same diet, for one whole year from henceforward to be fully complete, which we [Charles I.] are graciously pleased to allow to the equerries of our hunting stable." The grant was to remain in force, and the money to pay for their rations to continue until "such time as our pleasure shall be signified to the contrary."

From these circumstances there can be no doubt that every element conducive to give good sport with the Royal pack was in a thoroughly efficient state. It would also appear the pace was a cracker, and "grief" by no means infrequent. Accidents among the followers of the Royal Buckhounds in those, as in subsequent times, must have been a common occurrence in the hunting field, otherwise the services of Richard Vincent and Edward Kingsley, the "bonesetters" in ordinary to the pack, would not be required. These gentlemen probably filled a position similar to Dr. Frazer, "the hunting chirurgeon" to James II. And in those times there were casualties in the hunting field which are impossible in our day. For instance: on Friday, September 16, 1636, when the Royal Buckhounds were hunting in Windsor Forest, Mr. Henry Percy—younger brother to Algernon, Earl of Northumberland, created afterwards by Charles I. Baron

monies by him disbursed for the taking of them in Toyles and for the carriage of those deer to H.M. new park at Richmond, which service continued from November then past to Michaelmas following [*i.e.*, 1640], 212*l*. 16*s*. 4*d*." [The salary of the Master of the Toyles was 66*l*. 13*s*. 4*d*., that of the two yeomen 1*s*. a day wages, and 40*s*. each per annum for livery.]

Percy of Alnwick—and the King were up simultaneously when the stag was pulled down. Percy drew his *coteau-de-chase* to grarlloch the stag. His glove being wet, caused his hand to slip down to the blade, which cut two of his fingers so severely, that the surgeon by whom the wounds were dressed feared " he would hardly ever recover the use of those two fingers."

Charles I. was a fine horseman. His knowledge of the *manège* is testified by the Duke of Newcastle in his great work on the art and mystery of equitation, so far as perfect horsemanship was understood in those (the last) days of the Cavaliers. His equestrian portrait by Van Dyck is all dignity and grace. Indeed, he was the personification of culture and refinement, and of every attribute indigenous of the "real gentleman" of that era. He was devotedly attached to hunting and field sports, in which he could hold his pride of place against all comers. Like other mighty monarchs, he took his hounds with him in his military expeditions (*Cal. Belvoir MS.*, vol. i., p. 520); but as these expeditions ended in disaster and ruin, the less we say of them the better. During the brief period dating from the League of the Covenant to the assembling of the Long Parliament, when the nation was comparatively free of acute agitation, Charles I. formed the New Park, at Richmond, with the intention to make it the headquarters of the Royal Hunt, and stocked it with herds of red and fallow deer, which were derived chiefly from Windsor and Epping Forests. It appears, however, the enclosure of the New Park could not be accomplished without the consent of those parishes which had a right of common on the wastes, and the owners of estates intermingled with them; consequently the King was obliged to purchase their rights to 265 acres belonging to the Manor of Petersham, and 483 acres in that of Ham, for 400*l.* Exclusive of these, Richmond New Park consisted of 650 acres in Mortlake, 230 acres in Putney, about 200 acres in Richmond and Kingston, in all about 2,253 acres. But this intention of Charles I. was not carried out to the contemplated extent, and the ensuing Civil War rendered its accomplishment impossible for the time being. Nevertheless it is a singular circumstance that the New Park, Richmond, was destined to become the headquarters of the Royal Hunt about a hundred years after this time, when the hereditary heir of Charles I. was a fugitive, and when another dynasty reigned in his kingdom.

The domestic troubles so prominent in those days militated against the enjoyment of rural sports, consequently we hear very little of the proceedings of the Royal Buckhounds in the hunting field. The antagonism of the King with the majority of his subjects left few harmonious intervals during his unhappy reign. He had hardly ascended the throne when the Plague began to depopulate the land. Then, in rapid succession, followed the affair of Diggs and Eliot, shipmoney, Buckingham's fiasco at Rhé,—whereby the prestige of the nation was ruined for the time being,—troubles with the Parliament, the brief interval of quiescence from the Peace with France and Spain down to the appointment of Stafford and the republication of the "Book of Sports." Then John Hampden appeared, the Star Chamber, pillory and mutilation, the League of the Covenant, the expedition against the Scots, which happily ended in a Royal hunting journey, more trouble in Parliament, another Royal hunting journey to the North, the King in league with the Lords, the Long Parliament, the impeachment of Strafford and Laud, the Royal flight from London, the Standard set up at Nottingham, followed by eight dreary years of blood, fire, and rapine, terminating on the scaffold at Whitehall, January 30, 1649, with the word "Remember." Alas! we only remember to forget; and often when we endeavour to ascertain what the Remembrancers have recorded, the official dog in the manger snarls defiance, whining incoherentific yelps.

On the outbreak of the Civil War, fish, game, and poultry in the British Islands had a bad time of it. However, rabbits and Roundheads seem to have got on pretty well, to the prejudice of higher game. About this time the constableship of Windsor Castle, with custody of game in the forest and parks thereto appertaining, was conferred on the Earl of Pembroke, "basest among the base," but not until very little game was left for protection, as poaching was indulged in on a holy and a wholesale scale, truly commensurate with enlightened views inculcated by the worthy citizens who saved their country from such dire consequences in those Cromwellian days. Frequent orders were issued for the preservation of game. Sheriffs and justices of the peace were ordered to suppress all unlawful hunting of deer, nevertheless the abuse continued unabated. On February 18, 1641, the Earl of Holland informed the Lords "of the great destruction and killings of His Majesty's deer in the Forrest of Windsor, especially in the New Lodge, where the people of the country, in a continuous and tumultuous manner, have lately killed a hundred of His Majesty's fallow deer, and besides red deer, and do threaten to pull down the pales about the said lodge." Investigations were ordered; some transgressors were occasionally ammerced, but poaching became so general that Cromwell, on September 4, 1649, was compelled to issue a proclamation prohibiting soldiers (who were the principal offenders) to keep hounds or greyhounds for killing deer in chases, parks, or warrens. According to a survey of Windsor Forest, made by order of Parliament February 27, 1649-50, there had been no deer in it for "several yeares past";* but rabbits were represented to be abundant. The deputy-keeper of the forest about this time narrates as follows: "I sent out my keepers into Windsor Forest to harbour a stag to be hunted to-morrow morning (August 23); but I persuaded Colonel Ludlow that it would be hard to show him any sport, the best stags being all destroyed, but he was very earnest to have some sport, and I thought not fit to deny him." A stag being found, his Republican friends met Colonel Ludlow next morning by daybreak. He adds, "it was a young stag, but very

* According to a survey of the estates, etc., "of the late Charles Stuart," made, by order of Parliament, March 20, 1649-50, the deer in Windsor Great Park were then estimated to be of the value of 951*l*.

lusty, and led the gallants at the first ring above twenty miles." (*Memorials*, p. 424.)

It is a pure conjecture as to the hounds or the hunt-servants that followed the lusty young stag in the rare run enjoyed, on that occasion, by Colonel Ludlow and his Cromwellian friends. As above mentioned, nothing is heard of the Royal hounds after the Civil War began. It is probable the hunt-servants, loyal to, and adhering to the King, would hardly participate in this "ring of above twenty miles." Who can tell where the latter were on that particular day? Sad to say, the ultimate fate of some of those good and faithful servants is put beyond a doubt. Soon after the Restoration, a question arose in the department of the Great Wardrobe as to the liveries of the servants of the Buckhounds *redivivus*. It then and there transpired that the following " dyed before ye King's arrival "—viz., Thomas White, Edward Stanton, Anthony Holland, William Lowman, William Bathe, Edward Lambert, Edward Kingleys, John Hakes, John Cockers, William Cocker, William Ludman, George Fryer, Henry Dover, William Hopkins, G. Williams, George Fowler, and Ralph Read. Truly a sad finish to a sad chapter! (*Lord Chamberlain's Records*, Series III., Bundle 2.)

CHAPTER VII.

HOUSEHOLD BRANCH—CHARLES II., 1660-1685.

John Cary, Esq., Twelfth Master : July 7, 1661 to February 5, 1685.—The Hunt-Servants.—Their Salaries, Fees, and Emoluments.—The Cost and Affairs of the Pack during the Reign of Charles II.—Deer.

JOHN CARY, ESQ., Twelfth Master of the Household branch of the Royal Buckhounds, *temp.* Charles II.—from July 7, 1661, to February 5, 1685—was the son and heir of Sir Philip Cary, of Chaddington, county Herts. Who his mother was we are unable to say, as she is not even mentioned in any of the family pedigrees in print or in MS. available for reference, neither is her son, the subject of this memoir, whose life and career is a blank in biographical literature. His father was knighted by James I. at Greenwich, on March 23, 1605; he died in June 1631. Sir Philip Cary's eldest brother, Sir Henry Cary, first Viscount Falkland, was killed in Theobald's Park in September 1633, through the collapse of a stand upon which he was viewing some hunting or racing match. As to his Lordship's nephew, the Master of the Buckhounds to whom we are now referring, the earliest occurrence of his name in the State Papers of this period is in reference to the appointment, conferred upon him by James I., to the Custody of Marylebone Park, in the county of Middlesex—an office that had been held by his ancestors from the time of Queen Elizabeth. In his patent to this office (which is dated at Westminster Palace, February 7, 1622), he, or his sufficient deputy, or deputies, obtained a grant (of the custody) of the whole of Marylebone Park for the natural term of his life, with the deer therein; also all the lodges, barns, stables, houses, and edifices therein, with a salary of 8d. per day; pasture for 32 cows, 2 bulls, 10 geldings, 4 breeding mares, one mare called a stalking mare, and one ox called a stalking ox; 30 loads of hay, to be moved yearly upon the premises, and 20 loads of wood, called browse-wood, and windfall wood yearly in the said park during his life. In those days Marylebone Park was full of wild deer and other game; a royal preserve that frequently afforded the King and foreign potentates rare sport.* It is now known as Regent's Park, situated almost in the heart of London; a delightful retreat on a summer's evening, but at the very time when it is most enjoyable the public are expelled, why or wherefore it is impossible to say, except it is in fear they might (according to precedent) go stalking the lions or similar big game in the Zoo. Soon after the accession of Charles I., Mr. Cary obtained from that monarch a confirmation of the Custody of Marylebone Park, with all fees, rights, and privileges thereunto belonging. At this time he was a prime favourite with the king, to whom he was one of the Gentlemen of the Privy Chamber. In this capacity he was in frequent attendance upon His Majesty until a few months before the surrender of the royal garrison at Oxford, in June 1646. It seems, however, that four years before the royal cause was absolutely lost, he was appointed to the office of Master of the Privy Buckhounds to Charles, Prince of Wales, with the

---

* The Duke of Holstein, "the Queen's Majesty's Brother," paid a hunting visit to England, and "sondrie times" enjoyed the pleasures of the chase in company with King James in the vicinity of the Metropolis, Windsor, etc. When in London the Duke lodged at the Earl of Derby's house in Channel Row, then noted for its stables, etc. The Constable of Calais was also a distinguished visitor in the hunting field at this time.

"To Sr Richarde Connigesbie Knighte Gentleman vsher dailie waitor for thallowaunce of himselfe one yeoman usher fower yeoman twoe groomes of the chamber twoe gromes of the wardrobe and one groome porter for makeinge readie at Whitehalle for the Kinges Matie and the Duke of Houlsten twoe severalle times when his Matie rode a huntinge vnto Maribone parke by the space of viij dayes mense Aprilis 1605 viij^{li} xij^{s}. iiij^{d}." (*Wardrobe Acc. T. of C., Lord Stanhope, B. 3, m. 133 d. See, further, Ibid., m. 135 d.*)

fee of 20*l.* a year and a pension of 100*l.* per annum. We can find no patent or enrolment of this appointment; the office must have been a nominal one during those days of civil strife, and from 1641 to 1660 it was necessarily in total abeyance. We cannot find any payments to Mr. Cary by right of this office, nor to the hunt-servants under him; but those officials asserted their respective claims after the Restoration, and had their claims allowed, as we find they were promoted to somewhat similar posts in the regal pack, when the Royal Buckhounds were re-established in 1660–61.

As we have already mentioned in the preceding chapter, according to the terms of the capitulation of Oxford, Mr. Cary had the option of quitting the country, or to compound for his estates within six months. He adopted the latter course, apparently with great reluctance, having delayed to avail himself of the period of grace allowed to delinquents until the last moment. This conduct excited the suspicions of the Parliamentarians, by whom he was accused of infringing the terms of the treaty of Oxford; and although he escaped at the time, the charge was subsequently renewed, which involved him in serious consequences. By order of both Houses of Parliament he obtained licence, on December 12, 1646, to continue within the cities of Westminster and London, or elsewhere within the lines of communication, or within twenty miles distant of the said lines, for the purpose of proceeding with the composition of his estate. This proved a tedious affair, as his petition to the Committee for Compounding was not presented until April 20, 1649. In this document he describes himself as "John Cary, of Maribone Park, in the county of Middlesex, Esq.," and he sets forth that, being a sworn servant in ordinary to the late King, he did by His Majesty's command attend his person at Oxford, and other garrisons held against the Parliament, and did adhere to the King, but never was in arms.* He then

---

* It seems, nevertheless, he took an active part in the affairs of the King, and transacted, under cover, some delicate correspondence with the Loyalists outside of Oxford, as appears from Baillie's *Letters and Correspondence.*

gives a statement of his estate, which comprised a moiety of the Manor of Minster, county Kent, of the yearly value before the wars of 700*l*., the Manor of Hinslet, county York, and other lands and mills there, to the yearly value of 126*l*. 13*s*. 4*d*.; a life interest in Maribone Park, by patent of the late King, which was to him before the war worth, yearly 250*l*.; a right to the Manor of Stanwell and its rectory, and a warren in Colnebrook, county Middlesex, of the yearly value of 300*l*., which was decreed against him in Chancery in Trinity Term 1649, and therefore he prayed a saving to compound for it, until such time as he could recover it; an estate in the counties of Cardigan and Carmarthen, worth 300*l*. a year, for which he had compounded with the sequestrators for South Wales. His debts and obligations amounted to several thousand pounds. Upon this statement he was amerced in a fine of 600*l*. This fine was confirmed in January 1651, when he was ordered to pay it with interest within fourteen days.

In the interval pending the final settlement of Mr. Cary's delinquency, the tenants of his estate in Kent were ordered to hold the harvest and account to the sequestrators for the same. Thus we get the following agricultural curiosities of farm produce, as it stood in this part of Kent for the season ended at Michaelmas 1649: 23 acres 12 perches of wheat 3*l*. 10*s*. per acre; 24 acres of barley, 2*l*. 2*s*. per acre; 21 acres ditto, 2*l*. 6*s*. per acre; 7 acres of tares, 2*l*. 11*s*. per acre; 1 acre 3 roods of beans, 2*l*. 15*s*. per acre; 14 acres 3 roods of peas, 3*l*. 3*s*. 6*d*. per acre.

The Parliament having granted, in 1645, 8,000*l*. a year to H.H. Charles Ludovic, Prince Palatine of the Rhine, and decreed that the vote was to be charged upon certain estates in delinquency, the sum of 381*l*. was paid out of the estate of John Cary, Esq., in the county of Middlesex, for that purpose, in the year ended January 20, 1649. On November 19, 1650, Mr. Cary took the national oath, and after this date we hear nothing further of him till the Restoration.

Soon after Charles II. ascended the throne in 1660, Mr.

John Cary was among the first to welcome his quondam Royal Master on his return to his native land. The King thereupon included his ex-master of the privy Buckhounds in the general amnesty, by which he was purged of any treason, overt or intended, against His Majesty's sacred person and prerogatives. This was more a matter of form than of necessity, seemingly quite unnecessary for a person of Mr. Cary's undoubted loyalty, save so far as the circumstance of his having subscribed to the National Convention in 1650, which might possibly be afterwards raked up to his disadvantage, but this "pardon" rendered such a contingency impossible, even in the intrigues of the corrupt Court of the Merry Monarch. Mr. Cary did not lose much time in pushing his claims on the royal bounty, as we find that he petitioned the King in August 1660 to be restored to his right of the custody of Marylebone Park, of which he was deprived in 1642, as well as a grant of the timber felled therein and still on the ground, for repairing the lodges * in the said park. In this matter he was successful; consequently, he at once resumed his duties, and enjoyed the profits and privileges of the post until Marylebone Park was disparked as a royal game preserve exactly eight years afterwards, when he and all the gamekeepers under him were discharged from further attendance or service in or concerning the same. On November 6, 1660, a special warrant was issued to the Lords of the Treasury to pay John Cary, Esq., and others, the sum of 1,000*l*. for His Majesty's service—for what purpose is not mentioned. As we shall presently see, this grant referred to re-stocking the Royal forests, parks, and chaces with deer. The reinstitution of the Royal Buckhounds had been engaging the attention of the King and the Court officials for some time, although Mr. Cary was not actually appointed Master of the Household branch of the pack until July 7, 1661—the date of his patent to that office. This document sets forth that he was entitled to hold the Master-

---

* The chief, or royal lodge, erected for James I., at the entrance of St. John's Wood, within the precincts of Marylebone Forest, is now the property of the Marquis of Bute.

ship for the natural term of his life, with the wages and fee of 33*l*. 6*s*. 8*d*. per annum, payable quarterly out of the Exchequer, at the usual feasts, and to hold the office in as full and ample manner as his predecessor, Robert Tyrwhitt, Esq., "aut aliquis al' offic'm ill' antehac." About a month prior to the date of this patent we find the following royal warrant bearing the King's signature was issued in Mr. Cary's behalf:—

"CHARLES R.

"Our will and pleasure is That you prepare a Bill for our Royall Signature conteyning a Privy Seale to Warrant & authorise Our high Treasurer and vnder Treasurer of Our Exchequer for the time being, out of such treasure as shall from time to time bee & remaine in Our Receipt of Exchequer to issue and pay vnto Our Seruant John Carey Esq[r] Master of Our Buckhounds the Sum' of fower hundred pounds a yeare upon Accompt for the keeping of Our said Buckhounds and all other the charges incident and belonging to y[e] keeping of them excepting only the feeding for w[ch] there is an allowance of one hundred pounds a yeare formerly given vnto Francis Dodsworth by Lres Patents from Our Late Father of glorious memory. The said Summe of fower hundred pounds to be paid vnto the said John Carey or his sufficient Deputie or Deputies quarterly by euen & equall Por'cions; the first payment to begin from the Feast of S[t] Michael last past, and to continue during Our pleasure. For wh[ch] this shalbee yo[r] Warrant. Giuen at Our Court at Whitehall the   day of June 1661.

By his Ma'[s] Command,
EDW. NICHOLAS.

To the Clerck of
Our Signet attending."

There are some conflicting circumstances in these two documents not easy to reconcile. The Master's salary, according to his patent, is only 33*l*. 6*s*. 8*d*. a year, and he was only paid at that rate "for one quarter of a year ended at Michaelmas 1660, viz., 8*l*. 6*s*. 8*d*." By the royal warrant his stipend is increased to 400*l*. a year. But on the ensuing August 24 his salary on the Civil List Establishment was further increased to 500*l*. a year during the King's pleasure, as appears by the subjoined royal warrant :—

Charles the Second by the Grace of God King of England, Scotland, France, and Ireland, Defender of the Faith &c. To the Treasurer and Under Treasurer of Our Exchequer now and for the time being Greeting. Our will and pleasure is and we do hereby require and authorise you out of such our treasure as shall from time to time remain and be in the receipt of our Exchequer to pay and cause to be paid unto our servant John Cary Esq. Master of Our Privy Buckhounds or his asignees the sum of Five hundred Pounds of lawful money of England by the year, without account, for and towards all charges incident and belonging to the keeping of our said Buckhounds (excepting only the feeding for which Francis Dodsworth hath an allowance of One hundred Pounds by the year formerly granted by Letters Patents from Our Royal Father of glorious memory and lately confirmed by Us). The said sum of Five hundred Pounds to be paid to the said John Cary or his assinnee or assignees at the usual Feasts or Terms of the year, that is to say, the Feasts of the Birth of Our Lord God, the Annunciation of the Blessed Virgin Mary, the Nativity of St. John the Baptist, and St. Michael the Archangle, quarterly by even and equal proportions. The first payment thereof to begin from the Feast of St. Michael the Archangle last past before the date thereof. And to be continued unto him for and during Our pleasure, In consideration of which allowance the said John Cary hath resigned and given up his right or pretence to any pensions or privy seals which were granted or intended him as Master of the Buckhounds to Us when We were Prince of Wales, and since our happy Restoration amounting to Two hundred and twenty Pounds by the year. And these our letters shall be your discharge. Given under our Privy Seal at Our Palace of Westminster the 24th day of August in the 13th year of our reign.

Samuel Pepys Dep^t Com^{tir} de Sandw^{ch}.

Mr. Cary's pension of
500*l.* per annum.

To the Treasurer and Under-treasurer
of our Exchequer now and for the time being.
—*State Papers Domestic*, Charles II., vol. xl., No. 53.

The second payment to him in the accounts of the Treasurer of the Chambers is at the rate of 500*l*. a year, as appears by the following entry :—

"To John Cary Esq. Master of His Majesty's Buckhounds for his wages and in consideration of all other charges incident and belonging to the keeping of the said Buckhounds (except only the feeding) by vertue of a warrant under the Privy Signet dated the 13th of May 1662, and due to him for half a year ended at Lady Day 1661—250*l*."

His remuneration continued at 500*l*. a year from 1661 to the year ended at Christmas 1678, except for the year 1677, when he appears to have only received 125*l*. for one quarter's salary. After the year 1678 his name does not again occur in the accounts of the Treasurer of the Chamber. This final payment was not made to him till 1682, most of the payments to this Master and the hunt-servants being usually several years in arrears.

Now, as to the yearly cost of this branch of the Royal Buckhounds, as we find it re-established by Charles II. in the years 1660–61, it is almost impossible to get at the exact amount for any given year during the reign of the Merry Monarch. Not that the accounts of the pack are inaccurate or badly kept; but the payments to the hunt-servants having been continually in arrears is where the difficulty lies. As will be seen in the subjoined details, the cost of the pack on the Establishment of the Civil List up to March 1668 was (nominally) 2,248*l*. 9*s*. 7*d*. per annum.* This sum was apportioned to defray the charges of the Master, and thirty-four hunt-servants under him—viz., one sergeant, first and second yeoman, six yeomen prickers, thirteen yeomen, eight grooms, one harbinger, and two helpers. Each of those officials obtained their respective appointments for life ; their salaries were supposed to be paid quarterly out of the Exchequer of the Household, but they were only too glad to get any portion of their wages long after it was due, just as the finances of the

* Add. MS. 28080, fo. 63.   S.P.D., Car. II., Bundle 239, No. 374.

royal treasury permitted. It seems the hunt-servants were entitled to sell, or otherwise dispose of their offices to any sufficient deputy—provided the King or the Lord Chamberlain approved of the transference; but as the security was so equivocal very little business was done in that respect. Mr. Francis Dodsworth, the sergeant of the pack—who held the same office by patent in the reign of Charles I., with a salary of 50*l.* a year, a pension of 50*l.* a year, and an allowance of 100*l.* a year for keeping and feeding sixteen couple of buckhounds—now surrendered that patent into the High Court of Chancery to be cancelled, whereupon another patent was granted to him to hold the same office with the wages of 10*s.* 11½*d.* per day, "which amounteth to the said sum of 200*l.* a year formerly allowed to him, wanting only the twice halfpenny, to be paid to him, his assignees, &c., during the natural term of his life."* The other officers of this branch of the royal pack were entitled to a salary ranging from 4*s.* 2$\frac{1}{2}\frac{3}{2}$*d.* to 10*d.* a day each, and in most cases certain annual allowance for two suits of livery a year. To these sums must be added the King's free gift and reward to the huntsmen for their attendance from Midsummer to Michaelmas, an annual donation usually amounting to about 156*l.* 16*s.* 4*d.* However, those halcyon days did not long continue. The Treasury of Charles II., always in a strained condition, exhibited grave symptoms in 1677, for which year the total allocated to the officers of the Buckhounds was no more than 790*l.* 12*s.* 4$\frac{3}{8}$*d.*, principally arrears, and even this sum was not distributed until three years later (in 1680). The payments for 1678 were still worse—total 427*l.* 19*s.* 4½*d.*; while those for the following year dropped to 162*l.* 14*s.* 2*d.* As a matter of fact, the Royal Exchequer was practically bankrupt—the Civil List being almost suspended—most of the Court officials "utterly undone." Yet the King continued to lavish vast sums on his favourite mistresses! At the same time he had hardly a shirt to his own back, still he kept half-a-dozen laundresses who

* He died some weeks before Midsummer 1662.

had no work to do, and got nothing for doing it. Truly Old Rowley was a strange character.

Reverting from the financial affairs of the pack to some other events in the career of John Cary, Esq., the twelfth Master of this branch of the pack, it behoves us, in the first place, to record that about the time of his appointment to the office of the Buckhounds he obtained a similar post to the King's Harthounds, in as full and ample manner as any of his predecessors in the said employment, with the usual fees thereunto payable annually by the Sheriffs of Somerset and Dorset. He soon after relinquished this appointment to Mr. Pott (who had been Master of the Beagles to Charles, Duke of York). On July 26, 1661, Mr. Cary obtained an exclusive licence, or monopoly, to transport all sorts of hounds and sporting dogs beyond the seas, free of duty, and without let or hindrance, for the natural term of his life, as appears by the subjoined patent :—

Charles the Second by the grace of God &c. To all whome these psents shall come Greeting Whereas it hath been a Custome to transport and carry beyond the Seas all manner of Doggs Hounds Beagles and Greyhounds of severall kinds and names to the hinderance of our owne store the decay of Breed and p'iudice of our Game and sport of hunting. Knowe yee therefore that Wee for p'vention thereof of our speciall grace and favour haue given and granted and by these p'sents for our heires and Successors doe give and grant vnto our trusty and Wellbeloved servant John Cary Esquire Master of our privy Buckhounds full and free libertie lycence and authority for soe long tyme as he shall continue in that place to carry over convey and transport by himselfe his deputie or deputies asignee or assignes beyond the Seas out of this Realme of England and Dominion of Wales such and soe many hounds Beagles or hunting Doggs of what kinde or nature soever as he shall thinke fitt and then to goe sell and dispose of at his pleasure. And Wee doo hereby require and comãnd the Comissioners of our Customes and other the Officers of our Customes to permitt and suffer the said John Cary his Deputy or Deputies to transport the said Doggs accordingly without any account custome or other dutie to be rendered or paid to vs our heires or successors for the same. And our further will and

pleasure is and Wee doe hereby comãand that noe other p'sons
Whatsoever during the said tyme doe p'sume to transport and convey
any Doggs of what kinde soever without a passe from vs or the
lycense of the said John Cary or his Deputies first had and obtained
in that behalf And these our tres Patents shalbe as well vnto the
said Cary as to all others whome it shall or may concerne sufficient
Warrant and discharge in this behalfe. In witnes &ᵃ Witnes our selfe
att Westm̃ the fiue and twentieth day of July. Ipsā Regem.—
Patent Roll, 12 Car. II., part 17, m. 12.

About the same time he was appointed, conjointly with Lord
Ogleby and others, to receive all moneys formerly collected in
the county York, the Bishopric of Durham, the counties Northumberland and Westmoreland remaining unpaid to the King,
the receivers to have a moiety of all sums so collected. On
November 30 he was authorised to dispose, as he thought fit,
of several herds of deer, to be provided both at home and
abroad, for stocking the royal parks and forests. In December
1663 he received a warrant on the Exchequer for 500*l*., "His
Majesty's free gift and princely bounty." On October 28,
1669, he was appointed to the office of Ranger, called the
Riding Forester, in the New Forest, with the fee of 6*d*. a day
during His Majesty's pleasure. About this time he obtained
a grant of the benefit of a covenant between the king and
Sir Francis Crane for keeping 300 deer, and convenient browse
and shade for the same, in Stoke Bruerne Park, co. Northampton, with power to sue in case of breach of the said
covenants, and to take the benefit thereof for his own use.

It would appear by the subjoined Royal Letter that about
this time the Master of the Buckhounds had to observe and
report when any damage was done to the vert within the
precincts of the Royal Forests to the prejudice of the deer:—

Lᵈ Treaūr. ⎫ Right Trusty &ᶜᵃ Whereas Wee have been giuen
Mr. Cary of ye ⎬ to und'stand That William Browne of Framby in
Buckhoundes ⎪ Our County of Surrey is about grubbing some parts
    desire.   ⎭ of a Cops called Merishwood in the Balywicke of
Surrey belonging to Our Castle of Windsor, the same being Our
Demesne, & grubbing being contrary to law, Wee haue thought good

to signify Our Pleasure to y^u and accordingly Our Will and Pleasure is, That forthwth upon Receipt hereof, You giue order to, & require him ye s^d Wm Browne of Framley to forbeare grubbing any part of the said Cops Wood called Merishwood being Our Demesne as aforesaid. And Whereas Wee are likewise giuen to understand, That Richard Taylor of Chersey is about to cut & fell a Cops Wood called Great Grove in the Parish of Chersey in Our County of Surrey, the growth of wch Wood is und^r seuen yeares, being also Our Demesne, & not Warrantable by Law, Our further Will and Pleasure is, y^n give notice to ye said Richd Taylor, that he forebeare from henceforth to cutt or cause to be cutt or felled the s^d Cops Wood called Greate Groue, or any part therof, as he shall tender Our Displeasure. For w^{ch} &^{ca} December 5th 1672.

By his &^{ca}
ARLINGTON.

To ye Ld Clifford
Ld High Treas^r
of England.
—*Dom. Entry Book. King's Letters*, vol. xxxi., fo. 99^h.

In March 1677 Mr. Cary obtained (in conjunction with Sir Walter St. John, Sir Ralph Verney, and Sir Richard Howe) a grant of " all that peice or parcel of ground with the buildings thereon in St. James's Park, nigh the Cockpit, to them and to their heirs for ever." As above mentioned, the final payment, recorded in the accounts of the Treasurer of the Chamber to this Master of Buckhounds, occurred in the year 1682, viz., 500*l*. " for one year's wages ended at Michaelmas, 1678." Whether he received the arrears due on account of this office it is impossible to ascertain; at any rate, there is no evidence forthcoming of his having ever done so. In all probability he retained the horn of this branch of the royal pack until the end of the reign of Charles II. On June 12, 1685, James II. reappointed Mr. Carey to the office of Ranger and Riding Forester in the New Forest, county Southampton, which office he held during the pleasure of the late King, with the fee of 6*d*. a day, payable out of the Exchequer, and all privileges pertaining thereto. He did not enjoy his reappointment to that office as this Master of the Royal Buckhounds was "lately dead" on or about October 19, 1685. (*Luttrel's Diary, sub dato.*)

In the meantime, there is one circumstance connected with the Mastership of this portion of the Royal Buckhounds to which we must briefly allude. In June 1675 Thomas Elliot, Esq., and John Neville, Esq., obtained the reversion of the office: "To hold and enjoy the same office successively after the determination of the estate and interest of John Cary, Esq., therein (who now enjoys the same) together with the usual fees and privileges to the same office belonging for and during the terms of their respective lives, and the life of the longest liver of them." But as neither of those gentlemen attained the post, it is sufficient to mention that Mr. Elliot was the chief manager of the racing establishment of Charles II. at Newmarket, and one of the Grooms of the Privy Chamber. Mr. Nevill was a "natural son of Richard Nevill, of Billinber, co. Berks, Esq." (*vide* Patent).

Before concluding this memoir we must mention the following singular event. In August 1679 Messrs. Powney and Cary, " of the Royal Buckhounds," were put forward as candidates to contest the Parliamentary representation of the borough of Windsor, in support of the Court party, in opposition to Messrs. Winwood and Starkey, the late members. The Court candidates were returned by a considerable majority through the votes of the retainers and servants of the Castle. On a petition to the House of Commons the royal huntsmen were unseated, and the old members reinstated, because their opponents were illegally returned " by the voice of the King's servants, who have no pretence of voting there but as such." *
Another version (probably more accurate) is given by Messrs. Tighe and Davis in the *Annals of Windsor*, vol. ii., p. 381— viz., " Parliament was dissolved by a proclamation dated at Windsor, the 12th of July, 1679, and in August 1679 Mr. Starkey and Mr. Winwood were again returned by the inhabitants paying scot and lot, and John Carey and John Powney,

* *Diary of the Hon. Henry Sidney*, vol. i., p. 89.

Esqs., were returned by the mayor, bailiffs, and select burgesses." On November 4 the Committee of Elections and Privileges reported that in the Borough of New Windsor the inhabitants only who pay scot and lot had a right to vote in the election of burgesses to serve in Parliament for the said Borough; that Messrs. Winwood and Starkey were duly chosen to serve in that Parliament for the Borough of New Windsor; and that Messrs. Carey and Powney were illegally returned and should be unseated, which report was adopted by the House. Probably this John Carey was the Master of the Buckhounds, but as there was another gentleman of the same name connected with the Court at this time, we are unable to say positively which of them was the person in question.

The following is a summary of the financial affairs of the Household branch of the Royal Buckhounds during the reign of Charles II., beginning with the payments for the year 1660-61:—

1660-61.—John Carey, Esq., Master, for his wages at 33*l.* 6s. 8d. ⅌ ann., payable quarterly, and due for one quarter of a year ended at Michaelmas, 1660—8*l.* 6s. 8d.

Francis Dodsworth, sergeant, for his wages at 200*l.* ⅌ ann., due for one whole year ended at Midsummer 1661—200*l.*

Edward Hart, late sergeant, for his annuity at 90*l.* 14s. 4d. ⅌ ann., due to him for like time.

John Davies, oldest yeoman, for his wages at 4s. ⅌ day, and 20s. ⅌ ann. for his livery, due at Christmas—74*l.*

Bartholomew Montague, second yeoman, for wages and livery at the same rates, and due to him for three quarters of a year, ended at Midsummer—55*l.* 15s.

Robert Hancock, yeoman pricker, at 4s. 2½ 11/8 d. per day for his wages, and 2*l.* ⅌ ann. for his livery, due to him for one year ended at Midsummer 1661— 79*l.* 7s. 5¼d.

Robert Walker, yeoman pricker, for his wages at 3s. 8d. ⅌ day, and 2*l.* for his livery, due to him for like time—68*l.* 18s. 4d.

James Kipling, yeoman pricker, at 3s. 4d. ⅌ day for his wages,

and 1*l.* ℔ ann. for his livery, due to him for like time—
61*l.* 16*s.* 8*d.*

William Pitman, yeoman, for his wages at 3*s.* 2*d.* ℔ day and
2*l.* 10*s.* ℔ ann. for his livery, due to him for the like time
—59*l.* 15*s.* 10*d.*

Richard Allington, yeoman pricker, for his wages at 3*s.* 1½*d.* ℔
day, and 2*l.* 10*s.* ℔ ann. for his livery, due to him for like
time—59*l.* 0*s.* 7½*d.*

Henry Dodsworth, yeoman, for his wages at 2*s.* 1*d.* ℔ day and
2*l.* ℔ ann. for his livery, due for the like time—40*l.* 0*s.* 5*d.*

Henry Bone, William Callis, William Wetherell, Thomas Oacely,
and Thomas Field, 5 yeomen, to each of them at 2*s.* ℔ day
for their wages, and 1*l.* each ℔ ann. for their liveries, due
to them for a whole year ended at Midsummer 1661—
187*l.* 10*s.*

John Branch, Thomas Woolmer, John Crockford, Robert Lane,
and John Batchlour, 5 other of the said yeomen, to each of
them at 1*s.* 8*d.* ℔ day for wages, and 1*l.* each ℔ ann. for
their liveries, due for the like time—157*l.* 1*s.* 8*d.*

Thomas Thorne, yeoman, at 1*s.* ℔ day, and 10*d.* ℔ day for his
wages, and 6*l.* 13*s.* 4*d.* and 8*l.* 4*s.* 10*d.* ℔ ann. for his
summer and winter liveries, due to him for the like time—
48*l.* 7*s.* 4*d.*

Robert Potter, yeoman, at 1*s.* 6*d.* ℔ day, and 1*l.* for his livery
due at Christmas, due to him for the like time—28*l.* 7*s.* 6*d.*

James Metcalfe, Thomas Flowers, and Richard Brock, grooms,
for their wages at 1*l.* ℔ ann. each, and 1*l.* ℔ ann. each
for their liveries, due for the like time—63*l.*

William Goodwin, groom, at 26*l.* 13*s.* 4*d.* ℔ ann. for his wages,
and 1*l.* ℔ ann. for his livery, for like time—27*l.* 13*s.* 4*d.*

George Ilening, George Simpson, John Cant, and Wooley Minterne,
4 grooms, 1*s.* 1*d.* ℔ day wages each, and 1*l.* each for their
liveries, for the like time—84*l.* 1*s.* 8*d.*

Richard Eldrige, for his wages at 40*l.* ℔ ann., and 2*l.* 10*s.* for
his livery ℔ ann., for like time—42*l.*

Henry Sames, for his wages at 19*l.* 2*s.* 4*d.* ℔ ann., due to him
for like time—19*l.* 2*s.* 4*d.*

Edward Roe [Harbinger], for his wages at 1*s.* ℔ day, due to him
for like time—18*l.* 5*s.*

Robert Longville, yeoman, for his wages at 10d. ℙ day, and 19l. 2s. 4d. ℙ ann., and 1l. for his livery due at Christmas for like time—25l. 6s. 6d.

Under head of "annuities" we find extra payments to Henry Taylor, late groom of the Buckhounds, for his pension at 8d. a day, and to Francis Dodsworth, sergeant of the pack, "for his charges in feeding and keeping the said hounds by way of addition to his former allowance," 156l. 14s. 4d., for "his Majesty's free gift and reward, as formerly usually allowed to the huntsmen of the Buckhounds, for their attendance from Midsummer to Michaelmas 1661."

1662. Year ended at Midsummer 1662, made up of arrears for one year and a quarter. Total, 2,378l. 11s. 1¾d.
1663. Total, 1,950l. 19s. 9½d.
1664–65. All payments in arrear.
1665–66. Ditto.
1666–67. Ditto.
1667–68. Ditto.

On March 16, 1668, it was ordered that the usual liveries and allowances heretofore enjoyed by the hunt-servants were to be discontinued after the ensuing Midsummer quarter, and that the cost of this portion of the pack was to be retrenched from 2,248l. 9s. 7d. to 1,500l. a year (*Add. MSS.*, 28,080, fo. 63), whereupon they petitioned the King to annul the order and to restore them the remuneration which they were entitled to receive according to the original establishment on the Civil List. To this petition the King graciously assented; but, so far as receiving any pecuniary advantages, the unfortunate hunt-servants were no better off than they were before. We subjoin the details of those curious transactions as they are found in the documents cited:—

Statement by John Cary Esq. to the Council of State, August 22, 1667, relating to the cost of the Household branch of the Royal Buckhounds:—

May it please your Lordships

This is a true account of facts stipends and salaries as are paid to the Master and huntsmen of His Majesty's Buckhounds by the Treasurer of the Chamber, wherein there is no alteration of what was paid thereunto them in the late Kings time of ever blessed memory, but to the Master of the Office and John Davies and Bartholomew Montague, two of the huntsmen.

The Master that now is, John Carey, had the same office in the year 1642, under his Majesty that now is when he was Prince of Wales, with a stipend of 20*l*. and pension of 100*l*. per annum.

At the happy return of his Majesty, his Majesty was graciously pleased to continue the said John Carey in the said office, and in consideration of many years service past, and the great expense incident to the execution of the said office, together with a relinquishment of the 120*l*. per annum, before mentioned, and all other stipend, salary and pensions, such as Sir Timothy Tyrell, Sir John Tyrringham, Mr. Turwight (*sic*) (formerly Masters of the said office) had (who had several pensions out of his Majesty's Exchequer).

First, to give to the said John Carey a pension of 500*l*. per annum during pleasure, after during life, to be paid by the Treasurer of the Chamber for the time being.

' John Davies and Bartholomew Montague were huntsmen to his Majesty when he was Prince of Wales, and upon their petitions to his Majesty, and relinquishing all former stipends did obtain their salaries before mentioned in the list, during their lives, but no others are to succeed in their places.

Some small yearly pension should be paid to the huntsmen out of the Great Wardrobe: The particulars whereof I suppose your Lordships have an account of from thence; very little of that had been paid: not so much as one years allowance.

When his late Majesty of ever blessed memory had the ancient purveyance for his household, the Masters of the Buckhounds had a commission yearly from the Officers of his Majesty's Green Cloth, to require the High Constables of such Hundred as his Majesty's huntsmen and hounds were lodged in, during the time of summer hunting: which was from about the 20th of April to the 20th of September to bring in, to the Master and huntsmen, at easy rates provisions of hay, oats and straw, viz., hay at 6*d*. the truss, oats at 12*d*. the bushel, straw at 2*d*. the truss: which was so great a benifit to the said Master and huntsman, that after the said purveyance was no more taken by his

Majesty, his Majesty was graciously pleased to give in lieu of the said commission to the Master of the Buckhounds 30*l.* per annum, to the Sergeant 20*l.*, to each yeoman 10*l.*, and to the grooms 5*l.*; but since his Majesty's happy return that now is, they have not received any recompence for want of the same commission.

Your Lordships
Most humble servant,
J. CARY.*

Appending list of the officials of the pack in 1667, of the salary, etc., of each, amounting altogether to 2,249*l.* 4*s.* 4¾*d.*, all of which were in arrears for 2½ years at Midsummer 1667.

1637–67. *Memorandum from Mr. John Carey, Master of the Buckhounds, showing the difference between the ancient and present charges* [*of the pack*]. *Received August* 27, 1667.

These are to certify [to] whom it may concern, that in the year 1637, the Huntsmen of the Privy Buckhounds were paid the sum of 1,485*l.* 13*s.* 8½¼⅛*d.* as appeareth by the account of that year, Remaining in the Treasurer of the Chambers Office.

	£	s.	d.
Paid in 1637	1,485	13	8½¼⅛
Mr. Carey's increase	466	13	4
Mr. Davies and Montague	146	0	0
	£2,098	7	0½¼⅛
Reward	153	7	10
	£2,251	14	10½¼⅛

Order for retrenching the cost of the Buckhounds:—

Whereas We have found fitt in the present state of Our Affaires with the Advise of Our Privy Counsell, to make some considerable Retrenchment of Our Expenses in all the parts thereof, and amongst others in that of Our Buckhounds and Harriers which We have thought fitt henceforth to reduce according to the particulars hereunto annexed with direction to the Treasurer of Our Chamber where Wee will that all those Allowances for Our Buckhounds shall bee placed,

* S. P. D., vol. ccxiv., No. 75, August 22, 1667.

and likewise a further Significaçon of Our Pleasure to Our Master of Our Horse that all Liueryes, Horse Lueryes and other Allowanses whatsoeuer out of Our Aurey, as also to the Master of Our Standing Wardrobe and Officers of Our Greencloth, that all the Allowances, Lueryes, and Horse Lueryes usually made for Our Buckhounds & Harriers out of the said Offices respectively should from henceforth cease and determine; which Wee haue thought fitt hereby to signify to you, To the end you may for the future giue Order accordingly in the Payments that shall bee made out of Our Exchequer for the Expences and Entertainements of Our Buckhounds & Harriers aforesaid. Which Reductions Wee will that they begin & take place from Our Lady Day now next ensuing. For wch this shall bee yor Warrant. Guen att Our Court att Whitehall y^e 16th day of March, 166$\frac{7}{8}$.

By his Matie Comãnds.*

1669.—*The Order for retrenching the cost of the Buckhounds to be repealed.*

At the Court at Whitehall
the 16th of July 1669.
Present:
The King's most Excellent Ma^{ty}

His Royall Highness y^e Duke of Yorke.	Earle of Orrery.
His Highness Prince Rupert.	Lord B^p of London.
Lord Arch-B^p of Canterbury.	Lord Arlington.
Lord Keeper.	Lord Newport.
Duke of Buckingham.	Lord Ashley.
Lord Chamberlain.	Mr. Treasurer.
Earle of Craven.	Mr. Sec^{ry} Trevor.
	Mr. Chancellor of ye Dutchy.

Vpon reading this day at the Board the humble Petition of his Ma^{tys} Servants belonging to the Privy Buckhounds, who were lately retrenched, Praying that his Ma^{ty} would be graciously pleased to giue Order for setling the Pet^{rs} in their respectiue Offices as formerly, and that they may receive their respectiue Salarys in the like manner as they did before any Retrenchment thereof; their Wants being very great and pressing. It was Ordered by his Ma^{ty} in Councill, That

---

* *S. P. D.*, Bundle 239, No. 360, Ms. P. R. O.

the Pet^rs be continued in ye Establishment of his Ma^tys Privy Buckhounds, And that Sr Edward Griffin Kn^t Treasurer of his Ma^tys Chamber be, and he is hereby authorized and required to pay unto the Pet^rs their respective Salarys due unto them, as formerly, notwithstanding his Ma^tys Warrant of the 16th of March 166⅞ for retrenching the same, or any other Order or Directions to the contrary His Ma^ty being graciously pleased to declare that the said Warrant (as to his Maties Servants belonging to ye Privy Buckhounds) be, and accordingly it is hereby repealed & made voyd.

Whereof the said Treasurer of the Chamber & all others whom it may concerne are to take notice & governe themselves accordingly.

JOHN NICHOLAS.

Endorsed: "A Repeale of the Order for Retrenching the Huntsmen, 16 July, 1669."

1668-69. As will be seen from the subjoined account of the Treasurer of the Chamber for the year 1668-69, the huntservants obtained the several sums of money mentioned in payment of some of the arrears due to them according to the original scale :—

John Cary, Esq., Master, for his wages at 500*l*. ℔ ann., payable quarterly, due to him for two whole years and a half ended at Christmas 1665—1,250*l*.

William Pitman, sergeant, at 200*l*. ℔ ann., for his wages, payable quarterly, and due to him for 2¾ years ended at Michaelmas 1669—950*l*.

Robert Hancocke, yeoman, for his wages at 4*s*. 2$\frac{111}{248}$*d*. ℔ day, payable quarterly, and 40*l*. ℔ ann. for his livery, payable at Christmas, and due to him for 2½ years ended at Midsummer 1666—197*l*. 8*s*. 6½*d*.

Robert Walker, yeoman pricker, for his wages at 3*s*. 8*d*. ℔ day, payable quarterly, and 40*s*. ℔ ann. for his livery, payable at Christmas, and due to him for 2½ years ended at Midsummer 1666—171*l*. 5*s*. 10*d*.

Henry Dodsworth, another yeoman pricker, for his wages at 2*s*. 1*d*. day, payable quarterly, and 40*s*. annum for his livery, payable at Christmas, and due to him for one quarter of a year ended at Lady Day 1664—9*l*. 10*s*. 1*d*.

PAYMENT OF ARREARS TO THE HUNT-SERVANTS. 169

George Simpson, junior, another yeoman pricker in the room and place of the said Henry Dodsworth, deceased, for his like wages and livery payable as before, by vertue of H.M. warrant under the Signet, dated the 26th of July anno R.R. Caroli 16th, and due to him for 2¾ years ended at Christmas 1666—110*l.* 11*s.* 1¾*d.*

John Wotton, another yeoman pricker, for his wages at 3*s.* 2*d.* ℔ day, payable quarterly, and 40*s.* ℔ ann. for his livery, payable as before, and due to him for 3 years ended at Christmas 1666—179*l.* 7*s.* 6*d.*

Harry Bond, one of the yeomen of His Majesty's Buckhounds, for his wages at 2*s.* ℔ day, payable quarterly, and 22*s.* ℔ ann. for his livery, payable at Christmas, and due to him for 2 years ended at Christmas 1665—75*l.*

John Plummer, another of the said yeomen, in the room and place of Harry Bond, deceased, for his like wages and livery payable as before, by vertue of H.M. warrant under the signet, dated March 16th, anno. R.R. nunc Caroli sedi 12th, due to him for half a year ended at Midsummer 1666—17*l.* 5*s.*

William Callie, Thomas Catley, and Thomas Feild, three of the yeomen of H.M. Buckhounds, to each of them for his wages at 2*s.* ℔ day, and 20*s.* ℔ ann. for his livery, payable quarterly as before, and due to them for 3 years ended at Christmas 1666—337*l.* 10*s.*

William Netherville, another yeoman, for his wages and livery, payable as before, and due to him for 2 years ended at Midsummer 1666—93*l.* 5*s.*

William Goodwin, one of the grooms of H.M. Buckhounds, for his wages at 26*l.* 13*s.* 4*d.* ℔ ann., payable quarterly, and 20*s.* to him for his livery, payable at Christmas, and due to him for 2¼ years ended at Midsummer 1666—68*l.* 13*s.* 4*d.*

Robert Porter, another groom of the said Buckhounds, for his wages at 1*s.* 6*d.* ℔ day, payable quarterly, and 20*s.* ℔ ann. for a livery, payable at Christmas, and due to him for 3 years ended at Christmas 1666—85*l.* 2*s.* 6*d.*

John Palmer, yeoman of the waggons, for his like wages and livery, payable as before, and due to him for the said time—85*l.* 2*s.* 6*d.*

Thomas Thorne, another yeoman of the Buckhounds, for his wages at 12*d*. and 10*d*. ₱ day, and 6*l*. 13*s*. 4*d*. and 8*l*. 4*s*. 10*d*. ₱ ann. for his summer and winter liveries, all payable quarterly, and due to him for 2½ years ended at Midsummer 1666—120*l*. 18*s*. 4*d*.

Richard Eldridge, for his wages at 40*l*. ₱ ann., payable quarterly, and 40*s*. ₱ ann. for his livery, payable at Christmas, and due to him for 2½ years ended at Midsummer 1666—104*l*.

John Davis, eldest yeoman of H.M. Buckhounds, for his wages at 4*s*. ₱ day, payable quarterly, and 20*s*. ₱ ann. for his livery, payable at Christmas, and due to him for 2½ years ended at Midsummer 1666—184*l*. 10*s*.

Bartholomew Mountague, second yeoman of the said Buckhounds, for his like wages and livery, payable as before, and due to him for 3 whole years ended at Christmas 1666—222*l*.

John Kiplin, yeoman pricker, for his wages at 3*s*. 4*d*. ₱ day, payable quarterly, and 20*s*. ₱ ann. for his livery, payable at Christmas, and due to him for 3 years ended at Christmas 1666—185*l*. 10*s*.

Richard Allington, another of the said yeomen, for his wages at 3*s*. 1½*d*. ₱ day, and 40*s*. ₱ ann. for his livery, payable as the former, and due to him for the same time—177*l*. 1*s*. 10½*d*.

Robert Longville, another of the said yeomen, for his wages at 10*d*. ₱ day and 19*l*. 2*s*. 4*d*. ₱ ann., payable quarterly, and 20*s*. ₱ ann. for his livery at Christmas, and due to him for 2½ years ended at Midsummer 1666—87*l*. 16*s*. 3*d*.

John Crockford, Thomas Wolmer, and John Branch, three other of the said yeomen, for their wages at 1*s*. 8*d*. each ₱ day, payable quarterly, and 20*s*. each for their liveries, payable at Christmas, and due to them for 3 years ended at Christmas 1666—282*l*. 15*s*.

Robert Lane and John Batchelor, two other of the said yeomen, for their wages and livery, payable as before, and due to them for 2½ years ended at Midsummer 1666—156*l*. 1*s*. 8*d*.

Thomas Fowkes and Richard Brocke, two of the grooms of H.M. Buckhounds, for their wages at 20*l*. each ₱ ann., and 20*s*. each a year for their liveries, payable as before, and due to them for 3 years ended at Christmas 1666—126*l*.

John Plummer, another of the grooms of H.M. Buckhounds, for his like wages and livery, payable as before, by vertue of H.M.

PAYMENTS TO MASTER AND OFFICERS.

warrant under the signet, dated the 26th of August, Anno 16th R.R. Caroli Scidi, and due to him for $2\frac{1}{2}$ years ended at Midsummer 1666—52*l*.

George Simpson, Wolley Minterne, and John Cant, three other of the said grooms, for their wages at 1*s*. 1*d*. ℞ day each, and 20*s*. each ℞ ann. for their liveries, payable as before, and due to them for 3 years ended at Christmas 1666—186*l*. 18*s*. 9*d*.

George Penning, another of the said grooms, for his like wages and livery, payable as before, and due to him for $2\frac{1}{2}$ years ended at Midsummer 1666—51*l*. 8*s*. $6\frac{1}{2}d$.

And to Edward Roe, harbinger, for his wages at 1*s*. ℞ day, payable quarterly, and due to him for 3 years ended at Christmas 1666—54*l*. 15*s*.

Sum total, 5,622*l*. 16*s*. $10\frac{1}{2}d$.

Summary of payments to the Master and officers of the Buckhounds (continued):—

1670. JOHN CARY, Master, received 1,000*l*. in payment of his salary at the rate of 500*l*. a year for 2 years ended at Christmas 1667.
Other hunt-servants as before paid salaries more or less in arrear for some time back.
Total amount 2,510*l*. 15*s*. $8\frac{3}{4}d$.

1671. Master's salary paid for $1\frac{1}{2}$ years ended at Midsummer 1669.
Other hunt-servants as in foregoing accounts.
Total 2,099*l*. 12*s*. 8*d*.

1672. Master's salary paid for 2 years ended at Midsummer 1671.
Other hunt-servants certain arrears as before.
Total 2,159*l*. 1*s*. $10\frac{1}{4}d$.

1673. Masters paid, and in consideration of all other charges incident to the keeping of the said Buckhounds (except only the feeding) at 500*l*. ℞ ann., and payable quarterly during his life, and due to him for a year ended at Midsummer 1672—500*l*.
Other hunt-servants as before.
Total 1,987*l*. 1*s*. $6\frac{3}{4}d$.

1674. Master 500*l*. for his salary as before for the year ended at Midsummer 1673.

1674. William Pittman, now Sergeant, for his wages at 200*l*. ℔ ann. payable quarterly, and due to him for a year ended at Michaelmas 1674; and 50*l*. more for feeding and keeping the Buckhounds for the same year.
Other hunt-servants, certain payments for salaries and liveries due and in many cases in arrear
Total 1,979*l*. 6*s*. 4*d*.

1675. Master 250*l*. ½ year ended at Christmas 1673.
Others as before.
Total 1,694*l*. 17*s*. 5¾*d*.

1676. Same ½ year ended at Midsummer 1674.
Others as before.
Total 1,278*l*. 18*s*. 6¾⅛*d*.

1677. Same 500*l*. for year ended Midsummer 1675.
John Branch, sergeant in the place of Wm. Pitman, 200*l*. for year ended at Michaelmas 1677.
John Field, assignee to the said Mr. John Branch as huntsman to the Buckhounds, for his wages at 3*s*. 2½*d*. ℔ day and 40*s*. ℔ ann. for a livery at Christmas, due to him for ¾ of a year ended at Lady Day 1674, 59*l*. 1*s*. 0¹¹⁄₂₄₈*d*.
Total 1,789*l*. 12*s*. 4¼*d*.

1678. Master 500*l*. for year ended at Midsummer 1676.
Others paid some arrears as before.
Total 1,999*l*. 8*s*. 7¹¹⁄₂₄₈*d*.

1679. Master 500*l*. for year ended at Midsummer 1677.
Others as before.
Total 1,685*l*. 13*s*. 4⅜*d*.

1680. Master 125*l*. for ¼ of a year's salary due to him ended at Michaelmas 1677.
Others in arrears as before.
Total 790*l*. 12*s*. 4⅜*d*.

1681. Master 500*l*. for 1 year's wages ended at Michaelmas 1678.
Others paid in part as before.
Total 1,134*l*. 13*s*. 6⅜*d*.

1682. Master 500*l*. for year ended at Christmas 1478.*

* In John Chamberlain's *Not. Ang.* for 1682 he gives "John Cary, Esq., Master of the Buckhounds, and under him a Sergeant, John Branch, and 34 other persons."

A few payments of arrears to others as before.
Total 427*l.* 19*s.* 4½*d.*

1683. No Master mentioned. A few of the hunt-servants paid their salaries in arrear up to various times, including the sergeant, whose fee is still returned at 200*l.* a year and 50*l.* a year for keeping the hounds.
Total 162*l.* 14*s.* 2*d.*

1684. No Master mentioned. The Sergeant and three other hunt-servants only were paid their several salaries and livery money, altogether amounting to 180*l.* 3*s.* 4*d.*

Now, with reference to the quarry, we have seen, in the preceding chapter, that in consequence of excessive poaching and other abuses during the Commonwealth, the deer in the Royal forests, parks, and chases had a bad time of it in those days. At, and for some time after, the Restoration, the Royal preserves were almost denuded of *cervus* of all species, consequently most energetic action had to be taken to "replenish" the stock of those antlered monarchs of the glen. To accomplish this a patent was issued on November 7, 1660, authorising the Royal Exchequer to provide and advance the sum of 1,000*l.* for H.M. service in that behalf, the same to be payable to John Carey, Esq., and Sir William St. Ravy, who were commissioned to carry it into effect.

Operations commenced in December 1660 and January 1661, by removing certain deer from St. James' Park to Wanstead, at a cost of 107*l.* 16*s.* 10*d.* Removing deer from Sir John Cutts' park at Chelderley, county Cambridge, and conveying them to several of H.M. parks and forests, cost 68*l.* 5*s.* For taking deer in the Earl of Warwick's park at Lees, and other places in April and May 1661, "and for hay and oats to keep them, with several other charges incident thereto," entailed an expenditure of 37*l.* 3*s.* 10*d.* For taking deer in Hunsdon Park, and conveying them into several of H.M. parks and forests, "and for taking 33 Jermayne Deere out of a shipp at Tower Hill and Conveying them in five waggons to Waltham fforest with several other charges incident thereto," 148*l.* 1*s*. Harman Splipting, Master of the ship *Angel Gabriel*, for freight of the stags that came from the Duke of Oldenburgh, was paid 44*l*. The officers of the Toils received 22*l*. 11*s*. for keeping the said stags at Sir Thomas Connisby's. Sir Richard Ford was paid 176*l*. 8*s*. 8*d*. for the freight and other disbursements at Hamburgh, "for a parcel of deer that were sent to H.M. by the Duke of Brandenburgh in the year 1661, with other charges relating thereunto, as by Sir Richard Ford's account and receipt the said appears." A sum of 75*l*. was paid to several keepers for their fees at 5*s*. per head for 300 deer, presented to H.M. by several noblemen and others, and delivered into Windsor Forest, Waltham Forest, and Enfield Chase. The incidental expense of feeding with hay and oats the King's deer at Hunsdon Park, from February 1660 to May 1663, was 108*l*. 4*s*. 3*d*. Sir William Hicks, "for keeping the Germaine Deere at Wansted in the winter [of] 1662," received 15*l*. Bringing "three brace" of fallow deer from the Earl of Lindsey's to St. James' Park cost 5*l*. Three new "Dog waggons," which were bought in the year 1660 to remove the deer from place to place, "and several repairs for them since, with 26*s*. 6*d*. for rent of a house to set them in," involved an expenditure of 42*l*. 5*s*. 6*d*. Mr. Cary's coach hire and travelling charges to view the King's deer, "with 6*l*. paid to a Dutchman for freight of the deer that were taken by Mr. Pittman," amounted to 10*l*.

A few items of miscellaneous accessories were mixed up with and included in the total of this account—viz., Twelve brass horns for the King's Huntsmen, 18*l*. To a mariner that brought "fowle" from "Roane,"* in Normandy 30*s*. To the King's gardener in the New Garden at St. James' 100*s*. To a woman that brought strawburys and cherries to H.M. 20*s*. Freight and cellarage of wine that came out of France for

---

* The *caneton de Rouen* was, in those days, as in these, highly appreciated by the *bon vivant*. But the gastronomic excellence of the Rouen duck is solely acquired by gentle suffocation, through closing the mouth and nostrils until it is dead, by which process no blood escapes from the body, all the flavour being thereby retained. The "Humanitarian League" should abolish the French Republic for permitting such "cruelty."

H.M. own use, 21*l*. 10*s*. And, for the fees paid in the Exchequer to the accountants and tellers upon receipt of the money charged upon this account, and for a copy of the Letters Patents, and two impressed rolls, 18*l*. 11*s*. "In all the aforesaid several charges and disbursements according to two accounts upon oath, the first made by both the said accountants upon their oaths jointly, taken before Sir Christopher Turnor, Knight, late one of the Barons of H.M. Court of Exchequer, the 25th day of May, 1663, and the other made by the said John Cary alone upon his oath, taken before Mr. Baron Spelman the 14th day of February 1677-8 (after the decease of the said Sir William St. Ravy) as by the said several accounts together with the several bills, acquittances and other vouchers maintaining the same appeareth the sum of 980*l*. 2*s*. 5*d*."

Besides the deer mentioned in this document occasional supplies were given to the King by many noblemen and gentlemen, of which the particulars need hardly be gone into here. An informal close time, comprehending a period of from three to five years, was ordered to be observed in all the Royal forests, during which it was decreed that no fallow or red deer were to be killed therein.

During the reign of the Merry Monarch there are very few specific references to be found relating to the operations of the Royal Buckhounds in the hunting field. In the seasons immediately ensuing after the Restoration, the scarcity of deer must have somewhat impeded sport with this particular pack. In those days the King was not impartial to the pleasures of the chase, in which he not only held his own but moreover distanced the field.* He was a thorough good horseman, but preferred to display his prowess in the saddle on the flat. He bred, run, and rode his own racehorses. Later in his reign he attained notoriety "on shanks' mare," his favourite morning walk being from Westminster to Hampton Court. His recommendation to the Prince of Denmark was: "Walk with me, hunt with my brother, and do justice to my niece." His

* *Pepys' Diary*, August 10, 1661.

brother, the Duke of York, at that time was passionately devoted to the chase—probably the most ardent huntsman in the kingdom. His correspondence invariably contains allusions to hunting, but as H.R.H. had a separate pack of Buckhounds, it is impossible to determine when he was referring to the King's pack or to his own. And lack of money must have been an obstacle of difficult negotiation with the officials of the Royal Buckhounds in those days, for sport hath its proverbial "sinews," as well as war. As an example of the characteristic good nature so frequently manifested by the Merry Monarch, we may instance his appeal to "all the nobility and gentry" and "all other loving subjects of what degree and quality whatsoever," on behalf of Richard Blome's ponderous folio volume on field sports, entitled *The Gentleman's Recreation*, which H.M. enjoined such persons, by their subscriptions, to encourage the author, "to perfect and finish the said work." This royal advertisement is dated Whitehall, February 14, 1682-3. Blome boiled down all the old writers on the "Art and Mistery of Venery," and effectually murdered them in the process. It is a wretched compilation, nevertheless a perfect copy is now worth 100*l*. It was published in 1686.

CHAPTER VIII.

THE HOUSEHOLD BRANCH: JAMES II. (1685-1688).

Colonel James Graham, Thirteenth Master: March 25, 1685, to September 29, 1688—Expenses of the Pack during the Reign of James II.

WITH the termination of the reign of Charles II. all the interesting details given in the Accounts of the Treasurer of the Chamber from the time of Elizabeth, of the hunt-servants, their several salaries and emoluments, come to an abrupt end. The accounts of this department of the Royal Household are continued (save a few lapses) to July 5, 1782, but the particulars relating to the hunt-servants formerly given are omitted in them from the accession of James II. to the 22nd year of the reign of George III. Instead of finding the name, office, and remuneration of every hunt-servant as heretofore recorded, we now only get the name of the Master for the time being, and the payments to him in a lump sum (apparently) to defray all the ordinary charges incident to the pack.

The Masters of the Household branch of the Royal Buckhounds were appointed for life, with the power to them to transfer or otherwise dispose of the office to a sufficient deputy or deputies, subject to the Sovereign's approval, from the time of Edward VI. to the time of Charles II.; but in the last-mentioned reign the patent salary of the Master was supplemented by an additional grant on the Civil List establishment, the latter to be held during the King's pleasure. When James II. ascended the throne, the patent office of the Master of the Buckhounds was discontinued; consequently no patent to the

Mastership can be found after that granted to John Cary in 1661, and that relating to the reversion of his office in 1675 (which became null and void by the death of Charles II., in 1685); and from henceforward the Masters were appointed by the sovereigns during their pleasure, and so continued until the appointment subsequently became a quasi-political office, changing with a change of ministers. Thus the first payment recorded in the Accounts of the Treasurer of the Chamber of the Household, on the accession of James II., is as follows : " To James Grahme, Esq., Master of His Majesty's Buckhounds, for the wages of himself, the serjeant, and huntsmen of the said Buckhounds, according to the establishment, at 1,320*l*. per annum, payable quarterly, to continue during his Majesty's pleasure, by warrant under the Signet dated the 1st of September, 1685, and here allowed for the first quarter of a year ending at Midsummer, 1685, 330*l*." This Master's annual allowance on the Civil List was paid at full for the years ended at Midsummer 1686 and 1687, and for the year ended at Michaelmas 1688, when he ceased to hold the office : James II. having been deposed, and William of Orange elected by the Parliament to fill the vacant throne.

Before closing these Accounts of the Treasurer of the Chamber, we may mention that 100*l*. was paid in 1686 to Thomas Frazer, " His Majesty's chirurgeon, to ride with him a-hunting." This " hunting chirurgeon to his Majesty " was sworn into his office by the Lord High Chamberlain on May 8, 1685; he was promoted to the office of Surgeon to the Household (with a salary of 280*l*. a year, to begin at Christmas 1686), when Francis Beaulieu was sworn as his successor " to attend his Majesty in hunting." So far as we are aware, James never required their services in the hunting field; but William III. certainly did, as we shall have occasion to record presently.

COLONEL JAMES GRAHAM, M.P., thirteenth Master of the Household branch of the Royal Buckhounds, *temp.* James II.— from March 25, 1685, to September 29, 1688—was the second son of Sir George Graham, Bart., of Esk (Netherby), county Cumberland, and Lady Mary Johnstone, his wife, eldest daughter of James, first Earl of Hartfield. Towards the end of the reign of Charles II. we find him holding several posts in the establishment of the Duke and Duchess of York, by whom he was sent to Paris in August 1682, to congratulate Louis XIV. on the birth of the young Duke of Burgundy, son of the Dauphin. In the month of December he obtained the office of ranger and keeper of Bagshot Park, with the house and appurtenances thereof, with the fee of 5*l*. 6*s*. 8*d*. per annum, payable out of the Exchequer during his Majesty's pleasure, and of all other fees, profits, and advantages connected therewith. In February 1683 a warrant was issued on the Exchequer to pay him any sum not exceeding 1,200*l*. on account, for repairing his Majesty's house called Bagshot Lodge, and impaling the said park, and the contingent charges thereof. In May 1685 he had a similar warrant for 2,688*l*. 9*s*. 11½*d*. in consideration of money by him expended in those works; and on December 5, 1687, he obtained a patent of renewal of that office, "and of the laundry, coveywarren, and warren-house therein, with the rangership, etc. with the fee of 5*l*. 6*s*. 8*d*. by the year, and all other privileges, etc., appertaining to the same, to hold for a term of thirty-one years, according to his Majesty's pleasure signified by warrant, etc." * According to the Establishment Book, he was sworn into the office of "Master of the Buckhounds and Harthounds" by the Lord Chamberlain on March 31, 1685, and Keeper of the Privy Purse on April 4 following (vol. 482)—he having held the latter office to the Duke of York from the year 1682 —and in July a warrant was issued on the Exchequer to pay him, or his assignees, any sum or sums of money not exceeding 20,000*l*. for the use and service of the Privy Purse. In January 1686 he had a similar warrant for 20,000*l*. on account of that office.† During the brief reign of James II. Colonel Graham's hands were kept busy with official work.

* His accounts for these buildings and palings, which are preserved in the Exchequer Lord Treasurer's Remembrancer (Roll 463), give all the particulars of the materials used, and the wages of the workmen engaged thereon. An item occurs for repairing the ponds and the taking of deer amounting to 94*l*. 7*s*.

† Compare Harl. 5010, fo. 5.

After James was deposed, his ex-Master of the Buckhounds was actively engaged in the Jacobian cause, as was his elder brother, Viscount Preston, and in fact all of the Graham clan. In January 1689 Colonel Graham was committed to the Tower. In the ensuing month of August he received a conditional pardon, was released from prison, and retired to Scotland, where he and other Jacobites conspired to overthrow King William and his government. In order to execute the plot, Colonel Graham came to London, where his presence was soon known to the authorities, and in January 1691 "great search was made for him," but he evaded pursuit, and "got over into France." On February 6 a proclamation was issued for his apprehension, and in May the Attorney-General was ordered to proceed against him "to the outlawry for high treason." Soon after he was formally "proscribed by Act of Parliament." In February 1692 he was again pardoned by the King, took up his residence in London, and resumed his designs to overthrow the Government. This plot was discovered; in April his house in Norfolk Street was surrounded by troops; the intrepid Jacobite escaped, "but left behind several chests of money and plate intended to be sent to King James," which were seized and forfeited to the Crown. On May 10 another proclamation was issued for the apprehension of Colonel Graham, and to commit him for high treason.* However, on June 1, he and the Earl of Scarsdale surrendered to the Secretary of State, and were committed to the custody of a messenger pending their recognisance at the King's Bench. It seems he remained quiescent for some few years, as we hear

* These are, &c. Search in the Yorkshire house ye Signe of the King on horseback near Charing Cross, for James Grahame or any other suspected person or persons, and him or them having found you are to apprehend and seize for Suspition of High Treason and Treasonable practices & to bring them, etc., according to Law. And you are likewise to Search diligently in the said House for Arms, and if you find any such you are to seize and Secure them. In the execution hereof, etc., Whitehall 6 May, 1692.

NOTTINGHAM.

To Ralph Young or any
other of their Ma^{rs}
Messengers in Ordinary.

Warrant Book, Home Office Records, vol. vi., p. 321.

nothing further of him until March 3, 1696, when he, the Hon. Bernard Howard, and other Jacobites, were again in durance vile. Probably deeming the cause to which he had hitherto so steadfastly adhered hopeless, he took the oath of allegiance of King William in 1701, and henceforth attached himself to Whigs. In December 1702 the Government obtained a judgment in the Court of Exchequer against Colonel Graham for the recovery of 1,250*l.*, which sum, it was alleged, he had informally received from the Treasury for providing "healing medals" (used in the function of touching for the King's Evil) for the late King's Privy Purse. The Sheriff of Westmoreland, in due course, was directed to execute this judgment, whereupon Colonel Graham petitioned the Lord High Treasurer (Sidney Godolphin) to order the Queen's Remembrancer of the Exchequer to stay proceedings until the first day of the next term, by which time he hoped to be able to make up and pass his accounts. This application was apparently granted; and on April 19, 1703, he further petitioned Queen Anne to be discharged from the liability, to which Her Majesty graciously acceded, consequently these proceedings of the Treasury were quashed (*Treasury Papers*, vol. lxxiii., fo. 57). The large sums of money which this Master of the Royal Buckhounds had to distribute for "healing medals" may be inferred from the circumstance that James II., during his brief progress in the summer of 1687, "touched" no less than five thousand persons, many of whom were charged with fraudulently representing themselves scrofulous in order to obtain the pecuniary benefit incidental to the ceremony. He represented the county Westmoreland in the several Parliaments summoned in the years 1701, 1702, 1705, 1708, 1710, 1713, 1715, and 1722. About the year 1685 Colonel Graham bought Levins and other lands in the county Westmoreland of Allan Bellingham, Esq.—" an ingenious but unhappy young man who consumed a vast estate " *—and after 1701 he seems to have chiefly resided there during the

---

* Evidently a hunting family, as their arms were argent, three hunting horns: crest, a buck's head couped or.

remainder of his life. He married Dorothy, eldest daughter of the Hon. William Howard, fourth son of Thomas, Earl of Berkshire, by whom he had an only child, Catherine, who married her cousin-german, Henry Bowes, Earl of Suffolk and Berkshire.

In hunting up the life of this Master of the Buckhounds we are losing sight of the Royal pack, the moving incidents of the hunt, and the subordinate officers thereof. Unfortunately there is very little available information under this head. All we know is that Lawrence Babill and Lancelot Carlisle were yeomen prickers, in the receipt of 85*l.* each per annum. As we have already recorded, the cost of the household part of this pack, during Queen Elizabeth's reign, amounted on an average to about 140*l.* a year. In the reign of James I. its annual cost came to about 750*l.*, exclusive of extras. Up to the time of the "troubles" it cost the exchequer of Charles I. about 1,300*l.* a year. Under Charles II. it involved an annual expenditure of about 2,000*l.*; but as the officers of the pack were so irregularly paid—their salaries, etc., being constantly in arrears—it is hard to say precisely what the cost was for any clear year during the Merry Monarch's reign. In the reign of James II. the pack was supported at an annual charge of 1,341*l.* 5*s.* But it must be noted that this King also kept up a pack of foxhounds—a royal revival of the Plantagenet era—which cost 700*l.* a year, and a pack of harriers which cost 1,000*l.* per annum, a pack of otter and other hounds, while Felton and Chiffinch, "Keepers of the Hawks," received 1,372*l.* 10*s.* per annum. consequently his hunting establishment was more expensive than those of his predecessors.

During the reign of Charles II. his brother, the Duke of York, was one of the most enthusiastic sportsmen in the Kingdom. In those days he not only hunted on every available occasion with the King's hounds, but also maintained four packs of his own. His familiar letters to the Prince of Orange* abound in allusions to hunting, racing, and field sports. Unfortunately he rarely indicates the particular

* King William's Sealed Bag, 1674-86, Bundle iii.

pack which he was out with in those days, consequently it might be misleading to ascribe to the Royal Buckhounds a run which may have been given by some other pack. The same may be said of his letters to his niece, the Countess of Lichfield. When he ascended the throne the political and polemical affairs of the Kingdom absorbed his time and attention so much as to admit of few opportunities of participating in the pleasures of the chase. Hence we hear very little of the Royal Buckhounds or of hunting during his short and sad reign. He was evidently out with the Buckhounds at Windsor on August 11, 19, and 27, 1685, when three "hunting dinners" were provided for him at a cost of 70*l.* 5*s.* 3½*d.* At any rate, every accessory of the chase at the headquarters of the Royal Hunt was maintained in a state of efficiency, and there was abundance of deer to show sport.* But, the cares of state, disaffection, and the almost overt disloyalty which prevailed in England from this time (when the little rebellion of Monmouth was suppressed) to the time when the great rebellion of 1688 put an end to his reign and dynasty, James II. almost abandoned the predilection which he formerly manifested for the chase. Indeed, the only other instance we have met with was in 1687, when it was officially announced in the *London Gazette*, September ₁₂⁸, that His Majesty had left Bath, *en route* to Winchester, "to take his divertisement of hunting." This royal venatic expedition was soon over, as the King was back at Windsor on the evening of September 17.

* John Branch was appointed Circuiteer and Bailiff of Battles Walk in Windsor Forest, with the usual fees and emoluments appertaining to that office, and a further annual allowance of 50*l.* per annum for provision of hay for the deer within the same. R. Hannington, Senr., and R. Hannington, Junr., and David Tyndall, were appointed underkeepers of the three "red deer walks" within the bailiwick of Finchamsted, within the forest of Windsor, at 20*l.* a year salary "to every one of them, payable out of the revenue of our honour and Castle of Windsor."

CHAPTER IX.

THE HOUSEHOLD BRANCH.—WILLIAM III.

1689—1702.

James de Gastigny, Fourteenth Master: September 9, 1689 to c. July 1698.—Reinhard Vincent, Baron Van Hompesch, Fifteenth Master: July 6, 1698, to March 8, 1702.—Annual Cost of the Pack.—Hunting in Holland.—Hunting in England.—Fatal Accident to the King when hunting with the Pack.—Various Accounts of the Spill, and a Poor Record of the Runs towards the End of His Reign.

WITH the last regnal year of James II. the accounts of the Treasurer of the Chamber of the Royal Household were suspended, consequently we cannot have recourse to the unique facts and figures recorded in that series down to the year 1688 until they were again resumed in 1694.

The Whigs treated William of Orange very shabbily. They brought him over here to champion their cause, placed him on the vacant throne, but only allowed him a civil list from year to year. At first he had no permanent regal establishment, nor any permanent salary or income to sustain his dignity. Subsequently the Parliament settled the customs on him for four years only, and the hereditary excise for life. Apart from the ministerial and political officers of State, William's personal attendants were chiefly foreigners, who had no sympathy and little intercourse with this kingdom. Hence many of the ancient institutions of the Court remained for some years inoperative, if not actually in abeyance. For instance, we hear very little of the Royal Buckhounds during his reign. In the first Establishment Book of Robert, Earl of Sunderland,

Lord High Chamberlain, James de Gastigny, Esq., is given as "Master of the Harthounds and Buckhounds" with a salary of 1,036*l*. a year. In the margin the date of his appointment is entered, "September 9, 1689"; and in a later Establishment Book of this Lord Chamberlain the following entry occurs: "Richard Vincent, Baron d'Hompeche, Master of ye Harthounds and Buckhounds upon ye surrender of James de Gastigny, Esq." This entry is repeated in the Establishment Book of the Earl of Jersey, Lord High Chamberlain, *circa* 1700, with a supplementary inscription showing that John Branch was re-appointed Sergeant of the Royal Buckhounds on February 13, 1691-2, with a salary of 200*l*. a year, "payable out of the Treasury Chamber" (vol. 485, fo. 25). We can find no payments to the officers of this branch of the pack in the Accounts of the Treasurer of the Chamber from the time of their resumption in 1694 to 1701, except in a special one, which exclusively deals with arrears of salaries due on the Establishment from 1698 to Midsummer 1701, in which the following entry occurs:—

"James de Gastigny * (and Richard Vincent Baron de Hompesch succeeding him), in the place of Master of the Buckhounds at m^{l}m^{l}cccxlj^{li} ₽ ann. for themselves and servants and other charges, and due for floure yeares & a quartor, ended at Midsumer, 1701, ix^{ml},ix^c,xlix^{li} v^s."

From this it appears that, from the year 1698 to 1701, those Masters were entitled to the sum of 2,341*l*. a year for defraying all the cost incident to the pack; but as to whether they received the amount prior to the year 1698, or after the year ended at Midsummer 1701, we are unable to say; at any rate, there is no entry of such save the one above mentioned. Apparently, the Lords of the Treasury evinced reluctance to pay the cost of the pack in those days, probably because they had no money to spare; perhaps they never saw those Masters, and

---

* In John Chamberlain's *Anglie Notitia* for 1691 we find the following paragraph: "James de Gastigny, Esqr., Master of the Hart and Buckhounds for himself and the Huntsmen is allowed 2,341*l*. per annum."—Pp. 140, 164.

when the King was absent on the war-path the Royal Buckhounds rarely assembled to hunt in England. On July $\frac{5}{15}$, 1697, Mons. de Blathwait, Secretary of War, in attendance on the King in Holland, wrote to the Lords of the Treasury, stating that his Majesty recommend them to make "some speedy provision for the Buckhounds, which is greatly wanted"; and on August 20, 1701, Baron de Hompesch also wrote from the Royal Palace at Loo to De Blathwait (who was then at Dieren), requesting him to ask the King for the salary due to him on account of his office. De Blathwait wrote again to the Lords of the Treasury stating that the King signified his pleasure that the money should be paid forthwith; but we can find no payment or acquittance to that effect, except in the subjoined minute, by which it appears the Baron's claims in respect to this office had been satisfied down to Christmas, 1701.*

* DIEREN the 26 Aug. 1701 N.S.

S^r,—

Having laid before the King the enclosed Paper from the Baron de Hompesch, Master of the Buck Hounds, His Majesty has been Pleased to Command me to Signify His Pleasure to the Right Honble the Lords Com^{rs} of the Treasury, That what is Due to that Office to Midsummer last, be forthwith paid, as His Majesty was Pleased to say, He had Directed before his coming from England, wherewith you will please to acquaint their Lo^{ps}.

I am, Sir,
Yo^r most humble servant,
WM. BLATHWAYT.

MR. LOWNDES.

Indorsed.—Fro' Mr. Blathwayt $\frac{16}{26}$ Aug., 1701, for paying half a year to y^e Buckhounds due at Midsum^r last.

Inclosing— (COPY).

MONSIEUR.—

Sa Maissût m'ayent ordonaér, de voûs dire de vouloir érerire ûne order qû on payè la demiee anné cehenc poûr son Eqûipage du Cerf le 70' de suin, je viens prier d'avoir la bontée de voûs en soûveirn poûr la faire expedier : é moi croûre.

Monsieûr,
Votre tres hûmble et tres obiesans Cerûnt,
(*Signed*) R. V. BARON D'HOMPESCHE.

Loo le 20 Aûeut, 1701.

Indorsed.—Pour Monsieur de Blatwright, Secretaire de gûre de sa Maiesti de Bretainge, &c., &c.

ANNUAL COST OF THE PACK, REIGN OF WILLIAM III.

Now as to the details of the *personnel* of the Household branch of the Royal Buckhounds in the reign of William III., the accounts of the Treasurers of the Chamber for the time being are silent upon the subject. But in the Records of the Lord Treasurer's Department we find by an interesting retrospective minute, dated March 26, 1706, some useful information, and as the particulars are unique for this period, we venture to give the document *in extenso*.

To the Right Honble Mylord High Treasurer of England.

    May it please Yo^r Lo^p.

These are most humbly to Certify yor Lordship. That the respective allowances under men'con'd were payable on the Establishment of the Treasurer of the Chamber's Office to the Master of his late Ma^{ts} Buckhounds for the services therein specified (vizt)—

To the Master of the said hounds for his wages, buying of Horses and maintaining them Servants Lodgings and other Extraord^{rys} whatsoever	£500	
To him more for maintaining 100 hounds at 3^d per diem each hound as well for their meat, as Couples, Grease, physick, and all other small things whatsoever for 100 hounds . . .	£456	
To him for maintaining a waggon wth 4 Horses .	£80	
		£1036
To the Serjeant of the Buckhounds . .	£200	
For a Horse Huntsman for his wages . £85		
For the Entertainment of 3 Horses . £54		
For buying one horse every year . . £20		
For a Servant £20		
For a brass horn and the repairac'on thereof . £2		
	£181	
		£381
To 4 Horse huntesmen £181 each ꝑ ann' . .		£724
To 5 Foot huntsmen £40 each ꝑ ann' . . .		£200
Besides 2^d ꝑ diem for keeping young hounds.		
	In all	£2341

And that all the said allowances are fully satisfy'd to Baron Hompesche or his assignes to Christmas 1701. But how long the said Baron continued after that time to Execute the office or to defray the Charge of the above mencõned Establishment for the Buckhounds doth not appear in this office. Nevertheless I am inform'd at the Prince's Treasury where the charge of the Buckhounds is now Establish'd that the same com'enced in Her Ma^{tys} Reign from Midsomer 1702.

Treasurer of the Chamber's Office, 26th March 1706.

Mos. GIRAUDEAU.

Indorsed.—" Trea'r of the Chamber's Certificate concerneing what remains due to his late Ma^{ts} Buckhounds 26 March 1706."

As to those Masters of the Royal Buckhounds very little can be told. Of JAMES DE GASTIGNY, 14th Master of the Household branch of the Royal Buckhounds, we know nothing, except that on February 27, 1688-9, he obtained a patent from William III. for " one annuity, pension, or yearly sum of 500*l*. of lawful English money from Christmas, 1697, and to continue henceforth during the natural term of his life "; and that he was ordered to be sworn into the office of Master of the " Harthounds and Buckhounds " on September 9th, 1689, as appears by the subjoined royal Warrant issued in that behalf :—

William R.

Our Will and Pleasure is that you forthwith swear and admitt, or cause to be sworn and admitted, Our &c., James de Gatigny, Esq., into ye place of Master of Our Harthounds and Buckhounds, To have, hold and enjoy ye same, together wth all ffees, allowances, perquisites, and priviledges belonging to y^t place, in as full and ample manner as John Cary and James Grahme, Esq^{rs}., or any other person hath formerly held and enjoyed ye same. And for so doing, &c. Given, &c. Hampton Court, 9th September, 1689.

By &c.,
SHREWESBURY.

To Our &c. Councellor Charles Earl
of Dorsett and Midd^x, Our Chamberlain of Our Household.*

* *Home Office Records*: *Warrant Book*, vol. 22 (R. L., No. 14), p. 453.

BARON VAN HOMPESCH, FIFTEENTH MASTER.

REINHART VINCENT, Baron Van Hompesch, 15th Master of the Household branch of the Royal Buckhounds, was born in 1660, at Guliksch, near Aix-la-Chapelle. According to the subjoined Royal Warrant, the Chamberlain was ordered to swear him into the Office of Master of the "Harthounds and Buckhounds" on July 6, 1698, the oath having been administered to him on the eleventh of that month :—

William R.

Our Will and Pleasure is that you forthwith Swear and admit, or cause to be sworn and admitted, Our Trusty and Wellbeloved Richard Vincent, Baron d'Hompesch into ye place of Master of our Harthounds and Buckhounds, to have, hold and Enjoy the same, together with all fees, allowances, perquisites and privileges belonging to y^t place, in as full and ample manner as James de Gastigny, Esq., or any other person hath formerly held and enjoyed the same. And for doing, &c. Given, &c. Kensington, 6th July, 1698.

By his Matie Command,
JA. VERNON.

To Our R^t Trusty and Wellbeloved
    Councell^r Peregrine Bertie, Esq.,
    Our Vice-Chamberlain of Our
    Household.*

Theses are to Certifie that I have sworn † and admitted Reinhard Vincent, Baron d'Hompesch, in the place and Quality of Master of his Majesty's Harthounds and Buckhounds, to have, hold and Enjoy y^e same with all Rights, Profits, Priviledges, and advantages thereunto belonging, in as full and ample manner as James Gastigny,

---

  * *Home Office Records*: *Warrant Book*, vol. $\frac{20}{21}$, p. 213.

  † All the Court officials in the Lord Chamberlain's Department had to take the following oath on their appointment to their several offices :—" You shall swear on the Holy Evangelist, and by the contents of this Book to be a true servant to our Sovereign Lord William by the Grace of God King of England, Scotland, France and Ireland, Defender of the Faith. You shall know nothing that may be any ways hurtful or prejudicial to the King's Majesty's royal person, state, crown, or dignity, but you shall hinder it what in you lies, or else reveal the same to his Majesty, or some of the Most Honourable the Privy Council. You shall serve the King faithfully in the Place of Master of the Buckhounds, &c., you shall be obedient to the Lord Chamberlain in his Majesty's Service. So help you God, &c."

Esq., or any other person hath formerly held and enjoy'd y" same. Given under my hand and seal this eleventh day of July in the Tenth Year of his Maties reign.

PERE BERTIE.*

He held the rank of a Major-General of Horse in the allied forces during the campaigns of William III. and Queen Anne against the French incroachments in the Netherlands. He was evidently a great favourite with William III.

The Baron was, invariably, in attendance on the King during his frequent sojourns in Holland. Thus we find at least one specific instance recorded. It is such a characteristic bit of hunting intelligence, we give it here *verbatim et literatim*. It would be spoiled in any other way :—

"*Loo*, October 28, 1698. On *Saturday* last *Monsieur d'Auverkirk*, being pretty well again, arrived from *Zell*, as did likewise Count *Aversberg* from the *Hague*. His Majesty, notwithstanding the late fatigue, hunted a brace of Stags, the first of which taking into a Morass full of bogs, escaped with his life. Baron *Hompus*, Master of the King's Buckhounds, following him too far lost his Horse, being stilted in one of the said bogs, and was himself in some danger. *Sunday* the Elector of *Bavaria's* Saddle Horses came hither, being 24 in number, of which 18 were led for his Highnesses own Riding to hunt &c., with his Majesty, and he is daily expected, whose coming will occasion his Majesty's stay in these parts longer than was designed, provision being ordered for 3 weeks, the Baggage arrived all from *Zell*, and the King's Horses will be here from thence the latter end of this week. Yesterday the King hunted a Hare, went afterwards shooting, and this day hunts a Stag. The Elector of *Bavaria* is to be here to-night, and likewise the Great Pensionary, and the Count *de Tallard*."

The Elector arrived at the Royal Palace on the 4th of November, attended by "his Grand Master of his Stables" and the Master of his Hounds. They were received by the Earl of Portland and conducted to the King's bed-chamber,

---

* *Lord Chamberlain's Records*: *Warrants for Servants from* 1697 *to* 1714, vol. 20, R. L. 756, p. 8.

where his Majesty welcomed them with all the marks of esteem and affection. The following day they hunted together "and kept the Feast of St. Hubert." The Elector was delighted to see the English hounds "run so fine." In one run with this pack the King proceeded so far from the Palace that he was very late before he reached home. The next day the King was to hunt the stag again; if it ran towards Dieren his Majesty was to lye there for a day or two. The result of this day's hunting is not recorded; but it seems the stag was a loyal stag and headed in the wished-for line, as the King returned from Dieren to Loo on the 15th of November, whence he returned to England soon after.

In the Accounts of Richard, Earl of Ranelagh, Paymaster-General of the Forces, for arrears of pay chargeable on the Forfeited Estates in Ireland, 1692–99, the Baron de Hompesch, "for his pay as Brigadeer General," is credited with the sum of 1,987*l.* 2*s.* 6*d.*

The Baron de Hompesch was also in attendance on the King soon after his arrival in Holland in the spring of 1700. The Intelligencers of the London newspapers announced that "some of his Majesty's horses have arrived at the Hague from England, and the Baron de Hompes, his Chief Huntsman, is speedily expected from Germany at Loo" (*The Flying Post*, March $\frac{7}{8}$, 1700). "The King of Great Britain's horses, that lately arrived here from England, are sent to Loo, whither the Baron de Hompes, who arrived here from Germany, will also suddenly go." It may be here noted that the Intelligencers probably spelt the name of this Master of the Royal Buckhounds as it was by them pronounced.

On the success of the Allied forces against the French and Spaniards in the lines at Vleerbeck, near Louvain, in July 1705, the Duke of Marlborough sent the Baron de Hompesch with despatches to the States General announcing the victory, in which the Duke says: "I thought this good news deserves to be sent to your High Mightiness by a person of note, and I have chosen Lieut.-General Hompesch, who had a great share therein."

Thereupon the States General presented the Baron " with a golden chain and medal " for the welcome news he brought to them. The Baron soon after returned to the camp.

The Baron having got in some disgrace, in October 1706, he importuned the Duke of Marlborough's intercession, who at once wrote to the Elector Palatine in his friend's behalf, testifying to his valour and worth, trusting he would be forgiven and restored to favour. The most important feature in this letter is that the Duke alludes to the Baron as having been " Son grand veneur " to Queen Anne.*

On March 16, 1707–8, pursuant to the subjoined Royal Warrant, the Baron was authorised to receive 468*l*. 2*s*. 6¼*d*. ; being the balance of his salary due to him as Master of the Buckhounds to the late King, the same to be paid out of the issues of North and South Wales; but it remains an open question whether or not gallant little Wales gallantly paid the little bill.

ANNE R.

Baron d'Hompesch
468*l*. 2*s*. 6¼*d*.

{Our Will and Pleasure is and We doe hereby Authorize and Command that out of the moneys which You have or Shall receive from the Receiver or Rec[ts] of Our Land Revenues in North or South Wales or any or either of them by Virtue and in pursuance of Warr[ts] from Our R[t] Trusty and Right Welbeloved Cousin and Counselour Sidney Earl of Godolphin Our High Treasurer of Great Brittain to the said Receivers in that behalfe respectively directed (which said Warr[ts] whereof one bares date y[e] seventh day of January last past and the other bears date the 3d day of March instant Wee do hereby according to the Tenors thereof in all respects ratifye and Confirme) you pay or cause to be paid unto Our Trusty and Welbeloved Reinhard Vincent Baron d'Hompesch or to

---

* The complimentary term applied by the Duke to the Baron, although strictly speaking correct, carried little signification, as he can only be considered the Queen's " grand huntsman " through having been included among all the high officers of state, etc., holding office at the death of William III., who were confirmed in and ordered to exercise their respective functions until their successors were appointed, pursuant to the Queen's proclamation of the 9th of March, 1702.

his Assignes the Sume of 468*l*. 2*s*. 6¼*d*. in Lieu and discharge of the like Sume which do remaine due to the said Baron d'Hompesch upon the Allowances Amounting to 2,341*l*. 7ᵖ añn which were payable to him in the Office of the Treasurer of the Chamber of Our Late Royall Brother King Willm ye 3^d of Blessed Memory as he was master of the Buckhounds to his said late Ma^{ty}, to wit, from Christmas 1701 the time to which he was last paid to ye 8th day of March following being the day of the Demise of the s^d late King, taking care That the said Baron d'Hompesch upon Rec of the s^d Sum do release unto us by writing under his hand & Seale all Claims and Demands touching the said Arrear which release is to be Entered with the Auditors of Our Imprests, and in the Office of Treasurer of Our Chamber to Avoyd double payments, And this together with the Accquittance of the s^d Baron d'Hompesche or his Assignes shall be as well to you for the payment as to all Others concern'd in Allowing thereof upon Your Acco^{ts} a sufficient Warr   GIVEN at Our Court at S^t. James's the 16th day of March 1707-8 in the 7th Yeare of Our Reigne.

By her Ma^{ts} Comand
GODOLPHIN.

To Our Trusty and Welbeloved Chis^{te} Tilson, Gent', Rec^r of ye Land Revenues due at or before Michās 1698 and to the Auditor of Our Land Revenues in North and South Wales and to the Rec^r & Rec^{rs} of the Same Revenues & all & every of them now & for ye time being.

In May 1708 he formally relinquished his claim against the Crown for the arrears due to him in his capacity of Master of the Buckhounds from Christmas 1701-2 to March 8 following, amounting to 468*l*. 2*s*. 6¼*d*., as appears by the subjoined assignment :—

Baron Hompesh's Release to the Queen { To ALL to whom these presents shall come Reinhard Vincent Baron d'Hompesche sends Greeting. WHEREAS there is due and owing unto me from his late Ma^{ty} King William the Third of Glorious memory the sum of Four hundred and Sixty Eight pounds two

Shillings and Six Pence Farthing upon my Allowance of 2341ˡⁱ ℔ ann. payable in the office of Treaſcr of the Chamber as Master of the Buckhounds to his said late Maᵗʸ (to wit) from Xᵗmas 1701 the time to which I was last paid to the 8th of March following, being the day of the demise of the said late King. Now KNOW YEE that I the said Reinhard Vincent Baron Hompesch for good and valuable causes and consideracõns me hereunto moving have Remised, Released, and for ever quitt, claimed and do by these pʳsent for me my heirs Executors Admʳˢ, and assignes and every of them clearly and absolutely Remise, Release, and for ever quit claim unto the queens most Excellent Maᵗʸ that now is her heirs and Successors, the said sum of 468ˡⁱ 2ˢ. 6¼ᵈ. due and owing to me in the said Office of Treasurer of the Chamber upon my said allowᶜᵒ as Master of the Buckhounds to His said late Maᵗʸ as aforesaid. In witness whereof I have hereunto set my hand and seal the $\tfrac{9}{20}$ day of May in the 7th year of the Reign of her Maᵗʸ Anne, Grace of God Queen of Gᵗ Britain, France, Ireland, Defendʳ of the Faith, &c., Anno Dom. 1708.

R. V. COMTE D'HOMPESCH.

Signed, Sealed, and Delivered, in the presence of
Fr: Hare.
A: Cardonnell.*

The Baron was engaged in the battle of Ramillies and other hard fought fields during the Dutch wars, and subsequently became Governor of Geertruidenberg in 1731, a post he held to his death, which occurred in 1733.

Now, having said so much of the two Masters of the Household branch of the Royal Buckhounds in the reign of William III., we must not omit to pay our little tribute to the memory of this monarch solely as a sportsman. This is a difficult task, because, in the first place, there are so few particulars to be found on the subject in the literary remains of that era, and secondly, because the historical writers deal almost exclusively with the campaigns, military and political, which are so prominently associated with the reign of the only "glorious, pious, and immortal sovereign who has had

---

* *Lord Chamberlain's Records, Assignments,* vol. $\tfrac{111}{22}$, pp. 38, 39.

the misfortune to reign over the only realm upon which the sun never sets and whose subjects never, never will be slaves." Notwithstanding these obstacles, we must here briefly state that William of Orange was every inch a sportsman. When the cares of state and the loud alarms of war permitted, he rarely missed an opportunity of participating in rural sports. He was a good shot at winged game, preserved pheasants, "wild Turkeys" (probably the capercailzie?) and "such small deer" at Hampton Court, Windsor, Richmond, and other royal manors; he delighted in a main of cocks; was attached to "setting dogs"; went in for coursing; patronised the Turf; bred his own "running horses" and backed them, occasionally, to the tune of 2000 guineas a match; founded the Royal Stud at Hampton Court, and instituted royal plates to encourage and improve the breed of horses. But what most concerns us here is William III. as a follower of the chase, mounted on a fleet horse in pursuit of the quarry. In the hunting field he must have had the appearance of a veritable masher, as he was supplied with sixteen "hunting cravats" a year. These consisted of 40 yards "of ground and looped lace," which, at 4*l.* 10*s.* a yard, cost him 180*l.* per annum. (*L. C. R. Bills*, vol. 209, No. 11.) In all the mysteries of hunting he was thoroughly proficient; he took great delight in it, both at home and abroad, and—like many a good and true man, before and after him—met his death in the hunting field when he was following the Royal Buckhounds near Hampton Court on Saturday, February 21, 1702. Upon this point all contemporary authorities are unanimous. Macaulay, however, rejects this evidence, and does not attribute the accident which eventuated in the King's death to have been in any way connected with the hunting field. As it is hardly within our province to discuss this point, our object will be best accomplished by simply submitting the subjoined versions, from which the reader can form his own conclusion:—

"On the 20th of February William was ambling on a favourite horse, named Sorrel, through the park of Hampton Court. He urged his horse to strike into a gallop just at the spot where a mole had been at work. Sorrel stumbled on the mole-hill, and went down on his knees. The King fell off, and broke his collar bone. The bone was set; and he returned to Kensington in his coach. The jolting of the rough roads of that time made it necessary to reduce the fracture again. To a young and vigorous man such an accident would have been a trifle. But the frame of William was not in a condition to bear even the slightest shock." *—*Hist. England*, ch. xxv.

" KENSINGTON, Feb. 28. His Majesty had last week an unhappy Accident by a Fall from his Horse in Hunting; but is, God be praised, very well again."—*London Gazette*, Feb. 26— March 2, 1701-2.

" As the King was taking the Divertisement of Hunting a Deer near Hampton Town on Saturday last his Horse slipt, so that His Majesty fell, and had the misfortune to hurt his Collar Bone, after which he Dined at Hampton Court, and at night came in his Coach to Kensington, where he rested well that Night, and did likewise on Sunday night."—*Post Boy*, Feb. $\frac{21}{24}$, 1701-2.

"On Saturday last as the King was hunting near Hampton Court, his horse fell with him, by which His Majesty's Collar-bone was hurt, but immediately set right again."—*Flying Post*, Feb. $\frac{21}{24}$.

" LONDON, February 25. His Majesty is, God be thanked, very well, notwithstanding the fall he got on Saturday a Hunting."— *The Post Man*, February $\frac{24}{26}$.

" LONDON, March 10. On the 8th Instant, about 8 a Clock in the Morning, King William III. of ever blessed Memory, departed this Life at his Palace of Kensington, after a Fortnight's Indisposition. It was occasioned by his Horse's falling with him as he was a Hunting near Hampton-Court on Saturday the 21st of February last. . . . "—*The Flying Post*, March $\frac{7}{10}$, 1702.

"On Saturday last, as his majestie was hunting a stagg near Kingston upon Thames, his horse fell with him and broke his collar bone; which was soon after sett, and is now pretty well again, and is expected in few dayes at the house of peers to passe what bills are ready."—*Luttrell's Diary*, February, 1701-2, vol. v., p. 145.

" The unhappy Accident that occassion'd his Majesty's Sickness

---

* Macaulay does not give any authority for this statement. It would be interesting to know the source from which it was derived.

was this. On the 21st of *February* being a Hunting near *Hampton Court*, his Majesty's Horse unfortunately stumbling, fell down under him with great Violence, throwing him on a rising Ground, which broke his Collar-bone, and was immediately set again by his chief Surgeon. . . ."—*The History of the Life and Reign of William III., King of England, Prince of Orange and Hereditary Stadtholder of the United Provinces* . . . by John Banks, of the Middle Temple. London, 1744, 8ᵈ., page 374.

" Feb. 21, 1701-2. The King, though ailing, frequently hunted in the neighbourhood of Hampton Court Palace, where he was then residing. After the accident he is reported to have said to Dr. Bidloo that ' while I endeavoured to make the horse change his walking into a gallop, he fell upon his knees. Upon that I meant to rise him with the bridle; but he fell forward on one side, and so I fell with my right shoulder upon the ground.' It is a strange thing, for it happened upon smooth level ground."—*Tindal's History of England, sub dato.*

According to the evidence cited above there seems to be very little doubt that William III. met with the mishap in the hunting field, from the effects of which he died at Kensington Palace, between seven and eight o'clock, on the morning of March 8, 1702. At any rate he, like all the monarchs of this kingdom who bore the name of William, met his fate in the saddle. It is somewhat remarkable to notice that in the reign of William III. staghunting and buckhunting were synonymous terms.* Nevertheless the former phrase usually applied to the latter in its technical sense. Officially, " buckhounds " was invariably the term from the earliest times down to the deposition of James II.; and when the Hanoverians came in, the correct appellation of this pack had necessarily to be employed to distinguish it from the Royal Staghounds north of the Trent, and so on until that pack was abolished and suppressed by Act of Parliament in 1782.

* It seems the Royal Harthounds were nominally amalgamated with the Royal Buckhounds, in the reign of William III., for the purpose of economy, and apparently placed under the latter Master and his staff. Hitherto these two packs were totally distinct: the former being partly supported out of the issues of Somerset and Dorset. In after times the Harthounds practically became a pack of Harriers.

Now as to the horses upon which the King, the Master and the hunt servants were mounted when following the Royal Buckhounds, we find occasional mention of the hunters that were bought for this particular purpose in the Accounts of the Masters of the Horse from time to time. Still we cannot conscientiously make any positive deduction as to the exact number of horses employed in this service, or what they cost; for in many cases some of them were bred or otherwise acquired by the Royal Stud,* and beyond the expenses incidental to keeping such therein, nothing further transpires.† With such scant materials to deal with, it would be useless to enter into speculations on this important and interesting adjunct of the Royal Hunt, therefore we must reluctantly pass the matter without further comment. Apart from the officiating staff, some of the old surviving hunt servants continued to enjoy their pensions; ‡ and upon the whole the

---

* The King's stables were full of magnificent horses "seized and taken of and from" the unfortunate Papists, who were prohibited by the Penal Laws to have or possess any horse above the value of 5*l*. Indeed, it has been a tradition of long standing at the Royal Mews that the hunter on which William III. came to grief belonged to this category.

	£	s.	d.
† Dec. 25, 1692, to June 24, 1700.—John Rawlins, Esq., H.M. sadler, for goods delivered and work done for H.M. hunters and pads at Loo and the Hague	665	6	0
March 22, 1692-3 to March 8, 1701-2.—4 geldings for the King's huntsmen and others, at several rates	101	0	0
10 horses for ditto, ditto	227	0	0
15 gelding for ditto, ditto	337	13	0
27 horses for ditto, ditto	435	5	2
1700 to Aug. 1702.—2 Huntsmens horses	46	0	0
2 bay geldings for the huntsmen	48	0	0
1 chestnut gelding for a huntsman	20	0	0
1 brown gelding, ditto	24	10	0
1 horse for a huntsman	20	0	0
1 grey gelding, ditto	21	10	0

The following horses were bought in Holland in the year 1700; huntsman's horse 364 guilders 8 stivers, 1 ditto, bought of the Earl of Romney, 330 guilders, 1 ditto, 264 guilders, 12 stivers, 1 ditto, 236 guilders 5 stivers.

‡ 1689.—The following "Hunting Grooms" to his late Majesty Charles II. were allowed and received a pension of £18 a year, each, in the year 1689, the same to continue during the King's (William III.) pleasure, in whose service

Royal Hunting Establishment was maintained in a thorough state of efficiency towards the end of the reign of William III. If we may draw any deduction from such an insignificant matter as the cover for the Hound-van, we find an order for a new one issued almost every year. These covers were made of red cloth and embroidered with the King's arms at the four corners with silk. In these unsettled times, it is probable the Royal Buckhounds only met when opportunity permitted; very little transpires as to the nature of the sport, as may be gathered from the subjoined contemporary reports :—

The King took the Divertisment of Hunting on Friday about Hounslow, and returned at Night to Kensington.—April $\frac{18}{21}$.

His Majesty went on Tuesday last to Richmond, and by the way he took the Divertisment of Hunting, and at night returned to his Palace at Kensington.—Oct. $\frac{29}{31}$.

The King was at Richmond on Saturday last to take his Divertisment of shooting.—Nov. $\frac{14}{17}$, No. 239.

1697. On Saturday last the King took the Divertisment of Hunting about Branstead Downs.—$\frac{\text{Feb. 27}}{\text{March 2}}$.

Mr. Stepney to Lord Lexington, London, November 21.—"The King got cold as he was hunting last Saturday. He had shivers last night as if he would have an ague, but to-day he is better."—*Lexington Papers*, p. 15.

1698. I hear His Majesty designs to go on Saturday to Windsor,

---

they were not employed. But in case any of them should be otherwise provided for, or in case of their death, their pensions were to cease and determine, viz. : Wm. Carpenter, Thos. Calcot, Christ. Sampson, Thos. Taylor, Geo. Burden and Rob. Franklin.—*Harl. MS.* 5010, fo. 17-36.

In this series we find the subjoined computation "of the charge and expence of the Horse Liveries, according to the following rates," viz. : Hay £4 per load, straw 30s. per load, oats 24s. per quarter, beans 6s. per bushel, shoeing and medicining 2s. per day ; more for each hunting horse 20s. per annum. Each horse was allowed 1 bottle of hay, 1½ peck of oats and ¼ peck of beans per day, and 8 trusses of straw per month. Four "hunting horses" and 36 "hunters coursers and pads" was the established yearly allowance in the royal stables.

The total cost of keeping each horse is set down at £52 10s. 3¾d. a year.

Yearly charge for diet, etc., commencing April 1, 1689. Yeomen of the field to the King and Queen on hunting days were entitled to receive from the royal larder 2 manchets of bread ; 2 bottles of Lambeth ale ; 1 bottle of champagne, 1 bottle of Rhenish, and 1 bottle of Spanish wines.—*Harl. MSS.* 5010.

to take the Divertisment of Hunting and Shooting, and some thinks the Czar will likewise go thither.—Feb. $\frac{1}{3}$.

On Saturday last His Majesty went from Windsor to Wooborn, the seat of the Right Honourable the Lord Wharton, to visit His Grace the Duke of Shrewsbury, who continues still very much indisposed. On Monday the King took the Divertisment of Hunting the stag.—March $\frac{22}{29}$.

The King got a small fall yesterday a hunting, but God be thanked, received no hurt. J. Ellis, Whitehall, March $\frac{4}{11}$ to Lord Ambassador Williamson, at the Hague.—*State Papers Domestic, Will. III.* 1698 March—April. Bundle 13, no. 26.

On Thursday last the King hunted at Hounslow Heath, where he had the misfortune to fall with his horse, but God be thanked received no hurt, though the Count de Nassau, who had the same misfortune, was forced to be let blood.—March $\frac{5}{8}$.

On Tuesday last the King's Hounds, as also those of the Prince of Nassau, were sent for New-market, and yesterday a Battallion of the Foot Guards marched thither likewise, to attend his Majesty during his stay there; there will be abundance of Persons of Quality &c. March $\frac{30}{31}$.

From the Hunting House at Goor (Holland), Oct. 7. On Friday about noon, the King of England arrived here, His Majesty having been 4 days on his way hither; he was met by the Duke of Zell,* and took yesterday the Divertisment of Hunting a Hart.—Oct. $\frac{4}{8}$.

Yesterday the King went a Hunting to Richmond, and 'tis said his Majesty goes next week for Windsor.—Dec. $\frac{22}{21}$.

On Tuesday his Majesty, who is now at Windsor, took the Divertisment of Hunting about that place, being attended by a great concourse of the nobility and gentry, who are gone thither to pass the Christmas holidays.—Dec. $\frac{27}{216}$.

1699. Yesterday His Majesty diverted himself with hunting at New Park, and returned to Konsington in the evening.—March $\frac{2}{4}$.

The King went on Tuesday to Richmond, where he took the divertisement of hunting.—April $\frac{6}{8}$.

On Saturday the King took the devertisement of hunting about Hounslow, and returned at night to his Royal Palace at Kensington.—$\frac{\text{April 29}}{\text{May 2}}$.

---

* "The Duke of Zell presented the King with 300 head of red deer to stock his forests in England."—*Luttrell's Diary*, August 1697.

Loo, *Sept.* 29. The King was at Diern all last week, and returned hither on Saturday with the Duke of Zell, having hunted the Stagg by the way. This day a horse-race was run here, betwixt Mr. Lalla and Colonel Rank for 100 Pistols, which was won by the former.—Sept. $\frac{28}{30}$.

On Sunday last his Majesty heard sermon at St. James's chapel, and yesterday took the Divertisement of hunting about Richmond, and returned to Kensington in the evening, and designs in a day or two to go to Hampton Court.—Nov. $\frac{11}{14}$.

Yesterday his Majesty took the divertisement of hunting about Windsor.—Nov. $\frac{18}{21}$.

This day his Majesty diverted himself with hunting about Richmond, notwithstanding the rain.—Dec. $\frac{1}{4}$.

On Tuesday his Majesty diverted himself with hunting about Richmond, notwithstanding the rain.—Dec. $\frac{13}{13}$.

1700. His Majesty heard sermon on Sunday at St. James's and took the divertisement yesterday of hunting about Richmond.—Jan. $\frac{13}{16}$.

This day His Majesty went to Hampton Court to divert himself with hunting.—Jan. $\frac{26}{29}$.

On Saturday His Majesty took the divertisement of hunting about Richmond.—Feb. $\frac{12}{14}$.

His Majesty took the divertisement of hunting on Friday and Saturday about Hampton Court, and returns on Saturday night to his royal palace at Kensington.—March $\frac{9}{12}$.

On Tuesday His Majesty took the divertisement of hunting &c. about Hampton Court.—March $\frac{12}{14}$.

On Thursday His Majesty went in the morning to Hampton Court, in order to take the divertisement of hunting and shooting.—March $\frac{21}{23}$.

HAGUE, *May* 21.—Some packs of hounds are arrived here from England, which will be sent to Loo, and 'tis said the hunting horses will follow in a little time.—May $\frac{10}{13}$.

Several fine horses and a number of hounds are bought up here [London] for the Elector of Brandenburgh.—June $\frac{11}{13}$.

His Majesty took the divertisement of hunting last Saturday at Cranbon Chase; afterwards he dyn'd at Windsor, and returned at night to Hampton Court.—June $\frac{7}{11}$.

Loo, *Aug.* 3.—The King arrived here from Soes-dyke the 28th past [Ultimo] in the evening, and the next day hunted and killed a stag. His Majesty came home afterwards on horseback, and found himself very well after the chase. Yesterday his Majesty hunted the stag again, and continues in good health.—July $\frac{25}{29}$.

Loo, *Aug.* 6.—His Majesty continues in perfect health, and is now hunting the stag, and designs to lie this night at Dieren, and continue some days there.—Aug. $\frac{1}{5}$.

Loo, *Aug.* 20.—Yesterday his Majesty hunted the stag and returned hither this day from Dieren.—Aug. $\frac{12}{17}$.

Loo, *Aug.* 27.—His Majesty continues in perfect health, and intends to-morrow to divert himself with hunting the wild-boar.—Aug. $\frac{19}{29}$.

DIEREN, *Sept.* 14.—The Electoral Prince was abroad with his Majesty yesterday morning at the rousing of the stag.—Sept. $\frac{5}{9}$.

Loo, *Sept.* 23, N.S.—Yesterday His Majesty and the Electoral Prince of Brandenburgh were diverted with two horse races, after which the Electoral Prince took his leave.—Sept. $\frac{16}{19}$.

Loo, *Oct.* 4.—On Friday His Majesty hunted and killed two stags, and in the evening returned to Dieren.—Sept. $\frac{26}{30}$.

Yesterday his Majesty diverted himself with hunting the fox and hare.—Nov. $\frac{0}{5}$.

Mr. Cardonnel (Secretary to the Earl of Marlborough) to the Privy Council, London. Loo, Oct. $\frac{7}{18}$.—"Thô the weather has been but very indifferent to-day yet the King has been abroad from morning till night, and had the pleasure of killing two staggs."—*Add. MS.* 28,917, ff. 305, 306.

Yesterday 20 of the King's hunting horses came to town from Harwich where they had been debarqued.—Nov. $\frac{12}{15}$.

(No reference to hunting from Nov. 1700 to June 21, 1701.)

1701. LONDON, *June* 24.—The King took the divertisement of hunting a buck last Saturday about Hampton Court, which he killed, and yesterday His Majesty came from thence to Kensington.—June $\frac{21}{24}$.

HAGUE, *Oct.* 28.—The King of Great Britain diverted himself yesterday a hunting beyond the Sorgoilet.—Oct. $\frac{22}{24}$.

His Majesty took the divertisement of hunting last Friday about Hampton Court.—Nov. $\frac{22}{25}$.

1702. LONDON, *January* 27.—The King took the divertisement of hunting about Hampton Court, and returned at night to Kensington.—Jan. $\frac{24}{27}$.

CHAPTER X.

THE HEREDITARY BRANCH: CHARLES I.—ANNE.

Sir Lewis Watson, First Baron Rockingham, Fourteenth Master.—Edward Watson, Second Baron Rockingham, Fifteenth Master.—Lewis Watson, First Earl of Rockingham, Sixteenth and Last " Hereditary " Master.

SIR LEWIS WATSON, Bart., first Baron Rockingham, fourteenth Manorial or "Hereditary" Master of the Royal Buckhounds, *temp.* Charles I. (from June 6, 1633, to 1652), was the eldest son of Sir Edward Watson, Knight, of Rockingham Castle, county Northampton, and Anne, daughter of Kenelm Digby, Esq., of Stoke, county Rutland. The date of the birth of this Master of the Buckhounds is not recorded; indeed, there is hardly any information to be found in print of his life or pursuits; we are therefore obliged to plod through a mass of State papers, and cognate contemporary documents, to obtain some few facts relating to his career. Of his early years very little information can be gleaned, but there is little doubt that he freely intermixed with the courtiers of the time of James I. That sporting monarch, like many of his predecessors, was very partial to hunting in Rockingham Forest. When in the vicinity James rarely missed paying a venatic visit to those happy hunting grounds. Thus, in August 1604, we find the King was hunting in this forest "for the space of two days," a " dyning-house " having been erected for his accommodation by the Court apparellers, at Sir Edward Watson's lodge in Rockingham Park, at a cost of 39s. 4d. It is consequently safe to assume that Sir Edward's youthful son and heir—who was afterwards destined to become a Master of the Royal Buckhounds—was at this early date acquainted, and mayhap a little favourite, with the British Solomon. The King was Sir Edward Watson's guest at Rockingham Castle "for the space of six days" in August 1605, when another "dyning-house" was put up for him in Rockingham Forest. Similar royal venatic visits to this forest may be passed over, as they do not directly relate to the subject of this memoir. However, on August 19, 1608, Lewis Watson was knighted by James I. at Grafton. Three years afterwards he obtained a licence to travel with money, horses, servants, etc., beyond the seas, and then did the grand tour characteristic of grand folks in England in those and later times. On the death of his father, in 1619, Sir Lewis Watson succeeded to the family estates; and during the month of July in this year he had the honour of entertaining, at Rockingham Castle, the King, who there and then knighted his host's eldest son, Edward, who must have been at this time a child of tender years. What a mania James I. had for dubbing! Barbers, innkeepers, and squires of the lowest degree were indiscriminately knighted, with the best blood in the land, by this prodigal monarch! But those honours were usually accomplished through the back-door influence of the King's followers, who put money in their pouch by this means. A few years afterwards (June 23, 1621) Sir Lewis Watson was created a Baronet—a dignity which cost him a thousand pounds in "lawful money of England."

For some years after these events we hear little of Sir Lewis Watson. He seems to have devoted himself to the enjoyments of country life, and to have principally lived at home, like many of the old English families, dispensing hospitality, improving his estates, and participating in the enjoyments of the chase and those rural sports in the mysteries of which he was so "well entered." But this pleasant mode of life was soon checked. The unconstitutional actions of Charles I. began to be manifested in various ways, that changed "Merry England" into "Melancholy

England." Thus in following the career of Sir Lewis Watson, we find him, in his capacity of Deputy-Lieutenant of the county of Northampton, called upon by the Council of State in London to make up a return of the money disbursed for billeting soldiers in that county in 1629, amounting to 700*l.*; and by a similar order he was enjoined to prepare a commission, within his jurisdiction, of martial law. These and similar events are antagonistic to our subject; they must have also been repugnant to Sir Lewis. Unfortunately there was the other phase of the sentiment yclept "loyalty" and "duty," which, of course, it was impossible to evade. However, the die was cast; there was no alternative but to side with either the Cavaliers or the Roundheads. Naturally Sir Lewis joined the former. What this step cost him we shall presently relate.

In the meantime, Sir Lewis Watson was pricked for, and officiated as, sheriff of the county of Northampton in 1633. During this year he purchased the Manor of Little Weldon, of Thomas Brocas, Esq., and through the possession of this holding he acquired the office of Hereditary Master of the Royal Buckhounds. Professor Montague Burrows says Sir Lewis paid 4,000*l.* for the property, and that it changed owners on June 6, 1633. The deeds being in private hands and not available for reference, we must assume the statement to be correct; nevertheless, the only consideration mentioned in the fine registered in the Court of Chancery is 240*l.* That document, which is dated July 8, 9 Charles I., sets forth that Sir Lewis Watson, knight and baronet, acquired the Manor of Little Weldon, *alias* Hunter's Manor, with the appurtenances, 2 messuages, 1 cottage, 3 tofts, 3 gardens, 3 orchards, 150 acres of land, 10 acres of meadow, 40 acres of pasture, 100 acres of wood, 20 acres of firs and heath, and common of pasture for all animals in Great and Little Weldon, Deene, and Corby; also the custody of the Bailiwick of keeping the King's dogs called Buckhounds, with the emoluments thereunto belonging as held by former owners. The dimensions and peculiarities of the manor, as set out in this deed, do not correspond with those mentioned in the settlement effected between Sir John Savage and the Earl of Rutland and others in the reign of Elizabeth, which we reproduced in Chapter IV. In both of these deeds the term "Master" is not used, but there is little doubt it was implied; and it is distinctly employed in the Pipe Rolls in the payments made to the holders of this manor in respect to the office appertaining to the tenure from the time of Henry IV. onward. It should likewise be noted here that the amount of the fine above mentioned does not necessarily represent the actual purchase money; in many cases the sums inserted in those fines were merely a deposit on account to bind the deal.*

Now, as to Sir Lewis Watson, in his capacity as Manorial or Hereditary Master of the Buckhounds, we find in the very year after he acquired this office, as holder of the manor of Little Weldon, he was paid the usual stipend of 50*l.* out of the issues of the county of Sussex. At this time (the 8th year of the reign of Charles I., 1634) his huntsman was Edward Remington, and the other two hunt-servants under him were Thomas Chaddock and John Morrall. Thus the Master and his men at this time were in receipt of the fees, allowances, and liveries as in the palmy days of the feudal ages. These payments continued to be derived from the same source in the two following years; but we can find no payment to Sir Lewis on the Pipe Rolls of the 11th of Charles I. However, in the ensuing one (12 Charles I., 1638), the payment to him was again resumed, and it continued to be paid annually, without deduction, to the 15th year of Charles I.— *i.e.*, 1641. Instead of being paid, out of the issues of the county of Sussex, as in the preceding instance, the funds came out of the issues of the county of Surrey from the year

* According to an I.P.M. taken at Winchester on January 9, 25 Elizabeth (1583), the fourth part of the Manor of Little Weldon was valued at 4*l.* 6*s.* 8*d.* per annum, and the bailiwick of the custody of the "canes venaticos Regis in Anglice vocat the King's Buckhounds," with the fee of 50*l.* for the keeping of the same payable annually by the hands of the Sheriff of Surrey and Sussex.— *Harl. MS.* 759. 56.

1638 to 1641. The last-mentioned was the penultimate payment made to this Manorial or Hereditary Master of the Buckhounds. He received no salary, fees, or allowances for himself or his hunt-servants from the 16th to the 19th year of the reign of Charles I. The next and final payment to him was for the 20th year of the reign of Charles I., when he was paid 50*l*. by the Sheriff of the county of Surrey. However, he did not receive the money until April 9 1648, which was the 24th and last regnal year of Charles I.'s reign, which terminated on the scaffold at Whitehall, on January 30, 1649.

There are many unaccountable circumstances attending the payment of the salaries of the so-called Hereditary Masters of the Buckhounds, but that last-mentioned one is the most curious on record. At this date the Master was a belted baron of three years' standing, rejoicing in the title of Lord Rockingham, a knight and a baronet, and lately a Cavalier of undoubted fidelity to the King, in whose cause, as we shall presently see, he severely suffered. Yet we find him taking this paltry salary from the Roundheads at the very moment his King was a captive, arraigned before a tribunal where no mercy was possible. The most contemptible element in the case is the receipt given by the Master for the money to the Sheriff of Surrey, in which acquittance he signs himself plain Lewis Watson. From this entry we find that in 1644–45 the huntsman of this branch of the royal pack was Richard Kilborne, and that the other two hunt-servants were Robert Bowett and Edward Bradshaw, each of whom and the Master enjoyed the same fees, liveries, and allowances as accustomed heretofore.

Reverting to other events relating to Sir Lewis Watson, we find that he was commissioned on May 6, 1634, to report to the Council of State upon the endowments of certain Church lands in which he held an interest. On June 29, 1638, he obtained from Charles I. a confirmation of the lands, tenements, meadows, pastures, woods, and hereditaments known by the name of Rockingham Park, etc., in the county of Northampton, within the forest there, with licence to make and enclose the park and warren thereof. In the autumn of this year we find him officiating as one of the verderers of the bailiwicks of Rockingham and Brigstock in the forest of Rockingham, relative to Hassell's coppice thereon, belonging to Sir Christopher Hatton, who had applied to the Earl of Holland, Chief Justice in Eyre, of all the forests south of the Trent, for leave to fell the covert of the said coppice in the ensuing fall. Thereupon the verder was requested to report if Sir Christopher's application could be allowed without destruction to the vert, or prejudice to the royal game. The verderer having certified that the coppice might be felled for that year only by its owner, without prejudice to the King's deer, or destruction to the vert, Hatton's application was graciously granted. When the Civil War broke out, Sir Lewis Watson, at his own cost, garrisoned Rockingham Castle for the King; but he does not appear to have held any military command in the Royal service during "these troubles." Whilst actively employed in this work, a muster of horses took place in the county of Huntingdon, where he held some property. In consequence of his other occupation in Northamptonshire he forgot to send his "light horses" to the muster in Hunts. Whereupon he was returned as a delinquent, and threatened with the Royal displeasure, besides dire pains and penalties by the Council of State in London. Having, however, soon after conformed with the requirements in this respect, by producing before the Lord-Lieutenant and the other authorities of Huntingdon the number of cavalry mounts proper to his estate in that county, he was discharged from the delinquency which he unintentionally incurred.

Although this Manorial or Hereditary Master of the Buckhounds held no military office under the King, he was otherwise active in the Royal cause. The defence of Rockingham Castle must have entailed him in considerable expense. When it fell into the hands of the Parliamentary forces a great quantity of provisions and munitions of war was captured. Apart from this loss, it appears by an inventory made by Sir Lewis Watson, in which he set out in detail the particulars of his personal property in the castle, which was confiscated at the time, that it alone amounted to 3,903*l*. 10*s*. After the fall of Rockingham Castle Sir Lewis went to Ashby-de-la-Zouch and remained there until the Royal garrison surrendered early in March 1646. Thence he fled to Oxford, where he was cordially welcomed by the King and brilliant host of Cavaliers assembled in the University city. Sir Lewis was still a rich man; he contributed liberally towards the maintenance of the Royal forces in Oxford; took his seat in the Parliament, or Assembly, or Council then held there under the auspices of the King; but whether he sat as a peer or a commoner, or as one of the Masters of the Buckhounds, it is impossible to tell. He was a peer of the realm about this time beyond doubt; but we can find no patent conferring that dignity upon him. However, we read in Dugdale's " Baronium " that " Upon the 28th of January an. 20 Car. I. [1645], Sir Lewis Watson, of Rockingham Castle, in Com. North., knight and baronet; being a person well descended, and of an ample fortune : and likewise for many considerable services, especially in the times of the late unhappy troubles, much deserving of the King and country; was, in consideration thereof, advanced to the dignity of a baron of this realm, by the title of Lord Rockingham, of Rockingham, in Com. North., as by his Letters Patents, then bearing date at Oxford, appeareth." The Great and Privy Seals were found in Oxford after the surrender of the city, when they were sent to the executive government in London, and there ordered to be broken in pieces. The Sword of State was preserved. Charles was lavish in the dispensation of dignities, and while he was immured in the besieged city dubbed no less than 104 knights, thus breaking his father's splendid record in that line during his sojourns at Newmarket. At any rate, Lord Rockingham remained in Oxford until the city surrendered to the Parliamentary army on June 24, 1646.

For some months before the capitulation occurred the Royal garrison contained many of the most valiant among the Cavaliers. We can picture to ourselves a coterie of men who were wont to witch the world with noble horsemanship, frequently assembled on the ramparts of the beleaguered city, recalling reminiscences of the happier days passed in the hunting-field or on the racecourse. How many traits of former companionship must have been remembered in a group comprising Michael Hudson—that " Rev. Father" of the Turf; the dashing Prince Rupert; the two Masters of the Buckhounds, Lewis Watson and Robert Tyrwhitt, and jolly Jack Cary, who was destined to be hereafter Tyrwhitt's successor as Master of the Household branch of the royal pack under the Merry Monarch. Many a sad and dreary hour was thus beguiled, as Hudson recalled the races won by his famous mare, and his better " nag," with which he "broke" the ring in Hyde Park at a memorable meeting there. How Tyrwhitt could recapitulate his famous ride from Dover to Canterbury, or recount some notable incident with the Buckhounds, which he was fated never to follow again. These reminiscences must have recalled the memory of Edward Somerset, fourth Earl of Worcester (whose prowess in the saddle has been immortalised by Sir William Dugdale), and his valiant son, who was still bravely defending, in the Royal cause, Raglan Castle, on which the hopes of the Cavaliers were then concentrated. But those hopes were soon shattered. Raglan, Pendennis, and Worcester had to succumb to superior force, backed by the will of an outraged nation. Oxford surrendered on June 22, and to the praise of the conquerors it must be recorded that they did not stain their laurels with blood. General Sir Thomas Fairfax gave the royal garrison the most honourable terms. The Governor of Oxford, Sir Thomas Glemham, at the head of the officers and forces of the garrison, were allowed to march out with "their colours flying, drums beating and trumpets sounding, bullet in mouth, horse and arms," and to proceed fifteen miles before they laid down their arms. Each man received a pass similar to that already described in Robert Tyrwhitt's case. The distinguished prisoners included James, Duke of York; Prince Rupert, and his two brothers Maurice and Charles Lodovic, Lord Rockingham, Messrs. Tyrwhitt, Cary, etc., etc.

As to Lord Rockingham's career after these events had taken place, little more remains to be told. By virtue of the terms of the surrender of Oxford, he had either to leave the country within six months, or compound for his estate. He chose the latter; and on August 15, 1646, presented his petition to the Committee for Compounding. In this document he returns his property in the counties of Northampton, Leicester, Huntingdon, and Lincoln as being, "before these troubles, worth 2,225*l*. 8*s*. 10*d*. per annum; and that there was owing to him 1,802*l*. 4*s*. 9*d*." Upon this statement he was amerced in a fine of 4,312*l*., which he paid on November 2, 1646, "when he was restored to his estate." However, the sequestrators were not yet done with him. They found out that he undervalued his estate; ordered a survey of it to be made, which was completed on November 7, 1650, when it appeared that it was worth more by 653*l*. a year than stated in his former composition, whereupon they imposed an additional fine of 1,430*l*. This amount he paid off in three instalments—viz., November 20, 500*l*.; November 22, 430*l*.; and November 23, 500*l*. In the course of these investigations it transpired, in connection with some Church land which he transferred, that he signed the deeds "Rockingham," instead of Lewis Watson. This could not "by any means be allowed of," consequently he was ordered to further sign and seal the said deeds "by the name of Sir Lewis Watson, and not by the title of Rockingham." He did not long survive this indignity, as he died on January 5, 1652-3. His lordship married, first, Catherine, daughter of Peregrine Bertie, Lord Willoughby of Eresbury, but by her had no surviving issue; and, secondly, Eleanor, daughter of Sir George Manners, of Haddon, county Derby, and sister to John, Earl of Rutland, by whom he had a son, Edward, his successor, and three daughters.

We hear nothing further of the "Hereditary" branch of the Royal Buckhounds or of its Masters until the Restoration, when the usual payments were resumed to Edward Watson, second Lord Rockingham, the fifteenth Master. The first payment to this Manorial or Hereditary Master occurs on the

Pipe Roll of the county Surrey for the twelfth regnal year of Charles II. (1660), in which his Lordship is described as the holder of the Manor of Little Weldon, *alias* Hunter's Manor in the county of Northampton, Master of the King's dogs, called Buckhounds. His fee of 12*d.* per day, 2*l.* for his livery, ½*d.* a day for the food of 30 hounds from Michaelmas to Midsummer, 7½*d.* a day for his attendance at Court, and the wages and liveries of his huntsman and two other hunt-servants are recited as formerly allowed. Edward Bradshaw was promoted to the post of Huntsman with the usual wages of 2*d.* per day, and Robert Brightmore and Robert Ridall now were the two "varlets berners," with a salary of 1½*d.* a day each, in succession to Robert Bowett and Richard Kilbourne, who had filled those offices in the reign of the "Martyred Monarch." From the 12th to the 25th year of the reign of Charles II. Lord Rockingham received his annual stipend of 50*l.* a year in full out of the issues of the county Surrey; for the 26th year he only received 23*l.* 12*s.* 9*d.* on account, but the balance was paid, with other sums on account, to him in the following year, and in the 28th year all overstanding arrears were paid to him in full. In the 29th and 30th years he was also paid his stipend in full, but in the 31st year he only obtained 37*l.* 19*s.* 6*d.* on account. However, as he received 62*l.* 0*s.* 6*d.* in the next year, the balance due, with the full salary for the current year, was consequently satisfied down to date; and from the 33rd to the 36th years of the reign of Charles II. his stipend was paid promptly without deduction. As the 37th year of the reign of Charles II. only covered a few weeks (the King having died on February 5, 1685), the Pipe Rolls for that year are included in the 1st year of the reign of James II., in which we find that Lord Rockingham was paid 50*l.* out of the issues of the county Sussex, by the hands of the Sheriff thereof, as appears by his lordship's acquittance, dated June 7, 1687; he also received a like sum out of the issues of the county Surrey for the 2nd year of the reign of James II. (1686-7), but the amount was not paid until July 4, 1688. We can find no payments to this

Manorial or Hereditary Master of the Buckhounds on the Pipe Rolls of Surrey or Sussex for the 3rd or 4th years of the reign of James II. Probably the impending Revolution may have had something to do with the nonpayment of this Master's stipend in the 3rd and the 4th (and last) year of James II.'s reign, which terminated on December 11, 1688. And, as Lord Rockingham was a Whig, it is very likely the King or his ministers refused to pass the Privy Seal, and without the production of that writ the Sheriffs of Surrey and Sussex were not warranted to pay the Master or his staff the tax imposed upon those counties towards the support of this branch of the Royal Buckhounds. Compared with the Household portion of the pack, this Hereditary Master and his hunt-servants were much more fortunate in receiving their wages and allowances, which were paid from 1660 to 1687 without any arrears having been encountered, save in the few temporary instances above mentioned. This Edward Watson, second Baron Rockingham, Manorial or Hereditary Master of the Buckhounds, *temps*. Charles II., James II., and William and Mary, from 1653 to 1689, married Lady Anne Wentworth, daughter of Thomas, first Earl of Strafford, by whom he had four sons and four daughters. He died in 1689, and was succeeded by his eldest son, Lewis Watson, third Baron and first Earl of Rockingham, sixteenth and last Manorial or Hereditary Master of the Royal Buckhounds. He nominally officiated in the first year of the reign of William and Mary, and was paid 50*l*. by the Sheriff of the county Surrey for that year only, as appears by his acquittance, dated July 10, 1691. We can find no further payments recorded to him on the Pipe Rolls of Surrey or Sussex again until the 2nd, 3rd, and 4th years of the reign of Queen Anne, when he received three several sums of 50*l*. out of the issues of the county Surrey for each of those years, as exhibited by his acquittances to the Sheriffs of that county, dated July 25, 1705, May 13, 1705, and May 13, 1707; the last being the final payment made to any Hereditary Master of the Royal Buckhounds by right of holding the Manor of Little Weldon, county Northampton, and the indispensable Writ of Privy Seal authorising the same.*

It only remains to mention, in connection with this branch of the Royal Buckhounds, that Watson Bradshaw was the huntsman, and Robert Brightmore and Robert Ridal the "varlets

* The following warrant, addressed by the Queen's command to the Lord Privy Seal, dated July 16, 1705, directing him to issue a writ under the signet, authorising the Sheriff of Surrey and Sussex to pay Lord Rockingham the usual stipend of his office, is the only *original* document of the sort we have ever met with:—

POUR LES BUCKHOUNDS.

Monseigneur, Vous plaist il faire tres de Guar and dessous le Seau Privé de sa Matie directes a le Vice-Comte de Surrey et Sussex, pour faire payment des Issues de la Baillage pour les Gages de Veneurs, et pour la pasture des Chiennes, en maniere dessous escript (c'est a scavoir) a Tres-honcureux Seigneur Lovis Baro Rockingham Maistre des Buckhounds a Sa Matie xij^d le jour, a Watson Bradshaw Veaultier ij^d le jour, a Robert Brightmore et Robert Ridal, Valets Barniers chacun d'eux j^d ob. le jour, pour leur Gages et pour la pasture de vj Leveriers et xxiiij Chiennes Courantes, pour chacun d'eux ob. le jour, commencantes a la Feste de St. Michael l'Arch-Ange 1703 jusques a xxiiij jour de Juin a donc prochain ensuivant, l'un et l'autre jour accomptes : Pour proviss la Pasture de xxiiij Chiennes courantes, pour chacun d'eux ob. le jour, et les Gages pour Valets Barniers pour xl jours en Caresme, quils sont au les costages du dict Baro Rockingham par les Statutes de l'Hostel de mesme Nostre Souvereigne. Et aussi qu'il fait Payment au dict Lovis Baro Rockingham pour les Gages en la Cour vij ob. le jour a prædic Watson Bradshaw, Veaultier ij^d le jour, et au dicts Robert Brightmore et Robert Ridal pour chacun d'eux j^d ob le jour, pour leur Gages vj Liveriers et xxiiij chiennes courantes chacun d'eux ob. le jour, de vxv^m jour de Juin devant dict jusques a le xxix^m jour de Septembre a donc prochain ensuivant, l'an et l'autre jour accomptes. Et plus outre qu'il fait payment au dict Lovis Baro Rockingham pour les deux Robes pour le dict Ann xl^s et a les dicts Veaultiers et Barniers pour leur Robes, chacun d'eux xiij^s iiij^d, et pour chauces pour chacun d'eux iiij^s viiij^d pour l'ann devant dict. Donné a le Chateau de Windsor le xvj^m jour du Mois du Juillet, en le iiij^m Ann de la Regne de Sa Matie Anne, par la Grace de Dieu, d'Angleterre, Escosse, France et d'Ireland Reine, Defenseur de la Foy &c.

A Tres-Noble Seigneur   W. fforester
Jehan Duc de Newcastle,   C. Scarburgh
Guardian de la Seau   Griffith
Prive de Nostre Sou-   C. Godfrey.
vereigne la Reine.

Two two shilling and sixpenny stamps in margin; and above red wax seal of a key transfixed by a bar on a shield, surmounted with letters A.R.
(*Harl. MS.* 7345, No. 68.)

berners," and that they enjoyed the same remuneration as heretofore allowed until the Hereditary Mastership of this pack ceased to exist in the fourth regnal year of Queen Anne's reign, ended on March 7, 1705-6; the appointment having been held successively by the holders of the Manor of Little Weldon for 345 years. This Edward Watson, third Baron and first Earl of Rockingham, the last Manorial or Hereditary Master of the Royal Buckhounds, died on March 19, 1724. He married, in July 1677, Lady Catherine Sondes, daughter and heiress of George, Earl of Feversham, by whom he had two sons and four daughters.

PART II.
THE UNITED PACKS.

CHAPTER XI.
ANNE (1702-1714).

The Hereditary and Household Branches amalgamated.—The United Packs placed on the Establishment of the Prince Consort.—Death of H.R.H.—The Buckhounds Re-established and Re-organised.—Appertains to the Lord Chamberlain's Department.—Annual Expenses of the Pack.—The Huntsmen and the Hunt-Servants.—The Hounds.—The Buck-hunting Season.—The Sport.—Ladies' Costume in the Hunting Field.—Sir Charles Shuckburgh, Thirty-second Master: June 6, 1703, to September 2, 1705.—Walter Chetwynd (Lord Rathdown and First Viscount Chetwynd), Thirty-third Master: October 4, 1705, to June 7, 1711.—Sir William Wyndham, Thirty-fourth Master: June 8, 1711, to June 27, 1712.—George, Third Earl of Cardigan, Thirty-fifth Master: June 28, 1712, to June 11, 1715.—Ascot Races instituted in connection with the Royal Buckhounds.—Reflections on Sport with the Pack during the Reign of Queen Anne.—Deer.—Officers of Windsor Forest.—Ascot Races.—"Queen Anne is dead."

AFTER a long and lingering illness the Hereditary Branch of the Royal Buckhounds died in desuetude on March 7, 1706. The two branches of this pack having merged into one, and become, what we may term, united, a new era and brilliant career soon after ensued. But, from the accession of Queen Anne till the death of "Est-il-possible," the pack was trammelled with uncongenial surroundings, which deprived it of many of its regal attributes. These obstacles were removed on the death of Prince George, the Queen's Consort, in the autumn of 1708, and during the following year the reconstructed pack resumed hunting under the most favourable auspices.

The Accounts of the Treasurer of the Chamber of the Household contain no payments relating to the Royal Buckhounds from the accession of Queen Anne (March 8, 1702) until the quarter of the year ended at Michaelmas 1709. This lapse was probably caused through the department of the Royal Hunt having been transferred to the establishment of George, Prince of Denmark, the Queen's husband, in 1702, to which establishment it appertained till the death of his Royal Highness. Unfortunately we have been unable to find the Establishment Books of the Prince of Denmark, consequently we are unable to give any *official* information of the Buckhounds, the Masters, the hunt-servant, or the cost of the pack during this period. But from other sources we learn that in June 1703 Sir Charles Shuckburgh and Sir Sewester Peyton were "made Masters of the Stag and Buckhounds to the Queen." We presume the two Masters above mentioned held the office directly from and under Prince George, as Walter Chetwynd, Esq., is the first Master of Buckhounds *officially* recorded in the reign of Queen Anne. According to Luttrell, Walter Chetwynd, Esq., M.P. for Stafford, was, on about October 4, 1705, "made Master of the Buckhounds, in room of Sir Charles Shuckburgh, deceased." We can find no official data relating to any of these gentlemen as having been appointed to or filling this office before June 13, 1709, when Mr. Chetwynd was nominated to the office and sworn on to it on the 24th of that month by the Lord Chamberlain. His salary was at the rate of 1,100*l.* a year, which he received in full down to June 7, 1711, when he resigned. He was succeeded by Sir William Wyndham, who was sworn into the post on June 8, 1711.* Sir William officiated for little over a year, as he was succeeded in the Mastership by the Earl of

* *Lord Chamberlain's Records, Warrants for Servants,* p. 269.

Cardigan on June 28, 1712, and he held the office during the remainder of Queen Anne's reign.

Leaving these Masters for the present, let us briefly glance at the expenses of the pack during this portion of Queen Anne's reign. As previously stated, the Royal Hunt was officially under a cloud during the interval extending from the Queen's accession to the year after the death of Prince George. But on June 24, 1709, the Royal Buckhounds were re-established with all the surroundings incident to this old and popular department of the Household. The Lord High Treasurer—thorough sportsman though he was—was the personification of economy in Governmental affairs. He was the terror of the Civil Service. He made the clerks employed in that service earn their wages; they had to attend to their respective offices, and personally perform their several duties; they were not allowed to delegate their labour to incompetent hacks yclept "writers"; and, what was the most important of his endeavours to reform the shameful abuses then rampant, he abolished, with the Queen's assent, the pernicious custom—a survival of the obsolete patent privileges—by which Governmental officials enjoyed the privilege of selling and transferring their situations to others who were able and willing to buy them. Actuated by this commendable policy of economy, Sidney Godolphin, with characteristic impartiality, cut down the established cost of the Royal Buckhounds from 2,341*l.*, at which it stood in the preceding reign, to 1,100*l.* a year when the pack was reinstated in June 1709, pursuant to the following Royal Warrant :—

Anne R.

An Establishment of the yearly charge of the Office of Master of our Buckhounds, which our pleasure is shall commence from the 24th day of June 1709 and be paid during our pleasure by the hands of the Treasurer of our Chamber and be allowed upon his accounts to be made to us and taken by our auditors of our imprests (viz.)

	Per Annum.
To the Master of Our Buckhounds for his own wages, buying of horses, and maintaining them, servants lodgings and all other extraordinaries whatsoever, Five hundred pounds	500ᵘ : 00 : 00
And to him more for keeping of hounds, wages of huntsmen, and all other charges relating to the said Office, Six hundred pounds.	600 : 00 : 00
In all eleven hundred pounds . .	£1100 : 00 : 00

Entered with both Auditors 17 June 1709.

By Her Majesty's Command,
GODOLPHIN.*

Upon this scale Mr. Chetwynd received the stipend of his office of Master of the Royal Buckhounds to defray the cost of the pack in full from the quarter ended at Michaelmas 1709 to June 7, 1711, the day on which he resigned. His successor, Sir William Wyndham, was paid at the same rate during his brief tenure of office—viz., from June 7, 1711, to June 25, 1712, when he resigned. But from this date the Master's allowance was raised from 1,100*l*., at which it stood from the year 1709, to the former minimum allowed in the preceding reign—viz., 2,341*l*., pursuant to the subjoined Royal Sign Manual:—

Anne R.

Earl Cardigan Master of the Buckhounds 2,341*l*. ℔ ann.

WHEREAS our Right Trusty and Right Wellbeloved Cousin George Earl of Cardigan was sworn and admitted into the office of Master of Our Buckhounds on the 28th day of June last 1712 And whereas we are Graciously pleased to allow unto him the like yearly sum of Two Thousand Three Hundred and Forty-one pounds for Salary and all manner of Charges and Expences any ways Incident or relating to the said office as was made for the same by Our Late Royall Brother King William the Third OUR WILL AND PLEASURE is and we do hereby

---

* *Lord Chamberlain's Records, Sign Manual Book*, Vol. ²⁰⁰⁄₂₂, fo. 57.

Direct Authorize and Comand that out of such money as shall be from time to time Imprested to you for the service of Your Office You pay or cause to be paid to the said George Earl of Cardigan or his Assignes the s^d Yearly sum of Two Thousand Three Hundred forty-one pounds by Quarterly paym^{ts} from the said 28th day of June 1712 During our pleasure as well for his Own Salary as for all other Charges & Expences whatsoever any ways relating to the s^d office of Master of Our Buckhounds And this shall be as well to you for Making the said paym^{ts} as to the Aud^{rs} of Our Imprests for allowing thereof from time to time Upon yor Accounts a Sufficient Warrant given at Our Court at St. James's the 13th day of May 1713 In the Twelfth year of Our Reign.

By Her Maties Comand.
OXFORD.

To the Treasurer of Our
Chamber for the time
being.

Ent^d with both Aud^{rs} 16th June 1713.*

The Earl of Cardigan received the remuneration of the office on the higher scale during the remainder of Queen Anne's reign, and in like proportion down to July 11, 1715, when he resigned in the first regnal year of the reign of George I. Some of the latter payments were considerably in arrears, as appears by the annexed summary of the Accounts of the Treasurer of the Chamber of the Household :—

To the Right Honble Sr William Wyndham Bart. at M^{l}C^{ll} ℔ ann from ye vijth June 1711 to ye xxvth of June 1712 in pursuance of her late Ma^{ts} Establishment commencing at Midsu^r 1709—M^{l}Clvij^{ll} ix^s vj^d ob.

To the Right Hono^{ble} the Earl of Cardigan succeeding the said S^r Wm Wyndham at M^{l}M^{l}CCCxlj^{ll} ℔ ann. from the xxviijth of June 1712 to the xxvth of December following in pursuance of her late Ma^{ts} Warr^t dated the xiijth of May 1713—M^{l}Clij^{ll} viij^s.

Total M^{l}M^{l}CCCix^{ll} xvij^s vj^d ob.

To the Right Hon. Charles Earl of Cardigan, for his salary and in lieu of all other charges whatsoever relating to the said Office at

---

* Lord Chamberlain's Records, Sign Manual Book, vol. $\frac{349}{725}$, fo. 75, dorso.

£2,341 ᵖ ann. for one year ended at Christmas 1713, by vertue of her late Majesty's Royal Sign Manual dated the 13th of May 1713.

Ditto—and here allowed from the 1st of August 1714 to Midsummer 1715—£2105 : 0 : 5¼.

1715—16—ditto at £2,341 ᵖ ann. from the 24th of June 1715 to the 11th of July following—£108 : 12 : 4½.

William Lowen Senior for keeping 30 couple of Buckhounds, Servants, and Horses at £600 per ann. from the 11th day of July 1715 (the time when the Earl of Cardigan resigned the Office of Master of the Buckhounds) to Lady Day 1716—£424 : 10 : 5.

More to him for keeping 20 couple of Buckhounds extraordinary at 3d. per day each hound from Christmas 1714 to the said time—£228 : 2 : 6. In both by a warrant under his Majesty's Royal Sign Manual dated the 13th of April 1716—£652 : 12 : 11.

John Hudson, Robert Armitage, William Lowen senior, and Wᵐ Lowen junior, Yeomen Prickers,* at 30l. per annum each, from the 9th day of July 1715 to Michealmas 1716—£381 : 3 : 10. William Lowen, Huntsman, for keeping 30 couple of Buckhounds servants and horses at £600 per annum from Lady Day 1716 to Michealmas following—£300. More to him for keeping 20 couple of Buckhounds extraordinary at 3d. per day each hound for one quarter of a year ended at Midsummer 1716 at which time the said additional number was reduced—£45 : 10s. Roger Webb, harbourer, at £20 per annum from the 6th of July 1715 to Lady Day 1716—£14 : 2 : 8¼. And to the said Roger Webb and John Webb two harbourers at £40 per annum each from Lady Day 1716 to Michealmas following —40l. In all by Warrant signed by His Royal Highness the Prince of Wales then Guardian of the Kingdom dated the 1st of October 1716—£785 : 16 : 6¼.

(*Arreas* R. 156.)

William Lowen, senior, Chief Huntsman to Her late Majesty in part of the sum of £360 : 16 : 5 due to him on his salary of £600

---

* William Lowen, late of the parish of Putney co. Surrey, Victualler, assigns to Charles Sparke of Wandsworth, Brewer and Attorney to ask demand and receive of any person appointed Master of the Buckhounds to King George, one half part of his salary of £80 a year as Yeoman Pricker until the sum of £80 be fully paid, and C. Spark shall give receipts for the same.

Dated Nov. 4, 1715.

(*In margin "paid off."*)   W. L.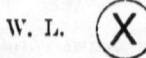

per annum for himself, servants, horses and hounds from Christmas 1713 to the 1st of August 1714—£289 : 8 : 10¼. John Hudson one of the Yeoman Prickers to the said Chief Huntsman in part of the sum of £48 : 2 : 2¼ due to him on his salary of £80 per annum for the same time—£37 : 7 : 9¼. William Lowen, junior, another of the said Yeomen Prickers for the like—£37 : 7 : 9¼. Robert Armitage, another of the said Yeoman Prickers, for the like—£37 : 7 : 9¼. And to William Lowen, junior, an Officer of the Buckhounds in part of the sum of £4 : 15s. due to him for his services within the same time—£3. In all (the said payments to be esteemed and taken no part of the debt owing to the Right Hon. the Earl of Cardigan on the sum of £2,341 per annum his established allowance as Master of her late Majesty's Buckhounds) by virtue of the warrant dated the 4th of July 1721—£404 : 12 : 2. The Right Hon. George Earl of Cardigan in part of the sum of £1,001 : 17 : 4¾ due in arrear on the allowance of £2,341 per annum, as Master of the Buckhounds to her late Majesty, by warrant dated the 26th of April 1723—£500 : 18 : 8¼.

Turning from the financial details of this Royal pack, as we find them on the establishment of the Household above cited, to the actual chronicle of the sport it yielded to its followers in those days, there are hardly any circumstantial records thereof to chronicle. So far as can be gathered from the facts above related, the officials of this pack—from the time when it was reorganised in 1709 to the end of Queen Anne's reign in 1714—consisted of the Master, the chief huntsman, five yeomen prickers, and two harbourers. Doubtless there were some other hunt-servants, such as grooms and helpers, not included in the above, who rendered casual assistance as part of their general duties at the Royal Mews and Kennels. The ordinary number of hounds in the pack was thirty couples, which were supplemented by twenty additional couples of "extraordinary" hounds, which we now hear of for the first time. The latter were, we presume, derived from the defunct Hereditary branch of the pack, and (under correction) we venture to submit that the amalgamation justifies us in now applying the term "United Pack" to the Royal Hunt at this period. At any rate, there was ample material to show good sport, so far as relates to the staff, the hounds, and the horses. The equine element is the most difficult one to tackle in dealing with this subject. According to the establishment of June 24, 1709, the Master had to find the horses for himself, the huntsman, and the yeomen prickers, and, in fact, to defray all the ordinary expenses incidental to the pack out of the annual allowance granted for the support of his office. The same arrangement prevailed under the increased scale granted to the Earl of Cardigan. But there were likewise occasional supplementary payments under this head, as we learn from the accounts of the Masters of the Horse.*

According to the ancient laws of venery the Buck-hunting season (proper) commenced on Holyrood Day and ended on Michaelmas Day. But there is incidental evidence frequently to be met with in the annals of the chase, proving the legitimate "season" was not rigorously adhered to, as "the hunting of the buck" was pursued, indirectly and at intervals, from Midsummer to Easter. For instance, Roger Palmer, in a familiar letter to Ralph Verney, dated April 6, 1706, says: "When

---

* 1711.—Samuel Masham for a grey gelding bought for the Master of the Harthounds, bought the 17th of September 1711—26*l*. 17*s*. 6*d*.

William Lowen, for a chestnut horse and a bay gelding for the Master of the Harthounds the 20th of the same month—41*l*.

Rowland Bright for a bay gelding for the use of the said Master bought the same day—25*l*.

Henry Pigot for a black gelding bought the 27th of the same month 28*l*.; more for a bay gelding for one of the huntsmen bought the 28th of the same month 26*l*.; more for a black gelding for her Majesty's chase bought the same time 25*l*.; more for a bay stone horse for the Master of the Staghounds bought the same day 32*l*. 5*s*. In all 111*l*. 5*s*.

1712-15.—To the Right Hon. the Earl of Cardigan, for three horses for the huntsmen of the Buckhounds, 75*l*. Cristopher Seymour for the hunting horses, 127*l*. 10*s*. 6*d*.; Robert Blount for a horse for the hunting stable, 43*l*.; Thomas Thompson for a bay horse for the hunting stable, 43*l*.

"Lately come to Town, a strong well-bred Mare, 7 Years old this Grass, about 14 Hands 3 Inches high, fit for either Hunting or the Course. to be seen at the Black-Horse at Hyde-Park Corner. Note, She has two Years keeping and is in good Order for Buck-hunting, or any present Business."—*Daily Courant*, Monday, June 30, 1712.

"At the sign of the 3 Cups in High Holborn, There is to be sold a very handsome strong Gelding, fed to Hunting, and fit to carry any Gentleman of 18 stone weight."—*Ibid.*, Monday, November 30, 1713.

yours came yesterday, I was a-hunting buck on Putney Heath with the Queen's buck hounds, there was a great appearance of gentlemen, tho' a bad day, they did not thin out before 1 o'clock, so we had fair riding and good, tho' short sport." Still, the legitimate season with the Royal Buckhounds, at and for many years after the period now under notice, began in July and continued until the end of September. When the cares of state permitted, Queen Anne and the high officers of the Court usually repaired to Windsor in July for the avowed purpose of buck-hunting. The Royal Diana Venatrix was early and "well entred" to the chase under the personal supervision of her Royal father, who (before he wore the weary crown) was the most ardent huntsman of his day. Imbued with such venatic associations, Anne became a mighty huntress. She continued to follow hounds on horseback until the gout precluded the continuance of that exhilarating exercise. Nevertheless her ardour for the chase remained undiminished; when she could not use the saddle she hunted on wheels. Her Majesty's hunting calash was a light two-wheeled carriage, containing a single seat, on which the Royal "whip" sate gracefully poised, skilfully "tooling" the splendid black roadster in the shafts.* In this vehicle she was enabled to follow a run with the Buckhounds through the forest glades † of Merry Windsor, sometimes covering forty miles in a single day. Her personal expenses, for hunting hospitality, during the buck-hunting season at Windsor—"from the first of July to the last of September"—usually came to about 550*l*., while the extra-

---

* The Duchess of Somerset, in a familiar letter to the Duchess of Devonshire, dated Windsor, September 29, 1707, mentions that when out with the Buckhounds on the preceding day, she was thrown from her calash; adding that "everybody thought I had broken my bones, but, thank God, I had as little hurt as was possible."

† To William Lowen for making 8 ridings 40 foot broad for the Queen's hunting at 20*l*. each, putting up posts and painting them, trenching Whitmore bog to lay it dry, brick arching, trenching and leveling Condit and South hill warrens, sowing them with fir-seed and broom-seed to make covers for the game, destroying the coneys, and other works within Windsor Forest, by command of H.R.H. Prince George of Denmark—300*l*.—*Treasury Papers*, vol. xcv., 122 (p. 415).

ordinary cost of the "Queen's stable for divers services and provisions for divers horses within the same time" amounted to about 105*l.* per annum. It is therefore evident that the usual followers of the Royal Buckhounds enjoyed good runs during the reign of Queen Anne; and although the literary remains of those times contain no details of the sport—the newspapers were muzzled on this and other current topics—a great contemporary poet tells us in "undying verse" that the fields were large and the pace a cracker:—

> " Now Cancer glows with Phœbus' fiery car:
> The youth rush eager to the sylvan war,
> Swarm o'er the lawns, the forest walks surround,
> Rouse the fleet hart, and cheer the opening hound.
> Th' impatient courser pants in ev'ry vein,
> And pawing, seems to beat the distant plain.
> Hills, vales, and floods appear already crossed,
> And ere he starts, a thousand steps are lost.
> See the bold youth strain up the threat'ning steep,
> Rush through the thickets, down the valleys sweep,
> Hang o'er their coursers' heads with eager speed,
> And earth rolls back beneath the flying steed.
> Let old Arcadia boast her ample plain,
> Th' immortal huntress, and her virgin-train:
> Nor envy, Windsor! since thy shades have seen
> As bright a goddess, and as chaste a queen;
> Whose care, like hers, protects the sylvan reign,
> The earth's fair light, and empress of the main."
>
> *Windsor Forest.*

Hunting predominated in every part of the kingdom. The example set by the Royal pack found emulation in all quarters; hounds were ridden to by all classes, from lords and ladies of high degree to the sturdy yeoman farmer.

The celebrated Lady Mary Wortley Montague refers to the people with whom she came in contact in Wiltshire as being " insensible to other pleasures than hunting and drinking," adding that their mornings were spent among hounds and their nights " with what liquor they can get in this country, which is not very famous for good drink." Her ladyship did not follow hounds at the time, although she became very partial to the chase in the ensuing reign. In another of her letters she incidentally bears witness to the popularity of hunting in Notts; and mentions how a bishop married a fair Diana (a daughter of Lord Lexington) " whom he fell in love with for falling backward from her horse leaping a ditch, where she displayed all her charms, which he found irritible."*

Now as to the four Masters of the Royal Buckhounds of Queen Anne's reign, it is difficult to define the status of the first two, as they were not *officially* recognised as such, although they *de facto* filled the office, and probably performed their duties with zeal and ability for the time being. The interregnum (if we may use the term) from March 8, 1702, to June 13, 1709, during which the Royal Hunt was directly connected with the establishment of Prince George of Denmark, the Queen's Consort, it received no official cognisance in connection with the Royal Household Departments. Hence we do not find the slightest reference to the Royal Buckhounds or their masters or the servants of the pack within that period. But from informal sources we are told that on or about June 8, 1703, " Sir Charles Shuckburgh and Sir Gwester Peyton are made Masters of the Stag and Buckhounds to the Queen." †

SIR CHARLES SHUCKBURGH, Bart., only son and heir of John Shuckburgh, Esq., of Shuckburgh, county Warwick (who was created a Baronet by Charles II. on June 26, 1660 ‡), and

---

* John Hughes, in the *Spectator* of June 29, 1711, describes " the Amozonian hunting habits " worn by ladies on horseback at this time as consisting of a coat and waistcoat of blue camlet trimmed and embroidered with silver, with a " petticoat " of the same materials. The hair was curled and powdered, hanging to a considerable length on the shoulders and " wantonly tied " with a scarlet riband. A little beaver hat edged with silver, made sprightly by a feather, was worn on the head " in a small cock."

† Luttrell's Diary, *sub dato.*

‡ About the time Sir Charles Shuckburgh came of age it was found that there was a claim of 1,095*l.* on his estates, alleged to be due to the Crown since the occasion of his father's creation to the dignity of a Baronet in 1660. Sir Charles, in a petition to the King, pointed out that the fees incidental to that creation had been remitted by Royal grace and favour, whereupon the King gave orders, on November 29, 1679, to the Lords of the Treasury not to press the claim, notwithstanding a recent order to enforce the collection of 20,000*l.*, which was due and payable for the use of the Great Wardrobe by the creation of Baronets.

Catherina, daughter of Sir Hatton Freeman, Knight, was born in 1659. He became the first Master of the Household and Hereditary packs of the Royal Buckhounds, which were united during his tenure of office under one Master and staff; hence we place him here as the thirty-second Master, in succession of the two branches, from the time of Sir Bernard Brocas. Sir Charles was High Sheriff for Warwickshire in 1687, and elected M.P. for that county in the Parliaments of 1698-1700, 1701, 1701-2, 1702 to April 1705, and from May 16, 1705, to the day of his death, September 2nd in this year. He married, first, Catherine, daughter of Sir Hugh Stukeley, Bart., of Hinton, by whom he had issue, John his successor, and two daughters; and secondly, Diana, daughter of Richard, third Lord Willoughby de Broke, by whom he had three sons and five daughters. Under the circumstances already related we are unable to give any reliable information concerning his administration as Master of the Buckhounds, an appointment he seems to have held from June 6, 1703,* to September 2, 1705. However, we may venture to say he did full justice to the office; and judging from the following incident it would appear he was in constant attendance on the Court during the hunting season. On the morning of August 28, 1705, the Queen, accompanied by the Prince Consort and the royal *entourage*, set out from Windsor to pay her first regnal visit to the ancient city of Winchester. Her *suite* comprised many of the high officers of State, including the Master of the Buckhounds. On the borders of the county the Royal party were met by the High Sheriff of Hampshire with ninety javelin men in armour, and others of his retinue in liveries, by whom the royal visitors were conducted to the Downs, where the Duke of Bolton, Lord-

---

* "Windsor, June 6, Sir Charles Shuckburgh and Sir S. Payton kis'd the Queen's Hand, being made Masters of the Stag and Buck Hounds."—*The Post Man*, London, June 8, 1703. As will be here seen, the chronicler is rather obscure. There is no doubt, however, that Sir Charles was the Master of the Buckhounds and Sir Swester Peyton the Master of the Staghounds. The latter died in 1717. Luttrell says: "Sir Charles Shuckburgh, M.P. for Warwickshire, *and Master of the Buckhounds to the Queen*, is dead of an apoplexy at Winchester" (Diary of Sept. 4, 1705).

Lieutenant of the County, with the Deputy-Lieutenants, Justices of the Peace, and a numerous company of the local nobility and gentry fell into the procession, which arrived at the east gate of the city at 6 P.M. Here the Mayor, Recorder, Aldermen, and the rest of the Corporation received them "in their formalities." The Duke of Somerset presented to Her Majesty the Duke of Bolton (as Lord High Steward of the city), who then presented the Corporate dignitaries. The Mayor presented the keys, maces, and other symbols of his trust, which the Queen received and returned to him. Next the Recorder made a speech, expressing their thanks for the honour she did them, and their duty, loyalty, and affection to Her Majesty and Government. The Mayor afterwards, in the name of the Corporation, presented the Queen with a hundred guineas in a rich purse, as a mark of their true loyalty, and in recompense he had the honour of kissing her hand, as had also the Recorder, Aldermen, and several others, whom the Queen received very graciously. The cavalcade re-started and passed through the streets, which were lined with the City Trained Bands, under the command of Lord William Powlet; all the people expressing "louder acclamations and greater joy on this occasion than ever before known on any other occasion in this city." At the close the Dean (in the absence of the Bishop, who was ill and unable to attend) presented a loyal address, which Her Majesty received very kindly. The following day the Mayor and Commonalty waited on Prince George, on whom they conferred the freedom of the city. After this function was done and performed the Royal visitors mounted their horses and went out with the local harriers,* the whole of the arrangement having been conducted under the supervision of the Master of the Buckhounds. No record of what sport ensued has transpired, nevertheless it probably proved enjoyable, as

---

* Mr. Bridges's, Mr. St. John's and Capt. Cornwall's huntsmen when Her Majesty was at Winchester, 6*l*. 9*s*. ; the harefinders there by Her Majesty's command, 7*l*. 10*s*. 6*d*. John Hudson, Huntsman to Her Majesty's Small Beagles, with servants and horses at 200*l*. per annum, from the 30th of July, 1713, to the 30th of July, 1714, 200*l*.—*Accounts M. H.* (R. 27).

Her Majesty's largess to the local huntsmen would seem to indicate. Unfortunately a gloom was cast over the proceedings. Sir Charles Shuckburgh was prostrated by an attack of apoplexy, from the effects of which he succumbed in the course of the day. This unexpected fatality dimmed the enjoyment of the Royal visit. The races on the Downs the two following days were not graced with the presence of the Queen,* to the great disappointment of those who had made great preparations to give the Royal Patroness of the turf a cordial welcome. Still it was a grateful tribute to the memory of the late Master of the Buckhounds. Having conferred the honour of knighthood on the Lieutenant-Governor and the Commissioner of the Navy of Portsmouth, the Queen's visit came to a somewhat abrupt termination, as Her Majesty took leave of the ancient city and the hunting fields of the vicinity—with which she was so familiar in her father and mother's time—and returned to Windsor on September 8.

According to an entry in Luttrell's Diary, under date October 4, 1705, "Walter Chetwind, Esq., M.P. for Stafford," was "Made Master of the Queen's Buckhounds, in room of Sir Charles Shuckburgh, deceased." This was probably the fact; still, like his predecessor in office, he had no official status at this time, nor indeed until June 13, 1709, when he was first recognised in his capacity of Master of the Buckhounds. Nevertheless we may take it that Mr. WALTER CHETWYND became the thirty-third Master of the Royal Buckhounds at the time mentioned by Luttrell; that he performed the duties of the office while it appertained to the establishment of Prince George, but under what circumstance we are unable to say; and so on until the Royal pack was officially reorganised according to the Sign Manual, above given, which was to commence on June 24, 1709.

On June 13, 1709, in pursuance of the subjoined Royal Warrant, addressed to the Lord Chamberlain, Mr. Walter

* The programme consisted of two plates: one of 20*l.* for horses under seven years old, 12 stone, Gentlemen to ride; and one of 10*l.*, 10 stone, the winner to be sold for 10*l.*

WALTER CHETWYND, THIRTY-THIRD MASTER.

Chetwynd was ordered to be sworn into the office of Master of the Buckhounds and Harthounds to the Queen:—

Anne R.

Our Will and Pleasure is, that you forthwith Swear and Admit, or Cause to be Sworn and Admitted, Our Trusty and Wellbeloved Walter Chetwynd, Esqr., into the Place of Master of Our Harthounds, and Buckhounds: To have hold and Enjoy the same, together with such Salary or Allowances as are or shall be Settled by Us, and all such other Fees, Perquisites, and Privileges as belong to the Place, in as full and ample manner as John Cary, James Grahme, James de Gatigny, Esq^{rs}., Reinhard Vincent Baron d'Hompesch, or any other Person hath formerly held and enjoyed the same. And for so doing this shalbe your Warrant.

Given at our Court at St. James's, the Thirteenth day of June, 1709, in the Eight year of Our Reign.

By Her Maties Command.

H. BOYLE.

To Our Right Trusty and Entirely
beloved Cousin and Councellor
Our Chamberlain of Our Household.*

Thus we find Mr. Chetwynd's immediate predecessor is officially given as Baron de Hompesch. Sir Charles Shuckburgh and Mr. Chetwynd, up to date, are ignored as having held this office, save in the allusion to "any other person," which is only a matter of form.

Now, turning to the accounts of the Treasurer of the Chamber for the year 1708-9 (Roll 145), the first payment in Queen Anne's reign relating to the Royal Hunt is as follows: "To Walter Chetwind Esq., Master of Her Ma^{ts} Buckhounds, at M^l C^{li} ℔ ann. at the established allowance, and here allowed him for one quarter of a year ended at Michaelmas 1709, CClxxv^{li}." Mr. Chetwynd's salary, at the rate of 1,100*l*. a year, was paid annually in full down to June 7, 1711,

---

* *Home Office Records, Warrant Book,* vol. xi., p. 47.

when he was succeeded by the Right Hon. Sir William Wyndham.*

Mr. Chetwynd was returned M.P. for the borough of Stafford on May 9, 1705, and at the General Election in May 1708. He was re-elected on November 25, 1709, "after his appointment as Master of the Hounds." He was returned by the same constituency in January 1712, "vice Thomas Foley Esq., called to the Upper House"; again returned on August 28, 1713. On November 19, 1724, "Walter Lord Viscount Chetwynd in the Kingdom of Ireland, vice John Dolphin Esq. deceased," was returned for that borough; and again on August 18, 1727. These details are important, as they establish the fact that when he was appointed Master of the Buckhounds in October 1705 he had not to vacate his seat in Parliament; therefore we may conclude that at the time his office was not one of profit under the Crown; and that it was held under the Prince Consort, by whom the emoluments of the office were defrayed out of the grant accorded to him for the support of his establishment. He was appointed chief ranger and keeper of St. James' Park on January 19, 1715, and ambassador at the Court of Turin for some time after he resigned the Mastership of the Buckhounds, and on June 29, 1717, was elevated to the peerage of Ireland as Baron Rathdown, county

---

* On April 20, 1711, Mr. Chetwynd received an order on the Treasury for 500*l*., but for what purpose is not stated.

Anne R.

Mr Chetwynd
Ma^r of the
Buckhounds
500*l*.

Our Will and Pleasure is, That out of any Our Money or Treasure that is or shall be Impresed to You at the Rec^t of Our Excheq^r You pay, or cause to be paid, unto Our Trusty and Welbeloved Walter Chetwynd Esqr Master of Our Buckhounds or to his Assignes any Sum or Sums of money not exceeding in the whole the sum of 500*l*. without Acc^t in such proportions as the Comm^{rs} of Our Treary or high Trear for the time being shall direct in that behalfe. The same being to be applyed to such Uses as We have directed. And this together with the Acquittance or Acquittances of the said Walter Chetwynd shall be as well to you for paym^t as to the Auditor for allowing thereof upon your Acco$_t$ a Sufficient Warr^t. Given at our Court at St. Jams's, the 20th Aprill 1711. In the tenth year of Our Reigne.

By her Ma^{ts} Command,
P: H. P. T. M.

Dublin, and Viscount Chetwynd of Bcrehaven, county Cork. In 1720 Lord Chetwynd and Lord Londonderry * obtained from George I. a grant of the island of Providence, in America, on condition of fortifying and planting it with English subjects. On July 2, 1722, Lord Chetwynd sold his house "adjoining to St. James's Palace" to the King. On the accession of George II. Lord Chetwynd was very harshly deprived of his Rangership and office of "Keeper of the Mall"; probably the "sale" of his residence in St. James's was only a courtesy term for "eviction." He was not a favourite with the Court or the Ministers; and from this time his name is rarely mentioned in connection with political and social transactions, beyond the circumstance that he and his family were notable members of the Charlton Club, and consequently mighty fox-hunters. His lordship died, without heirs, on February 21, 1735, when his estates and dignities went to a collateral branch of the family.

SIR WILLIAM WYNDHAM, thirty-fourth Master of the Royal Buckhounds, was appointed to the office on June 8, 1711,† and sworn in by the Lord Chamberlain the same day.‡ The warrant of his appointment is word for word similar to the document above cited in the case of his predecessor, except, of course, in the names and dates. His allowance was on the reduced scale of 1,100*l*. per annum, out of which he had to defray the ordinary expenses of the pack as then established. As he only held this appointment for little more than a year very few incidents of his Mastership have transpired. However, he had to continue the superintendence, which appears to have been carried on from the Queen's accession, of making the forest rides, and improving the going on those rustic roads for the Royal hunting *calash*. Thus, on June 29, 1711, the Lord Treasurer informed Mr. Chetwynd that it was Her Majesty's pleasure that "he was to pay over to Sir William Wyndham, Master

---

* His eldest son, and successor, Thomas, second Earl of Londonderry, broke his neck whilst hunting with the Royal Buckhounds near Richmond, on Saturday, August 24, 1734.

† *Home Office Records*, *Warrant Book*, vol. xi., pp. 244-5.

‡ *Lord Chamberlain's Records*, *Warrants for Servants*, p. 267.

of Her Majesty's Buckhounds, the money which remains in his hands out of the 500l. which he had lately had from Mr. Compton, to defray the charge of repairing the bridges over the bogs, and cutting ridings through the Heath in Windsor Forest for the conveniency and care of Her Majesty's hunting there."* This part of his duty likely extended to supervision attending the formation of the racecourse at Ascot at the first race meetings ever held there, in the months of August and September 1711, where some of his horses ran ; and, what is perhaps the most novel circumstance in the case, is the probability that he was the first Master of the Buckhounds who officiated in the ceremony, which is now familiar to all attending those Royal reunions on the famous Berkshire heath.

Sir William Wyndham, Bart., only son of Sir Edward Wyndham, Bart., and Catherine, daughter of Sir William Levison Gower, Bart., and sister to John, Lord Gower, was born about the year 1687. He was educated at Eton, and afterwards at Christ Church, Oxford, where he took high honours. After he left college he travelled abroad, going frequently out of the beaten track usually followed in the "grand tour." About this time we find the young traveller at the battle of Ramillies, where, as he afterwards related, he heard a trooper utter the briefest prayer on record : " If I forget Thee, O Lord, in the hour of battle, do not forget me." Soon after his return to England he was elected M.P. for the county of Somerset on April 26, 1710, a constituency which he represented during the remainder of his parliamentary career. These elections call for no comment at our hands save on the occasion of his return on July 4, 1711, consequent on his recent appointment of Master of the Buckhounds, which was "an office of profit under the Crown." In the senate he soon became a prominent statesman. On June 30, 1712, he was appointed Secretary of War, and on August 21, 1713, Chancellor of the Exchequer. He was sworn a Privy Councillor on November 1, and on the 9th of that month took his seat at that Board, then assembled in Windsor Castle. Upon the breach between Harley, Earl of

---

* *Treasury Papers. Letter Book*, vol. xiii., p. 383.

Oxford, Lord High Treasurer, and St. John, Lord Bolingbroke, in July 1714, Sir William adhered to the latter. Upon the death of Queen Anne, on August 1, 1714, he signed with others the Proclamation of George I.; nevertheless his Jacobian sympathies were viewed with distrust by the Hanoverian party, and in October following he was removed from his post of Chancellor of the Exchequer. In the next Parliament, which met on March 17, 1715, he appeared very vigorous in opposition to the measures of the Administration, and was, in consequence, reprimanded by the Speaker. On the outbreak of the rebellion in Scotland under the Earl of Mar, in August 1715, Sir William fell under suspicion, was impeached for alleged complicity in that rising, and, upon an alleged charge of escaping from custody, he was proclaimed a traitor, and 1,000*l*. offered for his arrest. Having soon after surrendered, he was examined by the Privy Council, and committed to the Tower, but was never brought to trial. In this respect he seems to have passed through much the same ordeal as Colonel Graham, the whilom eleventh Master of the Household branch of the Royal Buckhounds. After he had regained his liberty he continued his opposition to the several administrations under which he lived, though he is believed to have altered his opinion with regard to the Government itself, from the Jacobite notions which he might formerly have espoused, to a more large and popular system; and that upon this ground he afterwards formed his whole political conduct. It was universally allowed that he possessed all the qualifications requisite to form an able senator,—sagacity, to discern the strength or weakness of every question, and eloquence, to enforce the one and expose the other; skill and address, to seize every advantage in the course of a debate, without affording any; and a proper degree of warmth and vivacity in speaking, necessary to secure the attention of an audience, without such an excess as might embarrass himself and expose him to the cooler observation of his antagonists. Apart from his political career, this famous statesman was socially the best of company, equally distinguished by an unaffected civility and politeness and conversational ability, enhanced by an easy flow of wit, and supported by a various and extended scope of useful knowledge. Sir William Wyndham was a good all-round sportsman; a bold, straight rider to hounds, and thereby incurring many a spill in the hunting field. He was a great favourite with Queen Anne, by whom he was allotted a splendid suite of apartments in Windsor Castle, as well as the stately mansion belonging to the Crown, "near St. James's, wherein the Duchess of Mazarine formerly lived," from which he was evicted soon after the accession of George I., when it was sumptuously furnished "on the occasion of the coronation for the use of the Court."* He was one of the most popular politicians of the old school, of which Godolphin was the head; and, had he chosen to stoop to the court corruption of the Hanoverian *régime*, might have attained the highest ministerial honours. But, as Pope very truly states, he preferred to remain

". . . just to freedom and the throne,
The *Master* of our passions and his own."

Sir William died, greatly lamented, at Wells in Somerset, after an illness of a few days, on June 17, 1740.

GEORGE, THIRD EARL OF CARDIGAN, thirty-fifth Master of the Royal Buckhounds, was appointed to the office soon after the resignation of Sir William Wyndham, on June 28, 1712, in pursuance of the annexed Royal Warrant:—

Anne R.

OUR WILL AND PLEASURE is, that you forthwith Swear and admitt or cause to be Sworne and admitted Our Right Trusty and R^t Welbeloved Cousin George Earl of Cardigan into the Office and Place of Master of our Buckhounds, to have hold and enjoy the same during Our Pleasure, with all rights, ffes, Salarys, Profits, Priviledges and Advantages thereunto belonging in as full and ample manner to all Intents and purposes as Our Trusty and Welbeloved Sr William Wyndham B^t or any other person heretofore hath held and enjoyed, or of right ought to have held and enjoyed ye same. And for so

* *Lord Chamberlain's Records, Warrants for Servants,* vol. xxiii.

doing this shall be your Warrant. Given at Our Court at Kensington the Eight and Twentieth day of June 1712, in the Eleventh Year of Our Reigne.

By Her Ma^{ty's} Command,

DARTHMOUTH.

To Our Right Trusty and Right entirely beloved Cousin and Councellor Charles Duke of Shrewsbury Our Chamberlain of Our Household.*

As set forth in the Sign Manual above cited his allowance as Master of the Buckhounds was increased from the sum of 1,100l. a year to 2,341l. per annum; and he received this remuneration in full until he resigned office, soon after the accession of George I.

The Earl of Cardigan seems to have been as great a favourite with Queen Anne as the Earl of Leicester was with Queen Elizabeth. In another respect there was a similarity between these two Masters of the Buckhounds—viz., that of being the youngest amongst those who filled the office. Lord Cardigan was only in his twenty-fifth year when the official insignia of the Royal pack was confided to his charge. During the two years he officiated under Queen Anne everything was *couleur de rose*; but in his third and last year of office, under George I., he encountered so many checks that they drove him to resign.

George, third Earl of Cardigan, eldest son of Lord Francis Brudenell and Frances, daughter of James Saville (last), Earl of Sussex, was born in the year 1687. His father pre-deceased him during his minority. His father, and his uncle also, were most improvident, and through their dissipation almost impoverished the second Earl, of whom the following curious story, which is characteristic of the times, is told. During the dreadful hurricane of February 7, 1699, while Robert, second Earl of Cardigan, was at prayers in his chamber in Cardigan House, Portugal Row, Lincoln's Inn Fields, a large stack of

* *Home Office Records, Warrant Book,* No. 12, p. 223.

chimneys was blown down, and crushing right through the centre of the mansion levelled all before it, but his lordship providentially escaped uninjured. "This wonderful and almost miraculous deliverance did doubtless happen to him for his great piety, and unconstrained generosity, in paying, as fast as he could, his son's debts, which came to 30,000*l.* or 40,000*l.*, the most of which, had he died, being left as yet unpaid, would have been the undoing of multitudes. A noble and Christian example for other great men to imitate!"

On the death of his grandfather, "aged about a hundred," on July 16, 1703, George, third Earl of Cardigan, succeeded to the family honours and estates. He married Lady Elizabeth Bruce, eldest daughter of Thomas, second Earl of Ailesbury, by whom he had four sons and two daughters. He was brought up in the Roman Catholic faith, which he abjured when he came of age on January 11, 1708, "and received the Sacrament in St. James's Church; and on the following day took his seat in the House of Peers, introduced by the Lord Chancellor." About this time he and his wife appeared to have hankered after the then new and novel sport of fox-hunting in Oxfordshire. Adle, Countess of Shrewsbury, writing from Heythorp, November 8, 1707, to the Viscountess Longueville, Easton, Northamptonshire, says: ". . . My Lord and Lady Cardigan are at present here, and we discourse of nothing but fox-hunting, but,"—on her own part the Countess modestly adds,—"I have not yet arrived to the perfection of fox-hunting." In the meantime Lord Cardigan became a great favourite with Queen Anne, by whom he was appointed Custos Rotulorum of the county Northampton, on April 11, 1711. His appointment to the Mastership of the Buckhounds followed on June 28, 1712, as above shown, when he at once entered upon the duties of his office. In connection with this post everything seems to have been in a thoroughly efficient state, except an occasional hitch, now and then, with regard to the quarry. It is evident that the ancient predilection of making free with the Royal deer, which were deemed the lawful spoil of the predecessors and the successors of Robin Hood and his merry men, continued in those days as in the days of yore, as poaching was rampant in the vicinity of Windsor Forest. Great exertions were now made to suppress this abuse, and poachers retaliated by putting dogs into the pen containing the bucks intended for uncarting at the opening meetings of the Royal pack in 1712, when Lord Cardigan first assumed the official insignia of the hunt.* It would further appear that the herds of the antlered lords of the forest were increased during this year, by importation, as in May, William Lowen, the chief huntsman, received 166*l.* 10*s.* for taking one hundred red deer at Houghton Park, and conveying forty of them to Windsor Forest. Another important draft was obtained under the following curious circumstances: Squire Legh, of Lyme, having offered to make a heavy wager that his huntsman could drive a herd of his deer to any part of England. The bet being snapped up as a good thing, orders were issued to the foresters and huntsmen at Lyme Park to undertake what appeared to be a hopeless task. Nevertheless a herd was soon drafted from the stock at Lyme, and thence conducted, without loss or damage, over highways and byways, until they eventually reached Windsor, with the greatest ease and safety. Thus, this remarkable wager was won. The means employed must have been superhuman, or connected with subtle art of venery and woodcraft now unknown; for it's

---

* "KENSINGTON, July 2, 1712.—Whereas on Tuesday the 17th of June last, some Dogs were put into the Pen at Swinly Rails in Windsor Forest, and killed six Deer; Her Majesty, for the better Discovery of those who are guilty of this Presumption, hath been pleased to direct, That any Person or Persons who shall at any time within one Month, to be accounted from this Day, discover the Offenders or any of them, so as they or any of them may be convicted of the said Crime, shall over and above the Reward allowed by the Statute, receive a further Reward of Fifty Pounds, to be paid by the most Honourable the Lord High Treasurer of Great Britain. And in case any Person or Persons concerned in the said Offence, shall discover any of his or their Accomplices therein, so as to be Convicted thereof, Her Majesty is pleased to promise Her Gracious Pardon to such Person or Persons making such Discovery.

"H. ST. JOHN.

"*London Gazette*, July 1/3, 1712."

a million to one that it would now be impossible to drive a herd of timid deer from Cheshire to Windsor without losing every head before a quarter of the journey was accomplished. The Royal Forest having been "well replenished" by these drafts there was no lack of game to give sport. Large fields and brilliant runs appear to have ensued, but unfortunately no details of the sport have been preserved. However, we incidentally hear that on the conclusion of the run, on August 1, 1712, the noble Master received the joyful intelligence that his Countess had just presented him with a son and heir, whereupon he was heartily congratulated, and the Queen herself promised to become godmother to the welcome little stranger. This promise was fulfilled on the ensuing August 26, when Her Majesty presented her Master of the Buckhounds with a warrant on the Royal Jewel Office to obtain 130 ounces of plate as her gift at the christening of his child, the plate to be made into such vessels and after such fashion as his Lordship should direct. The order was executed at the Jewel Office on April 28, 1713, when his Lordship received "one large gilt cup, cover and salver," weighing 132 ounces 11 dwts., for which the Treasury was charged 76*l.* 9*s.* There is every reason to assume that the followers of the Royal Hunt continued to enjoy the pleasures of the chase, and that the Forest and its vicinity resounded with the merry music of hound and horn during the remainder of Lord Cardigan's somewhat brief term of office. But, by the Queen's death on August 1, 1714, hunting was stopped; nor was it again resumed for some time. George I. re-appointed the Earl of Cardigan to the Mastership on November 6, 1714, "to hold the office in as full and ample manner as he, the said Earl of Cardigan or any other person, hath held and enjoyed the same."* He was sworn into the office by the Lord Chamberlain on the same day, as appears by the subjoined certificate in that behalf:—

---

* *Home Office Records, Warrant Book,* vol. xiii., p. 163.

The Earl of Cardigan Sworn Master of His Majesty's Buckhounds in Ordinary. } These are to certify that I have Sworn and Admitted the Right Honble the Earl of Cardigan into the Place and Quality of Master of his Majestys Buckhounds in Ord^ny To have hold Exercise and Enjoy the said place together with all the Rights Profits Privileges and Advantages thereunto belonging; in as full and Ample manner as any person that formerly held, or of Right ought to have held and Enjoyed the same. Given under my hand and seal this 6th day of November 1714, in the first year of His Majesty's Reign.

SHREWSBURY.*

In the troubles that ensued, Lord Cardigan, like most of his old and honourable friends, fell under suspicion of favouring the Jacobian cause. These political and partizan proceedings we need not discuss, as they should not intrude in the hunting field, where they are not wanted, as they are antagonistic to our theme. Nevertheless, this baneful element deprived the Royal Hunt of Lord Cardigan's services, and was the indirect cause of the pack being "all masterless" for twelve years. No specific reason can be assigned for Lord Cardigan's "resignation," "removal," or "dismissal" from office. At any rate, his official connection with the Royal Buckhounds terminated on July 11, 1715. Beyond a casual allusion to the circumstance nothing further transpired in the current news of the day. The public press was scrupulously reticent on passing events of this class, and as his Lordship was not directly impeached on any charge of disloyalty to the new dynasty no reason was vouchsafed as to why or wherefore he relinquished office. Nevertheless, it must have occasioned much gossip, as His Excellency Giacomo Querini, the Venetian Ambassador at the Court of St. James', in a despatch to the Inquisitors of State, dated London, July 17, 1715, considered it of sufficient importance to announce that Lord Cardigan had "resigned into the King's hands the post of Master of the Buckhounds, a very profitable charge, and one which he obtained as a very great favour at the commencement of the reign." He retired soon

* *Lord Chamberlain's Records*, vol. $\frac{175}{8}$, p. 30.

242 HISTORY OF THE ROYAL BUCKHOUNDS AND ASCOT RACES.

after into the enjoyments of private life, and we hear nothing of him during the remainder of the reign of George I. Shortly after the accession of George II. he was created LL.D. of Cambridge on April 25, 1728. He died on July 5, 1732, after his return from Bath, at Lord Bruce's seat in Tottenham Forest, Wiltshire, and was interred at Dean, Northamptonshire.*

The following is a " List of Officers and Under Keepers of Windsor Forest," in 1704 :—

	Salaries ⅌ annum.		
	£	s.	d.
The Duke of Northumberland, Lord Warden	20	0	0
Richd Nevill, Esqr, Lieu^t of the Forest	10	0	0
Fra Negus, Woodward of the Forest	25	0	0
Maj^r Negus, Bayliffe of Finchamstead Bailywick, Rainger of Bigshot Railes & Sandhurst, Allowance for Hay for the Deer of those two Walks	30	0	0
Charles Mildmay, Riding Forester	5	6	5½
Ditto, Keeper of Swinley Railes, and Bayliffe of Battles Bayliwick, Allowance for Hay	50	0	0
Robt Hanington, Under Keeper of Bigshot Railes	20	0	0
Augustine Hanington, Senr, Under Keeper of Sandhurst Walk	20	0	0
Augustine Hanington, Junr, Under Keeper of Easthamstead Walk	20	0	0
Ditto as Vermin Killer	9	2	6

* It would appear by the Accounts of the Treasurer of the Chamber that a quarter's salary remained unpaid to Lord Cardigan. Whether this had ever been paid to his assignee or no we are unable to say.

These are to desire you to pay to Mr. Robert Webber all such sum and sums of money as shall from time to time become due and payable unto me as Master of Her Majesty's Buckhounds and his receipt shall be your discharge till further order. Witness my hand and seal this 21st day of November 1713.

CARDIGAN.

To John Holbech Esq. and the Right Hon. Lord Delawarr, Treasurer of Her Majesty's Chamber.

Witness—CHARLES KIRKHAM.
F. HACKET.

₊ Similar power of attorney from Sir William Wyndham to Christopher Desbrow, of St. James's, Westminster.

Lord Chamberlain's Records, Assignment Book, vol. (R.I.) cxcvi., p. 104.

	Salaries ℔ annum.
	£ s. d.
Wm Lowen, Under Keeper of New Lodge Walk	20 0 0
Ditto as House Keeper there	6 1 0
John Barnes, Under Keeper of Sunninghill Walk	20 0 0
Richd Lovegrove, Under Keeper of Billing Bear	20 0 0
Wm Miles, Under Keeper of Old Windsor	20 0 0
John Thorn, Under Keeper of Bear Wood	20 0 0
Geo: Holder, Under Keeper of Linchford	20 0 0
Benjⁿ Irmnonger, John Sawyer, Senr, John Sawyer, Junr, Under Keepers in Cranborn, each 20l. ℔ ann.	60 0 0
Andrew Streek, Under Keeper at Swinley	20 0 0
William Beaumont, Game Keeper of New Windsor	40 0 0
Francis Bancroft, ditto, of Old Windsor	30 0 0
Geo: Prudham, ditto, of Bagshott	40 0 0
Wm Carter, ditto, of Shrubs Hill	12 0 0
	£537 9 11½

George Churchill, Esq., Deputy Ranger, was allowed 100l. a year for hay for the deer in the Home Park, Windsor.

It seems the original intention was to have two horse-races at ASCOT in the month of August 1711. The first was for a Plate of 50 guineas, to be run for on Monday, the 6th, by any horse, mare, or gelding, that had never won the value of 40l. in money or plate; each animal to carry 12 stone, in three heats. They were to be entered on the preceding Wednesday at the Town Hall, New Windsor, "or with the Town Clerk or his Deputy, paying 2 guineas, or at the time of starting paying 6 guineas to the said Clerk or Deputy." The entrance money was to go to the horse running second in this race. On Tuesday, the 7th, "Her Majesty's Plate of 100 guineas" was to be run for "round the new Heat on Ascott Common, near Windsor," by any horse, mare, or gelding, "being no more than six years old the grass before, as must be certified under the hand of the breeder, carrying 12 stone, 3 heats; to be entered the last day of July at Mr. Handcock's, at Fern-Hill, near the starting-post."

For some reason or other these races were postponed from

the 6th and 7th to the 11th and 12th of August. The number of horses which started and the winners have not been preserved, so far as we can ascertain. All we know is that for the Queen's Plate of 100 guineas (= 107*l*. 10*s*.) four horses were entered—viz., Lord Raylton's brown bay; Lord Craven's grey horse; Sir William Goring's brown bay; and Mrs. Orme's bay horse. The 50 Guinea Plate obtained a better entry— viz., the Duke of St. Albans' chestnut horse, Doctor; Mr. Elwell's grey horse, Have-at-All; Mr. Smith's grey gelding, Teauge; Mr. William Hall's bay-stone horse, Dimple; Mr. John Biddolph's brown bay horse, Flint; Mr. Charles May's grey gelding, Grey Jack; and Mr. Merrit's iron-grey stone horse, Grim. As an accessory to the races there was to be "back-sword playing for pieces of plate"—this entertainment to begin "at eight o'clock in the morning."

There is very little doubt that this was the first race-meeting ever held at Ascot; for we learn from the Declared Accounts of Charles, Duke of Somerset, Master of the Horse, that the sum of 558*l*. 19*s*. 5*d*. had been paid "to sundry workmen employed in making and perfecting the round Heat on Ascot Common in the months of July and August 1711"; that a carpenter received 15*l*. 2*s*. 8*d*. "for setting up posts and other carpenter's work on the said common in the month of September 1711"; and that 1*l*. 1*s*. 6*d*. was paid to Mr. John Grape "for engrossing the Articles for Her Majesty's Plate, run for at Ascot Common."

A second race-meeting was held at Ascot in the ensuing month. On Monday, September 17, a Plate of 30 guineas was run for by any horse, mare, or gelding, carrying 10 stone, that never won in money or plate the value of 20*l*. On Tuesday, the 18th, a Plate of 20*l*. was run for by any horse, etc., that never won 20*l*. For the 30*l*. Plate the following were entered: The Duke of Somerset's grey horse, Crofts; Mr. Barber's chestnut gelding, Speedy Cut; and Mr. Edmund's dark-brown gelding, Hoboy. The 20*l*. Plate, run for on the following day, secured a like support — viz., Sir William Wyndham's grey gelding, Cricket; Lord Lifford's nutmeg gelding, Sharpes; Sir Thomas Palmer's bay gelding, Lumber; and Mr. Newman's grey gelding, Have-a-Care. Like the preceding meeting, no records of the runners or winners of these races have been preserved.

These inaugural race-meetings at Ascot were honoured with the presence of the Queen and all the Court Officials, including the reigning beauty, Miss Forester, one of the Maids of Honour, mounted on her "palfrey," and "dressed like a man"—that is, in the *equestrienne* attire of the period—viz., a long white riding-coat, a full-flapped waistcoat, and a small cocked hat, three-cornered, bound with broad gold lace, the point placed full in front, over a white-powdered, long flowing periwig. This beautiful and accomplished young lady met her fate at these races, and was soon after married, when the Queen presented her with a marriage portion of 3,000*l*.—the "dot" always given by Her Majesty to her Maids of Honour on their wedding-day.

1712.—In the last week of July 1712 it was formally announced "that Her Majesty's Plate of 100 Guineas" was to be run for on Ascot Common, near Windsor, on Friday, August 25, by any horse, mare, or gelding, being no more than six years old the grass before, "as must be certified under the hand of the breeder." The horses were to carry 12 stone each, in three heats, and had to be entered on the Friday before the race day, between the hours of ten and two, at Mr. Hancock's, on Fern Hill, near the starting-post. By a further semi-official notification a Plate of 50 guineas, "by subscription," was to be run for on that course on Monday, September 1, by any horse, mare, or gelding, that never won 40*l*. in plate or money. The horses were to carry 12 stone each in three heats, and to be entered at the Town Hall, with the Town Clerk of New Windsor, on Friday, August 29. Two guineas entrance had to be paid by the owners of intending competitors, or 6 guineas if entered at the starting-post on the day of the race. The articles "to be as usual," and the second horse to receive the entrance money. The Queen's Plate was won by "Robert Fagg, Esq., son of Sir Robert Fagg,

Baronet, of Sussex." Six horses started, four of them having been distanced in the first heat. The result of the 50 Guinea Plate, competed for by the followers of the Royal Buckhounds, has not transpired; at any rate, we can find no further notice of it. The Queen, accompanied by all the Court Officials, attended this meeting, as also several of the nobility and gentry who were sojourning at Windsor for the purpose of presenting Her Majesty with the inevitable "Loyal Address" on the occasion of the Peace with France and Spain; amongst whom were the Duke of Beaufort, Duke of Hamilton, Lord Chancellor Harcourt, Sir Simon Stuart, and numerous M.P.'s, besides a regular invasion of High-Sheriffs, Grand Jurors, J.P.'s, "and other gentlemen and freeholders" from every part of the kingdom.

1713.—In the ensuing year the Queen's Plate of 100 guineas was similarly announced to be run for "on Ascott Common, near Windsor," on Wednesday, August 12; the conditions as to age, weight, distance, etc., being the same as in the preceding year. But should any difference arise it was to be determined by "the Hon. Coyners Darcey, Esq., and the Hon. Col. George Feilding, Esq., Commissioners to execute the Office of Master of the Horse, or in their absence by Richard Marshall, Esq., Master of Her Majesty's Studd." The 50 Guinea Plate was to be run for on Thursday, August 13, by any horse, mare, or gelding that never won 100*l.* in plate or money "since they were six years old"; the best of three heats, carrying 10 stone each. They had to be shown and entered at Windsor by the Town Clerk on Monday, August 10, otherwise they were disqualified to run for this plate. Early in this month Windsor was *en fête*, in consequence of the installation of six new Knights of the Garter—viz., Henry, Duke of Beaufort; Henry, Duke of Kent; John, Earl Poulett; Robert, Earl of Oxford; Thomas, Earl of Strafford; and Charles, Earl of Peterborough. On the 5th the Queen arrived from Kensington at Hampton Court, where she remained until the 10th. On the following day Her Majesty and the Court were at Windsor Castle, and proceeded thence, on the 12th, to see the last Royal Plate run for at Ascot during her reign. We are unable to give the faintest description of this meeting, nevertheless we may be sure it proved a merry reunion to those who were so fortunate to participate in the sport. An autumn meeting was announced to take place at Ascot on October 20, when the Windsor Town Plate of 20 guineas, open to any horse, mare, or gelding, carrying 10 stone, that never won 30*l*. in plate or money. The result of this race has not been recorded in the annals of the turf. The Queen and Court were at Windsor Castle at this time, but we have no information whether or not the event in question had been honoured by the presence of royalty.

1714.—The last Queen's Plate of 100 guineas given by Queen Anne to be run for at Ascot was announced to take place on Friday, August 13, 1714, under the same articles as obtained there during the three preceding years. The 50 Guinea Plate was to be run for on Monday, the 16th. But good Queen Anne died on August 1, 1714, consequently these proposed races at Ascot were postponed. The meeting was eventually abandoned, and we hear nothing further of "Royal Ascot" for some years to come.

It has been truly said that Queen Anne "was every inch a sportsman." During her youth, and in those happy days when the Duke of York, her father, allocated his spare time to the pleasures of the chase, both she and her elder sister became proficient riders to hounds on the spacious downs and in the sylvan groves which extended from historic Winton to the New Forest. In those happy hunting fields, and subsequently at Windsor and Richmond, the two young princesses were "well entered" in all the arts and mysteries of the chase, under the supervision of their Royal father, than whom a more competent mentor could not be found for that particular purpose. During the time when the hunting establishment of Charles II. was under a cloud (through financial and other circumstances), that of the Duke of York was in the most flourishing condition. Indeed, if one could get at the records of the Establishment of H.R.H. at the time in question, it would probably transpire that his buck, stag, hare, fox, and other packs exceeded the King's; and from a comparative point of view the former undoubtedly yielded superior sport. Unlike the King, the Duke was in receipt of a large permanent income, free and unencumbered, and untrammelled by the peculiar devouring demands which soon exhausted the resources of the Royal Exchequer. Notwithstanding all his faults, James invariably paid twenty shillings in the pound. Thus the "sinews" of sport were strong and healthy within the verge of the Prince's Court, and under the watchful care of Colonel Graham every department of this establishment was—to use the nautical expression of the Duke—"in ship shape." Consequently no reasonable expense was grudged in efficiently sustaining this hunting establishment, in which H.R.H. evinced the utmost solicitude during this interval of rural enjoyment, down to the time of his eldest daughter's marriage with the Prince of Orange. Then came a check. That spoil sport—political and polemical agitation—had to run its course. When the political and sectarian fanatics regained their senses, the Duke of York again re-entered on the even tenor of his way, and, accompanied by the Princess Anne, resumed hunting with his hounds. His letters to the Prince of Orange, and to his familiar friends likewise, testify to the pleasure and relaxation they derived from those rural sports. But the demon of discord again came upon the scene. The father and daughter were separated for a time. Then to the former came "the weary crown," and the cares of state; no time for hunting for him, and very little for his favourite child.

It is not necessary here to again refer to the career of the Royal Buckhounds during the troubled reign of James II. When William and Mary jointly occupied the throne the latter was jealous of her sister's personal popularity, and of the love and devotion she inspired in all with whom she came in contact. Mary was envious of Anne's prowess in the saddle, and even endeavoured to prevent her following the Royal Buckhounds in the hunting field. Fortunately, however, she failed to accomplish this vindictive intention; but by her enmity the Princess was excluded from all approach to Windsor Castle and Park. Beyond the confines of Windsor Park the Royal Hunt was free to all who desired to join in with the hounds, a boon which even the "Knights of the Road" appreciated. In this juncture Anne cleared the obstacles placed in their path without turning a hair. Hunt she would, and hunt she did. She purchased a cottage near the Castle, and from this humble *villa venatica* joined in with the Royal Hunt every summer, from 1689 to 1694, in which latter year, by the death of Queen Mary, the unnatural severity to which she had been subjected by her sister was removed. As heir-apparent to the Crown, she was from this time onward treated with all respect and deference at the Court of William III. During those seven years we may depend she missed few opportunities of hunting with the Royal Buckhounds. Unfortunately the chroniclers and Court gossips of the day rarely condescended to notice passing events of that description; indeed, the only specific instance we have met with being recorded in September 1700, on which occasion, the heat being excessive, the Princess was suddenly taken so ill that Dr. Hanns was summoned from London to attend her. But before the Court physician arrived, "an apothecary at Windsor, by letting blood and other applications," quite restored her; and what appeared to be of equal importance, the Court physician "mightily approved of what the apothecary had done"; consequently, as those doctors did not differ, H.R.H. was able to resume hunting on the following Monday.

When she ascended the throne in the spring of 1702, Queen Anne, or her Ministers, committed an unintentional mistake in placing the Royal Buckhounds on the Establishment of her consort, the Prince of Denmark. As above explained, the adoption of that course tended to diminish the dignity and impair the efficiency of the Royal Hunt from the Spring of 1702 to the Midsummer of 1709. During those seven years, it appears to have been customary with Queen Anne to drive in her calash from Windsor Castle, Hampton Court, or

Richmond Park, as the case may be, to the rendezvous where the Royal Buckhounds assembled for the chase, which was usually in Windsor Forest. That procedure invariably prevailed during the life of the Prince Consort. "There is a noble oak," writes Miss Strickland, "among the glades of Windsor Forest which used to have a brass plate affixed to it, intimating that it was called 'Queen Anne's Oak'; for beneath its branches she was accustomed to mount her horse for the chase, and view her officials and dogs assembled for the hunt." Towards the end of her reign the gout and other complaints, which she had held at bay by frugal fare and active exercise, gradually made undeniable assaults on her usually robust constitution, and with the greatest reluctance she was eventually compelled to give up riding to her hounds. Nevertheless she continued to follow them up to the last in her hunting calash. There is a tradition to the effect that, in anticipation of her favourite Buckhounds falling into disrepute on the score of the expenses incidental to the pack, she set aside a fund, sufficient for their future maintenance, independent of any grant from the Civil List or demand on the Royal Exchequer. To what extent the validity of that fund proceeded it is now apparently impossible to ascertain. A version once obtained currency that this hunting endowment should have been reserved out of the money she allocated to the Established Church, known as "Queen Anne's Bounty." At any rate, it was worked out on the simile of robbing Peter to pay Paul, or, to be precise, of mulcting that patient beast of burden, the British taxpayer, for the benefit of "the scantily endowed clergy of the Established Church"—this "bounty" money having been allocated towards the expenses of the Royal Household from the time of the "Reformation" down to the year 1703, and from thence onward to our own times the taxpayers have been obliged to make the deficiency good.

Like Elizabeth, Anne lived in the hearts of her subjects. Apart from her individual predilection for the chase, she seems to have acted on the principle recorded by the old chronicler, that among "common people" (that is, the citizens and gentry living in and about London, such as, for instance, the ancestors of the Duke of Leeds and numerous noble lords*) hunting with the Royal Buckhounds was esteemed as a greater kindness than a greater benefit would have been. Like many of her predecessors, Queen Anne delighted to see these "common people" "hunt and be merry" when riding to her hounds in the vicinity of Windsor and Epping Forests. Miss Strickland says that prior to the Union with Scotland, she was depicted on the Great Seal, mounted on a fleet hunter at the head of the Royal Buckhounds. Dean Swift records that, in August 1711, he had seen Queen Anne hunting near Windsor in her calash, which she drove "furiously like Jehu, and is a mighty hunter like Nimrod"; adding that on that occasion Her Majesty followed the chase until four o'clock in the afternoon, during which she drove not less than forty miles. On the whole her reign was glorious in military triumphs; conspicuous in the eloquence and patriotism of her ministers; notable in the development of literature, science, and art; commerce flourished; while hunting and rural sports expanded to and were enjoyed by all classes. Thus in a blaze of glory set the sun of the last Stuart sovereign, amid the lamentation of her subjects, in that terse and enduring epitaph : " Queen Anne is dead ! "

* See Orridge's *Citizens of London.*

CHAPTER XII.

GEORGE I. (1714—1727).

The Earl of Cardigan re-appointed Master of the Royal Buckhounds, November 6, 1714.—Resigns Office July 11, 1715.—No Official Master onward during the Reign of George I.—Mr. William Lowen, Senior, appointed Huntsman to the Pack.—The Hounds.—The Hunt-Servants.—The Pack re-organised.—Annual Expenses of the Establishment during the Reign of George I.—Some Records of the Runs.—Popularity of the Hunt.—Is in great Favour with the Fair Sex.—Dearth of Hunting Intelligence during the Reign of George I.—Alderman Humphrey Parsons.—Ascot Races.

THE circumstances attending the reappointment of the Earl of Cardigan to the office of Master of the Buckhounds by George I. on November 6, 1714, and his resignation thereof on July 11, 1715, having been circumstantially recorded in the last chapter, it will be sufficient here to mention that the 247 days in which he officiated in the capacity of thirty-fourth Master of the Royal Buckhounds, under the first Hanoverian Sovereign, passed away without leaving the slightest indication of the proceedings of the Royal pack in the hunting field during the time mentioned. The probability is that, owing to the political complications, he never officiated or took any practical part in the administration of the office under the new régime. After his resignation or removal had been accomplished, no one was appointed to fill the vacancy; consequently we hear of no official Master for the remainder of the reign of George I.

After the death of the Duke of Somerset, no Master of the Horse was appointed for several years, the profits of that office being paid to the king's head mistress, Herrengard

Melesina von Schulenburg, who was created Duchess of Munster in the Peerage of Ireland, and afterwards Duchess of Kendal in the English. Her rapacity was very great and very successful; and there is no doubt that her secret emoluments for patronage and recommendations far surpassed any outward account of her receipts. Sir Robert Walpole more than once declared to her (but this was after the death of George I.) that she would have sold the king's honour for a shilling advance to the best bidder. Still, with the accounts of the Treasurer of the Chamber open before us, we are bound to exonerate the rapacious duchess of having any finger in the sparse expenses allocated to the support of the Royal Buckhounds; although it was surmised she was the means of keeping open the Mastership of that pack until a favourable opportunity presented for its disposal to the highest bidder. At any rate, no recognised or official Master to the Royal Buckhounds was appointed until the accession of George II., when Colonel Negus—who had been commissioner for executing the office of Master of the Horse throughout the reign of George I.—was promoted to the post.

In the meantime the Royal Buckhounds were not idle. In the year 1716 the pack consisted of 50 couples of hounds. This number was soon after reduced to 30 couples, when the annual cost of the pack was 1000*l*. per annum. Out of this yearly allowance the huntsman had to defray all the incidental expenses, as set forth in the subjoined summaries of the accounts of the Treasurer of the Chamber of the Household, and cognate records for the time being:—

George R.

Kings Warr^t.
Mr. Lowen for Keeping the Buckhounds £652 : 12 : 11

Our Will and Pleasure is And We do hereby Direct Authorise and Command that Out of Such our Treasure as is or Shall be Imprested to You at the Rec^t. of Our Excheq as Treā̃rer of Our Chamber and for the Use & Serv^{ce}. of that Office You pay or cause to be paid unto Willm. Lowen Senr. or to his Assignes the Sum̃e of Six hundred fifty two Pounds Twelve Shillings & Eleven Pence in

Satisfaction of his Service care pains & Expences in looking after, keeping and maintaining Our Buckhounds free of all further Charge to us; either for S'vants, horses or otherwise howsoever with in and for the Severall Periods of Time, hereunder menčõned That is to say

For keeping 30 Couple of Buckhounds, Servants and horses, from the 11th July 1715 the day on wch the Earl of Cardigan resigned his Office of Master of Our Buckhounds to X'mas ffollowing, the same being computed after the rate of 600^{lb} ℔ ann., £274 : 10 : 5.

For keeping the like number of hounds, servants, horses, for one quarter from X'mas 1715 to Lady Day 1716 at the rate of 600^{lb} ℔ ann., £150.

For keeping 20 Couple of Buckhounds Extroord^{ry} to make up 50 Couple in all from X'mas 1714 to Lady Day 1716 being one year & a quar' at ye rate of iij pence a day each hound for all Expences w'soever, £228 : 2 : 6. Total £652 : 12 : 11.

And for so doing this together with the Acquittance of the said William Lowen or his Assignes shall be as well to you for making the said payment as to the Auditor of Our Imprests and all Concern'd in passing and allowing thereof upon Your Account a Sufficient Warrant.

Given at Our Court at S^t. James's this 13th day of Aprill 1716 in the Second Year of Our Reigne

By His Ma^{ts}. Command

To Our Right Trusty & Right Welbeloved Cousin Bodville Earl of Radnor Treãrer of Our Chamber

Will: S^t. Quintin
P: Methuen
T: Newport

—*Lord Chamberlain's Records*, S.M.B., vol. $\frac{200}{723}$, fo. 107

Arrears due to the huntsman to Lady Day, 1716 :—

William Lowen, the huntsman, for himself, servants, horses, and hounds, was paid by the Lord Cardigan to July 10, 1715.

By the Treasury to Lady Day last :—

The Yeomen Prickers and Harbourer was paid by the Lord Cardigan to July 10, 1715, at 80*l*. each Yeoman Pricker per annum, and 20*l*. to the Harbourer; but then he found the Harbourer a horse.

Due to John Hudson, from July 11, 1715, to Lady Day following, being 258 days at 80*l*. per ann., 56*l*. 10*s*.

To Robert Armitage, William Lowen, brother to the Huntsman, William Lowen, son to the Huntsman, at 56*l*. 10*s*. each; and to Roger Webb, Harbourer, at 20*l*. per annum, 14*l*. 2*s*. 6*d*.— 240*l*. 2*s*. 6*d*.

From Lady Day to Midsummer last:—

To William Lowen, the Huntsman, 1 quarter, for himself, 6 servants, 9 horses, and 30 couple of Hounds, at 600*l*. per annum, 150*l*. For 40 additional Hounds, at 3*d*. per day each, 45*l*. 10*s*. (but these are to be reduced from this time)—195*l*. 10*s*.

Four Yeomen Prickers, at 20*l*. each, 80*l*.; two Harbourers at 10*l*. each, £20 (and they find their own horses)—295*l*. 10*s*.

One quarter to Michaelmas, 1716:—

To William Lowen, the Huntsman, 150*l*.; four Yeomen Prickers, 80*l*.; and two Harbourers, 20*l*.—250*l*.—T. P., vol. 205, no. 38.

According to another account the hunt servants were paid in full down to Michaelmas, 1716, 785*l*. 16*s*. 6¼*d*.—L. C. R.; Sutl. B., vol. ²⁰⁰⁄₇₃₉, fo. 131*d*.

1717
William Lowen, huntsman, for himself, six servants, nine horses, and thirty couple of Buckhounds, at 600*l*. per ann., for one year, ending at Christmas, 1717—600*l*.

John Hudson and three other yeomen Prickers at 80*l*. per ann. each for the same time—320*l*.

Roger Webb and John Webb, two Harbourers, they finding and keeping their own horses, at 40*l*. per ann. each for the same time—80*l*.

1718 ditto, total, 1000*l*.
1719 ditto „ 1000*l*.
1721 do. for 1¾ years, ended at Christmas, 1721, 1050*l*.
    4 yeomen prickers, do., 560*l*.
    2 harbingers, do., 140*l*.
1722 do. for ¾ of a year, ending at Mich. 1722—
    do. 4 yeomen Prickers, at 80*l*. per ann.; do. 2 harbingers—total for ¾ year, 750*l*.
1723 ditto for a year ended Michaelmas 1723—total, 1000*l*.
1724 ditto for a year and ¼ ending at Christmas 1724—total, 1250*l*.
1725 do. ½ year to March, 500*l*.

1726 do. for 1½ year, from Midsummer 1725 to Christmas 1726,
900*l*.
4 Yeomen Prickers for same time, £480.
2 Harbourers, Wm. Ives and Robt. Shorter, for same time,
120*l*.—total, 1500*l*.

As may be gathered from the preceding summaries of these accounts the chief huntsman out of the annual allowance of 1000*l*. a year defrayed the whole cost of the pack as we find it on the establishment of George I. This sum covered the cost of keeping thirty couples of hounds, the wages of the huntsman, six servants, nine horses, four yeomen prickers, and two harbourers. There were, however, contingent expenses, not included in the above calculations, such as pensions, fees to the keepers of Windsor and Epping Forests, cost of carting deer, extra horses, saddles, food for deer in Windsor, etc., etc., as indicated in the following extracts from the Accounts of the Commissioner of the Master of the Horse:—

1715-1717. A hunting mare and a pad 22*l*. 0*s*. 9*d*. each. 1 hunting mare 27*l*. 8*s*. 3*d*., one ditto 16*l*. 14*s*. 9*d*., 1 ditto 13*l*. 3*s*.

1717-1719. William Lowen, sen., for 2 hunting horses, 25 Aug., 1717—64*l*. 10*s*.

[Several saddle horses bought, but for what object not mentioned, in most cases.]

A mare and 2 geldings for the chief huntsmen 67*l*. 16*s*., and 2 geldings 37*l*. 10*s*. 6*d*.

New saddles, bridles, and other furniture for the accustomary new sets of sadlers' wares allowed yearly by way of livery to the huntsmen and other attendants upon his Majesty, etc. (various miscellaneous sums).

10 couples of Buckhounds 52*l*. 10*s*. For freight and other charges in sending to Hanover 5 horses, 10 couples of Buckhounds, and a Spanish pointing spaniel, 100*l*. 7*s*.

Cost of 10 couples of Buckhounds 42*l*. 10*s*. (R. 33.)

To the widdow and children of Wm. Lowen, late chief huntsman, 100*l*.; of Edward Ives, late yeoman pricker, 40*l*.; and of Robert Webb, harbinger, 20*l*.; being his Majesty's allowance in lieu of all other pretensions whatsoever, by warrant dated the 31st of May, 1725—160*l*.

ABSENCE OF HUNTING INTELLIGENCE.

To the several keepers of Windsor and Epping Forests for their fees for deer killed by his Majesty's hounds between the 10th of February, 1721-2, and the 25th of December, 1725, viz., 105 stags at 40s. each, 19 hinds at 20s. each, and 23 bucks and 2 does at 10s. each, by virtue of a warrant under the royal sign manual dated the 25th of October, 1721—241*l*. 10s.

To Charles Howard for the hire of teams of horses and men, and other expenses in removing stags and hinds from the paddock at Kensington to Swinley-rail walk in Windsor Forest in the year 1725—57*l*. (R. 33.)

To Mr. Wm. Lowen for hay for the deer at New Lodge, Windsor Forest, from Midsummer 1713 to Midsummer 1717—219*l*. 16s. (*Treasury Papers Letter Book*, vol. xvi., p. 321.)

Now, as to the sporting element. There are very few allusions to the proceedings of the Royal Buckhounds in the hunting fields to be found in the literary chronicles of those times. As in the past, political troubles militated, indeed we may say " crowded out," intelligence of passing events bearing upon our subject. Hence for the first two seasons following after the accession of George I. hardly a single word transpires upon the hunting of this pack. If the King ever went out with the Buckhounds the circumstance would probably be mentioned in the newspapers at the time, but they are absolutely mute on any such subject. Nevertheless George I. was a fairly good rider to hounds; but, as we shall subsequently have occasion to record, he showed a marked predilection for the chase in his native country in preference to that of his new kingdom. During the time that the ministers were carrying their measures in Parliament they had to struggle with the King's impatience to revisit his German dominions. It was in vain that his confidential advisers pointed out to him the unpopularity that must attend, and the dangers that might follow, his departure at such a crisis : their resistance only chafed instead of curbing his Majesty, and at length the ministers let go the bridle. In his absence the Prince of Wales was appointed Guardian of the Realm instead of Regent, an office unknown in England since the days of the Black Prince.

At this time the Prince of Wales occupied Hampton Court Palace, where he principally held his court during his father's absence in the autumn of the year 1716. Although the season for buck hunting opened on Midsummer Day, the first inkling of it did not appear until the 21st of August, when it was announced that his Royal Highness and several of the nobility and gentry were then enjoying the chase in the vicinity of Windsor Forest. The following week the meets were held in Richmond Park, and in the ensuing one the Prince was hard again hunting at Windsor, where "a great concourse of nobility attend him." About the same time the King was reported to be hunting at Göhrde, Hanover.

During the buck hunting season of 1717 the King was in England. On July 9 it was publicly announced that "Richard Barker, Esq., was made Master of his Majesty's Buckhounds,"* but, if true, it was not ratified nor ever officially confirmed. On the 19th the King went to Hampton Court, where he continued on and off the premises till towards the middle of September. While the court remained there a post went twice a day from London. Open house was kept for those who had business to transact, and something akin to regal state unexpectedly broke out. It is not our province to pursue the diurnal of this royal visit, except on occasions when it was associated with hunting. Unfortunately no news of the chase occurs until September 9, when the King "hunted in Windsor Forest and killed a brace of bucks, and afterwards dined at Cranborn Lodge, belonging to the late Earl of Ranelagh." At the end of the month the King and Court "departed hence" for Newmarket.

Turning from the King's Court to its rival held by the Prince of Wales, it is somewhat satisfactory to notice that, although the King and the Prince were at daggers drawn on political issues, they were on good terms in the hunting field. Alexander Pope, in a letter to Miss Martha Blount, dated September 13, 1717, tells his fair correspondent that he had recently encountered at Hampton Court the Prince with all the maids of honour on

* "The Historical Register," vol. ii. [iv.]; Chron. Table, p. 30.

horseback coming from hunting. He adds, " to eat Westphalia ham in a morning, ride over hedges and ditches on borrowed hacks, come home in the heat of the day with a fever, and (what is worse a hundred times) with a red mark in the forehead from an uneasy hat! all this may qualify them to make excellent wives for foxhunters and bear abundance of ruddy-complexioned children." Thus we learn that the fair sex continued to follow the royal hounds as they were wont in past and future times.*

1718.—August 28. The King went from Hampton Court to Windsor to hunt. October 3: " Stormy weather prevents the King hunting and shooting as he frequently do's at other times." In September the Prince of Wales and his children were at Richmond. On bad terms with his father. Rival courts very factious. Servants of the Prince's children not allowed to wear scarlet liveries; only yellow ones permitted, "according to precedent."—1719. The King absent in Hanover during the buckhunting season. Prince of Wales and family at Richmond. Not a word about hunting.—1720. The King absent in Hanover. July: the Prince at Richmond. His court, attended by great numbers of the nobility and gentry, " which brings prodigious profit to the country people thereabouts." No hunting intelligence, nor, for that matter, of anything except the South Sea Bubble, which was now in full cry. Every one gambled in this specious swindle. Folks begged, borrowed and stole to dabble in the myth. Everything upon which the wind could be raised was pawned to invest in the

---

* " Yesterday-Night, the Prince diverted himself with Hunting about Hampton Court, where he kill'd a Buck. He was accompanied by several Ladies on Horseback, who took part in the Diversion."—*The Weekly Journal or British Gazetteer*, Saturday, August 31, 1717.

" On Monday the King diverted himself with Hunting in Bushy Park near Hampton-Court, after which His Majesty, alighting from his Horse, walked above three Miles, with a Fowling-Piece in his Hand, and kill'd several Braces of Partridges flying."—*Ibid.*, September 14.

" On Saturday the Prince hunted a Buck in Windsor Forest. The Buck ran as far as Staines, where he was killed. On Sunday the Earl of Roseberry carried the Sword of State before his Majesty to the Chapel Royal at Hampton Court, where Dr. Holland preached."—*Ibid.*, September 14.

stock—hounds and horses included.* The Jews made their first appearance on the turf, and came through the ordeal with credit, Baron Schwartz and Mr. Gomes Arras having carried off the principal honours at Epsom.—1721. The King at Hampton Court for the summer season; the Prince at Richmond. No hunting news.—1722. In September George I. paid his first formal visit to Windsor Castle. No reference to hunting.—1723. The King reported to be hunting in Hanover. The Prince held his court at Richmond during the buck-hunting season, but no details of the sport transpire. It seems, however, that the Royal Buckhounds pretty frequently hunted in the vicinity of Windsor and Epping Forests.

In July 1724 it was publicly announced that several fine hunting horses were bought for his Majesty, who intended going to Windsor to reside there for some time, "to take the diversion of stag-hunting." This state visit was postponed until the 14th of the ensuing month, when his Majesty, accompanied by "the young princesses," arrived at the Castle. In the meantime an installation of the Garter was held there, the first of this reign, which was largely attended. "Never was such a scene of roguery carried on in so short a space, and with such wonderful dexterity; for, in short, allmost everybody was robbed, and yet nobody in particular seen or suspected of doing it." On the first Sunday after his arrival at the Castle the King dined there in public, "when a great number of the country people came thither, and were admitted to see his Majesty at dinner." During this royal sojourn the King, "attended with divers of the nobillity and other persons," frequently went shooting and coursing in the Great Park and Forest. On August 27 his Majesty was reported to be "shooting from 8 in the morning till almost 5 in the afternoon"—the royal bag comprising the sum total of 2½ brace of pheasants and 1½ brace of partridges. On September 5,

---

* "They write from Newmarket that several of the fine Race Horses have been converted into Notes and Specie for their more convenient Running in Change-Alley."—*The Weekly Journal*, July 2, 1720.

the King, accompanied by the "young princesses," and all the Court officials, paid a visit to, and dined with, the Earl of Orkney at Cliefden. On his return, all the villages through which the Royal *cortège* passed were illuminated; and, on entering the Home Park, it was met there by the inhabitants of the Royal Borough, who turned out *en masse*, and thence His Majesty, T.R.H., and *suite*, were conducted to the Castle surrounded by a torch-light procession, which is described to have produced a novel and picturesque effect. We cannot find the slightest allusion to hunting, from his arrival at Windsor till his departure for Kensington on October 1, "in perfect health."

In 1725 the Ministry submitted a royal message to Parliament, requiring 508,367*l*. 19*s*. 4*d*., to discharge the debts of the Civil List. This enormous arrear had been incurred in the short space of three years, because, as the message stated, his Majesty had found it impossible to make any considerable retrenchments. The nation was amazed at this demand, but, notwithstanding Pulteney's plucky protest, the grant was passed by 239 votes against 119. Probably not one farthing of this sum went into the King's pocket; most of it was gobbled up by the corrupt administrators of the state and their hungry hangers-on. At any rate, the only arrears outstanding on account of the Royal Buckhounds were for one year and a quarter, amounting to 1250*l*. Consequently this department of the Civil List was free from extravagance and innocent of peculation. Disgusted with the management of state affairs in his new dominions, which he could not understand, George I. left England for Hanover in August. He spent most of the ensuing month hunting at Göhrde, in the company of Prince Friedrich and some of the English nobility of his suite. There the chase usually commenced at 7 a.m. and continued till 5 p.m.

In the meantime the Prince of Wales had proceeded to Richmond, where he held his court amid the most enjoyable surroundings. As usual, hardly an item of hunting intelligence was mentioned in the chronicles of the time; nevertheless there is ample reason to believe that the Royal Buckhounds were showing good sport.

Lady Mary Wortley Montagu, in a letter to the Countess of Mar, tells her that at this time she rode a good deal, and had "got a horse superior to any two-legged animal, he being without a fault." In another epistle to the Countess she says: "I think this is the first time in my life that a letter of yours has lain by me two posts unanswered. You'll wonder to hear that short silence is occasioned by not having a moment unemployed at Twickenham; but I pass many hours on horseback, and I'll assure you, ride stag-hunting, which I know you'll stare to hear of. I have arrived to vast courage and skill that way, and I am as well pleased with it as with the acquisition of a new sence: his Royal Highness hunts in Richmond Park, and I make one of the *beau monde* in his train. I desire you after this account," she humorously adds, "not to name the word old woman to me any more: I approach to fifteen nearer than I did ten years ago, and am in hopes to improve every year in health and vivacity." Thus, in the sixty-fourth year of her age this accomplished lady first took to ride to hounds; with what result the modesty of her letter is commendably silent.

On July 30, 1726, it was announced that Colonel Negus had sent several sets of horses to Windsor, and that other preparations were making for his Majesty's going thither in a little time. However, the projected royal sojourn at the Castle was eventually abandoned. The King went to Hampton Court instead; and thence, during a short visit, made shooting excursions to Bushey and Richmond Parks. The Prince held his court at Richmond, which was probably still associated with the Royal Buckhounds during his sojourn there in the hunting season. Although no records of the sport leak out, there is nevertheless one circumstance mentioned which establishes the fact that the pack must have been in a working way—viz., the races at Ascot by horses "that staghunted with the King's hounds." And, during the last four seasons, 147 stags and hinds had been hunted with the pack.

On June 3, 1727, the King set out for Hanover, accompanied by the Duchess of Kendal, Lord Townshend, and suite. On the 9th the royal travellers arrived at Delden, the King apparently being in perfect health, as he resumed his journey at 4 a.m. next morning. But as he was travelling that forenoon he was seized with an apoplectic fit in his coach, and was dead in a few hours afterwards. Thus suddenly closed his chequered and eventful, but, on the whole, prosperous and indulgent reign. Like William of Orange, George the First was brought hither to fill the English throne by a political faction mainly for their own purposes. He had no sympathy with the inhabitants of these islands, whose manners and customs he could not understand and whose language he could not speak. He was to all practical intents and purposes a mere puppet in the hands of his unprincipled ministers. Many hard things have been said of George I., a few of which may be true. Most of them are foul calumny. It is absurd for us to accuse him of callousness or indifference in connection with the exalted station we compelled him, much against his inclination, to fulfil. We were alone to blame in the matter; if things did not turn out to our liking, why, serve us right. Without his crown and sceptre George I. was not a bad fellow. He was a good sportsman, though his conception of sport was not our sport. Evidently he intended to participate in the pleasures of the chase at the time when he built the New or Stone Lodge in Richmond Park, from a design by the Earl of Pembroke, with the intention to use it as a *villa venatica*, "after the fatigues of the chase." He was a good judge of a horse; liked racing, but disliked the surrounding of our racecourses. He won the first race in which any of his horses ran—*i.e.*, in the Plate of 50*l.* at Guildford, on Tuesday, June 5, 1715, for which six horses competed; and he named the winner before the start. He never saw this horse before, did not know to whom it belonged, and picked it out as the best of the lot solely from knowledge of horseflesh. True, he discontinued the gold cups which were given to be run for in Queen Anne's reign; but in lieu of them he gave several sums of 100 guineas annually, to be run for on different courses throughout the Three Kingdoms. It is bootless to inquire why he did not fill up the office of Master of the Buckhounds; perhaps he did not understand what it meant. His belief was that as every general should lead his own forces to battle, so also every sportsman should be his own huntsman; and if we cannot gainsay it, wherefore complain?

Turning from the royal and noble celebrities associated with the Buckhounds in those days, we must pay a brief tribute to "the common people," who, according to the old chronicler, were steadfast followers of the pack almost from time immemorial. During the reigns of George I. and George II. these "common people"—the merchant princes of the city, the lawyers, the doctors, the clergy, and the rich though humble bagman, mounted on the now obsolete "nag," on which he travelled, on business thoughts intent, throughout the land—rarely missed a favourable opportunity of hunting with the Royal Buckhounds. Among, and at the head of, the metropolitan patrons of the Hunt was Humphrey Parsons, twice Lord Mayor of London. His prowess in the saddle, and his ability in the hunting-field, was not only notorious among the followers of the pack; it was recognised on the Continent, and, in fact, his reputation as an intrepid rider extended to every part of Europe wherever hunting men might chance to congregate. Towards the end of the reign of George I. Humphrey Parsons became very conspicuous through an incident which took place when he was hunting with the staghounds of Louis XV. in the forest of Fontainebleau, in the month of September 1725. On this occasion we are told that Alderman Parsons, "being mounted on a spirited English horse, contrary to the etiquette of the French Court, outstripped the rest of the field, and was first in at the death. The King inquiring who the gentleman was, one of his adulatory attendants indignantly answered that he was *Un Chevalier de Malte*. The King, however, entering into conversation with Alderman Parsons, asked the price of his horse, which the *Chevalier*, with true politeness, answered that it was beyond any price otherwise than His Majesty's acceptance. The King could not resist the acquisition of so perfect a hunter, even upon such terms; consequently, it was duly delivered at the Royal Stables. As a *quid pro quo*, Louis XV. gave Alderman Parsons—who was a famous brewer—an exclusive monopoly "of serving the French nation with his *Extract of Malte*," yclept in the vernacular "London Stout." It further transpired that in the course of this novel audience in the forest of Fontainebleau, that His Most Christian Majesty asked Alderman Parsons if all the Aldermen of London were as good sportsmen. We have not heard what the answer was, but we can vouch that at least the then Alderman of the Ward of Farringdon Without, Sir Francis Child, was a thorough sportsman, and fairly rivalled Alderman Parsons in the hunting-field. The former, however, principally patronised the City Hunt, which gave grand sport at this time (and, in fact, during the whole period it was led by Mr. Cuttenden, the "Common Hunt," from the time of his appointment to that office in September 1723 onward), and was rarely out with the Royal Buckhounds except when the latter pack hunted in Epping Forest. On those occasions, at Sir Francis Child's house at Brentwood, there usually assembled a large number of hunting men who (*more civitatus*) were regaled with a sumptuous banquet—the *menu*, the side dishes and the wines being circumstantially described by the intelligencers of the period; but, sad to say, never a word transpires relating to the runs. Although Alderman Parsons was a "common person" according to the supercilious ethics of "great" folks and centurions of those and later times, he could, nevertheless, boast of a pedigree dating from the Anglo-Saxon era. He was a good linguist, and could adapt himself to any society at home or abroad. He was a fine type of the metropolitan followers of the Royal Buckhounds of his day. His portrait, in hunting attire, is a rare and interesting souvenir of the chase of the early Georgian era. He was M.P. for London; served as Sheriff with Sir Francis Child in 1722; was Lord Mayor of London in 1730 (Sir Richard Brocas having preceded, and Sir Francis Child succeeding, him in the civic chair); and was again Lord Mayor of London in 1741. He died on March 21 in that year, lamented by all who had the pleasure of his acquaintance.

As to Ascot Races—which were first instituted in connection with the Royal Buckhounds in the reign of Queen Anne— there is very little doubt attending the assumption that those meetings had taken place annually during the reign of

ALDERMAN PARSONS IN HUNTING ATTIRE.

George I. Unfortunately we are unable to follow the annals of those races succinctly year by year. Nevertheless, some news of them was occasionally recorded by the chroniclers of those days. Thus we ascertain that on August 15 and 16, 1720, two Plates of 30 guineas were announced to be run for "on Ascott-Heath, in Windsor Forest," by hunters "used in hunting 12 months last past," which had never run for money or plate. The horses were to carry 11 stone on the first day, and 12 stone on the second day. They were to be entered "with Barlow, in Hatchet Lane," prior to August 8. The entrance fee was 2 guineas, or 4 guineas if entered at the starting post; but a "contributor" (to previous races of this sort?) had only to pay 1 guinea, "the entrance money to go to the second winning horse." The result of these two races has not transpired.

Early in August 1722 it was announced that "Forty Guineas" were "to be run for on Askott Heath, the 18th Instant, by Horses that have Stag-hunted in Epping or Windsor Forest with the King's hounds before the 2nd Instant, and have never won Five Pounds, to carry 11 Stone, three times round the four Miles Course at one Heat; to be entered at John Tempiro's at Sunning-Hill Wells, on Friday the 17th Instant; the Subscribers to pay one Guinea Entrance, no Subscriber two, or four at the Post; the Stakes to go to the second Horse." The result of this race has not been preserved, at least so far as our researches can penetrate the obscurity by which it is environed.

Fortunately, in 1724 and 1726, although we miss the "card," we find the winners. On Monday, July 11, 1724, the first Stag-Hunters' Plate of 30 guineas was won by Mr. Darby's Clubfoot; "next day the Lord Harry Beauclair's Puppet won the second of 20*l*." On Monday, August 8, 1726, the "staghunters' plate of forty guineas was run for on Ascot Heath, and won by Mr. Meggott's chestnut mare, carrying twelve stone"; and on the following day a Plate of 30 guineas was run for and won by Sir Thomas Reynolds' chestnut horse, carrying 10 stone.

CHAPTER XIII.

GEORGE II. (1727—1732).

Colonel Francis Negus, Thirty-sixth Master: June 11, 1727, to September 9, 1732.—Annual Cost of the Pack.—Records of the Runs from 1728 to 1732.—Ascot Races.

THE circumstances attending the accession of George II. are more or less detailed in all the standard works published on the history of England, which see. With the political surroundings recorded therein we have very little concern, consequently we shall confine ourselves to the reconstruction of the Royal Household so far as it bears upon our subject. One of the first appointments made by George II. was that of the Earl of Scarborough to fill the long-vacant office of Master of the Horse, which was received with acclaim. The intelligence produced exuberant delight at the Royal Mews, where the effigy of the Duchess of Kendal was burnt amid great rejoicings. The Earl was very popular with every one who had the pleasure of his acquaintance. He was a great favourite with the new King, by whom he was presented with a warrant on the Jewel Office to receive, by virtue of his office, 1,000 ounces of silver plate, "the same to be made into such articles and after such fashion as his Lordship shall direct." The next important office in the Household, which was practically vacant during the whole of the preceding reign, was the Mastership of the Buckhounds. To fill this post Colonel Francis Negus was apparently promoted on the very day of the King's accession. Although we have not been able to find the warrant of his appointment to the office of Master of the Buckhounds, we know beyond doubt he received the stipend of that post from June 11, 1727, "by virtue of an Establishment under His Majesty's sign manual dated December 20, 1727." The established allowance of this office was now fixed at 2,341*l.* per annum, out of which the Master had to defray all the ordinary charges of the pack from year to year. Some other incidents relating to his appointment are mentioned in our brief memoir of this Master, consequently we may leave him here for the present to follow his doings at the head of the Royal Buckhounds.

Partly owing to the Court being in mourning, political affairs, and the domestic arrangements of the Royal Family, no formal meetings of the Royal Buckhounds appear to have taken place in the season of 1727. Nevertheless we have official authority showing that at least 18 stags, 8 hinds, and 4 bucks had been hunted by the pack. Assuming each of those deer gave more than one run the sport must have been fairly good. Another proof of the popularity of the hunt, even in the unavoidable absence of royalty, is derived by the circumstance that on July 31 a plate of forty guineas was run for at Ascot, by such horses as had, during the season, carried their owners to the death of a leash of stags in Windsor Forest, twelve stone each; which race was won by Mr. Walter's grey horse Hobler, beating four others. For some reason or other the King evinced reluctance to inhabit Windsor Castle, and in the hunting seasons usually occupied, when he was in England, Hampton Court Palace and Richmond Lodge. As we have already seen, the latter was his local habitation and his home in summer, during his father's reign. In those days Richmond Lodge was quite unworthy to be occupied by any member of the Royal Family of the greatest nation in the world. The situation was good, the park charming, the house a wretched place swarming with vermin.* It went from bad

* "Richmond House having been very much pestered with vermin, one John Humphries, a famous Rat Physician, was sent for Dorsetshire by the Princess, through the Recommendation of the Marchioness of Hertford, who collected together above five hundred rats in His Royal Highnesses' Palace, which he brought alive to Leicester House, as a proof of his art in that way."—*Brice's Weekly Journal*, No. 29.

to worse, and was only tolerated now pending the projected improvements and enlargements designed to be carried out thereon.

In June 1728 the King paid intermittent visits to Richmond, and on the 8th of that month it was publicly announced "that His Majesty designs to take the diversion of Hunting in Windsor Forest in the month of August." The Prince of Wales—who subsequently became a staunch follower of the Royal pack—was languishing in a sort of political exile in Hanover. His Royal Highness was now expected "home." There was much ado, and little done, about arranging his establishment; and beyond the appointment of twenty-two livery servants belonging to the late King's stables, who had been discharged upon the setting up of the Household, were now taken into the service of His Royal Highness, no further steps were taken in that direction. On July 4 the King and most of the Royal Family arrived at Hampton Court, and on the 14th they dined in public for the first time. All comers were admitted into the banqueting room. The pressure of the public caused the rail surrounding the table to break, whereby many persons fell in upon the Royal Family, when the scramble for hats and wigs caused much diversion, "at which their Majesties laughed heartily." This incident shows, and subsequent ones prove, that the Royal Family were very affable, and did not disdain to mingle with the masses during the hunting seasons with the Royal Buckhounds.

Great preparations were being made, in the meantime, at Windsor against the opening day, which was fixed for June 27, at Hounslow Heath. The rendezvous was attended by the King and the Royal Family. His Majesty and the elder princesses were on horseback, the Queen in a calash and single horse, "in the same manner as Queen Anne used to hunt in Windsor Forest." There was a large attendance at the meet; unfortunately no news of the run transpired.

Hounslow, August 1, was the next fixture at which the King was present.

August 3, Richmond Park. — Their Majesties, Duke of

Cumberland, and the Princesses, attended by a great concourse of the nobility and gentry, hunted a stag, which was killed "after four hours' sport." The Royal party were very affable with the country people, "by conversing with them and ordering them money." The highwaymen were very attentive, some of the fraternity hunting belated hunting men even within the sacred precincts of Windsor Park! Owing to the death of Prince Ernest Augustus of Brunswick, the King's uncle, the Court went into mourning, and no hunting took place until Saturday, August 17, which was a red-letter day in the annals of the Royal pack. Between 10 and 11 o'clock "their Majesties, together with His Royal Highness the Duke, and their Royal Highnesses the Princesses, came to the new park by Richmond from Hampton Court, and diverted themselves with hunting a stag, which ran from 11 to 1, when he took the Great Pond, and defended himself for about half an hour, when, being killed and brought out by the help of a boat, the huntsman sounded the French horns. The skin was taken off, and the carcase given to the dogs. His Majesty, the Duke, and the Princesses Royal hunted on horseback; Her Majesty and the Princess Amelia hunted in a four-wheel chaise, and the Princess Carolina in a two-wheel chaise, and the Princesses Mary and Louisa were in a coach. Several of the nobility attended, and among them Sir Robert Walpole, clothed in green as Ranger. When the diversion was over, their Majesties, the Duke, and the Princesses refreshed themselves on the spot with a cold collation (as did the nobility at some distance of time after), and soon after two in the afternoon returned for Hampton Court."

Saturday, August 31, Sunbury Common.—Their Majesties and the rest of the Royal Family present. The stag took them across the Thames, and was killed in the Earl of Lincoln's park, after a chase of several hours. The Princess Royal came to grief, "but received no hurt."

Saturday, September 7.—Sir Robert Walpole and several noblemen "diverted Count Kinski,* the Imperial Ambassador,

---

* Count Philip de Kinski was at this time the Austrian Ambassador to our Court.

with Hunting in Richmond Park. The King's Buckhounds, being out of order they made use of Lord Viscount Palmerston's [harriers], and between 9 and 12 o'clock they Kill'd 2 brace of Hares." On this day the King, Queen, and Royal family paid their first State visit to Windsor Castle. "They went in the Park Way to the great Disappointment of the Mayor, Aldermen and Burgesses, &c., who were ready to receive them in their Formalities" at the State entrance. The next day their Majesties "dined in Publick as they will continue to do during their stay." The Castle was refurnished for this royal sojourn; among other necessaries one hundred new beds were put up for the servants.

Saturday, September 14, The Little Park.—The King, Queen, and all the Royal Family, attended by an immense concourse of nobility and gentry, roused a stag, which was killed about nine miles from Windsor. In honour of the occasion—it was Holy Rood Day—an elk was uncarted, and gave a brilliant run, which was worthy of the festival. "The sport was not over till 8 in the Evening when their Majesties returned to the Castle." The Royal Family were said to be well pleased with Windsor. "The Right Hon. Sir Robert Walpole is sending over to His Royal Highness Prince Fredrick a Hunting Suit made after the English manner"; and the Lord Chief Justice in Eyre presented Prince William with "a fine hunting horse."

On Saturday, September 21 and 28, their Majesties and all the Royal Family at Windsor followed the Buckhounds, and "were exceedingly diverted with that exercise."

Saturday, October 5.—Through some mistake their Majesties lost sight of the stag for three hours, and only cut in at the death.

Wednesday, October 9.—Their Majesties, accompanied by the Duke of Grafton, Sir Robert Walpole, "and many others of the Nobility and Quality hunted about Windsor Forest for several Hours, till the rain coming on, when their Majesties returned to the Castle to Dinner without having killed the stag." At this banquet the *piece de resistance* consisted of three herring-pies, which were presented, according to the ancient custom, by the Mayor, Aldermen, and Capital Burgesses of the town of Great Yarmouth, according to the charter of that corporation.

Saturday, October 12, was the last meet of the season at which the Royal Family assisted.

According to the official certificate 31 stags were provided to give sport with the pack during the season.

On Monday, October 14, the Staghunters' Plate was run for at Ascot. It was won by Colonel Negus' Grey Turk, beating Brigadier Honeywood's Marks Hall, Mr. Hankey's Foxhunter, and Mr. Yark's Hopeless. None of the Royal Family were present, they having arrived at St. James' for the winter season on the day in question.

1729.—At the opening of the hunting season of 1729 the King was absent in Hanover. The Queen was somewhat indisposed. The Prince of Wales had recently returned, after a long exile in Hanover, to assume his proper position in England, in which he acquitted himself as well as could have been expected.

When Frederick Prince of Wales arrived "home" from Hanover there were many expressions of public joy and local congratulations upon this untoward event. For some reason not very clear, but probably to gratify the Hanoverian party, the young Prince had never been allowed to visit England in the lifetime of George I. He now came over at the age of twenty-one, a pledge of the Protestant succession, and not without qualities to captivate the multitude, who were prone to love an heir-apparent better than a King. Unfortunately this fair prospect was clouded and darkened by faction. A corrupt clique of Jacks-in-office soon induced Fred to follow his father's example in caballing against his sire, and thus embittered what would have otherwise proved many pleasant days with the Royal Buckhounds. The Civil List was now in arrears, alleged to amount to 115,000*l.*; and although it was afterwards proved there was no such deficiency, yet the Government of the day persevered, and carried the bogus vote by a large majority.

Early in the month of August the Prince of Wales and the Princesses arrived at Richmond. The King was in Hanover. The first meet of the Royal Buckhounds, in this brief season, took place in Richmond New Park on Saturday, August 11, which was attended by Her Majesty, the Prince of Wales, the Duke of Cumberland, the Princess Royal, and the Princesses Amelia and Caroline, and a large field of all sorts and conditions of brave men and fair women. Notwithstanding the rain the run proved enjoyable; Her Majesty, attended by the Duchess of Hamilton, being in at the death of the stag, and then they returned to Kensington to dinner.

Thursday, August 14, Windsor Forest.—Present all the Royal Family (bar the Sovereign) and a large field. Short but fast run, and at finish all those who were up "were entertained with a magnificent dinner and a fine desert at the Lord Malpas's seat at Windsor." (His Lordship was Master of the Horse to the Prince of Wales.) The following day the King arrived in England; and on Wednesday, October 2, "their Majesties hunted in Richmond Park" for (so far as we can ascertain) the last time this season.

As appears, by the official certificate of the Master, 35 stags and 14 hinds were hunted by the pack in the vicinity of Windsor and Epping Forests during this season.

1730.—In the month of July we find the Court at Windsor Castle, and the highwaymen reaping a golden harvest from those whom pleasure or business obliged to journey thither from town. Detachments of cavalry were ordered to patrol the road from Hyde Park Corner to Windsor in order to protect the public. In the Forest a large body of military was encamped; to each of the officers' mess the King presented a fat buck. The troops had very little to do beyond levelling the Forest and making roads in the vicinity. Those military roads were admirably constructed; indeed, they soon became famous throughout the Three Kingdoms, and (especially in Ireland) still retain their reputation. Among the Royal guests at this time were two Indian chiefs. Their portraits were painted by order of the King, and at their departure he presented each of them with 100 guineas. The first mention of hunting was on August 1, when the Duke of Cumberland hunted the ram (according to ancient but brutal custom) with the Eton boys; a great concourse of fathers and mothers and sisters and brothers being present to see the fun, which was very cruel "sport." It had, however, one redeeming feature. The cap was sent round, as usual, and a considerable sum collected for the College Library.*

So far as we can ascertain, it appears that all the meets of the Royal Buckhounds which have been reported in this hunting season were held in the vicinity of Windsor Forest. The first took place on

Saturday, August 8, at which their Majesties and the rest of the Royal Family were present. A stag was roused near Colonel Crosby's house. A good run ensued. The Royal Family are said to have been in at the death, after a chase of about two hours.

Saturday, August 15.—All the Royal Family present; no details of this run. The Prince of Wales took a liking to Mr. Fleetwood's "very fine hunter, which he bought for 100 guineas."

Saturday, August 29.—The King and most of the Royal Family hunted a stag, when "an extraordinary accident happened. Two stags breaking herd together ran so for several miles, till at last the foremost (provok'd at the other's following him) turn'd at him, and with his brow antlers gor'd him in the side with such a great force, that he kill'd him on the spot. The other they hunted down, but carried him in a Cart to Sunning-hill, in order to save his life for another time, he being a very fine one."

Saturday, September 5.—Their Majesties, the Prince of Wales, and the rest of the Royal Family at the meet. A stag was roused near the Bear and Bell; ran to Bagshot, thence

* No offence meant. Eton is such a swell school now that this begging business in her antecedents may appear to be *infra dig*. But the fact is (*teste* Charles Kingsley) all our colleges were once charity schools endowed for the masses, but subsequently (and in these cases, at any rate) most appropriately appropriated by the "classes."

back to Swinley Pond, and got upon the island. The hounds brought him to bay there; but he defended himself so well that the King spared his life.

Wednesday, September 16.—"The Queen having some Returns of the Gout upon her, their Majesties did not hunt last Wednesday as usual. But the Prince of Wales put up a Stag at Low-Pond in the Great Park, which ran several Hours, and having given great satisfaction, his Royal Highness order'd his Life to be spared. On Monday Sir Robert Walpole bought a fine Pad, and made a Present of it to the Princess Amelia."

Saturday, September 19.—Their Majesties and "all the rest of the Royal Family" roused a stag at Cæsar's Camp; run three hours; all in at the death.

Early in October the Royal Family left Windsor for Richmond, and soon after returned to Kensington for the winter season. In the meantime some other circumstances occurred to which we must briefly allude. On August 30 the Earl of Carlisle was appointed Master of the Harriers and Foxhounds. This Royal pack had not been on the establishment of the Royal Household since the reign of James II. The revival was well received, as foxhunting was now becoming very popular. And we get the following particulars of Ascot races in connection with the Royal Hunt:—

To be run for by Hunters on Ascot Common, in Windsor Forest, on Monday, the 31st of August, 1730, Fifty Guineas; and on Tuesday, the 1st of September, Forty Guineas, by any Horses, Mares, or Geldings which have been or shall be at the Death of three Staggs hunted by his Majesty's Hounds in the Forest of Windsor, between the 1st of March last and the day of Running, carrying 12 Stone for the 50 Guineas, and 10 Stone for the 40 Guineas, the best of three Heats, each Heat being once round the Four Mile Course. No Horse, Mare, or Gelding which has won the Value of Fifty Pounds at any one Time in Plate or Money shall be entitled to either of the Prizes abovementioned. No Horse, Mare, or Gelding now kept in training or feeding for running for Plates or Matches shall be entitled to run for either of the aforesaid Prizes, notwithstanding they may be used or rode as Hunters at the Death of three Stags after this Advertisement. The manner and Rules for running to be according to the Rules used in running for the King's Plate at New-market; and if any Dispute or Difference about entring or running arise, the same shall be determined by the Judges of the Course, who shall be appointed Judges by the Duke of St. Albans. The Horses, Mares, and Geldings designed to run must be shewn and enter'd before the Judges at John Tempra's, at Sunning-hill Wells, the 28th of August, between the Hours of Ten in the Morning and Four in the Afternoon. If any Subscriber enters a Horse, Mare, or Gelding he shall not pay any Entrance Money; but any Person who has not shall pay two Guineas Entrance for the Fifty Guineas, and one Guinea for the Forty Guineas.

These races were afterwards postponed to September 7 and 8, when they took place with the following results: For the 50 Guinea Plate 9 horses started; it was won by a horse owned by the Duke of Newcastle, who gave his groom the stakes for his care and diligence, "and the Prince of Wales gave him 30 guineas more." The 40 Guinea Plate was won by Major Honeywood's mare.

According to the certificate of the Master of the Buckhounds, 48 stags were provided to give sport with the pack during this season, pursuant to the subjoined Royal Warrant:—

GEORGE R.

Underkeep^{rs} of his Ma^{ts} Forests for Kill^{g} Staggs, Hinds & Bucks wth his Ma^{ts} Hounds

Whereas we are well Informed that Our Roy^{l} predecessors thought fit to allow unto the Under Keep^{rs} wthin their Forests a Fee of 40^{sh} for each Stagg—20^{sh} for each Hind—and 10^{sh} for each Buck killed by their Stagghounds, and that, by means thereof the said Under Keepers were Encouraged to be diligent in their Offices, and to Harbour and preserve those Beasts of the Forest wthin their respective Walks, for the Royal Sport and Diversion; Now We being minded to Revive the said Fees, which have been discontinued to be paid to the said Under Keep^{rs} ever since our Accession to the Throne, have had an account laid before Us of all the Staggs, Hinds, and Bucks, killed by Our Stagg-hounds between the 11th day of

June 1727 and the 14th day of October now last past 1730, which Acco^t is hereupon Indorsed; And there by it appears that there is due and payable unto the said Under Keep^{rs} whose names are specified in the said Acco^t the Sum̃ of 286^{li}, as followeth :—For 131 Staggs at 40^s each, 262l.; 22 Hinds at 20^s each, 22l.; and 4 Bucks at 10^s each, 2l. Total, 286l.

Our W[ill] & Pl[easure] is and We do hereby Authorize Direct and Require you, out of any Monies coming to your hands for the Extra^{ry} Expense of Our Stables, to pay, unto the s^d Under Keep^r the said Sum̃ of 286l. in full of the s^d Fees, and of all Claims and Demands what so ever on Account thereof, from Our Accession to the Throne to the s^d 14th day of Octob^r last past. And Our further Will and Pleasure is that, out of the like Mo[neys] from time to time being and remaining in your hands; you pay unto the Under Keep^{rs} of the Walks within Our Forests yearly and every year, or at the end of every hunting Season in each year, so much as the same Fees of 40^{sh} for each Stagg—20^{sh} for each Hind—and 10^{sh} for each Buck shall amount unto for each Species happening to be Killed by our Stagg-Hounds in every such year or Hunting Season upon Certificates of the Numbers Killed, and the Names of the Under Keep^{rs}, with their Walks, to whom the same are or shall become payable, to be Signed from time to time by the Ma^r of Our Buck Hounds for the time being or otherwise attested to your Satisfaction. And for so doing this with proper Acquittances for the Sum̃s which shall now and from time to time be paid, pursuant to Our pleasure afore declared, shall be as well to you for paym^t as to Our Aud^{rs} for Allow^g thereof from time to time upon your Acco^{ts}, a sufficient Warr^t. Given at Our Court at St. James's this 14th day of March 1730 [-31] in the 4th year of Our Reign.

By his Majesty's Command

R. WALPOLE.
G. DODINGTON.
G. OXENDEN.

(Lords Commissioners of the Treasury.)

To the Earl of Scarborough,
Ma^r of the Horse.

Appending :—" An Account of the Staggs, Hinds, and Bucks

Hunted and Killed by his Ma^ts Hounds since his Ma^ts Accession to the 13th day of Octob^r 1730, viz.,

	1727			1728			1729			1730		
	S.	H.	B.	S.	H.	B.	S.	H.	B.	S.	H.	B.
In Windsor Great Park				3						3		
„ Cranborn Walks			3	1			1					
„ Swinley Walk	1	1		1			5	5		10		
„ East Hampstead Walk	2	2						1		4		
„ Bagshot Rails & Sandhurst Walks	1			5			3			6		
„ Billingbear Walk	1						1	1		5		
„ Newlodge Walk	5	2	1	12				4		3		
„ Old Windsor Walk	2			4			4			2		
„ Fan Grove Walk	1			1			3			3		
„ Twelve Oaks' Walk							1			1		
„ Richmond Park	6	2		4			5	2				
„ Epping Forest, viz.:—												
Epping Walk							3			4		
Waltham Stow Walk										3		
Park Hall Portico							2			2		
Hannault Walk							2			2		
Lowton Walk							4					
Ongar Portico							1					
Chinkford Walk							1					
	18	8	4	31			35	14		48		

Staggs, 131 at 40^s each, 262*l*.
Hinds, 22 „ 20^s „ 22*l*.
Bucks, 4 „ 10^s „ 2*l*.
Total, 286*l*."

—*Treasury Records.* K.W.B., vol. xxx., pp. 154–5.

Ladies continued to indulge immoderately in the pleasures of the chase, and the long, fast, and furious runs with the Royal Buckhounds occasionally superinduced more or less ill effects. Thus, in August 1729, we find Lady Hervey writing to Mrs. Howard (soon afterwards Lady Suffolk): "As your physician, I warn you against such violent exercise as you tell me you take. All extremes are, I believe, equally detrimental to the health of the human body, and especially to yours, whose strength, like Sampson's, lies chiefly in your head. If you continue your immoderate hunting, depend upon it, it will prove prejudicial to your constitution, as I find it does to my entertainment, and will in time rob you of as much satisfaction as it has already deprived me of."

Lady Suffolk, in a familiar letter to Mr. Gay (the poet) dated July 31, 1730, tells him that the ladies of the Court "hunt with great noise and violence, and have every day a very tolerable chance to have a neck brok." Lord Chesterfield, writing to her Ladyship, August 17, 1733, pays an unintentional compliment to the popularity of the hunt, which the pompous cynic says, "give the lie to those who complain of the uncertainty and instability of courts, since the same joyous recreations have, for these sixteen revolving years, been steadily pursued without interruption."

1731.—About the middle of July the King and the Royal Family arrived at Hampton Court Palace, where great preparations were being made for the projected Royal progress to York. This journey was soon after abandoned, to the great disappointment of the good folks in those parts, who had made elaborate preparations to give the Royal Family a welcome worthy of the occasion. The first meet of the Royal Buckhounds was announced to take place on July 28 in Windsor Forest, "weather permitting"; and on August 4 and 7 Bushy Park was the fixture. Beyond these bare announcements nothing further transpires. In the meantime, the hunting horses, used by the Royal Family in the chase, were being exercised and got into proper fettle;* the deer well looked after, and poachers, when taken, were punished with extreme severity.†

* "Last Thursday (July 29) one James Varo, a helper to his Majesty's grooms, was riding a grey horse, called *Walker*, in Bushy-park, which his Majesty generally used to ride a hunting: the horse started, and ran full speed against the pallisades before the Lord Hallifax's house, with such force, that he dash'd his brains out, and died immediately, and threw the rider on the spikes, where he hung a considerable time, but received little damage. A swan in the L. Hallifax's canal flew out of the water at the horse, who thereupon took flight. The same swan some time before flew at his Royal Highness, but did his Royal Highness no hurt."

† "On Sunday last John Nun and Baptist Nun, his brother, keepers of Windsor great and little parks, went with a complaint to Hampton Court, viz., That the two men condemned at the late Assizes for the county of Berks, for Deer stealing, had threaten'd their lives in case they should obtain a pardon, which they were in hopes of procuring, through the intercession of a Nobleman. The said Malafactors have since been ordered for Execution."—*Grub-street Journal*, August 19, 1731. [They were executed at Reading on the evening of Friday, October 7, following.]

Saturday August 14, Richmond Park.—The King, Queen, Prince of Wales, Duke of Cumberland, the Princesses Amelia and Caroline, accompanied by several lords and ladies, "took the Divershon of Hunting for the first time this Season." A stag was roused in Fan Grove. "In the midst of the sport, Sir Robert Walpole's fell just before the Queen's chaise and threw him in the dust, but he was soon remounted, and Her Majesty ordered him to bleed, by way of precaution. When the stag was run down, the King commanded the hounds to be call'd off."

Saturday, August 21, Richmond.—Their Majesties and the Royal Family, attended by the Earls of Scarborough and Grantham, Lord Malpas, and several other persons of distinction, roused a stag at Fan Grove; and after a chase of about three hours returned to Hampton Court. On the following Tuesday night "some rogues got into Richmond New Park where their Majesties hunt, and breaking one of the Sluices belonging to the Pond, let all the water out, to the great inconvenience of the deer."

Wednesday, August 25, Richmond.--The King, Queen, Duke of Cumberland, Princesses Amelia and Mary, and a large field arrived at the meet in the New Park. The Princess Amelia was thrown from her horse, but she received no hurt. Hon. Mr. Fitz-William, Page of Honour to His Majesty, also came to grief. Her Majesty and the Princess Mary on wheels were in at the death of the stag, after a good run of two hours. The Princess Royal was absent nursing the Prince of Wales, who was ill.

Saturday, August 28, Richmond. "On Saturday morning last the King, Queen, the Duke, and the Princesses, together with divers of the Nobility and Quality went again a staghunting in the New Park near Richmond. The Lord Delaware's Lady and the Lady Harriot d'Auverquerque, Daughter to the Earl of Grantham, had the misfortune to be overturned in a Chaise, which fell with such violence, that the shafts were broken, and the Chaise went over the Ladies; but providentually they escaped any visible Hurt. Mr. Shorter, one of the King's Huntsmen, had a Fall from his Horse, and received a slight Contusion on his head. The Stag was lost five Several Times: Their Majesties, together in a Chaise, and the Duke on Horseback, having hunted between three and four hours left the Field at One o'Clock; but the Princesses and Col. Negus continued the Chase for an Hour longer, and killed the Stag."

Saturday, September 11, Richmond.—All the Royal Family, except the Princesses Mary and Louisa, accompanied by several persons of distinction and a large field, hunted a stag from the New Park. The run warmed up with a kill about two o'clock, when the Royal Family returned to Hampton Court to dinner.

Wednesday, September 15, Richmond.—The Duke of Cumberland, the Princess Royal, and the Princess Amelia, with several persons of quality and distinction, roused a stag in the New Park. During the run the stag charged, gored, and threw Equerry Coulthorpe Clayton's horse. Mr. Thomas Walker, one of the Commissioners of Customs, was thrown from his horse, but not much hurt. Lady Susan Hamilton, Lady of the Bedchamber to the three eldest Princesses, was also unhorsed, " and immediately let blood by a surgeon in the field." " The stag having run a delightful chase for nearly two hours, was kill'd about 10 o'Clock, when their Highnesses returned to Court."

Wednesday, September 29, Windsor Forest.—" On Wednesday the Royal Hunters did not return from Windsor Forest to Hampton Court till 6 in the Evening. Coulthorpe Clayton, Esq., had the misfortune to put one of his shoulders out by a fall from his horse in the Chase." No further news of this run, which was apparently a good one. Mr. Clayton was not able to hunt again during this season. At this date he was a cornet in the Horse Guards Blue and one of the King's equerries, and soon afterwards was appointed Avenor and Clerk Marshal in succession to Colonel Negus.

Wednesday, October 6, Windsor.—No information. The Prince of Wales was to have joined in the hunt, " but being taken ill the preceeding night, the Guards were countermanded early in the morning." The neighbourhood was so infested with highwaymen that the Royal Family could not safely go from Hampton Court to Windsor without a strong cavalry escort.

Saturday, October 9, Windsor.—About 8 o'clock A.M. the King, Queen, Prince of Wales, and the three eldest Princesses set out from Hampton Court Palace to Old Windsor, where a stag was uncarted, "and ran but a short chase in the Great Park before it was kill'd." Major Selwyn, Equerry to Her Majesty, and Mr. Acourt, Page of Honour to Her Majesty, and "many others" of lesser note, came to grief without much hurt; but a youth, son of one of the hunt-servants, broke his neck, and died on the spot. The Royal Family returned between twelve and one o'clock to Hampton Court.

Saturday, October 16, Windsor.—This was a grand day. All the Royal Family were present, attended by the lords and ladies of the Court, and several of the nobility and gentry. H.S.H. the Duke of Lorraine, "who goes by the name of Count Blamont," was also present, accompanied by H.E. Count Kinsky and a distinguished suite, all well mounted, and eager for the chase. H.S.H. having a reputation of "a brisk sportsman, the hounds were order'd to run at full head; they roused a stag at Swinley, and kill'd at Blacknall; the chase lasted two hours, very hot." During the run James Lidderdale, M.D., physician to Lord Harrington, Master of the State Lotteries, was thrown, broke several of his ribs, "and beat one of his eyes almost out."

Mr. Delafaye, writing to the Earl of Waldegrave, then Ambassador at the court of Versailles, from Hampton Court Palace, October 15, 1731, gives the following particulars of the Duke of Lorraine's venatic visit, and the ulterior proceedings thereof:—

"The Duke of Lorrain is come at last, under the travelling name of Count Blamont. Count Kinsky brought him hither. They came to court in chairs (having alighted at Baron Hartoff's lodgings upon the Green): the guards took no notice of them, I mean by way of being drawn up or saluting. They alighted at the first gate and walked through the court, up stairs, through the grand chamber and the next room, into the cartoon gallery, at the door of which the housekeeper was placed to keep everybody else from going in. My Lord Hervey (vice-chamberlain to the King) waited in the cartoon gallery, and carri'd him that way into His Majesty's private apartment. Then I saw my lord chamberlain conducting his highness through the admiral gallery to the queen's apartment, where he saw (in private) her majesty and the royal family, except the prince of Wales, to whom he afterwards paid a visit, being carry'd also the private way. I imagined count Blamont would from thence have slunk away, but he was more gallant; went to the queen's circle, and saw the dining in publick, standing behind their majesties, or rather in some measure between their chairs. About a quarter of an hour's stay there, he went and dined at count Kinsky's at Isleworth, and so back to London to count Kinsky's house there, whither all the ministers went early this morning to pay their court to his highness, before they came to the King's levy here. The duke of Lorrain was not here this day; but to-morrow he is to meet their majesties and the royal family at the hunting in Windsor forrest, and they dine together, as I hear, at Cranborn lodge. The Duke of Newcastle will give his highness a great entertainment next week at Claremont. They talk of count Blamont's going to Newmarket at the end of next week, and that we shall then remove to town; but that is not certain."

In a postscript the intelligencer informs Lord Waldegrave that :—

"The hunting was last Saturday, as I wrote to your excellency was intended, but the dinner was here. There sate at the table the King, the prince of Wales on his majesty's right hand, and count Blamont on his left, and the ministers and great officers, and such others as his majesty was pleased to appoint, who sate *pêle mêle* without any distinction. They were about fourteen in all. It was in the beauty room next the privy garden. A play is now acting here, to which count Blamont is come from count Kinsky's. Tomorrow the Duke of Devonshire entertains his highness at supper in town. Wednesday is to be another hunting, and another dinner here. Thursday count Blamont goes to see a ship launched, and will be entertained by the admiralty. Friday he dines with my Lord duke of Newcastle at Claremont, and is to be at a ball here at court. Saturday another hunting. This day sen'night his highness goes to Newmarket, and comes back to town for the birthday; after which the duke of Grafton will entertain him, as is said, for some days at Euston, and sir Robert Walpole at Houghton."

It seems that the hunters used by the Duke of Lorraine were provided by the Master of the Horse at the King's expense.*

According to the official certificate of Colonel Negus 57 stags, 20 hinds, and 7 bucks, were provided to give sport with the pack, between October 14 and November 5, 1731, for which the several underkeepers received the usual fees, amounting to 138*l*. 10*s*.

During this year George II. completed the purchase, and thereby acquired, by payment of 2,688*l*. 16*s*., to the trustees of the late Richard Earl of Ranelagh, Cranborne Lodge in Windsor Forest, "together with all fees and profits thereunto belonging, and the pictures, furniture, and household stuff in the said Lodge or in any outhouses or offices belonging thereto." His Majesty, about the same time, also bought for 3,161*l*. 18*s*. 6*d*., forty-five acres of woodland adjoining Richmond Park, from the executors of Nathaniel Halhed, deceased. Both of these places were associated before, at, and in after times with the Royal Hunt.

1732.—For some time prior to the beginning of the Buck-hunting season the King was away in Hanover, and on July 10 it was publicly announced that the Queen Regent and the Royal Family designed to hunt twice a week during the ensuing season. On July 20 several of the Royal grooms arrived at the New Park, Richmond, with the hunters, etc.; and on the following day Colonel Negus arrived there from

* Jasper Smith stud-groom, for his own and several other grooms, horse-hire and travelling charges in attending upon the Duke of Lorraine on hunting into Norfolk, and in fetching up from Falmouth to Hampton Court two Barbary horses which came from Tripoli, 51*l*. 12*s*. . . . Richard Powell for travelling charges and expenses of himself, two grooms and two helpers in conducting seven horses of the Duke of Lorraine to Calais, and for their expenses back 54*l*. 14*s*. 6*d*.—*Vide* Accounts of Richard Earl of Scarborough, Master of the Horse, July 1731 to June 30, 1732 (Roll 39). For 4 saddle horses bought in the year 1731, for a present to the Duke of Lorraine, 181*l*. 5*s*. (Roll 40).

Ipswich. Thus all the preparations have been completed for the opening meet of the season.

Saturday, July 22, at Richmond, where we find the Queen in a calash, the Prince of Wales, the Duke of Cumberland, and the three Princesses on horseback, attended by several lords and ladies of the Court. A stag was put up in the New Park, and hunted for two hours; the Queen and all the Royal Family that were out having been in at the death. The Royal party dined at Richmond, and in the evening the Prince of Wales, the Duke of Cumberland, the Princesses Mary Caroline and Louisa, went to the theatre there, and saw the comedy called *The Careless Husband,* " and about Eleven at Night the Queen with all the Royal Family return'd to Kensington, escorted by a Guard of Horse Grenadiers."

Those members of the Royal Family joined the hunt at the meets held in the New Park on July 26, August 12, 21, 28, September 4, 18, and 25, each of which yielded an average run of about three hours' duration. The King, having returned from Germany, joined the Queen and his children at Richmond, and was out with them at the New Park on Saturday, September 30. He missed the well-known face and figure of Colonel Negus, who died in his hunting harness on the 9th of this month. Sir William Strickland, Secretary of War, was now nominated to fill the vacant office, but this was not confirmed. During this, and some subsequent runs, Sir Robert Walpole acted as Field Master of the Buckhounds; but the vacant office was not officially filled until shortly before the opening of the ensuing season. Now, to return to this, the first run at which the King participated this season. The stag gave a good spin of three hours, and was killed near Ham Green. During the chase Captain Jackson, Deputy Ranger of the New Park, fell from his horse and was much bruised; and " a Domestick belonging to Sir William Strickland," was thrown, rode over, and killed. The Prince of Wales rendered every assistance to the poor fellow, " placed him in a chariot and ordered particular care to be taken of him."

Saturday, October 7, Richmond.—Their Majesties and all the Royal Family, except the Princess Amelia (who "sprained her ancle and did not go"), attended by the officers of the Court, and a large field of ladies and gentlemen, roused in the New Park a stag which gave them a good run of three hours. It rained incessantly all the time. Sir Robert Walpole again acted as Field Master of the Buckhounds.

Saturday, October 14, Hounslow.—Their Majesties and all the Royal Family joined the meet at the Powder Mills, where a hind was turned out in the presence of "over a hundred ladys and gentlemen." After a pleasant chase of two hours she was killed at Twickenham. Grief—a page of honour to the Queen "left for dead in the field."

Wednesday, October 18, Hounslow.—All the Royal Family at the Starting Post on the Heath, where a hind was uncarted. "There was a grand appearance of nobility and gentry in the field, and the chase lasted about three Hours, when the Hind was killed at the further end of Sunbury Common."

Saturday, October 21, Hounslow Heath.—The King, Prince of Wales, Duke of Cumberland, and the three eldest Princesses went from Kensington to the meet, where a hind was turned out. The Queen and the Princess Caroline were in a calash; the King and the rest of the Royal Family on horseback. "His Majesty was thrown out by a countryman giving a wrong scent, and lost sight all the way." The hind ran towards Harrow-on-the-Hill. The Duke of Cumberland and the Princess Royal rode in view till the death.

Wednesday, October 25, Richmond.—The King, Queen, and all the Royal Family, "attended by several of the Nobility and Gentry," left Kensington at 6 A.M. for the New Park, where they roused a hind, which gave a good run of three hours. All the Royal Family were in at the death, and then returned to Kensington to dinner, "except the Prince of Wales who dined at his house at Kew." During this run "Sir William Billers, Knight and Alderman, dislocated his collar-bone, but having timely assistance there are hopes of his recovery." Sir William Irby, Bart., Equerry to the Prince of

Wales, fell with his horse, but received no serious hurt; Mr. Buckworth, Gentleman Usher to His Royal Highness, narrowly escaped being gored by a stag " which started suddenly upon his Horse and brok off part of his Whip"; and William Aldridge, one of the grooms to the pack, was badly bruised by a fall from his horse. The pack did not meet on the following Saturday. Many of the principal followers of the Buckhounds were at the Newmarket races; and the King's birthday festivities were the great attraction in town. The State Ball in Kensington Palace seriously interrupted the proceedings of the racing division at headquarters; the demand on the posting establishments vastly exceeding the supply. The King " was pleased to express his satisfaction at the good order the Buckhounds appeared to be in," and Mr. Lowen, the huntsman, was to have the charge and care of the pack till such time as a Master shall be appointed. This announcement dashed the hopes of many courtiers who were soliciting the appointment.

Saturday, November 11, Richmond.—Their Majesties and the Royal Family having arrived at the Lodge on Friday, November 11, for a short sojourn, they attended the meet in the New Park on the following morning, when a hind was roused, which gave a good run for three hours. Their Majesties pulled up about half an hour before the end of the run; but the Prince of Wales, the Duke of Cumberland, and the Princesses were in at the death, and afterwards returned to Richmond to dinner.

Wednesday, November 15, Richmond.—The Queen having been indisposed did not hunt. The rest of the Royal Family were out, and enjoyed a brief run of one hour's duration. At the end of the week the Royal Family returned to town; and so ended the season with this pack.

Now as to the " HON. FRANCIS NEGUS, ESQUIRE, M.P." (as he was officially styled), the thirty-sixth Master of the Royal Buckhounds, *temp*. George II., from June 11, 1727, to September 9, 1732, we are unable to say " what was his race or whence he came." On December 24, 1715, he was appointed, jointly with Coyners Darcy, Commissioner for executing the office of Master of the Horse, with a salary of 800*l.* a year during His Majesty's pleasure. Those gentlemen jointly held this office (the profits of which went to the Duchess of Kendal during the reign of George I.) until March 25, 1717. Colonel Negus was appointed sole commissioner for executing the same office—which he continued to fill until March 27, 1727—by another patent, according to which his salary was to be paid quarterly out of the Treasury, from June 10, 1716, at the rate of 800*l.* per annum, "in lieu of all perquisites, etc., relating to the said office." It seems that this carried with it the post of Avenor and Clerk Marshal to the King. The duties Colonel Negus had to perform in his capacity of Commissioner of the office of Master of the Horse were very onerous, and embraced a wide field of action.* To enter upon this subject would involve writing the history of the Royal Stud for the time being, a labour we respectfully decline to undertake. Colonel Negus was also Ranger of Bagshot Rails and Sandhurst Walks, and Lieutenant and Deputy Warden of Windsor Forest. He had a suite of apartments in Hampton Court Palace; and on the accession of George II. he relinquished his commissionership upon the appointment of the Earl of Scarborough to the long-vacant office of Master of the Horse.

We have not been able to find the warrant or the Royal

* The following items are taken from one membrane of Roll 30 : " William Nelson Sturgeon for setting the leg of Thomas Phipps one of H.M. huntsmen, 10*l.* 10*s.* To a person to teach several huntsmen to sound the French horn 7*l.* 6*s.* John Harris for 10 brass French horns and mending two others for H.M. huntsmen, 26*l.* 16*s.* Wm. Lowen, senior, H.M. chief huntsman as H.M. free gift when he was at Cranborne on Holy Rood Day, 1717, 53*l.* 15*s.* Jax Vanderwarden, falconer, for wages, etc., 103*l.* 9*s.* 6*d.* A couple of buckhounds given to the Duke of Lorraine's Envoy, 15 couple of staghounds sent to Zell (cost 5 guineas a couple), 5 staghounds a present to the King of Sweden, 20 dogs for the Emperor of Germany, 2 boar dogs and 2 bitches for the Emperor of Morocco, feeding the wild turkeys in Bushy Park, turning down pheasants in Windsor Park, distributing King's Plates at race meetings," etc., etc. He had to superintend the Royal Menagerie in Hyde Park paddock where the King's tiger was fed every day with six lbs. of boiled beef and mutton.

Sign Manual by which Colonel Negus was appointed Master
of the Buckhounds to George II. There is no doubt, however,
that he received this preferment almost immediately after the
King's accession. From non-official but reliable contemporary
evidence we ascertain that he kissed the King's hand upon
"his appointment of Master of the Buckhounds," and that he
set out to Harwich to contest the seat at the General Election
about this time. Having been appointed to this office prior
to that election he had not to vacate his seat and offer himself
for re-election through having accepted a "place of profit
under the Crown," otherwise the return of the writ would
have confirmed it more amply. At all events, the accounts of
the Treasurer of the Chamber distinctly show that he received
the emoluments of this office in full, commencing on June 11,
1727, "by virtue of an Establishment under His Majesty's
Sign Manual dated December 20, 1727." The stipend of his
office of Master of the Buckhounds, as we now find it re-
established, was 2,341*l*. per annum "for his salary and in lieu
of all charges thereof"; and he was paid at this rate down to
the Michaelmas quarter in the year 1732, " by virtue of a
warrant under His Majesty's Royal Sign Manual, countersigned
by the Lord Commissioners of His Majesty's Treasury, dated
26th day of October, 1732." Then we come to the final payment
relating to this Master: "To Francis Whitworth, Esq., without account which is to be esteemed as part of the allowance
on the Establishment for His Majesty's Buckhounds (and
which was payable to Francis Negus, Esq., as Master thereof
since deceased), to be applied and paid over by him to clear
the expense on account of His Majesty's Buckhounds for three-
quarters of a year ended at Midsummer, 1733, by three
warrants under the Royal Sign Manual—1,452*l*. 1*s*. 6½ *d*."

As may be gathered from the above chronicle of the runs
the name of this Master of the Buckhounds is rarely mentioned. Indeed, it is somewhat remarkable to observe, Sir
Robert Walpole figures much more prominently in connection
with this pack. The latter was a most enthusiastic follower
of hounds, and, of course, his position at the head (and tail) of

the Government tended to obscure the lesser Ministers and Court officials when he condescended to appear among them. Nevertheless, Colonel Negus was an intimate and trusted friend of George I. On Christmas eve, 1718, the King " supped with the Commissioner of the office of the Master of the Horse at his house in St. James's Mews"; and on August 20, 1720, he was summoned to Hanover to consult the King on the impending financial crisis in England; and he usually superintended the arrangements when the King departed from, and arrived at Harwich in his journeys to and from Hanover. Colonel Negus was likewise a great favourite with George II. and the Royal Family; and during the time he officiated as Master of the Buckhounds the pack was in good fettle, and frequently gave good sport. The "official horn" which had been entrusted to Mr. Lowen, the huntsman, during the reign of George I., appears to have been retained by that able though subordinate officer; and it seems the " official insignia " of the Master was the well-known golden couples. On July 1, 1729, Colonel Negus received the sad news that his seat at Dallinghoo, near Wickham Market, county Suffolk, had been burnt to the ground, together with all the furniture, pictures, etc., therein, worth 10,000*l.* He was High Bailiff of Harwich, and represented that borough in Parliament. He was also one of the Commissioners of the Lieutenancy of Middlesex and the Liberty of Westminster, and a Director of the Royal African Company. He died in his hunting harness at Swinly Lodge, on September 9, 1732, and was buried "in the New Chapel in the Broadway, Westminster." He left an only son. This is all we have been able to ascertain of the thirty-sixth Master of the Royal Buckhounds. His career was surrounded with a certain amount of mystery and obscurity, which we have been unable to penetrate. Even the erudite Davey, in his exhaustive collection of historical, topographical, and genealogical documents relating to the county Suffolk, hardly mentions his name. Like Lord Cardigan, his predecessor in this office, Colonel Negus had a few horses on the turf; and, like him, he never won a race except with a *bonâ fide* hunter.

CHAPTER XIV.

GEORGE II. (*Continued.*) 1733—1736.

Charles, Earl of Tankerville. Thirty-seventh Master. June 21, 1733, to June 1737 —Annual Cost of the Pack—Records of the Runs—Ascot Races.

ON June 21, 1733, pursuant to the subjoined Royal Warrant, Charles, Earl of Tankerville, was ordered to be sworn into the office of Master of the Royal Buckhounds, *vice* Colonel Negus, deceased :—

GEORGE R.

Our Will and Pleasure is, that you forthwith Swear and admit, or cause to be sworn and admitted, our Right Trusty and Right Wel-beloved Cousin, Charles Earl of Tankerville into the Office and Place of Master of Our Buckhounds ; To have, hold and enjoy the same during Our Pleasure, with all Rights, Fees, Salarys, Profits, Privileges and advantages thereunto belonging, in as full and ample manner, to all intents and purposes, as Francis Negus Esqr deceased, or any other Person hath held and enjoyed, or of Right ought to have held and enjoyed the same, And for so doing this shall be your Warrant. Given at our Court at Richmond the 21st day of June 1733, in the Seventh Year of our Reign,

By His Ma^{tys} Command

HOLLES NEWCASTLE.

To Our Right Trusty and Right
Entirely Beloved Cousin and
Councellor, Charles Duke of
Grafton, Our Chamberlain of
Our Household.

—*Home Office Records, Warrant Book,* vol. xix., p. 245.

As we have seen, in the last chapter, the office had been in abeyance from the death of Colonel Negus, and during that interval the Prime Minister, Sir Robert Walpole, acted in the capacity of Field Master to the Pack. In the meantime

Mr. Lowen, the huntsman, very ably conducted all the details. His superintendence merited and received the approbation of the King, and with the followers of the hunt his assiduity was much appreciated. From the death of Colonel Negus to the appointment of Lord Tankerville, it would appear, by the annexed warrant, that the wages of the six horse and three foot servants of the pack amounted to 784l. a year, but, apparently, this was exclusive of the salary of the huntsman and the annual expenses incidental to feeding the hounds, etc.

GEORGE R.

Horse & Foot Huntsmen their Salaries Mich^a Qua^r 1732 in ye Vacancy of ye Master of ye Buck Hounds } OUR WILL and PLEASURE is that out of such our Treasure as hath been or shall be issued to You at ye Receipt of our Excheq^r for ye Use of our Chamber whereof you are Treasurer You pay or Cause to be paid unto our Horse and Foot Huntsmen hereunder named ye Sums set against their respective Names amounting in ye whole to One Hundred and Ninety Six Pounds, Viz.:—

HORSE HUNTSMEN: Geo. Lowen 25l. Wm Lowen, Robt Shorter, Wm Ives, Wm Holmes, and Charles Remus 26l. each.

FOOT HUNTSMEN: John Webb and Robt Bickar at 15l. 10s. each, and Saml Perrin at 10l. Total 196l.

Which sum is to be esteemed as part of ye Allowance on ye Establishment of Our Chamber for our Buck Hounds wch was payable to Francis Negus Esqr as Master thereof who is lately deceased & is to be taken by ye said respective Huntsmen for one Quarter on ye respective Sallaries allowed them by ye said late Master and due at Michaelmas last 1732. And for so doing this shall be as well to you for payment as to our Auditors of ye Imprests, or either of them, for allowing thereof upon your Acc^s a sufficient Warr^t. Given at our Court at Kensington ye 26th Day of Oct 1732 in ye Sixth Year of our Reign

By his Ma^{tys} Command

R. W.
G. D.
W^m C.

To our Right trusty & Well beloved John Ld Hobart Treãfer of our Chamber.
—*Treasury Records*, K.W.B., vol. xxx., p. 475.

Lord Tankerville's stipend as Master of the Royal Buckhounds was at the rate of 2,341*l.* per annum, out of which he was obliged "to defray all the charges of the same."

On June 7 Lord Tankerville set out from London *en route* to Windsor, "with a gard of retainers and troops," to take command of the pack, and to make all necessary preparations against the opening of the hunting season.* Special precautions had to be taken to protect the followers of the hunt from the designs of the highwaymen, who were, at this time, most aggressive in the neighbourhood of Windsor and Epping Forests. Deer-stealers, likewise, were so industrious that a proclamation had to be issued offering a reward of 50*l.* for every one convicted.

In August, their Majesties, the Royal Family, and the Court arrived from Kensington at Hampton Court Palace, and the first meet of the Royal Buckhounds was announced to take place in Richmond New Park on Saturday, August 4. We have found no allusion to the inaugural meet of the season beyond an announcement in the *Gazette* that " Their Majesties and all the Royal Family " partook of that diversion on that occasion.

Wednesday, August 8, same meet.—Their Majesties, Prince of Wales, Duke, and all the Royal Family, accompanied by several persons of distinction, again out. No particulars or incidents of the sport.

Saturday, August 11, same meet.—Their Majesties, the Duke, the Princesses Royal and Amelia, accompanied by

* "A common occurrance at this time befel the Countess of Tankerville almost simelteanously with her husbands portentious journey to Windsor. It appears she was then staying on a vistit with the Duchess of Richmond at Goodwood. While she was 'taking the air' in a carriage, accompanied by the Duchess, Lady Hervey, Mr. Stephen Fox and the Dean of Chichester, they were attacked on Rook Hill by two highwaymen who ordered them to stand and deliver. Mr. Fox and Lady Hervey lost their gold watches, the Countess her gold snuff boox, and the Dean ' about eight guineas.' Soon after this incident we read that as Mr. Atlee, groom of the chambers to the Earl of Tankerville, was riding over Honslow Heath on his way to the Earl's Lodge in Windsor Forest, a 'Gentleman disguised in liquor,' wounded him in the body with a sword in a very dangerous manner, upon pretence that he suspected him to be a highwayman."

several lords and ladies of the Court, roused a stag "which the King had hunted three times last year, which [now] gave them very good diversion for about two hours, when his Majesty was pleased to order his life to be spared, and their Majesties left the chase: His Royal Highness the Duke, who was up with the Hounds, ordered he should be killed; when Sir Robert Walpole, as being Ranger of the Park, desired his Grace would excuse it, his Majesty having commanded his life to be spared."

Wednesday, August 15, Windsor Forest.—The first meet of the Buckhounds in the forest gave rise to much apprehension as to the safety of the Royal Family and the ladies and gentlemen of the Court. Highwaymen and deer-stealers and exasperated politicians were very aggressive; so much so that the Ministers of State took the precaution to order detachments of Life Guards and Grenadiers to escort the Royal family and the lords and ladies of the Court from Hampton to the meet. No unpleasantness occurred; large attendance, and fair run ensued. All the Royal Family up at the death.

Saturday, August 18, Richmond Park.—All the Royal Family out. The King and Queen pulled up after two hours, "but the Duke and the Princess Amelia were in at the death in an hour after, and then follow'd to Hampton Court."

Saturday, August 25, Richmond Park.—All the Royal Family out, except the Prince of Wales, who was cricketing,* and the Princess Royal, who was ordering her trousseau, those out having enjoyed a capital run. The Duke of Grafton, Lord Chamberlain, had the misfortune to be thrown from his horse into a mill-race near Datchet, and was seriously ill from the effect of the spill for some considerable time afterwards.

Saturday, September 1, Sunbury Common.—Their Majesties and some members of the Royal Family participated in a good

* This match was for a silver cup given by His Royal Highness, and played for by Mr. Stead's 11 men of Kent r. The Prince of Wales' 11 men of Surrey. On August 28 the Prince's 11 played against Lord Gage's 11 for 100 Guineas. Cricket became very popular in the reigns of George I. and George II., though its progress is not recorded in the books of reference on the game.

run. The stag was taken near Harrow-on-the-Hill, and the Royal hunting party then returned to Hampton Court.

Wednesday, September 5.—"Their Majesties and the Royal Family hunting a Stag in *Surrey*, he passed the River Thames, and took into some strong Inclosures near *Staines* in *Middlesex*, belonging to one *Richd. Violet*, who clap'd up a Chain, and refused the Sportsmen Admittance, telling the Noblemen, who expostulated with him, *he was King in his own grounds*. Some of the courtiers were for violent Measures; but their Majesties being informed of it, ordered the Farmer some Gold, and then he took down his Chain, and the Stag was soon after Killed." The good sense and tact here exercised by the King and Queen was a severe reproof to the indiscretion of those who, smarting at the check, would have overridden the law. Considering the unpopularity of the Court at the moment, we must commend the farmer's conduct, as—

"One whose free actions vindicate the cause
Of sylvan liberty o'er feudal laws " (*Scott*).

Saturday, September 8, St. George's Hill (Surrey side).— Stag uncarted; gave a good run for nearly two hours, and killed on Red Hill. King, Queen, and the Royal Family reported to have taken part in the "diversion."

Wednesday, September 12, Richmond Park.—"The Stag that was roused at Fan-Grove, carry'd the Royal Family a Chase of about 40 Miles, four Miles beyond Bagshot. The King changed his Horses four Times, and at length order'd the Dogs to be call'd off: Their Majesties and the Royal Family dined with the Earl of Tankerville at Swinley Lodge, upon a cold Collation: The King commanded Lady Tankerville to sit down at Table; and their Majesties being highly delighted with the Sport as well as with their Entertainment, return'd about Five in the Evening to Hampton Court."

Saturday, September 15, Sunbury Common.—The first hind of the season was uncarted in the presence of their Majesties, the Prince of Wales, the Duke of Cumberland, the three eldest Princesses, and a large field of the nobility and gentry. "A

Contribution being annually made in Favour of the Huntsmen on the first Day of their Majesties hunting the Hind, the Earl of Tankerville, Master of his Majesty's Buckhounds, held the Purse, and collected about 360*l.* on the Spot, their Majesties giving 50 Guineas each, his Royal Highness the Prince of Wales 40 Guineas, the Princess Royal 30 Guineas, the Duke and the other Princesses 50 between them; the Ministers of State and others of the Nobility gave five Guineas each." This is the first circumstantial account we have met with of this custom. It seems to have yielded a good round sum, and if the liberality evinced on this occasion usually prevailed, it was very profitable to the deserving recipients. The hind was uncarted at 11 A.M., gave a good run of three hours, during which she crossed and recrossed the Thames several times, and at last was killed near Weybridge.

Saturday, September 22, Sunbury Common.—Almost a repetition of the preceding meet, except in the final incident. The King ordered the hind's life to be spared, and a silver collar to be put round her neck. She was not to be hunted again.

Wednesday, September 26, Sunbury Common.—Hind turned out; ran for three hours, when "their Majesties order'd the Dogs to be taken off between Egham and Old Windsor, and return'd about Two to Hampton Court to Dinner." *

Saturday, September 29, Sunbury Common.—Hind turned out. "Ran thro' Feltham, over part of Honslow Heath and Twickenham Common and through Hampton Town, where taking to the River, several of the Courtiers swam their Horses over, but then the Hind return'd, and crossed the Tames between Teddington and Twickenham, and after a most delitful Chace of about three Hours, was kill'd on Sutton Common

---

* Her Royal Highness the Princess Royal "lost a very curious wrought snuff-box, in the lid of which was a fine picture of great value, and the same was picked up by Mr. Wright, a Gentleman of the Life Guards, who was on duty to attend the Royal Party in the Chace. H.R.H. did not miss it till her return to Hampton Court, when upon Enquiry the Commanding Officer acquainted her who had found it, upon which Mr. Wright immediately attended with it, and H.R.H. was pleased to receive it from his own Hands, and to make him a Present of Five Guineas." Fortunate Princess! Lucky Guardsman!

between Kingston and Epsom. It was remarkable that at this Hunting the Huntsman mistook an Ass for the Hind * in the Chase, and led on the Dogs, who followed that Scent for about Ten Minutes, to the great Diversion of the Company, when it was discovered."

Wednesday, October 3, Feltham.—The King, Queen, Prince of Wales, Duke of Cumberland and some of the Princesses, " attended by the Great Officers and others of the Court, came to Feltham-Field, where a Hind was turn'd out of a Waggon, and after running about an Hour and a Half swam across the Thames between Sunbury and Hampton; the King and the Duke on Horseback, the Queen and the Princess Royal in a Chaise, ferry'd over at Hampton Town, with great numbers of others, and many swam their Horses thro'; the Hind turn'd back over the River between Weybridge and Shepperton, and between One and Two was killed in Chertsey Meads."

Saturday, October 6, The Rubbing House, Epsom.—Hind turned out in the presence of their Majesties and the rest of the Royal Family, " which led them a Chace of about 50 Miles, and was kill'd about Four o'Clock in the Afternoon, near Godstow, between Rygate and East Grinstead in Sussex. The Lady Arabella Finch was thrown from her Horse, and lay for some Time before she could get Help. The Royal Family dined with Lord Baltimore, at his House near Epsom, and returned about six to the Royal Palace at Hampton Court."

Wednesday, October 17, Sunbury Common.—Their Majesties, the Duke of Cumberland, and the three eldest Princesses present, accompanied by the usual suite, hunted a hind, which swam across the Thames towards Waltham, and then headed for Esher, when, after a chase of two hours, she was killed near Upper Moseley.

Saturday, October 20, Hounslow.—Their Majesties, the Prince of Wales, and the rest of the Royal Family, attended by several persons of quality, went from Hampton Court to Hounslow Heath, " where a Hind was turned out near the Starting-Post and hunted, which gave very good diversion for about four

* A somewhat similar instance is reported in the *Field* of September 3, 1887.

hours, and was at last Kill'd about half a mile from Hampton Town; after which their Majesties and the rest of the Royal Family return'd to Hampton Court to Dinner. Col. John Lumley, Brother to the Earl of Scarborough, fell from his Horse, but receiv'd very little damage. The Prince of Wales had like to have been unhors'd by a Country Fellow, who rode furiously against His Royal Highness. A Boy, son of the Earl of Berkeley's huntsman, happen'd to be thrown from behind a Coach, and Mrs. Andrews of Sunbury being in full Chace, the wheels of her Chaise ran over his Thighs, but the Child only received a slight bruise. The Queen order'd him a Guinea."

Wednesday, October 24, Hounslow.—Their Majesties and the rest of the Royal Family, except the Princess Louisa, went to the Earl of Isla's near Hounslow, where a hind was turned out, " but hurting one of her legs in coming out of the Waggon, ran a very short Chace, being Kill'd about 12 o'clock, near Hesson, two Miles beyond Hounslow." For some reason not mentioned we are told that "the Earl of Tankerville, as Master of the Buckhounds, removed Mr. William Lowen from being Yeoman-Pricker (or Marker of the Hounds Feet), which Place he and his Father had held for Fifty Years," and that "Sir Robert Walpole has made the said Mr. Lowen Huntsman of the Harriers in the New Park near Richmond."

Thus the last run of the season was associated with a considerable amount of grief. During the ensuing week the Royal Family returned to town, where great preparations were in progress anent the marriage of the Princess Royal. On November 7 the Prince of Orange arrived. Shortly before the wedding fixture he was prostrated by a fever; the nuptials had to be postponed, which caused great disappointment, and much sympathy was manifest for the bride elect, who was deservedly popular with all classes (particularly in hunting circles) throughout the length and breadth of the land.

According to the official record 100 stags and 64 hinds were "hunted and killed" by His Majesty's Buckhounds between November 5, 1731, and January 2, 1733-4. The fees payable thereon, "to the keepers of His Majesty's forests and parks," amounted to 267*l*.

William Lowen, G. Mathews, E. Booth, "and Theophilus Aldridge and Wm. Albut, successively gamekeepers for watching, keeping, and preserving the game of all kinds within and for the district of 10 miles about the Palaces of Richmond and Hampton Court at 30*l*. per annum each for their salaries and 10*l*. each per annum each for their liveries," received in 1733, 160*l*.

1734.—The Earl of Scarborough resigned his office of Master of the Horse to the King in February 1734, and was succeeded by the Duke of Richmond shortly before the opening of the hunting season in July. In March the long-deferred marriage of the Princess Royal to the Prince of Orange was celebrated in London. The happy couple departed for Holland soon after the ceremony. The princess returned to England a little before the buck-hunting season began, the first meet in the year 1734 having been announced to take place on Saturday, July 17, at Richmond New Park, at which their Majesties and all the Royal Family were expected to be present. For some reason or other the opening day was not honoured by any member of the Royal Family. The result of the run is not known, nor any incidents, except that Sir Robert Walpole was, as usual, to the fore, and officiated as field master of the pack.

Monday, July 29, Richmond.—The Duke of Cumberland and several persons of distinction enjoyed a moderate run; His Royal Highness afterwards dined with the Prince of Wales at Kew.

Wednesday, August 1, same meet.—Their Majesties, the Prince of Wales, the Duke, the Princess of Orange, and the Princesses Amelia and Carolina, "being attended by several Persons of Distinction, went from Kensington to Richmond New Park, and took the Diversion of hunting a Hind (being the first Time for this Season), which afforded excellent Sport for about two Hours; and his Majesty was pleased to order his (*sic*) Life to be spared: After which His Majesty and the Royal Family returned to Kensington to Dinner."

Saturday, August 3, same meet.—Except the Princess Amelia, all the members of the Royal Family which were in the preceding run were present again, and in at the death of the first stag: "They afterwards hunted another, but His Majesty ordered his Life to be spared, and about 3 o'clock returned to Kensington."

Wednesday, August 7, same meet.—The Princess Amelia, her brothers and sisters, with her father and mother, attended by several lords and ladies of the Court, hunted a stag, "which afforded very good sport for about three hours, and afterwards took the water; where the Dogs must have inevitably been drowned in pursuing, if the Yeomen Prickers had not taken to a Boat, and Killed the Stag in the Water."

Saturday, August 10, same meet.—The Duke of Newcastle, the Earl of Tankerville, Sir Robert Walpole, and several persons of distinction, hunted a stag and killed after a long chase. "They afterwards dined at Capt. Jackson's Lodge in the said Park. That morning being wet, the Royal Family did not hunt."

Wednesday, August 14, same meet.—Their Majesties and the rest of the Royal Family out. The King in at the death after a chase of two hours; "but her Majesty had but little share in the Diversion, she continuing in her Chaise best part of the Time under a Tree."

Monday, August 19, same meet.—The Duke of Cumberland attended by a great number of the nobility out. "The first Stag that was rous'd not being capable of giving Diversion, the Dogs were called off, and a second unharbour'd, which ran for three Hours, when his Royal Highness declaring his Pleasure to have his life sav'd, the Huntsman acquainted him that the Dogs would receive great Prejudice in being so often called off in full Scent, whereupon the Chase was continued some Hours longer, till most of the Field being thrown out, and all the Hounds to two or three Couple, his Royal Highness was Pleased to command the Stag to be spared."

Wednesday, August 21, same meet.—"Wednesday before Nine in the Morning their Majesties, together with the rest of the

Royal Family, went from Kensington to Richmond New Park, to hunt a Stag: During the Chase the Princess Amelia had the Misfortune to be thrown by her Horse, and her Petticoat hanging on the Pommel of the Saddle, she was dragg'd near 200 yards, but most providentially receiv'd no Manner of Hurt: The Right Hon. Harry Pelham took her up. Her Royal Highness afterwards remounted, in order to pursue the Chase, but the Queen would not permit it, so she returned to Kensington in a Coach an Hour before the Sport was over, and was blooded in her own Apartment by Mr. Ranby, one of the King's Surgeons. His Majesty order'd the Stagg's Life to be spared, to the End he might be hunted again. Several persons were unhorsed in the Chase."

Saturday, August 24, same meet.—Princess Amelia gone to Bath. Their Majesties and the rest of the Royal Family present at the meet, which attracted the usual crowd. "A Woman whose curiosity had carried her thither with a Child of about two Years old in her Arms, had the Infant thrown down by a Horseman's riding over her, and a Coach and Six Horses flying by at that Instant the Babe was trodden to Death and the Woman miserably bruised." The Earl of Londonderry *—"a Youth of about 17 Years of Age who was at School at Cheam"—joined in the chase, and after he had ridden about a mile was thrown and killed on the spot. This fatal accident threw a cloud over the run; beyond the record of the grief nothing else has been recorded, except that the field included Prince Charles, "nephew to his most Serene Highness the Elector of Treves," accompanied by two German noblemen; there were also present two Indian chiefs † from America, who had brought with them, as a present to the King, the "body of a flying horse," which died on the voyage.

Wednesday, August 28, Hounslow Heath.—The King having

---

* Thomas Pitt, second Earl of Londonderry.

† These were Tomo-chichi and another chief of the Creeks. They arrived from America to do homage at Court. They were "Buffalo Bill'd" by Colonel Oglethorpe. Query if the "Flying Horse" was a Bucker Mustang, and so called by the animal's ability to send its rider *flying*.

decided to make Hounslow his hunting headquarters for the rest of the season, all the hunters of the Royal Family were sent on there from Hampton Court. About 9 A.M. on Wednesday morning, their Majesties and all the Royal Family (except the Princess Amelia) set out from Kensington to the new fixture. On their arrival there a stag was turned out at the starting post. He headed for Staines, but being turned ran as far as Brentford, where he crossed the Thames, recrossed the river at Hampton Town, ran through Staines, and thereabouts crossed the river twice, "and was kill'd about half-an-hour after Three, at Water-Oakley near Windsor. Their Majesties gave out at Thorp, about a Mile from Staines, after following him above 30 Miles; but their Royal Highnesses the Prince and Duke were in at the Death." The latter dined at the "Red Lion" at Hounslow, "having been so fatigued with the Diversion of hunting the Stag that Day (who ran one of the most delightful Chaces ever known), that they could not reach the Palace at Kensington by Dinner-time."

Saturday, August 31, same meet.—Present their Majesties and all the members of the Royal Family above mentioned, accompanied by "the Lord High Chancellor and several other Persons of Distinction. The Stag ran them a Chace of about three Hours, and about twenty Miles, and was kill'd two Miles beyond Watford in Hertfordshire. He ran so very hard, and in such an enclos'd Country, that there were but six Gentlemen in at the Death, and but few of the Huntsmen; and to encourage the Dogs, they were suffer'd to eat the whole Stag. The Duke in riding pitch'd over his Horse's Head, but received no Hurt by the Fall, and was first in at the Death."

Wednesday, September 4, same meet. — Present, their Majesties and most of the Royal Family. No details of the run.

Saturday, September 7, same meet.—No information.*

Wednesday, September 11, same meet.—"Their Majesties and the rest of the Royal Family hunted a Stag on Honslow

---

* The Prince of Wales hunted with the City Hounds. The meet was at Cheshunt, Herts, "the Lord Mayor's Country House being near that Place."

Heath, which ran several times across the Thames, and about three o'Clock was Killed near Egham; after which their Majesties and the rest of the Royal Family accepted an Invitation to dine at his Grace the Duke of Newcastle's at his Seat at Clermont."

Saturday, September 14, same meet.—The King, Queen, and Royal Family present, "where a Stag was turned out of a Deer Waggon, and run by Hanworth, down French-street, in Sunbury, and cross'd the Thames below that Town, run up Walton Field, and so to Walton Common and over Redhill by Ockham, and was kill'd near Effingham in Surrey. The King cross'd the Thames at Sunbury, but the Stag was, when his Majesty landed, gone above half an Hour before. The Queen, Princess Royal, and Princess Caroline, cross'd the Thames in their Chaises at Walton, but all the Royal Family were not in at the Death. The Prince in his return from hunting stopt and refresh'd himself at Col. Wyvill's at Walton, and went afterwards and din'd at Sir John Chardin's at Kempton Park near Sunbury. This being Holy Rood Day when their Majesties leave off Stag hunting, and on which Day the Contribution or Bounty Money is usually given in Favour of the Huntsmen, the Right Hon. the Earl of Tankerville, Master of his Majestie's Buckhounds, held the Purse, and collected near 300 Guineas, their Majesties giving 100, the Prince of Wales 40, the Duke, the Princess of Orange, and the Princess Caroline, 50 between them, and most of the Noblemen five each."

Wednesday, September 18, same meet.—The Duke of Cumberland and numerous persons of quality had a good run of three hours, and killed the stag near Harrow. The Duke and several noblemen were mired in a bog near the Powder Mill on Hounslow Heath.

Saturday, September 21, same meet.—"Their Majesties and the Royal Family diverted themselves with hunting a Stag (that had been hunted several Times before) which afforded very good Diversion for near four Hours, when his Majesty order'd his Life to be spared, and returned with the Queen and Princesses to Kensington to Dinner. The Prince of Wales and the

Duke continued the Chase for some Time after, and at length the Prince return'd to his House at Kew, and the Duke to Kingston." As the Princess of Orange and the Princess Caroline were returning to Kensington a wheel came off of their carriage, and they were nearly spilled; but fortunately the coachman pulled up the horses in time, and thus prevented any accident to the fair Dianas, beyond a slight shock. As a precautionary measure the Princess of Orange "was let blood" on her arrival at the Palace. This was her last day in the hunting fields of old England.

Wednesday, September 25, same meet.—Duke of Cumberland and a large field out. Killed the stag near Harrow. His Royal Highness thrown, but without damage. Bad weather prevented their Majesties joining in the chase.

Wednesday, October 2, same meet.—Their Majesties and some of the Royal Family, attended by several lords and ladies of the Court, hunted a hind, "which afforded a pleasant chase of about 4 hours, and was killed near Brentford." The young Earl of Londonderry, who was on a visit with the Royal Family, was in this run, and had for his pilot the King and the Prince of Wales. With all their faults, this much-maligned King and Prince had their hearts in the right place when any circumstance deserving of sympathy came under their notice.

Saturday, October 19, Richmond New Park.—Their Majesties and some of the Royal Family at the meet. No details of the sport, which seems to have been eclipsed by the grief. "Mr. James Fouch, a Groom belonging to his Royal Highness, was thrown from his Horse, by which Accident he had the Misfortune to break his Collar-bone, together with one of his Legs; but they were immediately set by Mr. Ramby, the King's Surgeon. Mr. Lowen, head Groom to his Majesty, was likewise flung off his Horse, and broke his Arm." So much for the last run with the Royal Buckhounds in that season, so far, at least, as the reports of the proceedings of the pack have been chronicled. As in previous cases, many runs cannot be traced; but upon the whole the season appears to have been a good one, 60 stags and 17 hinds having been hunted and killed, as appears by the fees paid by the Master of the Horse to the Keepers of Windsor Forest, Windsor Great Park, Richmond Park, and Epping Forest, amounting, at the usual rates, to 155*l*.

1735.—Parliament was prorogued in the last week of July, when the Queen Regent announced her intention of hunting with the Royal Buckhounds on Wednesdays and Saturdays during the ensuing season. The first meet took place in the New Park, Richmond, on Saturday, August 9.

In the meantime the horses appear to have headed the hounds, so far as related to the races at Ascot, which were held in the preceding week. On Monday, August 4, the 40 Guinea Plate for hunters carrying 12 stone each was won by Mr. Moor's sorrel gelding Spot, from the Earl of Tankerville's bay stone horse Achilles, the Hon. Mr. Masham's chestnut gelding Farmer, and Captain Clayton's cropped gelding Squirrel. The next day the Huntsmen's Plate of 10 guineas for horses, etc., carrying 10 stone each, was won by Mr. Richell's grey gelding Augur-Eye, from Mr. Lowen's bay stone horse Whitefoot, Mr. Ives' bay stone horse Tantivy, Mr. Holme's bay gelding Mad Cap, Mr. Tempro's chestnut gelding Fearnought, Mr. Webb's black gelding Tinker, and Mr. Shorte's bay mare Tumble Down; and on the Wednesday the Duke of Marlborough's chestnut gelding Diver won the 30 Guinea Plate, for horses, etc., carrying 10 stone each, from Mr. Bowler's bay-brown mare Miss Rattle. This was the first meeting at Ascot that extended over three consecutive days, with one race per diem, including "a great Match of Cock-fighting at the sign of the Flower-de-luce in Hatchet Lane, for two Guineas a Battle, and Twenty Guineas on the odd Battle, between the Gentlemen of Hampshire and the Gentlemen of Berkshire." *Festina lente* seems to have been the motto of the C.C.

Let us now hark back to the opening day. First and foremost it was announced that "Upon Account of the great Crowds and Throngs of People that have attended the Stag-Hunting at New-Park, when the Royal Family were hunting there, which has rendered the Riding there not only very troublesome, but very dangerous, her Majesty has been pleased to order, That no Person shall be admitted into the Park without a Hunting Ticket, prepared for that Purpose, with the Date of the Day, and the Seal of the Ranger; to be given Weekly, by the Ranger or his Deputy, upon proper Application." The Prime Minister, who was Ranger there at this time, must have had his hands pretty full. (By the way, he had just presented the Princess Amelia with "a fine hunting horse.") With the exception of the King, who was boar-hunting in Hanover, and the Princess of Orange, who had recently presented her husband with an heir, all the Royal Family followed the stag, "which afforded excellent sport for near three Hours."

Saturday, August 16, same meet.—All the Royal Family above mentioned hunted a stag "for above two Hours; after the Death Her Majesty returned to Richmond to Dinner, and in the Evening to Kensington."

Monday, August 18, Windsor Forest.—The Duke of Cumberland and the Princess Amelia, attended by the Duke of Grafton, Sir Robert Walpole, and several persons of distinction, "took the Diversion of Staghunting in Windsor Forest."

Saturday, August 23, Richmond.—Her Majesty and the Royal Family out, and in at the death of the stag after a run of about two hours.

Wednesday, September 3, Windsor.—"On Wednesday morning about Four o'Clock [A.M.], their Royal Highnesses the Duke and Princess Amelia set out from Kensington, and about Eight rous'd a Stag in Windsor-Forest, which gave them very good Sport for near five Hours, when he was kill'd at Billingbear near Egham; soon after which they accidentally rous'd an outlying Stag, which continued their Diversion till about Four in the Afternoon, when their Royal Highnesses quitted the Chace, and did the Earl of Tankerville the Honour of dining with him at his Lodge at Swinley." The Prince of Wales lost this good run and 1,000*l.* besides, for which sum he backed his eleven against Kent in a cricket match.

Saturday, September 6, Richmond.—All the Royal Family

hunted a stag, which was killed in the pond "after a pleasant chase of three hours."

Saturday, September 13.—Two meets were announced for this day—viz., at Richmond and Hounslow. At the latter a hind was to be turned out for the first time this season. We cannot find any further reference to either of them.

Wednesday, September 17, Windsor. — The Duke of Cumberland and the Princess Amelia hunted a hind in the forest, which was killed after a pleasant chase of about two hours, and afterwards dined with the Master at Swinly Lodge.

Saturday, September 20, Richmond.—Her Majesty and the rest of the Royal Family hunted a hind, which was killed after a good run of three hours. The Queen dined at Kew, and afterwards returned to Kensington.

Saturday, September 27, same meet.—The Queen, Prince of Wales, Duke of Cumberland, the Princesses Amelia and Caroline, attended by several persons of distinction, hunted a stag. No details of the run mentioned.

Saturday, October 4, same meet.—All the Royal Family, "attended by several Nobles of the Court," hunted a stag for about two hours. Her Majesty afterwards dined at Kew, and returned to Kensington in the evening.

Wednesday, October 15, Windsor.—The Duke of Cumberland and the Princess Amelia, attended by the Dukes of Newcastle and Grafton, and other persons of distinction, "took the Diversion of hunting a Hind in Windsor Forest."

Saturday, October 18, Richmond.—The Queen and all the Royal Family hunted a hind, "which afforded a pleasant chase for two hours." This was the last run of the season with the Royal Buckhounds. The King arrived at Harwich from Hanover on Sunday, October 26, consequently he could not have hunted with this pack at all, although he had good sport at Gohree during his absence from England.

It is somewhat remarkable to notice that during this season there is not a single instance of grief recorded. Possibly the reporters had instructions not to go into details. If they offended, the hunting ticket might have been withheld, so far, at least, as the meets in Richmond Park were concerned.

The official record of sport with the pack for this season shows that 54 stags, 36 hinds, and 2 bucks were hunted and killed, and the fees paid thereon to the keepers amounted to 145*l*.

1736.—The Parliamentary Session having closed in May, the King proceeded to visit his German dominions, as he had likewise done in the preceding year, taking with him Mr. Horace Walpole as Deputy Secretary of State, and leaving the Queen as Regent in England. During his absence, the tranquillity which England had now enjoyed for so many years was slightly ruffled. A great number of poor Irish having come over in the summer, not merely worked at the hay and corn harvest as was usual, but engaged themselves at the Spitalfields looms at two-thirds of the ordinary wages. The cockney weavers, declining to have their wages reduced from 10s. and 12s. to 6s. or 8s. a week, raised riots on several nights during the first week of the buck-hunting season, and attacked a public-house where the Irish resorted. Similar riots occurred about Michaelmas, when the new Gin Act came into operation. But the presence of Sir Robert Walpole on both of these occasions checked these riots without bloodshed or injury or damage. In Edinburgh, however, a serious disturbance took place, culminating in the well-known Porteous riots, by which the Queen was greatly irritated, as she construed them to be an insult to her person and authority. There is a tradition that Her Majesty, in the first burst of her resentment, petulantly exclaimed to the Duke of Argyle, that, sooner than submit to such things, she would make Scotland a hunting field. "In that case, Madam," answered Argyle, with a profound bow, but with no courtly spirit, "I will take leave of your Majesty, and go down to my own country to get my hounds ready!" Eventually these difficulties were overcome, and domestic affairs again ran smoothly in the old grooves.

Unfortunately another obstacle had arisen in the bosom of the Court. Frederick, Prince of Wales, was now in open opposition to his father and mother's Court. Although in political alliance with many honourable patriotic members of the opposition, there was a back-stairs influence of unprincipled persons, by whom he was unwittingly led away from the right path. His marriage in April 1736, to Augusta of Saxe-Gotha, a princess of beauty and excellent judgment, did not, as was hoped, restore union to the Royal Family. His establishment was not one fitting to support his dignity, and the Ministry enforced this parsimony, not from economical motives, but to suit their own book.

Saturday, July 24, Richmond.—Her Majesty, the Prince and Princess of Wales, the Duke of Cumberland, and the rest of the Royal Family, "hunted (for the first Time this Season) a Stag in Richmond New Park, and in the Evening their Royal Highnesses the Prince and Princess of Wales, attended by several Persons of Quality, went to the Theatre at Richmond to see the Comedy of the *Tender Husband* and the *Honest Yorkshireman* (which was perform'd to a splendid Audience with universal Applause), and they afterwards returned to Kensington."

Wednesday, July 28, Windsor.—The Prince of Wales, Duke of Cumberland, and the two eldest Princesses, accompanied by a large field, hunted a stag for "above four hours," and killed him on Ascot Heath.

Saturday, July 31, Richmond.—The Queen and the rest of the Royal Family roused a stag in the New Park, which was run into and killed after "a chase of about three hours." In the evening the Prince and Princess attended the Theatre at Richmond, and afterwards returned to their residence at Kew.

Wednesday, August 4, Richmond.—Meet announced, but was not attended by the Queen or the Royal Family, as on this day, "the Queen, the Duke, and the Princesses came in Coaches from Kensington, and drove round Grosvenor, Hanover, and Soho Squares; and came afterwards to Lincoln's-Inn Fields to see the Works carrying on there." The following day the Prince and Princess of Wales went to breakfast at Windsor Castle, dined with Lord Archibald Hamilton at

Henley, and angled for salmon in the Thames. The Queen reiterated the order of last season, "that no Stranger be admitted at Richmond New Park on Hunting days without tickets, which are to be delivered by the Ranger there."

Saturday, August 7, Richmond.—The Queen, accompanied by the Duke of Cumberland, and the Princesses Amelia and Caroline, went from Kensington and were joined at the New Park by the Prince and Princess of Wales. A stag was hunted, but no particulars of the run transpired.

Wednesday, August 11, Richmond.—Neither the Queen nor any member of the Royal Family hunted on account of the intensity of the heat.

Saturday, August 14.—Heavy rain in the morning prevented the Queen, and probably many others, from hunting, although they were at the meet.

Wednesday, August 17, Windsor.—No intelligence.

Saturday, August 21, Richmond.—The Queen, accompanied by the Duke of Cumberland, the Princesses Amelia and Caroline, the Prince and Princess of Wales, hunted a stag, " and after a pleasant Chase of about three Hours, the Stag was killed by the Water-side. Her Majesty dined at Richmond, but returned to Kensington in the evening."

Saturday, August 28, Richmond.—Her Majesty and the Royal Family hunted a stag, " and after a Pleasant Chase of severall hours killed it near the Great Pond, after which the Queen, &c., went to Kew to Dinner, and returned to Kensington in the evening."

Wednesday, September 1, Windsor.—The Duke of Cumberland and the Princess Amelia arrived from Kensington at the Castle; but in consequence of the heavy rain did not join in the hunt.

Saturday, September 4, Richmond.—The Queen, accompanied by the Duke of Cumberland and the Princess Amelia, were present at the meet. The weather being "foul" Her Majesty did not hunt, and returned to Kensington in the evening. The meet was largely attended; many coaches were "delivered" by the highwaymen on their return to town.

Saturday, September 11, Richmond.—Her Majesty, the Duke of Cumberland, the Princesses Amelia and Caroline, were joined at the meet by the Prince and Princess of Wales, where a stag was uncarted, and "after a pleasant chase of two hours and a half was killed near the Pond."

Saturday, September 18, Richmond.—"On Saturday morning, about six o'clock [A.M.], Her Majesty, accompanied by their Royal Highnesses the Duke, and the Princesses Amelia and Caroline, went from Kensington to take the Diversion of hunting at Richmond New Park; where the Prince and Princess of Wales repaired from Kew; and after a Chace of about three Hours, the Stag was killed near the Waterside. Her Majesty dined there, and in the Afternoon walked about the Garden, and stay'd about half an hour at Merlin's Cave, to consider the properest Place where to put the twelve Bustos of the Queens of England, etc., and returned to Kensington about ten o'Clock at Night, escorted by a squadron of the Horse Guards."*

Saturday, September 25, Richmond.—Present, the Queen, Duke of Cumberland, and the Princesses Amelia and Caroline, when they hunted a stag. No details of the run.

Wednesday, October 6, Sunbury Common.—The Queen and the Royal Family (as previously mentioned) hunted a hind, "which was kill'd after a Chase of about Three Quarters of an Hour."

Saturday, October 9, Richmond.—"The heavy Rains that fell on Saturday last, prevented the Royal Family's Hunting in the New Park."

Wednesday, October 13, Hounslow.—The Duke of Cumberland, the Princesses Amelia and Caroline, and a very large field hunted a hind, which was turned out about 10 A.M. at Feltham, on Hounslow Heath. She ran by Hanworth to Sunbury, where she crossed the Thames, and made to Walton Common, then passed through Esher, and, after crossing the

---

* It was announced that a hind was to be turned out on Hounslow Heath on the date of this fixture, "when the annual Contribution will be gather'd for the Huntsmen"; but we can find no further reference to it.

river again, recrossed the Thames at Hampton Court. She next headed for the river, and swam across, when she was driven back, and, after a chase of four hours, "was Kill'd near the House of the Hon. Arthur Onslow, Esq., at Ember Court near Ditton. Their Royal Highnesses followed the Chace no further than Esher; and after dining with the Hon. Mr. Pelham, returned in the Evening to Kensington." Grief: the Earl of Lincoln thrown into a ditch, and very much brused; Mr. George Stanforth, "a Young Gentleman of good Family in Yorkshire," both legs broken.

Wednesday, October 20, Hounslow.—The Duke and the two eldest Princesses, attended by divers noblemen and gentlemen present. At the starting post a hind was turned out; she gave a good run for "several hours," and was killed near Hampton town.

Wednesday, October 27, Hounslow.—The same members of the Royal Family and a large field hunted a hind for about two hours, which they killed near Staines.

Saturday, October 30, Richmond.—"Tho' her Majesty has left off the Diversion of Hunting till his Majesty's Return to England; the Duke and the Princesses Amelia and Caroline, accompanied by several of the Nobility went from Kew to hunt a Stag at Richmond New Park; and, after a Pleasant Chase till one o'clock the Stag was killed near the Pond."

Thursday, November 4, Hounslow.—A hind was turned out at Fan Grove, in the presence of the Duke of Cumberland, the two eldest Princesses, and a considerable field. No details.

Saturday, November 6, Hounslow.—Ditto.

Thursday, November 11, Hounslow.—Ditto.

Saturday, November 13.—"On Saturday last her Majesty, accompanied by her Royal Highness the Princess Caroline, went to Kew, whither the Duke and the Princess Amelia repaired from Hounslow-heath, where they took the Diversion of hunting a Hind, which was killed after two Hours pleasant Chaise, and returned to Kensington in the evening."

Wednesday, November 17, Banstead Downs.—The Duke of Cumberland and the Princess Amelia, attended by several persons of distinction, hunted a hind, and, after a pleasant run of two and a half hours, killed on Forest Hill.

Wednesday, November 24, Barham Downs.—"Their Royal Highnesses the Duke and the Princess Amelia, attended by several of the Nobility, went to take the Diversion of hunting a Hind at Barham Downs; but the Weather proving very indifferent, they returned to Kensington without Killing the Hind."

Wednesday, December 1, Banstead Downs.—The Duke of Cumberland and the Princess Amelia, attended by several persons of distinction, hunted a hind, which was killed "near the Pond" after a pleasant run of about two hours. Although the young Duke and his hard-riding little sister were announced to hunt a hind on Banstead Downs on the following Saturday, that event did not take place. When the fixture was made it was probably forgotten that on that day the Princess Amelia entered her thirteenth year; consequently the family festivities on the happy occasion at Kensington prevented any hunting at Banstead. Hence December 1 was the last hunting day recorded (so far as we can ascertain) with the Royal Buckhounds in the year 1736. With this season came the dawn of that change, or rather prolongation, of staghunting, and the subsequent alteration of the hunting season as we find it now established. And it is to those two royal youths we owe, in a great measure, the result. The King set sail from Helvoetsluys on Monday, December 23, and, the wind being fair, he expected to be back in London on Christmas Day. After a run of about six leagues the wind changed, and blew very hard, the sea ran mountains high, and the Royal Yacht, with his Majesty on board, got within ten miles of Yarmouth, but could not reach the beach without great risk of going ashore; consequently she had to put about, and run before the wind back to Helvoetsluys, where the King disembarked. There he was detained by contrary winds and foul weather till February 13, 1737. The following day he arrived off Lowestoft, "where 40 Sailors in White Shirts, went into the sea up to their Chins, and as soon as the Boat, his Majesty was in, came at them, they took it out of the Sea, and carried it safe to Land." The King proceeded thence by road in his coach to London, where he arrived the following morning. During his stay in Hanover he frequently hunted the stag, but his principal sport was among the wild boars of the Westphalian mountains, the royal bag on September 24, near Gifhorn, having totalled no fewer than 70 head of those unclean though savoury tuskers.

The official record of sport with the Royal Buckhounds for this season shows that 101 head of deer were killed and hunted.*

The Ascot races took place in September. On Monday, the 20th, the purse of 40 Guineas for hunters carrying 12 stone, saddle and bridle included, which had been ridden by their owners, "being gentlemen, to the death of a leash of stags this season, and that have not won the value of 5*l*. in plate or money." The best of three heats (4 miles) was walked over for by Mr. Smith's bay horse Factor. On Tuesday, the 21st, the Town Plate of Windsor of 20*l*. for any horse, mare, or gelding, carrying 10 stone, that never won above the value of 20*l*. in plate or money at any one time, was won by Lord Gower's horse, Tumbler, by beating Mr. Downe's chestnut-grey mare Stay till I Come. On Wednesday, the 22nd, the Purse of 30 Guineas for hunters, carrying 10 stone, including saddle and bridle, "conformable to the qualifications of the first Article," was won by the Hon. John Spencer's bay horse, Robin Hood, beating Mr. Smallwood's grey mare, Lightfoot, and Mr. Long's chestnut horse Sly. The horses had to be entered on September 13 "at the house of Mr. John Tempro at Sunning-Hill Wells, at 4 o'clock in the afternoon," each horse entered for the 30 and 40 Guinea Plates, to pay one

---

* The keepers of Swinley Walk, New Lodge Walk, Bagshot, and Eastbamsted Walk, Billingbear Walk, Cranborn Walk, the Great Park, Richmond Park, and Epping Forest, for their fees for killing, with his Majesty's hounds 68 stags, at 2*l*. each, 29 hinds at 1*l*. each, and 3 bucks at 5*s*. each between December 31, 1735, and December 31, 1736, by virtue of a warrant dated March 14, 1730, and a certificate under the hand of Charles, Earl of Tankerville, of the number killed, 171*l*. 10*s*.

guinea entrance, if a subscriber; if not, two guineas. The entrance for the Town Plate was two guineas on the day of entrance, or three guineas at the post, "and no less than three horses to start which are esteem'd running horses." A good ordinary was announced on every day of the races "at the said Mr. Tempro's."

CHAPTER XV.

GEORGE II. (*continued*)—1737-1744.

Ralph Jenison, Esq., Thirty-Eighth Master : July 7, 1737, to December 25, 1744.
—Records of the Runs.—Ascot Races.

1737.—The hunting season of 1737 with this pack opened late and ended early. Mr. Ralph Jenison had succeeded Lord Tankerville as Master of the Royal Buckhounds shortly before the season began. About the first week in August the King and the Royal Family arrived from Richmond at Hampton Court Palace. The Prince and Princess of Wales were at Kew. The King was far from well. The Queen was slowly, but surely, approaching her death. The weather was inclement. Political affairs were in a worse muddle than ever, and the botheration over the financial allowance of the Heir-Apparent and the settlement of the Princess gave rise to much unnecessary unpleasantness in Court and political circles. Then the Princess of Wales was sent to St. James', and there safely delivered of a princess by "Mrs. Cannon, the Midwife of the Archbishop of York." These and other circumstances partly broke up and interrupted the hunting fixtures, so far as related to the Royal Family and the Court. When these interruptions were to some extent adjusted, Lady Walpole died, and she was soon after followed to the grave by another of the King's most intimate friends, Baron Hartoff, who was Secretary of State for Hanover, and a prominent follower of the Royal Buckhounds.

The first meet of this season took place on

Wednesday, August 3, Richmond.—The King, Queen, Duke

of York, and the Princesses Amelia and Caroline arrived at the New Park from Hampton Court. A stag was roused, " and Notwithstanding the Heaviness of the Rain they staid till Twelve o'Clock before they quitted the Field."

Saturday, August 19, Hounslow.—" His Majesty, the Duke and the Princess Amelia, attended by several Persons of Distinction, went from Hampton-Court to Hounslow-Heath, where a Stag was turn'd out of a Waggon at the Starting-Post, which afforded them excellent Diversion for about two Hours, and was Kill'd in Feltham Fields near Hounslow."

Wednesday, August 24, Twickenham Common.—" It rained so very hard, that his Majesty got into his Coach soon after the Hounds were laid on, and went to Hampton Court; this was the first Stag that has been brought from Windsor Forest, and turned out this Year. This Stag took the Enclosures directly, and shew'd little Sport; and it rained hard great Part of the Chase."

Saturday, September 3, Hounslow.—The King, Queen, Duke of Cumberland, and the Princesses at the meet, " where a Stag was turn'd out which had been brought from Windsor Forest. It gave a great deal of good Diversion for about four Hours, and was Kill'd near Hampton-Town; his Majesty chang'd Horses four Times."

Wednesday, September 14, Hounslow (?)—The King, Queen, Duke of Cumberland, and the Princesses Amelia and Caroline " took the Diversion of Stag-Hunting," where not mentioned. " It being Holy Cross Day, Ralph Jennison, Esq., Knight of the Shire for Northumberland, and Master of his Majesty's Buck-Hounds, held the Purse according to Custom to their Majesties, Nobility, Gentry, &c., when a considerable Contribution was made for the King's Huntsmen. After the Diversion was over their Majesties returned to Hampton-Court to Dinner."

Saturday, September 17, Sunbury Common.—The same members of the Royal Family, attended by several persons of distinction, hunted a stag, " which carry'd them from 9 to 1 o'Clock a Chace of about forty Miles, he crossing the Thames several times, and at last took to Windsor-Forest, where his Majesty order'd the Dogs to be call'd off and a silver Collar to be put about the Stag's neck, and order'd that he should never be hunted again; after which they returned to Hampton-Court to Dinner."

Monday, September 19, Sunbury Common.—Their Majesties, the Duke of Cumberland, and the Princesses hunted a hind, which gave a good run for two hours. Killed near Teddington. " During the Chace his Royal Highness fell from his Horse on Hounslow-Heath, and receiv'd a slight Hurt."

Wednesday, September 21, Sunbury Common.—The same members of the Royal Family hunted a hind, " which afforded them good Sport for two Hours, when it was Killed near Kingston-Wick."

Saturday, September 24, Hounslow Heath. — The same members of the Royal Family " took the Diversion of Hunting a Hind from Hounslow-Heath, which cross'd the Thames and ran beyond Guildford in Surrey, then turn'd back, and was taken as she was crossing the Thames near Staines; but his Majesty order'd her Life to be spared, and about Five o'Clock their Majesties and the rest of the Royal Family return'd to Hampton-Court to Dinner. The Duke of Cumberland fell with his Horse, and pitching on his Face, his Royal Highness had a great Effusion of Blood from his Nose." The highwaymen in the neighbourhood of Hounslow Heath were in battalions strong, and woe betide the straggling stag-hunter who fell into their clutches.

This was Queen Caroline's last appearance in the hunting field. She died on the ensuing November 20, to the deep and lasting grief, not only of the King, her family, and friends, but of the nation. During the ten years (1727 till 1737) in which she yielded so great an influence over public business, it continued to flow in a smooth and uniform current, seldom broken by obstacles, and bearing along comparatively few materials for history. It was her greatest pleasure to mingle with the people, and for many years she took especial delight in fraternising with the field at the meets of the Royal Buckhounds.

As we have already recorded, the unrestrained liberty which was so cheerfully accorded to every one to attend those happy reunions with the Royal Pack in the New Park at Richmond, was so grossly abused, chiefly by importunate Germans, that it became absolutely necessary to restrict the loafers and begging impostors, who frequently interfered with the real followers of the hounds. To stop these abuses the hunting tickets were a happy thought, as no one was allowed to enter the Park on these hunting mornings except those provided with one. All *bonâ-fide* followers of the pack obtained the necessary "permit"; indeed, no instance of any refusal is recorded. The young members of the Royal Family were "well entered" by Her Majesty in the art and mysteries of the chase, and their subsequent career in the hunting field proved how worthy they were of such an able preceptor. In strictly political matters holes can be picked in the Queen's conduct. She certainly governed by bribery. Her Ministers were corrupt and venal; they wanted their price, and got it. That was the Queen's misfortune, not her fault. Unprincipled politicians brought her name into unnecessary conflict with the people over the Excise Act; and although the Royal Family had really nothing to do with the Great Gin Question of the day, it was made a party cry to the prejudice of the Court. This, like many other libels on the personality of the members of the House of Hanover, must be ignored by the impartial and dispassionate analyst of their form in rural affairs.

It is asserted by the editor of Lord Hervey's "Memoirs of the Reign of George the Second," that Queen Caroline did not love hunting. Without disputing this statement, it would appear by the contemporary chronicles of the runs with the Royal Buckhounds that Her Majesty evinced more than a passing interest in the chase, and was solicitous that her children should be courageous and prudent followers of the pack. Possibly Lord Hervey may have found those Wednesdays and Saturdays, " which were the King's days for hunting," favourable opportunities of entertaining the Queen, " whilst other people were entertaining themselves with hearing dogs bark and seeing crowds gallop." We are told Lord Hervey did not love hunting, although he was mounted on those occasions on hunters placed at his disposal by the Queen. With Walpole so prominent in connection with the pack it is possible Lord Hervey deemed it prudent to avoid anything which might be construed to give umbrage to the Prime Minister, who could rarely brook a rival in the field or senate.

According to the official certificate of the Master of the Buckhounds, 55 stags and 15 hinds were hunted by the pack during this season.

1738.—Preparatory to the opening of the season of 1738, with our pack, the Duke of Kingston was gazetted to the office of Master of His Majesty's Staghounds " on the North side of Trent," *vice* the Earl of Carlisle deceased; and the Right Hon. Robert Lord Walpole to be Master of His Majesty's Harriers and Foxhounds. The Earl of Tankerville resigned his gold staff as one of the Lords of the Bedchamber to the King, and soon after embarked for Holland. George III. was newly born. The Prince and Princess of Wales and young George and his little sister arrived at Cliefden House " for the summer season," where they received a present, from the Earl of Chesterfield, " of Cato (his Black), who is recon'd to blow the best French Horn and Trumpet in England."*

Then we are told that there were " Shipp'd for Copenhagen six fine hunting horses and a Pack of Stag Hounds for the use of his Danish Majesty." " A Stag Hunter's Plate was run for on Honslow Heath, and won by Dr. Munro's ch. gelding All-decciv'd-in-Toby." The King's hunting horses were ordered to be in readiness against August 2 " for the stag and hind hunting on Sunbury Common."

---

* " Cato," previous to this time, had been in the service of Sir Robert Walpole. His portrait was painted in a group of hunting celebrities by Wooton, and is here engraved from the original picture in the possession of Walter Gilbey, Esq., at Elsenham Hall, Essex. The Prince of Wales appointed " Cato " head gamekeeper at Cliefden, and afterwards at Richmond Park. Among the novel presents sent to the Prince and Princess of Wales, on the birth of George III., was a " newly invented " perambulator, made by " Mr. Bassinet, the eminent upholsterer in Piccadilly."

The first meet with the Buckhounds was announced to take place in the New Park, Richmond, on Saturday, July 1, but nothing further about it, or any ensuing one, transpires until

Wednesday, July 26, Windsor Forest, when the Prince of Wales, the Duke of Cumberland, "and the eldest Princess took the Diversion of staghunting, which afforded them good Sport for several Hours."

CATO.

Wednesday, August 2, Windsor.—The King, Duke of Cumberland, and the Princesses Amelia and Caroline roused a stag, which gave a run of "several hours; after which His Majesty returned to Kensington to dinner."

Saturday, August 12, Richmond.—The King, Duke of Cumberland, and the Princesses arrived from Kensington at the New Park, where they roused a stag, "which carried them a Pleasant Chace of an Hour and a Half, and was killed as he was going to take the great Pond. After the Chace was over, the Duke and the Princesses returned to Kensington, his Majesty and the Lords of the Bedchamber in Waiting, went to view her late Majesty's House at Richmond, and at two o'Clock returned to Kensington."

Wednesday, August 16, Richmond.—No information.

Wednesday, September 20, Hounslow Heath.—The Duke of Cumberland and the Princesses Amelia and Caroline announced to hunt a hind. No reports.

Saturday, September 23, Hounslow.—The King, Duke of Cumberland, and the Princesses "went from Kensington to Hounslow Heath, where a Hind was turn'd out to be hunted; the Chace began at Ten o'Clock, and lasted 'till One, during which Time the Hind cross'd the Thames several Times, and after a fine Chace, was Kill'd near Staines. A Contribution being annually made, on the first Day of his Majesty's hunting the Hind, Ralph Jennison, Esq., Master of his Majesty's Buckhounds, held the Purse, and collected about 350 Guineas, his Majesty giving 100 Guineas, the Duke 30, and the Princesses 50 between them, the Ministers of State and others of the Nobility gave five Guineas each."

Wednesday, September 27, Hounslow.—The King, accompanied by the Duke of Cumberland, the Princesses Amelia and Caroline and suite, "took the Diversion of Stag-Hunting on Hounslow Heath as usual."

Monday, October 1, Richmond.—The King, the Duke of Cumberland, and the two eldest Princesses "took the Diversion of Hunting in Richmond New Park. Next Monday a Hind will be turn'd out on Epsom Downs, so much Company spoiling the Diversion on Hounslow Heath."

Wednesday, October 11, Richmond.—The same members of the Royal Family arrived at the New Park, where they hunted a hind, which gave a good run; "and therefore the King did not receive the Compliments of the Nobility, Quality, and Foreign Ministers, on the Anniversary of his Coronation," which were to be "performed" on the following day. The hunting fixture was more important than that function; a great honour for the chase! Sir Robert Walpole "and divers other persons of Distinction" were present. The Premier, who had lately been prostrated with illness at the New Lodge in Richmond Park (his Ranger residence), was heartily congratulated on his restoration to health.

Saturday, October 14, Richmond.—The Duke of Cumberland, the Princess Amelia, the Dukes of Newcastle and Grafton, Sir Robert Walpole, "several other persons of distinction," and a large field roused a hind in the New Park, "which was Kill'd after a fine Chace of two Hours."

Wednesday, October 18, Richmond.—The King, the Duke of Cumberland, the Princesses Amelia and Caroline, attended by several of the nobility and gentry, roused a hind, "which afforded a pleasant chace of two hours"; and thus (so far as the Royal Family were concerned) the season ended.

According to the official certificate of the Master of the Buckhounds, 51 stags and 26 hinds—which had been procured in Swinly, New Lodge, Bagshot, Easthampstead, Billingbeare Walks, Richmond Park, and Epping Forest—constituted the quarry during this season.

1739.—Preparatory to the opening of the season of 1739 Parliament was in full cry upon going to war with Spain. However, the belligerent legislators found time to pass a grant of 15,000*l.* a year for the Duke of Cumberland, and 24,000*l.* a year for the Princesses Amelia, Caroline, Mary, and Louisa, who had just successfully negotiated a bad bout of the measles. The Royal children attended in the House of Lords when the Bills received the Royal assent, whereupon they returned thanks in the usual manner. The Prince and Princess of Wales received an ovation at Guildford races. The hunting horses belonging to the Royal Family were ordered to Hampton Court stables, and put to rights there for the ensuing season, which opened on

Saturday, July 1, Richmond.—Early in the morning the Duke of Newcastle, Lord Harrington, Sir Robert Walpole, 'and divers other Persons of Quality and Distinction hunted a Stag in Richmond New Park, being the first Time of that Diversion this Season."

Saturday, July 21, Windsor.—The Duke of Cumberland, the Princesses Amelia and Caroline, attended by several persons of distinction, "went to Windsor New Forest, and took the Diversion of Hunting a Stag, which carry'd them a Chace of about thirty Miles, and was Kill'd between Wateroakly and Holyport."

Wednesday, August 15, Richmond.—The King and the Duke of Cumberland, attended by several persons of distinction, roused a stag in the New Park, which gave a good run of about two hours. "After the Sport was ended, his Majesty dined at Richmond, and returned in the Evening to Kensington." This was the first time George II. was out with the pack this season. Military preparations and frequent reviews of the troops in Hyde Park and on Hounslow Heath considerably interrupted the hunting arrangements of the Royal Family.

Wednesday, August 22, Richmond.—The same members of the Royal Family hunted a stag from the New Park, "which afforded excellent Sport till one o'Clock," when His Majesty returned to Kensington.

Saturday, August 25, Richmond.—"His Majesty and the Royal Family hunted a Stag in Richmond New Park, which was Killed after a Chace of Two Hours."

Saturday, September 1, Richmond.—The King, attended by the Dukes of Marlborough, Grafton, Newcastle, etc., hunted from the New Park. No details.

Wednesday, September 5, Richmond.—"His Majesty, the Duke, and the Princesses took the diversion of hunting a stag in Richmond New Park."

Saturday, September 8, Hounslow Heath.—The first meet of the season here gave one of the best runs. A large field assembled, including the King, Duke of Cumberland, and the Princesses, who were attended by "the Ministers of State, others of the Nobility, and Foreign Ministers." The Stag (which was brought from Epping Forest) was turned out at the starting post, ran directly to Sunbury, thence back to Hounslow Heath, thence to Southwell, and back to the Heath again. He then ran to Hampton, where he crossed the Thames, and proceeded by Moseley Hurst away to Walton, where he recrossed the Thames, and came back to Hounslow, where he was run into and killed "after a chace of above forty Miles." The King, Sir Robert Walpole, Lord Harrington, and Sir William Cope were up with the hounds during the whole of the run. "Mr. Serjeant, Master of the Crown Inn at Uxbridge, had the Misfortune to break his Thigh, by his Horse running away with him near Hampton Town," and was so ill that his life was despaired of. The Prime Minister was likewise laid up at his Lodge in the New Park, "having suffr'd a Great Fatigue in attending his Majesty in the long Hunting Chace."

Wednesday, September 18, Hounslow.—The King, Duke of Cumberland, "and several of the Nobility," were at the meet. No details of the run; nevertheless it must have been a "full head" one, as it was soon after announced that "His Grace the Duke of Newcastle recovers daily from his Indisposition, which was a violent Cold, he took in attending his Majesty a Hunting some Days ago." Sir Robert Walpole was also on the mending list, and congratulated accordingly. Sad to say, the Prime Minister's chief motive in so constantly hunting with the Buckhounds was not exclusively attributable to his love for the chase. His presence here drove the Prince of Wales out of the field, and Walpole perceived that every encounter between the Prince and his father, amid such harmonising surroundings, would tend to heal the rupture which kept them apart. His equestrian portrait, in the summer costume worn by the followers of the Royal Buckhounds in those days, is engraved after the original picture by Wooton. It is more interesting as a souvenir of the Royal Hunt in the reign of George II., than as a work of art. *Divide et impera* was the motto of this minister; in no instance did he practise that precept more successfully than in fomenting dissension in the Royal Family. The heir-apparent being thus boycotted, and practically prohibited of hunting with the Royal Buckhounds, which he so dearly

SIR ROBERT WALPOLE.

loved, His Royal Highness now purchased "a set" of Foxhounds, supplemented them with drafts from the then famous Lincolnshire strain, hired the Durdans for a hunting-box, and announced three meetings a week at Epsom Downs. To checkmate this move the Premier appointed his eldest son, Lord Robert Walpole (whom he had previously created a peer), to the office of Master of the Royal Harriers and Foxhounds, with a salary of 2,000*l.* a year. Foxhunting had now become the most popular pastime throughout the land. The famous Charleton Club had recently celebrated its second jubilee—the club having been the pioneer of this rising branch of the chase. The Duke of Cumberland had been formally inducted into its mysteries with the Duke of Newcastle's pack, two years previously, in Sussex. And it was introduced, "according to the English method of foxhunting," into France in 1737, by the Earl of Berkeley, who "hunted that Kingdom from Aubigny." His Lordship, therefore, had plenty of room to follow his hounds. We have no room here to devote to the subject, which we commend to the investigation of those who may be interested in the rise and progress of fox-hunting.

As may be inferred from the above account of the runs recorded with the Buckhounds during this season, the current of sport with the pack was frequently dammed by pressing political and cognate affairs of State. Only one hind is mentioned as having been hunted, and only two meets assembled at Hounslow Heath, when a stag was the quarry on both of these occasions. Before the season began great preparations were made in Windsor Forest, where the officers of the Board of Works were erecting "a large room adjoining to Swinley Lodge for his Majesty and the Royal Family to dine in on Hunting-days." But, so far as we can ascertain, only one meet was reported there in this season; hence it is possible this large room must have been better than the company. The King did not visit Windsor during this year.

It would, nevertheless, appear that this had been a brilliant season. It transpires, by the official certificate of the Master of the Buckhounds, that at least 87 stags and 35 hinds had been killed and hunted by the pack. Unfortunately, the records of the runs—even on those occasions when the King and the Royal Family were out with the hounds— do not seem to be fully reported, and when Royalty did not appear in the hunting field the chroniclers of those days invariably disdained to give publicity to the proceedings of the pack. Still, we must be thankful for such small mercies, and make the most of the intelligence thus placed at our disposal. From this season onward we shall be far worse off in this respect. War—that spoil-sport—was now upon us, and during the ensuing ten years very little about the proceedings of the Royal Buckhounds in the hunting field is to be found in our rural annals or cognate domestic history.

ASCOT races were held on July 9 and 10. On the first day of this meeting the 40 Guinea Plate for hunters carrying 12 stone was won by Colonel Horley's grey horse beating two others. On the second day the 20 Guinea Plate was won by Mr. Ives' (one of the yeomen prickers) grey mare beating six others.

We shall hear nothing of Ascot races for some years hence. They were, indirectly, suppressed by the Jockey Club, and by the Act of Parliament of 13 George II. c. 19. Nearly ten years prior to this time the members of the Jockey Club held a memorable meeting on August 1, 1729, at Hackwood, the Duke of Bolton's seat in Hampshire, for the ostensible purpose: " to consider of methods for the better keeping of their respective strings of horses at Newmarket." At this meeting of the (original) members of the Jockey Club it was agreed unanimously that steps should be taken to discountenance, and, if possible, to suppress the so-called race meetings which had, about this time, sprung up in every part of the country, on the ground that such race meetings were inimical to the true interests of the turf. In the metropolis several of those so-called race meetings were conducted in the most disgraceful manner. They were associated with disgusting scenes of gross profligacy, brutality, drunkenness, and robbery. During the decade ending 1739 these hole-and-corner racing fixtures—at which a thoroughbred race-horse rarely ran—attained unenviable notoriety, and were almost universally condemned by the public and in the press. At length the remonstrances of the members of the Jockey Club and others had the desired effect. A bill was introduced in Parliament, in which were embodied certain provisions calculated to put a stop to the atrocities perpetrated under the disguise of horse-racing. The outcome of this bill was the Act of Parliament, 13 George II. c. 19, pursuant to which it was enacted that from and after June 24, 1740, no person was allowed to enter, start, or run any horse, mare, or gelding for any race unless the animal so entered was the *bonâ fide* property of the person by whom it was entered. No person could enter more than one horse in any race. No plate could be run for under the value of 50*l*., any infringement of this stipulation being liable to a penalty of 200*l*.; five-year-old horses to carry 10 stone, six-year-olds 11 stone, and seven-year-olds, 12 stone each. The owner of any horse carrying less weight to forfeit 200*l*. The entrance money to go to "the second best horse," and not to what is now technically called the "Fund." The Act did not apply to Scotland or Ireland, nor to matches run for at Newmarket or York. The primary object of this Act was to hamper the objectionable hole-and-corner "race meetings" above referred to, at which one of the chief prizes was a cask of beer to the person who overtook and lifted a pig by the tail—the tail having been well greased for the occasion! For a time, at least, the purport of this Act had the desired effect, inasmuch as these objectionable "race meetings" could not conform to the dictates of the law. Unfortunately, in passing the Act, such genuine races as those run for at Ascot and elsewhere by horses owned by staghunters and hunt-servants—to whom a large stake was not a primary object—had been overlooked; consequently, as Ascot was too poor to raise sufficient money, or to increase the 40 and 20 Guinea Plates to two of 50*l*. each, this meeting had to drop out of the annals of the turf during the ensuing four years.

1740.—We were now at war with Spain. At home military

organisation, the camp at Hounslow, reviewing, massing, and shipping troops and sailors was the order of the day. The Royal Family were divided, and in doleful dumps among themselves. The Duke of Cumberland was not on friendly terms with the Prince of Wales, who rarely took any interest in the Royal Buckhounds, and devoted his spare time to his own particular pack. The Duke of Cumberland volunteered to serve in the naval expedition on the Spanish Main; sailed in the *Boyne* frigate, and returned victorious in October. In May the King set out for Hanover, and did not return to England until November. The Princess Mary, heretofore a conspicuous follower of the pack, was married to Frederick, Prince of Hesse, consequently Her Royal Highness was never seen again with the Royal Buckhounds. As to the other members of the Royal Family, they are not mentioned as having been out with the pack during this season. We can find no reports of the runs. It appears, by the official certificate of the Master, that the sport was good: 72 stags and 33 hinds having been "killed" by the hounds during this year.

1741.—The King set out for Hanover in May, and did not return to England until October. During this interval the Duke of Cumberland assumed a prominent position in home affairs, exhibiting much energy in directing military matters at the principal camps. However, His Royal Highness found time to hunt pretty frequently with the Royal Buckhounds; and he also organised a pack of staghounds of his own. It was publicly announced, on July 8, that "their Royal Highnesses the Duke and Princesses began last Monday to hunt a stag in Windsor Forest, which sport is to be continued two days in every week during the hunting season." How far this arrangement was carried out we are unable to ascertain, the records of sport with these packs having been almost eclipsed by intelligence from the battlefield and camps. Indeed, we can only trace two circumstantial reports from the hunting field— viz., on Saturday, September 17, when their Royal Highnesses the Princesses hunted a stag which ran from Windsor Forest to Guildford, "from whence their Royal Highnesses came to

St. James's in a hir'd coach, their horses being all tir'd with the chase"; and on Saturday, October 24, "H.R.H. the Duke took the diversion of hunting in Windsor Forest; but the company was a little retarded in the sport by one of his Highness's horses accidentally dropping down dead on the road near Hounslow." It does not appear that the Prince of Wales was out with the Royal Buckhounds during this season. However, His Royal Highness hunted for some time in the New Forest, and devoted a considerable portion of his spare time to cricket and yachting. According to the official certificate of the Master of the Buckhounds, it appears that, from Christmas 1740 to Christmas 1741, 92 stags, 61 hinds, and 30 bucks had been killed and hunted "by His Majesty's and the Duke of Cumberland's hounds." *

1742.—War. Hunting intelligence *nil*. In April the King formed an army in Flanders. Walpole's Government was overthrown, when he retired from office with a peerage and untold plunder, while his three sons held sinecures and places for their several lives amounting to nearly 20,000*l*. a year. The Prince of Wales and his father were reconciled. The Duke of Cumberland embarked for Flanders. Somerville—that glorious laureate of the chase—died at the beginning of the hunting with the Royal Buckhounds, whose praises he so often sang in undying verse. We can find no records of the runs during this season; nevertheless, it must have been a very good one, as, according to the official certificate of the

* We hear nothing of Ascot races in this year. The Staghunters' Plate of 40 guineas for "real hunters, that have been in at the death of two brace of deer with the King's hounds since the 1st of July last, carrying 10 stone, bridle and saddle, etc.," was to have been run for on Hounslow Heath on Tuesday October 4, but "by reason of the bad weather and the badness of the course" it was subsequently decided to change the venue to Mosley Hurst, in Surrey, when the race came off, and was won by the Duke of Newcastle's grey mare Surrey, she having beaten the Duke of Cumberland's horse Whitefoot, the Hon. Peter Wentworth's black gelding Come-tickle-me-lightly, and four others, belonging to Messrs. Jenison, Hammond, Jennings, and Raby. Notwithstanding the "badness of the course" at Hounslow, races were held there for some years after. This was contrary to the recent Act of Parliament; but it seems that Hounslow having been under martial law at this time, a civil writ could not run there.

Master of the Buckhounds, the quarry provided for this pack and that of the Duke of Cumberland, from Christmas 1741 to Christmas 1742, was 90 stags, 64 hinds, and 27 bucks.

1743.—War. George II. entered into an alliance with Frederick II. of Prussia, of which the most prominent outcome was the battle of Dettingen, where the Duke of Cumberland received a severe wound. We were threatened by, and greatly alarmed at, the imminent prospect of an invasion by France; while the almost overt movements of the Jacobites at home placed the safety of the Kingdom in a very precarious position. These events left no room for hunting intelligence; consequently we hardly hear anything of the proceedings of the Royal Buckhounds in the hunting field, except that the Princess Amelia was frequently out with the pack. It seems the Duke of Cumberland gave up, or put aside, his pack of staghounds, as we hear nothing of it in the official certificate of the Master of the Buckhounds during this and for some subsequent years. The number of "deer" killed by His Majesty's hounds in the year ended at Christmas 1743 was 54 stags and 30 hinds, from which we may infer the runs were good and the pace a cracker.*

1744.—On July 25 it was publicly announced that the Duke of Cumberland and the Princess Amelia "began to take the diversion of staghunting in Windsor Forest." In the ensuing month the Duke went to Hanover; consequently the Princess Amelia was the principal representative of the Royal Family to be seen out with the pack during the remainder of this season. The Duke did not return until October 18, the King having arrived from Hanover on September 1. In the meantime, the ordinary followers of the Royal Buckhounds appeared twice a week in force. The Duke of Grafton arrived at Sunning Hill early in August "for staghunting and to drink the waters of that place." The official certificate of the Master

---

* On October 13 the Duke of Bedford's hounds are reported to have roused a deer at Wooton Woods, near Bedford, which they ran for six hours without a check. "By the least computation they ran upwards of 60 miles, which by sportsmen is thought to be the greatest chase ever run by hounds."

of the Buckhounds shows that between Christmas 1743 and Christmas 1744 the pack had killed and hunted 63 stags, 17 hinds, and 20 bucks, and that the keepers of the several walks and parks from which the quarry was derived received in the usual fees 154*l*. This was Mr. Ralph Jenison's last year of office in the first period of his Mastership of the Royal Buckhounds. As we shall presently see, Mr. Jenison assumed the official couples for the second and last period of his Mastership two years after this time.

Ascot races were resumed on September 17 and 18. We have not been able to ascertain the entries or the results. Beyond the subjoined programme of the two 50*l*. plates and the announcement of the assembly and concert to be held in the Town Hall, Windsor, no further intelligence has apparently been preserved:—

"Ascot Heath Races, Berks.

"To be run for on Ascot Heath, in Windsor Forest, on Monday the 17th of September, Fifty Pounds, by any Horse, Mare or Gelding, that is at this Time in the Possession of the Huntsman, or one of the Yeomen Prickers of his Majesty's Buck Hounds, or in the Possession of the Keepers of the said Forest, or Windsor Great Park in the said County; to carry twelve Stone, Bridle and Saddle included, as never started for Match or Plate, and has been hunted in the said Forest between Lady-Day last and Michaelmas-Day. All Disputes for this Plate, relating to Entering or Running, to be determin'd by Ralph Jennison, Esq.; or whom he shall appoint.

"And on Tuesday, the 18th Instant, Fifty Pounds by Hunters, that never won either Match, Plate or Stakes, and that never started for any Thing except a Hunter's Plate, to carry twelve Stone, Bridle and Saddle included. No less than three deem'd Hunters to start, and if only one comes, to have Twenty Guineas, and the Plate not run for; and if two only, to have Ten Guineas each. No Person to enter two Horses.

"All horses that run for the first Plate must be enter'd on Monday next, the 10th of this Month, between the Hours of One and Six in the Afternoon, at Sunninghill Wells in Windsor Forest, by the Clerk of the Course, paying Half-a-Crown to him, Entrance Fee.

"And for the second Plate to enter at the same Time and Place, paying if a Subscriber One Guinea Entrance, if a Non-Subscriber Three Guineas, or at the Post Two Guineas if a Subscriber; if a Non-Subscriber Five Guineas, to go to the second best tho' distanc'd.

"All Horses to be kept from the Time of Entering to the Time of Running, at some Publick House within three Miles of the said Course; and all Horses, &c., to be plated by some Smith that lives within that Distance.

"All Disputes for this Plate, relating either to Entering or Running, to be determin'd by the Majority of Subscribers their present.

"There will be Ordinaries each Day, at Sunninghill Wells at One o'Clock."

"WINDSOR, *Sept.* 17, 1744.

"THESE are to certify the Gentlemen and Ladies, that there will be an ASSEMBLY at the Town-Hall there Tomorrow, the 18th instant, being the Day of the Horse-Race on Ascot-Heath, near Windsor."

"AT the Town-Hall, Windsor, this Day the 17th Instant, will be perform'd

SOLOMON.

A SERENATA, taken from the CANTICLES.
Set to Musick by Mr. BOYCE.

Tickets to be had at the Maidenhead, the Ball and Castle, and the White Hart."*

---

* This aristocratic gathering contrasts favourably with the entertainments of the upper ten in Belgravia on the same day, to wit: "*At May-Fair Ducking Pond.* This Day, precisely at Two o'Clock, three Dogs will hunt Six Ducks, for Three Guineas. And on Monday the 1st of October next, will be Goose Hunting; and the famous Flying Dean will hunt six Ducks, for Two Guineas, against the noted Nero, at the above Place, precisely at Two o'Clock."

CHAPTER XVI.

GEORGE II. (concluded)—1745-1760.

The Earl of Tankerville, Thirty-ninth Master: December 31, 1744, to June 25, 1746.—Ralph Jenison, Esq. (ii), Fortieth Master: July 2, 1746, to February 5, 1757.—Viscount Bateman, Forty-first Master: July 1, 1757, to October 25, 1760.—ii. March 17, 1761, to July 5, 1782(?).—Records of the Runs.—Annual Expenses of the Pack during the Reign of George II.—The Huntsmen and the Hunt-Servants.—Ascot Races.

ON the last day of the year 1744 the Earl of Halifax was appointed successor to Ralph Jenison, Esq., and his lordship consequently became the Thirty-ninth Master of the Royal Buckhounds on the day above mentioned. He retained the official insignia of the hunt during the years 1745 and 1746 down to the opening of that season, when he retired from this office. During Lord Halifax's mastership we find very few allusions to the proceedings of the Royal Buckhounds in the hunting field. His first season must necessarily be drawn blank, so far as concerns any records of sport with the pack. 'Twas '45, and "'45" explains the matter. Prince Charles Edward Stuart was making a gallant attempt to recover the kingdom which he, and many others, deemed to be his alone by inheritance and "right divine." The proceedings of the "Young Pretender" and his Jacobite adherents need no further reference here. In May George II. left for Hanover, and did not return to England for some months. The Duke of Cumberland was also absent, and was otherwise too much engaged to take any interest in hunting. Nevertheless, the pack had been out at least twice a week during the season, and apparently gave good runs. It does not appear, however, that any members of the Royal Family, except the Princess Amelia, participated in the sport. The official certificate of the Master of the Buckhounds indicates that 44 stags and 16 hinds had been killed and hunted by the pack during this year.

1746.—The Civil War practically came to an end with the Battle of Culloden in the spring of this year. Then followed the preparations for decorating Temple Bar with human heads. Midsummer and the opening of the hunting season arrived in due course, when it was found there was a deficiency in the Civil List amounting to 456,733*l*. 16*s*. 3¾*d*. This having been made good by Parliament, the Lords of the Treasury wrote to the Lord Chamberlain conveying His Majesty's commands that he should exercise economy and prudence, and to be careful in his expenses, and to use his utmost endeavour to lessen the incidental cost of the Household, and to prevent any addition of the expenses thereto. It does not appear, however, that the cost of maintaining the Royal Buckhounds had increased, or that there were any considerable arrears due or owing on account of the pack. The Duke of Cumberland proceeded to Windsor in July, the King went there on a flying visit soon after, " and view'd the Lodge in the Park there and that on the Forest, both of which are fitted up for the Duke." His Royal Highness sojourned in the vicinity during the month of August, and, apparently, hunted occasionally with the Royal Buckhounds. The Princesses were gone to Bath. Mr. Ralph Jenison became the Master of the Royal Buckhounds, for the second time, at the opening of this season; and according to his certificate 46 stags and 22 hinds had been killed and hunted by the pack from Christmas 1745 to Christmas 1746.

1747.—War. The King and the Duke of Cumberland absent in Hanover, etc. No hunting intelligence.* Never-

---

* We can only trace the report of one run with the pack this season, when it appears it was taken to Epping Forest, on Wednesday, August 24, which "being the day fix't for the Ladies' Hunt, a stag was rous'd, near the Green Man, which ran several hours, and afforded excellent Diversion. There were present a great number of Ladies finely mounted, many of whom kept in view the whole chase and came in at the death. Several in the chase were thrown from their horses, rode over and receiv'd much hurt."

theless, this season with the Royal Buckhounds must have been a fairly good one, as 45 stags and 28 hinds had been killed and hunted by the pack.

1748.—Peace and plenty—of racing at Ascot. "What were the fruits which Britain reaped from this long and dreadful war? A dreadful expense of blood and treasure, disgrace on disgrace, and the national debt accumulated to eighty millions sterling."—*Hume.* The King did not return to England until November 24. The Duke of Cumberland arrived at his hunting quarters at Windsor on August 20. His Royal Highness, who had been Ranger of the Great and Little Parks since July 1746, was now appointed Lieutenant of Windsor Forest during the life of the King and the Princess Amelia or the longest liver of them. Notwithstanding the attraction presented by the local duties belonging to the Lieutenancy of the Forest, the Duke soon left the locality and returned to Hanover. Meanwhile the Princess Amelia occasionally hunted with the Buckhounds; and although we are unable to unearth any records of the runs, it seems the sport was good, the fields large, and the pace a cracker.* The official certificate of the Master shows that 52 stags and 31 hinds were killed and hunted by the pack from Christmas 1747 to Christmas 1748.

At Ascot the races were resumed and run for on August 15, 16, and 17, as appears by the subjoined programme of this meeting:—

* Good runs seem to have prevailed in foxhunting and staghunting during this season. "On Monday (December 5) Lord Chedworth's and Mr. Dutton's confederate pack of Foxhounds had the most remarkable fox-chase that ever was seen in those parts (Camden, Gloucestershire). They ran a fox five hours without a check over the finest country in England; no chase could have afforded more entertainment, no hounds could pursue their game with more steadiness and resolution, no fox could more boldly run over a fine country, and no sportsmen could pursue with more spirit and judgment in riding; for it was remarkable that there was not a hunter at the unkenneling that was not at the death; and not five horses out of thirty able to go a mile further: many horses were obliged to be blooded to save their lives." On November 25 the Duke of Marlborough's staghounds had a run in Oxfordshire of "at least 50 miles." The Duke and many of his friends were in at the death. Most of the field, "though well mounted, tired their horses before the chase was ended."

"To be run for on Ascot-Heath, in Windsor Forest, on Monday, the 15th of August next, a Purse of 50*l.*, by actual Hunters of the past Season, that never started for Match or Prize, nor never had a Sweat before Lady Day last. Those of full age ten Stone and a half; all under that Age ten Stone; a Certificate of which to be produced at the Time of Entrance.

"On Tuesday the 16th will be run for, on the same Course, a Purse of 50*l.*, by any Horse, Mare or Gelding, carrying ten Stone; the best of three Heats; but whatever Horse, Mare or Gelding that wins two Heats shall have the Plate; the winning Horse to be sold, if demanded by any one of the Subscribers, for 80*l.*, but if demanded by more than one to be determined by a Raffle.

"On Wednesday the 17th a Purse of 50*l.*, by Horses, &c., which have been only Hunters, and Stag-Hunted in Windsor Forest this Year, and hunted by the Owners; and that never were in Training with Intention to run for any Match or Prize by an Hunter's Plate. Weight twelve Stone.

"Each Horse etc., that runs for the Hunter's Plate must be the Property of a Subscriber, and have been in his Possession from Lady Day last to the Day of Running.

"To enter at Sunning-hill Wells on the Monday se'nnight before the Race Week; if a Subscriber of two Guineas to pay one Guinea Entrance; if a Subscriber of only one Guinea to pay two Guineas Entrance. No less than three to start for each Plate.

"The winning Horse for each of the above Prizes to pay five Guineas towards mending the Course and Rails.

"To run according to Articles, which will be produced at entering.

"If any Difference should arise to be Determin'd by a Majority of the Subscribers then present.

"N.B.—There will be Assemblies at the Town Hall in Windsor, during the Races, as usual."

We can find no account or reference to the results of these races, except that one of the Plates or Purses of 50*l.* was won by Mr. Bowle's horse, of Windsor, which likewise won a match of 100 guineas run for at Ascot on Thursday, August 25, from a horse belonging to a Mr. Burton.

1749.—We cannot find any records of the runs with the Royal Buckhounds during this year. The Duke of Cumberland was at his hunting lodge in Windsor Forest for a short sojourn; he was absorbed in military affairs. The King and the Princesses stayed at Kensington Palace. The Prince of Wales gave his spare time to hunting in the New Forest and yachting about the Nore. The ordinary followers of the Royal Buckhounds apparently had a good season, there having (according to the official certificate of the Master) been killed and hunted with the pack 64 stags and 21 hinds.

ASCOT RACES were announced to come off on Tuesday, Wednesday, Thursday, and Friday, the 1st, 2nd, 3rd, and 4th of August. The race for the first day was for a Purse of 50*l*., by hunters that had never started for match or plate, and used as regular hunters, which had been in at the death of a leash of stags in Windsor Forest "this season," carrying 12 stone; the second day a Plate of 50*l*., free to any horses that had never won above 50*l*. at any one time (bar in matches), those of full age to carry 11 stone, six-year-olds 10 stone, five-year-olds and under that age, 9 stone; the third day 50*l*. was to be run for by the hunters belonging to the huntsmen, yeomen prickers, and keepers, carrying 12 stone; and on the last day the prize was 50*l*. for any horse, mare, or gelding carrying 10 stone. Each of these races was three heats of four miles a heat. The entrance money was as in the year 1744, but the winners were now called upon to pay five guineas "towards mending the course." Three to run, or no race. The competitors to be shown at Sunning-hill Wells on July 24, and to run according to the articles submitted on the day of entry. We can find no return of the results of this meeting except as to the Hunter's Plate, which was won by Mr. Withers' chestnut horse Windsor by the first two heats, defeating Mr. Buckley's bay gelding Speaker, and Mr. Fisher's bay horse Ramper. Possibly the other items in the programme did not fill.

1750.—The King was abroad; the Duke of Cumberland was principally occupied with military affairs, consequently we hear hardly anything of the Royal Buckhounds in the hunting field during this year. When the hunting season opened Windsor was *en fête* on the occasion of the installation of Prince George, K.G. ("who shall be King hereafter"). In September, two bucks and a stag having been killed by poachers within the parish of Bray "in the Forest of Windsor," the churchwardens and overseers of the poor, "desirous to declare their abhorance of such practices," offered a reward of 10*l*. for the discovery and conviction of any one concerned in the same. Dennis Gainer, saddler, in Long Lane, near West Smithfield, London, "and no where else," announced to all gentlemen and sportsmen that he had lately invented a new method of making velvet hunting and jockey caps, and also a neat light sort for ladies, without any seam or button, in one entire piece of velvet, which would not rip or wear bare, and the skull was so stout as to defend the head from any blow or fall. As appears by the official certificate of the Master only 40 stags and 4 hinds had been killed and hunted by the pack this year.

1751.—Horace Walpole, writing under date of June 25, 1751, in his "Memoirs of the Reign of George II.," says: "The Duke [of Cumberland] had a fall as he was hunting at Windsor, and was taken up speechless, and refusing to be blooded, grew dangerously ill with a pain in his side, and was given over by his physicians, but recovered. The King was inexpressibly alarmed, wept over him, and told everybody that was in his confidence that the nation would be undone, left to nothing but a woman and children! He said to Mr. Fox of the Duke, 'He has a head to guide, to rule, and to direct.'" . . . If Walpole is correct in his date the hunting season with the Royal Buckhounds must have opened rather early in this year. The accident to the Duke must not have been so serious as it was represented to have been, for His Royal Highness was out with the pack on July 18, on which occasion he was accompanied "by several persons of distinction." In the ensuing week there was consternation in London on receipt of the news that the Duke had died at Windsor. It was quite true the Duke was dead; his defunct grace was

a favourite charger of that name, which his Royal Highness
"rode in Scotland during the late unnatural Rebellion." A
groom reporting the circumstance in Windsor, "the Publick,
without enquiry catched the News, and with swifter currency
than the Tide, it came to Town." On the 10th of this month
the Princess Amelia was sworn into the office of Ranger of
Richmond New Park by the Chairman and High Bailiff of
the City and Liberty of Westminster, at Kensington Palace—
an appointment which, directly and indirectly, led to great
contention and lawsuits during the ensuing ten years. In
August, Cranborn Lodge—which had been occupied by the
late Duke of St. Albans—was given to the Duke of Cumberland
for the natural term of his life. On the 8th His Royal Highness
took possession of this Lodge, when the occasion was
celebrated with a cricket match between "the Duke of Cumberland's
XI. v. Sir John Elvill's XI., which the latter won by
an innings." On Monday, July 12, the Duke and a large field
were out with the Buckhounds, and this is the last allusion
we have met with relating to the runs with the pack during
this season. It is improbable that any of the Princesses hunted
with the pack before September 8, on which day the Court
went out of mourning for the late Prince of Wales. Poor Fred
had been devotedly attached to the Royal Hunt down to the
time when, by the specious policy of Walpole, he was forced
to seek other hunting quarters. Like the Princess Anne, in
the days of yore, he cast long lingering glances after the Royal
Buckhounds, and it is alleged that he employed scouts, during
the period of his banishment from Windsor, to inform him
(when he was in residence at Cliefden and Kew) whenever
the pack ran in those directions. A saddled hunter was continually
kept in readiness; and whenever an opportunity
of this sort presented, Fred unexpectedly fell in with the
hunt, and enjoyed the sport to his heart's content. During
his exile in Hanover he was trained on sausages and sowercrout
(orthography not warranted sound in wind or limb);
nevertheless there must have been a good current of true
British blood in his veins. On his arrival in England he

adapted himself, like a true son of the soil, to all our national sports and pastimes, and soon became proficient in hunting, cricket, yachting, racing, angling, and falconry. Unfortunately, he was somewhat addicted to betting; and, according to the custom of those days, he invariably had a heavy stake and a wager on every run made in a cricket match.* The primary cause of the fatal illness which somewhat unexpectedly carried off the Prince was attributed at the time to "a blow on his side with a ball about two years ago, playing at cricket, which diversion he was very fond of, and 'tis thought was the occasion of his death, having a bag [imposthume] near six inches long, down his side, full of putrescence."

Upon the whole, this season with the Royal Buckhounds must have yielded better sport than some of the preceding ones, 73 stags and 14 hinds having been killed and hunted by the pack.

The programme of the "Ascot Heath Races" for 1751 comprised the following events: On Tuesday, July 2, a plate of 50l. value, open to any horse, mare, or gelding that had been used as a regular hunter, and had been at the death of a leash of stags in Windsor Forest, "and rid by his owner this last season," and that never started for anything except a hunter's plate; to carry 12 stone, the best of three heats, and to be the property of a gentleman. On Wednesday, July 3, a plate of 50l. value, free for any horse, mare, or gelding; weight, 10 stone; three heats; open to all horses, etc., that never won more than 50 guineas at one time, matches excepted. On Thursday, July 4, a plate of 50l., free to any horse, etc., belonging to any or either huntsmen, yeomen prickers, or keepers belonging to any or either of the packs of Windsor Forest; each horse, etc., to carry 12 stone, saddle and bridle

* The notorious Bubb-Doddington incident, which every writer on the Hanoverian era, from Thackeray to McCarthy, has misconstrued, was a bet on a run in a game of cricket. In those days what are now termed "runs" were called "notches," the runs made by the batsmen having been cut or "nicked" on a piece of wood. Hence, a person in speaking of losing a bet on a run, said "So-and-so nicked me for so much."

included; the best of three heats; every horse, etc., to be the property of a huntsman, etc., and to be in his possession for six months at the time of entering, to be a known hunter, and never started for any plate but a hunter's plate, and that in Windsor Forest. On Friday, the 5th, a plate of 50*l.* for any horse, etc., that never won 50*l.*, matches excepted; six-year-olds 10 stone, five-year-olds 9 stone; three heats; certificates to be produced at the time of entrance; all horses to be entered at Summerhill Wells on Tuesday, June 26, between the hours of three and eight in the afternoon, and be subject to the Articles produced at the time of entrance. Every subscriber of 2 guineas to pay 1 guinea entrance; subscribers of 1 guinea to pay 2 guineas; a non-subscriber to pay 3 guineas entrance; which entrance money to go to a future Plate. Every horse entered to pay 5*s.* to the clerk of the course. No less than three horses to start for each of these Plates. If but one enters to be allowed 10 guineas; if two, 17½ guineas; and the Plate not to be run for.

No booths to be erected on the course, or carts, by any person unless a subscriber to the plates, and by the direction of the clerk of the course.

"No Horse, Mare, or Gelding that was on the 7th Day of April last the Property of Mr. Prentice (who was then the Owner of Trimmer), or shall belong to him at the Time of these Races, shall be admitted to start for any of these Plates."

"The Hunter's Plate on Tuesday last was won by Mr. Walker's chestnut gelding Slender, beating with great ease William Walker, Esqr.'s, Windsor; Col. Boscawen's Northallerton; Captain Phillips' Red Tail; and Mr. Osborn's Grist.

"The Aged Plate was not run for on Wednesday, to the great Disappointment of Multitudes, who went thither to see the Decision between Capt. Vernon's Grey Horse, Beau (late Lord Portmore's), and Mr. Marshall's Chestnut Horse, Diver, upon which great Sums were depending.

"There were but three Horses to start for this Plate; and Beau, since his Entrance, being match'd to run with some other Horse for a considerable Sum, Diver receiv'd Ten

Guineas; and is gone, as we are inform'd, to Hounslow; where 'tis said, he will meet Mr. Roger's Grey Horse, Garland, late Sir Ralph Gore's. The Odds are Five and Six to Four on Diver against Garland, the first Time they meet."

The following Horses started for a Purse of Fifty Pounds, and came in as follows: —

	1st Ht.	2nd Ht.	3rd Ht.
Mr. Benj. Rogers's grey horse, Pumpkin, late Lord Portmore's, got by Steady, five Years old	3	1	1
Mr. Swymmer's Bay Horse, Saturn, Babram's Brother, six Years old	1	3	2
Sir Charles Goreing's Chestnut Horse, Golden Locks, got by Golden Locks, five Years old	2	2	3

The Odds at starting were on Golden Locks.

1752.—The Duke of Cumberland occupied his hunting lodge in Windsor Forest during a considerable part of this year. A large body of troops were encamped there through the summer. The Royal Buckhounds met twice a week, as also did the Duke's Staghounds; and although we can find but few circumstantial records of the runs, it seems the sport was good from the first to the last meet, which was held on Wednesday, December 6. The King did not visit Windsor this year. He did his hunting in Hanover.* According to the official certificate of the Master of the Royal Buckhounds it appears that 49 stags and 16 hinds were killed and hunted by the pack during this year.

The horse races were held on Ascot Heath in the second week of August, when the programme comprised four events—viz., on Tuesday, the 11th, a plate of 50*l.*, "the Property of

---

* "His Britannic Majesty was highly pleased with the grand Hunting Match of the Boar, at which he was present on the 21st (of October), in the Forest of Osterwald. The Noblemen and Gentlemen that accompanied him in that Diversion, din'd after 'twas over under five several Tents, which were pitch'd in the Field on Purpose. His Majesty return'd hither (Hanover) that Evening about Five."

Gentlemen Subscribers, for Hunters, for which six horses were entered, resulted thus:—

	1st Ht.	2nd Ht.
Mr. Walker's bay gelding, Orphan	1	1
Sir Charles Ledley's grey gelding, Richmond	3	2
Col Boscawen's bay gelding, Poker	4	3
Lord Bury's black stone horse, Little Blaze	2	dr.
H.R.H. Duke of Cumberland's chestnut gelding, Button	5	dis.

Wednesday, the 12th, for Weight for Age Plate, Josiah Marshall's chestnut horse, Diver, and Mr. Bowle's bay horse, Johnny Armstrong, ran, which the former won. "These two Heats were exceeding good; but an Accident happened to Mr. Bowle's Horse at the End of the second Heat, after coming in, by a Man's being in the Way; whereby the Horse was flung down, and it is believed will die. The rider saved himself."

On Thursday, the 4th, for the Give and Take Plate, Captain Shaftoe's chestnut horse, Silver Legs, and Mr. Sparrow's grey gelding were entered; and the 50l. Plate for the keepers and yeomen prickers of Windsor Forest obtained an entry of three: Mr. Kennedy's brown gelding, Rat; Mr. Ricard's bay mare, Cat; and Mr. Ives' bay mare, Betsy-Feel-the-Tap. The results of the last two events are not recorded. No member of the Royal Family was present on this occasion. Lords Anson, Montfort, and Monson were mentioned as having attended the meeting on the second day.

In connection with this meeting we obtain the following additional information in a letter from Mr. Rigby to the Duke of Bedford, dated (London) August 13, 1752: "And now to send you what little news I have been able to pick up yesterday; for the day we landed, Ascott Heath races had engaged the few people that remained in town, and I could find no soul to dine or sup with. In short, I have seen but three intelligent beings, Lord Waldegrave, Fox, and Harris. The first . . . was at the above mentioned races on Tuesday, where the Duke of Cumberland's horse ran, and would have been distanced" [in the first heat] "if his master had not been higher bred than himself: there was much company there, and the Duke invited Lord Waldegrave and his companion *Lord Anson,* to Cranbourne that night, but they did not go. Sandwich was not there." * . . .

1753.—The Duke of Cumberland was at Windsor Forest for most part of this year; but it does not appear that the King or any other members of the Royal Family had been there. The Royal Buckhounds and the Duke's pack hunted as usual in the vicinity of the Forest, but we have found no reliable chronicle of the runs which ensued. The former pack met on one occasion, in March, in the New Park, Richmond. The Princess Amelia would not admit pedestrians, and only chaises, chariots, and persons on horseback were allowed to enter. The local inhabitants resented this restriction of their legal rights, and to vindicate their privileges instituted a suit which was tried at the Kingston Assizes on April 3, 1754, which ended in a verdict in favour of the claimants.† We believe the meet of the Royal Buckhounds, above mentioned, was the last which was held in Richmond Park with this pack. According to the official certificate of the Master of the Royal Buckhounds 38 stags and 22 hinds were killed and hunted by the pack in this year.

On May 26, 1753, a match was run over Ascot Heath new course, the best of three two-mile heats for 50*l.* "and 50*l.* bye," and was won by Mr. Fisher's bay gelding in the first two heats from Mr. Coat's roan filly.

The annual meeting was held on Tuesday, Wednesday, and Thursday, August 14, 15, and 16. On the Tuesday the 50*l.* Plate, "free only to such horses, etc., as had been in the pos-

* "Correspondence of John, 4th Duke of Bedford: selected from the originals at Woburn Abbey," by Lord John Russell, vol. ii., pp. 110, 111. In another letter from Mr. Rigby to the Duke, dated October 5, following, he mentions having lately been at "a turtle feast" at Windsor, where he saw both of the Duke of Cumberland's lodges in the forest, his hounds, and his wild beasts. He adds that the Newmarket October race meeting had then made London "emptier than it had been over the whole summer."

† Tim Bennet, "the honest Presbyterian cobler of Hampton Wick," who died in June 1756, "had a noble monument erected to his memory," for persisting and obtaining a right of way through Bushey Park, which had been closed to the public in the reign of William III.

session of the owner from October before starting, and had been regularly hunted with the Duke's hounds,* carrying 12 stone," was won by Captain Vernon's bay gelding, Blaze, by winning the first two heats from Mr. Walker's bay gelding, Orphan, and Mr. Wimbourn's bay gelding. The same day the 50*l*. Plate, for the huntsmen, yeomen prickers of the Royal Buckhounds, and Keepers of Windsor Forest, was run for, and won by Mr. Ricket's bay mare, Flora, by taking the first two heats from Mr. Ives' chestnut gelding, Saucebox, Mr. Canada's [Kennedy] chestnut gelding, Pea Cagen, and Mr. Johnson's bay gelding, Viper. On the Wednesday the Plate of 50*l*. was run for by four-year-old horses that never won above 50 guineas at one time (matches excepted), carrying 9 stone, two mile heats, and was won by Mr. Burford's bay horse, Coomb, by landing the second and third heats from Lord Craven's grey horse, Anthony (which got the first heat), and Mr. Everett's bay horse, Creeper (which came in last in each heat). On the Thursday the Plate of 50*l*. was run for, open to any horse, etc., that never won more than 50 guineas at one time (matches excepted), carrying weight for age—viz., five-year-olds, 9 stone; six-year-olds, 10 stone; and those of full age, 10 stone 9 lb. Three started for this race: Mr. Rogers' grey horse, Garland, and two others to qualify; but upon a dispute arising the Plate was withheld.

1754.—In July the King hunted with the Royal Buckhounds in the vicinity of Windsor Forest. The meets were well attended "by persons of distinction" during this season, and also by the usual followers of the pack. The Duke of Cumberland still represented royalty at the head of the hunt; nevertheless, His Royal Highness contemplated to yield that

* In the programme the conditions for this race stipulated that the horses had been "regularly hunted with H.R.H. the Duke's Hounds, or any real Pack of Staghounds, which must be certified by the Master of the Hounds he has hunted with, and has never won a plate or match but a Staghunter's plate." The horse that won two heats in any of those races not to be obliged to start for a third. Entries to be made at Sunninghill Wells, on August 6. The entrance remained unaltered, except for those entering at the post, which was raised from 3 to 5 guineas.

position to Prince George, the heir-apparent, and to seek for fresh hunting fields and pastures new in some other locality.* By the official certificate of the Master of the Royal Buckhounds, we learn that 58 stags and 22 hinds were killed and hunted by the pack during this year.

ASCOT RACES were held on Monday, Tuesday, Wednesday, and Thursday, June 17 to 20. On Monday, June 17, a Plate of 50l. for horses, etc., that had been in the possession of the owner since January 1 last past, and had been regularly hunted with "the King's Hounds, his Royal Highness the Duke's Hounds, or any real pack of Stag Hounds," and had never won plate or match, carrying 12 stone each, was won by

	1st Ht.	2nd Ht.
Mr. Jenison's grey horse, Why-not (late Mr. Hartley's, Bashful), got by Cartouch	1	1
Mr. Wither's bay gelding, Stag Hunter	2	2

"The odds at starting were 2 to 1 on Why-not, and very high at starting the second heat, which Stag Hunter would have won, it being 2 to 1 on him in running, but he died a Rogue."

On Tuesday, 18, a Subscription Purse of 90l. for four-year-old horses, etc., that were the property of a subscriber on March 25 last past, one four-mile heat, carrying 9 stone each, was won by the Duke of Cumberland's bay colt Shock, got by Shock, by beating Mr. Jenison's bay colt Regulus, got by Regulus. The odds at starting were 3 to 1 on Shock. On the same day, a Plate of 50l. for huntsmen, yeomen prickers and keepers of Windsor Forest, weight 12 stone, was won by

	1st Ht.	2nd Ht.
Mr. Ives' bay gelding, Warhawk	1	1
Mr. Ricket's bay mare, Flora	2	2
Mr. Johnson's grey gelding, Viper	4	3
Mr. Canadey's [Kennedy] chestnut gelding, Pickpocket	3	dr.

* In the first week of March it was publicly announced that the Duke of Cumberland was fitting out a hunting-box near Basingstoke, Hampshire, "where kennels are provided for 160 couple of Foxhounds to hunt 3 Days in a Week during the Season; and about 50 couple will always be taken into the Field."

The odds at starting were 6 to 4 on the field against Viper; 4 to 1 on the field against Warhawk; after the first heat, 6 to 4 on the field against Viper; 4 to 1 on the field against Flora; and even betting Warhawk won.

On Wednesday, 19, for the Free Plate of 50*l.*, the Duke of Cumberland's grey horse Crab walked over. His Royal Highness declined to accept the Plate, and gave it to be run for by hunters that were never sweated (*i.e.*, untrained horses), which was won by—

	1st Ht.	2nd Ht.
Mr. Walker's chestnut horse, Chance	1	1
Mr. Ives' black gelding, Crop	2	2
Mr. Jenison's grey gelding, Grantham	4	3
Hon. Levison Gower's bay gelding, Squirrel	3	4
Mr. Benwell's bay gelding, Last-of-all	dis.	

The third and last run on this day was a match for 50*l.*, between Mr. Lamego's bay Galloway mare, Whitenose, 13 hands high, carrying a feather, against Mr. Pond's brown gelding, Cripple, got by Swift, carrying 10 stone, the best of three four-mile heats, was won by Whitenose. The odds were 3 to 1 on Cripple.

On Thursday, 20, a Plate of 50*l.*—four-year-olds 8 stone 7lb.; five-year-olds 9 stone 7lb.—was run for by the following five-year-old horses, and won by—

	1st Ht.	2nd Ht.	3rd Ht.
Mr. Grisewood's grey horse, Teazer, got by Teazer	2	1	1
Mr. Burfoot's bay horse, Coomb, got by Janus	1	2	3
Duke of Cumberland's bay horse, Entrance, full brother to the Godolphin gelding	4	3	2
Mr. Jenison's black horse, Tawney, got by Shock	3	dr.	

At starting Teazer was taken against the field; 5 to 4 on the field against Entrance; 65 to 10 on the field against Coomb; after the first heat 5 to 4 on Teazer; 6 to 4 against Entrance; and 3 to 1 against Coomb; after the second heat, 4 to 1 Teazer won.

On Friday, August 30, 1754, a match was run on Ascot

Heath, between the Earl of Sandwich's chestnut gelding, Forester, by Forester, and Colonel Hodgson's bay gelding, Brisk, owners up, one four-mile heat, for 50 guineas, and was won by the former. 5 to 1 were laid on Brisk.

1755.—The King was in Hanover from April until September. The Duke of Cumberland was chiefly occupied in reviewing troops and conducting State affairs in his capacity of First Lord of the Regency Council, during the absence of the King. We are unable to trace any reliable records of the runs with the Royal Buckhounds during this year; but as the pack had killed and hunted 47 stags and 18 hinds, the regular followers of the hunt must have enjoyed good sport.

The races on Ascot Heath were held on Monday, Tuesday, Wednesday, and Thursday, May 26 to 29, of this year. On Monday, May 26, the Duke of Cumberland's grey colt beat the Earl of Gower's roan colt, weight 8 stone each, in one four-mile heat, over Ascot Course, for 200 guineas. "The roan colt run rusty." The same day a Purse of 50*l.* was run for, free, only for the huntsmen, yeomen prickers, and keepers of Windsor Forest, by horses, etc., carrying 12 stone, resulted as follows:—

	1st Ht.	2nd Ht.
Mr. Ricket's bay mare, Flora	1	1
Mr. Ives' bay gelding, Warhawk	2	2
Mr. Chapman's bay mare	3	dis.

On the 27th 50*l.* was run for, give and take, by horses carrying weight for inches, that had not won 50*l.* this year. They came in thus:—

	1st Ht.	2nd Ht.	3rd Ht.
Mr. Leeson's chestnut gelding, Bly, 14 hands and ¼ inch, weight 9st. 1lb. 12oz.	4	1	1
Mr. Marshall's grey gelding, Grey Stag (late Mr. Croft's Trinket), 14 hands and ¼ inch, weight 9st. 1lb. 12oz.	1	2	dr.
Hon. William Howe's grey mare, Poor Jenny, 14 hands 1 inch, weight 9st. 7lb.	2	dr.	
Mr. Humphrey's grey horse, 14 hands 2 inches, weight 10st.	3	dr.	

On the 28th 50*l.* was run for by six-year-olds and aged horses—the six-year-olds carrying 9 stone 7lb., the full aged 10 stone 3lb., and was won by

	1st Ht.	2nd Ht.	3rd Ht.	4th Ht.
Marquis of Rockingham's bay horse, Cato, aged	2	3	1	1
Mr. Lamego's chestnut horse, Diver, aged	4	1	2	2
Mr. Merdiths' brown horse, Shock, 6 years old	1	4	3	3
Duke of Cumberland's grey horse, Crab, aged	3	2	4	

"The second heat was hard run between Crab and Diver; the third and fourth as fine sport as ever was seen, Cato beating Diver but half a length."

On the 29th 50*l.* was run for, free for four-year-olds carrying 8 stone 7 lb., and five-year-olds carrying 9 stone 5 lb. This prize was won by Mr. Merdiths' bay colt, Monkey (four years old), by winning the first two heats from the Duke of Cumberland's brown horse, Shock (2nd), Mr. Marshall's brown horse, King Alfred (3rd), and Mr. Bowles' bay mare, Lady Ann (4th), as placed in each heat. The last three were five-year-olds.

The same day a Sweepstakes Match for 45 guineas, by four-year-olds, the property of subscribers, was run, and won by Lord Gower's bay filly, beating Lord Chedworth's brown colt, Bauble, the Duke of Cumberland's bay colt, Stamp Crab, and Captain Vernon's chestnut filly, in the order named.

Then followed two matches. The first, of 2 miles, was won by Lord Walgrave's bay colt, from the Duke of Cumberland's grey colt; the second was won by Mr. Ives' bay gelding, Warhawk, carrying 10 stone, from Mr. Ricket's bay mare, Flora, carrying 10 stone 5 lb.

1756.—War with France. No hunting intelligence. The Duke of Cumberland was absorbed in military affairs; consequently, the Royal Buckhounds were left entirely to the Master's devices and the pleasure of the permanent followers of the pack, who were frequently augmented by the metropolitan and military division, whose name was legion. It seems that all the meets took place in the vicinity of Windsor

Forest, the keepers of the walks therein having provided 44 stags and 12 hinds to show sport with the pack in this year, for which they received, at the usual fees, the sum of 100l.

The races on Ascot Heath came off on Monday, Tuesday, Wednesday, and Thursday, on June 14 to 17 of this year. On Monday, the 14th, Mr. Ralph Jenison's grey horse, Why-not (9 stone 6 lb.), beat Lord Rockingham's bay gelding, Anacreon (9 stone), in one four-mile heat, for 100 guineas. The same day 50l. was run for by horses, etc., carrying 12 stone, the property of the huntsmen, yeomen prickers, and keepers of Windsor Forest, and was won by Mr. Ives' bay gelding, Warhawke, beating Mr. Ricket's bay mare, Flora (2nd), and Mr. Shorter's brown gelding (3rd), in both heats.

On Tuesday, the 15th, 50l. was run for, free only for four and five-year-olds—four-year-olds, 8 stone 7 lb.; five-year-olds, 9 stone 5 lb.—in two-mile heats, and was won by—

	1st Ht.	2nd Ht.
Mr. Roger's chest. h. Newcastle Jack, 5 years old	1	1
Lord Gower's bay h. Coxcomb, 5 years old	2	2
Lord Portmore's chest. h. Steady, 4 years old	4	3
Lord March's grey h. Trial, 4 years old	3	dr.

On Wednesday, 16th, a sweepstakes match, by horses the property of subscribers on March 25 last, weight 8 stone 7 lb., the winner to receive 40l., the remainder to be disposed of as the subscribers thought proper, one four-mile heat was run, and won by Lord Orford's chestnut horse, Lucifer, beating Lord Portmore's grey horse, Centurion (2nd), Marquis of Granby's black mare (3rd), and the Duke of Cumberland's grey gelding, Caristina (4th). The same day 50l. was run for, six year olds carrying 9 stone 7 lb., and full aged 10 stone 3 lb. This prize was won by—

	1st Ht.	2nd Ht.	3rd Ht.
Mr. Blake's chestnut horse Slider, 6 years old	4	1	1
Mr. Swymmer's bay horse Tantivy, aged	1	2	3
Mr. Pytt's bay horse Liberty, aged	3	3	2
Duke of Cumberland's chestnut horse Ranger, 6 years old	2	4	4
Lord Eglington's bay horse Lightfoot	5	dr.	

On Thursday, 17th, 50l. was run for by hunters, weight 12 stone, four-mile heats, and was won by—

	1st Ht.	2nd Ht.	3rd Ht.
Mr. Boothby's bay horse Bobadil	3	1	1
Mr. Churchill's bay gelding Sportsman	1	2	dr.
Mr Hayes' black gelding Belzebub	2	dr.	

The same day the Duke of Cumberland's grey horse, Crab, beat Lord Gower's bay horse, Little David, weight 8 stone 7 lb., in one four-mile heat, for 100 guineas.

1757.—War. No hunting intelligence. Nevertheless, this season with the Royal Buckhounds opened at Midsummer 1756, and closed at Easter 1757. It seems the Duke of Cumberland intended to join the hunt in February, with the object of having a few days in the hunting field before going into the field of battle. But, on his arrival at his *villa venatica*, "the arch of the cellar under His Royal Highness' bed chamber fell in, which happily was attended with no other accident, notwithstanding that he was in bed; since which H.R.H. removed to Cranborne Lodge, at a little distance. Windsor Lodge is so out of repair, that it is necessary to be rebuilt, and a plan is prepared for that purpose." The Duke soon after returned to London, and left there on April 9 to take command of the expedition against the French. The Duke's forces were defeated at the battle of Hastenbeck. George II. immediately recalled him to England, and on his arrival treated him with the utmost coolness. The Duke resented this treatment, resigned all his military employments, almost abandoned hunting, and his only relaxation was on the turf. Henceforward he lived in comparative obscurity. He died 1765. This was Mr. Ralph Jenison's last season as Master of the Royal Buckhounds, he having resigned office on February 5, 1757. He was succeeded by Lord Bateman, who donned the official insignia of the hunt on the ensuing June 1.

ASCOT RACES took place on June 27, 28, 29, and 30. Five races were run for during the four days over which this meeting extended. On the 27th, a Plate of 50*l.*, for four-year-olds, 8 stone 7 lb., and five-year-olds, 9 stone 5 lb., in two-mile heats, was won by Mr. George's bay horse Juniper, beating in the second and third heats Mr. Humphrey's brown horse Snake, and Lord Portman's chestnut horse Steady.

On the 28th, a Plate of 50*l.*, for horses, etc., of the huntsmen, yeomen prickers, and keepers of Windsor Forest, was won by Mr. Ives' chestnut gelding Forester, in the first and second heats, by beating Mr. Ricket's bay mare Flora, and Mr. Kennedy's bay horse Sportsman.

On the 29th, a Plate of 50*l.*, for six-year-olds, 9 stone 7 lb., and full aged, 10 stone 3 lb., was won by Mr. Vernon's grey horse Myrtle, six years old, beating in the first and second heats Mr. Shelly's grey horse Success, Mr. Bennet's bay horse Trifle, and Lord Craven's grey horse Anthony.

And on the 30th, a Plate of 50*l.*, Give-and-Take, 14 hands, 9 stone 7 lb., allowing 7 lb. for every year under seven, was won in the first two heats by Mr. Dutton's bay horse Tim, five years old, 14 hands, carrying 8 stone 7 lb., beating Mr. Adams' chestnut horse Crispin, Mr. Chapman's bay horse Sylvia, and Mr. Cox's chestnut horse Trip.

A sweepstakes match for four-year-olds, weight 8 stone 7 lb., one four-mile heat, was won by Mr. Jenison's bay colt, beating Lord Portman's black colt Pug, and Lord Granby's grey colt.

1758.—During this year we were implicated in war through all the four quarters of the globe; consequently one may seek in vain for any hunting intelligence worth recapitulation. Except the Prince of Wales, who attended the meets frequently and was in the runs occasionally, no other member of the Royal Family hunted during the season with the pack, which, it would appear, by the following official statement, showed fairly good sport to the ordinary followers of the hunt: "Robert Nunn, for the Keepers of Windsor Forest, for their fees on 59 stags, at 2*l.* each, and 20 hinds at 1*l.* each, which were hunted and killed by His Majesty's staghounds in Windsor Forest from the month of January, 1757, to Midsummer, 1758. by vertue of a warrant, &c., and an account thereof certified by Lord Viscount Bateman, Master of His Majesty's hounds, and the receipt appears, 146*l*."

ASCOT RACES were held on May 29, 30, and 31, and June 1. During the four days only six races were run for at this meeting. On the 29th, a Plate of 50*l*. was run for by five-year-olds, carrying 9 stone 5 lb. each, in two-mile heats, and was won, in the second and third heats, by Mr. Dutton's bay horse Quid Nunc, beating Lord Craven's bay horse Aquillo, and Mr. Stewart's chestnut mare.

On the 30th, a sweepstakes was run by four-year-olds, carrying 8 stone 7 lb. each, in one four-mile heat, and was won by Lord Orford's grey filly, beating Lord Gower's bay colt Moses, and Lord Portman's bay colt, the Duke of Cumberland's black colt, and Lord Chedworth's Spot.

The 50*l*. Plate for the hunt-servants and keepers of Windsor Forest for horses carrying 10 stone each, was won by Mr. Ives' chestnut gelding Forester, beating in the first and second heats Mr. Nunn's bay horse Babram, Mr. Shorter's brown gelding Bullock, and Mr. Ricket's bay horse Dumpling.

On the 31st, a Plate of 50*l*. was run for by six-year-olds, 9 stone 7 lb., and full aged, 10 stone 3 lb., was won in the second and third heats by Mr. Jones' roan horse Adolphus, beating the Duke of Cumberland's bay horse Blacklegs, Mr. Vernon's chestnut horse Forester, Mr. Brooks' chestnut horse Rainbow, and Mr. Larkin's black gelding Sloe.

On June 1, a 50*l*. Give-and-Take Plate was run for by five horses, and was won in the third and fourth heats by Mr. Wynn's bay horse Compton, carrying 9 stone 4 lb. 6 oz.

And then the meeting terminated, when the Duke of Cumberland's black colt, Jet, beat Lord Gower's bay colt, Coxcomb, in two matches, the first of two miles, the second of half a mile, weight 8 stone 7 lb. each, for 100*l*. each match.

1759.—War abroad— at home an expected invasion by the French--put hunting intelligence altogether out of the question.

Nevertheless, we ascertain by the official certificate of the Master of the Buckhounds that 50 stags and 38 hinds had been hunted and killed by the pack "in one year ended the 24th of June, 1759."

Ascot Races were announced to take place on June 12, 13, 14, 15, and 16, but on Friday, the 15th, the only race on the card for that day—viz., a Plate of 50*l.* for six-year-olds and aged horses—was not run for, "for want of horses to enter for the same." However, on Tuesday, June 16, a Plate of 50*l.* was run for by five-year-olds, carrying 9 stone 5 lb., in two-mile heats, and was won, in the first and third heats, by Sir Hugh Smithson's* bay horse Persius, beating Mr. Gore's bay horse Snap, Mr. Vernon's chestnut horse Stow Hill, Mr. Pytt's mare Sportly, Mr. Barrot's chestnut horse Scrub, Lord Albemarle's black gelding Jet, and Mr. Snell's dun mare Atalanta.

On the 13th, a Plate of 50*l.* was run for, free only for horses of huntsmen, yeomen prickers, and keepers of Windsor Forest, carrying 12 stone each, which was won, in the second and third heats, by Mr. Shorter's grey horse Babram, beating Mr. Ives' chestnut gelding Blameless, and Mr. Nunn's bay horse Babram. The next and last race on this day was for "the great sweepstakes," by four-year-old horses, carrying 8 stone 7 lb., in 1 four-mile heat. This race was won by H.R.H. the Duke of Cumberland's brown colt Dapper, beating Lord Portman's grey colt Grey Jack, Mr. Shaftoe's chestnut colt Hooke Nose, the Duke of Ancaster's grey colt, Mr. Blake's colt, Lord Rockingham's colt, and Lord Gower's chestnut colt, which "fell sick in running and pull'd up," the competitors passing the winning post in the order named.

On the 14th, a Plate of 50*l.* was run for by five and six-year-old mares, carrying, according to their age, 8 stone 7 lb. and 9 stone 3 lb. respectively, which was won, in the second and third heats, by Mr. Rogers' Fair Rechael, beating Mr. Harvey's,

---

* He married, in 1740, Elizabeth, only child of Algernon Seymour, Earl of Northumberland, and was created Earl Percy and Duke of Northumberland October 22, 1766. He died in 1784. From the time of his marriage to the date of his elevation to the peerage he was commonly styled Lord Northumberland.

the Duke of Kingston's, Mr. Pitt's, Sir Richard Grosvenor's and the Duke of Cumberland's mares, which ran in this race. A four-mile match between Mr. Grant's Spotted Roan mare, 10 stone 8 lb., and Mr. Early's chestnut gelding, 10 stone 13 lb., was won by the former. As previously mentioned, the 50*l*. Plate for six-year-olds and aged horses did not fill.

On the 16th, a Give-and-Take Whim Plate of 50*l*. was won by Mr. Adam's chestnut horse Crispin, 9 stone 7 lb., beating Sir J. Lowther's chestnut horse Whitelegs. And thus the meeting ended.

1760.—Saw the end of the reign of George II., His Majesty having expired on October 25 in that year. During the thirty-four years of his reign, the regular followers of the Royal Buckhounds thoroughly enjoyed and highly appreciated the exhilarating sport provided by the pack. As in the preceding year we have not found any records of the runs that had taken place in this season, nevertheless, it appears by the certificate of Master of the Buckhounds, that down to June 24, 44 stags and 39 hinds had been killed and hunted in the vicinity of Windsor Forest by the pack.

The Ascot Race Meeting was celebrated on the Tuesday, Wednesday, Thursday, Friday, and Saturday, June 10 to 14, in 1760.

On Tuesday, the 10th, a Plate of 50*l*. for four and five-year-olds was run for, in two-mile heats; four-year-olds 8st. 7lb., five-year-olds 9st. 5lb., resulted thus:—

	1st Ht.	2nd Ht.
Lord Gower's bay filly, 4 years old . . .	1	1
Mr. Churchill's chestnut horse, 5 years old .	2	2
Mr. Aldridge's bay horse Americus, 5 years old	6	3
Duke of Grafton's grey gelding Cocker, 5 years old	5	4
Duke of Cumberland's bay horse Pam, 5 years old	4	5
Lord Waldegrave's bay gelding Skim, 5 years old	3	dr.
Mr. Cooke's bay horse Bolton Boy, 5 years old .	7	dr.

1760: ASCOT RACES.

On Wednesday, the 11th, a 50l. Plate was run for by horses belonging to the yeomen prickers and keepers of Windsor Forest, carrying 12 stone each, the best of three heats, which was won by Mr. Shorter's grey horse Babran,* by beating Mr. Ives' grey horse Stag Hunter in the first two heats, and Mr. Ricket's bay gelding Dumpling, distanced.

During the interval between the first and second heats for this race, the "Great Subscription" or "Sweepstakes" for four-year-olds, carrying 8st. 7lb., one four-mile heat, was run for, and won by Lord Portman's grey colt Tiney, from the Duke of Ancaster's grey colt (lamed) (2nd), Mr. Shaftoe's chestnut colt (3rd), Lord Northumberland's grey colt (4th), Lord Waldegrave's grey colt (5th), Lord Bolingbroke's bay colt (6th), Mr. Churchill's bay colt (7th), and the Duke of Cumberland's grey colt (8th).

On Thursday, the 12th, a 50l. Plate for mares which never won a Royal Plate; five-year-olds 8st. 7lb., and aged 10st. 3lb., was won by—

	1st Ht.	2nd Ht.	3rd Ht.
H.R.H. the Duke of Cumberland's bay mare Madam	1	3	1
Mr. Fortescue's bay mare Lady Carolina	3	1	3
Lord Chedworth's bay mare	2	2	2

"The odds at starting were 5 to 1 against the Duke, and 5 to 4 on Lady Carolina, who took the rust, and left the knowing ones on the wrong side of the post. J. Marshall did not ride for the Duke on account of a sore knee." We seldom hear of the jockeys in those days; Marshall's name is occasionally mentioned.

On Friday, the 13th, a Plate of 50l. was run for, the best of three heats, six-year-olds carrying 9st. 7lb., and aged 10st. 3lb., and was won by—

	1st Ht.	2nd Ht.	3rd Ht.	4th Ht.
Mr. Elliott's bay horse Trifle, aged	3	2	1	1
Mr. Crosoer's chestnut horse Elephant, aged	2	1	2	2
Mr. Adam's chestnut horse Stanby, 6 years old	1	3	dis.	

* This horse is frequently returned by the name of Walmouth Tom.

On Saturday, the 14th, the 50*l.* Give-and-Take Plate, 14 hands, weight 9st. 7lb., allowing 7lbs. for every year under 7, resulted as follows:—

	1st Ht.	2nd Ht.	3rd Ht.
Mr. White's brown horse Gamester, aged	4	1	1
Hon. Mr. Howe's bay horse Spotless, 5 years old	1	4	3
Sir R. Grosvenor's bay horse Dragon, aged	5	2	2
Mr. Watt's Chestnut horse Crispin, aged	3	3	dr.
Mr. Fisher's bay mare	2	dis.	

It appears the Duke of Cumberland, the Duke and Duchess of Ancaster, and a large assemblage of the nobility and gentry attended this meeting.

Now we must hark back here and say "a few words" about the four Masters of the Royal Buckhounds, who flourished and filled this office successively, after Colonel Negus, during the reign of George II.

CHARLES BENNET, second Earl of Tankerville, was sworn into the office of Master of the Royal Buckhounds on June 21, 1733. His stipend was 2,341*l.* per annum, out of which he had to defray all the ordinary expenses of the pack. He bore the official insignia of the pack for only a brief term, his Lordship having resigned it in June 1736. During those three years the Prime Minister, Sir Robert Walpole, invariably acted as Field Master, and, of course, when he was in the saddle the actual master was more or less left in the shade. Charles, second Earl of Tankerville, thirty-seventh Master of the Royal Buckhounds, from June 21, 1733, to June 1736, the eldest son of Charles, first Earl of Tankerville, by his wife, Lady Mary Grey, only daughter of Ford, Viscount Grey of Glendale, succeeded to the family honours and estates on the death of his father, May 21, 1722. He was born in 1696, educated at Eton, was a colonel in the army, a Lord of the Bedchamber to Frederick, Prince of Wales, from 1729 to 1733, and was appointed to a similar office in the Household of George II. in 1737. He was made Lord-Lieutenant of the

RALPH JENNISON, ESQ. M.P.
Master of the Royal Buckhounds, to H.M. King George II.
June 18, 1737 – December 30, 1744. (ii) July 2, 1746 – July 4, 1756.

From the original picture by Sir Joshua Reynolds in the possession of Col. Alexander Adair, Heatherton Park, Wellington, Somerset.

county Northumberland, February 11, 1740, and created LL.D. of Cambridge University, July 3, 1749. He was one of the original members of the Jockey Club, and was present at the great meeting of that Turf Senate, which was held at Hackwood on August 1, 1729. His Lordship had some good horses on the turf: Sophonista, Bay Wilkinson, and Tippet, winners of King's Plates, while his galloway, Harlequin, was famous for his inches and triumphs on many courses. His Lordship was taken suddenly ill on Tuesday, March 13, 1753, in a post chaise on the road between Aldborough Hatch, Essex, and London; and, notwithstanding all the assistance that could be rendered, he died on the following night, and was interred at Hounslow "among his ancestors in a private and decent manner."

In 1737 Lord Tankerville was succeeded by RALPH JENISON, ESQ., M.P., who became the thirty-eighth Master of the Royal Buckhounds; and, pursuant to the subjoined Warrant, was sworn and admitted to that office, and entered upon the duties appertaining thereto, commencing on July 7, 1737.

GEORGE R.

Our Will and Pleasure is, that you forthwith swear and admitt or cause to be sworn and admitted Our Trusty and Well beloved Ralph Jenison Esqr into the Office and Place of Master of our Buckhounds; To have, hold and enjoy the same, during Our Pleasure, with all Rights, Fees, Salaries, Profits, Privileges, and Advantages thereunto belonging, in as full & ample manner, to all Intents and Purposes as Charles, Earl of Tankerville, or any other Person hath held and enjoy'd, or of Right ought to have held and enjoy'd the same. And &c. Given &c. the eighteenth day of June 1737, in the Eleventh Year of our reign.

By His Majesty's Command
HOLLES NEWCASTLE.

To his Grace the Duke
of Grafton &c.

—*Lord Chamberlain's Records: Warrants of Several Sorts*, vol. xxviii., p. 333.

As appears by the Accounts of the Treasurer of the Chamber of the Royal Household, Mr. Jenison's stipend was 2,341*l*. a year, out of which he had to discharge the ordinary annual cost of the pack. He was paid at this rate down to Christmas 1744, when he went out of office, and was succeeded by the Earl of Halifax.

Mr. Jenison was reappointed about eighteen months after this time, and in pursuance of the subjoined Warrants was sworn in, and thus *de facto* became the fortieth Master of the Royal Buckhounds:—

GEORGE R.

Our Will and Pleasure is, that you forthwith swear and admit, or cause to be sworn and admitted, Our Trusty and Welbeloved Ralph Jenison Esqr into the Office and Place of Master of Our Buckhounds; To have, hold and enjoy the same, during Our Pleasure, with all Rights, Fees, Salaries, Profits, Priviloges, and Advantages thereunto belonging, in as full and ample manner, to all Intents and Purposes, as George Dunk, Earl of Halifax, or any other Person, hath held and enjoyed, or of Right ought to have held and enjoy'd the same. And for so doing, This shall be your Warrant. Given at Our Court at Kensington the 2^d Day of July 1746, in the Twentieth Year of Our Reign.

By His Majesty's Command
HOLLES NEWCASTLE.

To Our Right Trusty
and Right entirely
beloved Cousin and
Councillor Charles,
Duke of Grafton, Our
Chamberlain of Our
Household.
—*Home Office Records: Warrant Book*, vol. xxiv., p. 119.

(Seal of the Duke of Grafton.)

COPY.

Stamp xl. shillings.

Stamp xl. shillings.

Stamp xl. shillings.

These are to Certify that I have sworn and admitted Ralph Jenison Esquire into the Place and Quality of Master of His Majesty's Buckhounds (in the room of the Rt. Honble. The Earl of Halifax) To have hold exercise and enjoy the said place together with all Rights Profits Privileges and Advantages thereunto belonging in as full and ample manner as the said Earl of Halifax formerly held or of right ought to have held and enjoyed the same.

Given under my hand and Seal this 2nd day of July 1746 in the Twentieth year of His Majesty's Reign.

GRAFTON.

ENTRED in the Office of Treasurer of His Majesty's Chambers the 10th September 1746.

AN^k FOLLETT, Junr., Dep^{ty}.

Entred in the Office of Wm Aislabie Esqr Aud^r October 31st 1746.

JA^s THOMAS, Dep^{ty} Aud^r.

Entred in the Office of Wm Benson Esqr Aud^r the 26th day of February 1746[-7].

EDW^D BANGHAM, Dep^{ty} Aud^r.*

About this time he was accorded a noble suite of apartments overlooking the bowling green,† in Somerset House, and of

* Copied from the original Warrants, and communicated, by Colonel Adair, Heatherton Hall, Wellington, Salop.

† THESE are to require you to deliver to Ralph Jennison Esqr the Keys and possession of the Lodgings in His Majesty's palace of Somerset House late held by Mr. Jervase. And for so doing this shall be your Warrant.

Given under my hand this 14th Day of November 1747 in the Twenty-first year of His Majesty's Reign.

GRAFTON.

To Mrs. Grovenor (*sic*) Under Housekeeper
of His Majesty's palace Somerset House.

The bowling green at Somerset House had been accessible to the public from course he occupied Swinly Lodge, in Windsor Forest, during the hunting season, where he frequently dispensed, in an ultra-liberal manner, the official hospitality of the Master to the followers of the pack, and occasionally to the King and the Royal Family, whenever the latter honoured him with their presence, before the chase began and after it was over.

We believe (but not quite certain before 1782, when Viscount Hichingbroke undoubtedly obtained the allowance) that all the Masters of the Royal Buckhounds, from the time of Colonel Negus onwards to the time of the Marquess of Cornwallis in 1812, received 300*l.* a year in addition to their established salary to provide "breakfasts" for the followers of the Buck-hounds at Swinly Lodge.* This also reminds us that the Masters occasionally received a supplementary grant of 700*l.* on account of their extraordinary expenses in providing hunters and other necessaries, as, for example, in the subjoined Warrant issued in favour of Mr. Jenison in 1747, and a similar one in 1748-9 :—

GEORGE R.

Ralph Jenison Esqr 700*l.* for Extrā as Master of the Buck-hounds for the year ended Mids^r 1747

{ OUR WILL and pleasure is that By virtue of Our General Letters of privy Seal bearing date the 26th day of June 1727 You issue and pay or cause to be issued and paid out of any Our Treasure or Revenue in the Receipt of Our Exchequer applicable to the uses of Our Civil Government unto Our Trusty and Welbeloved Ralph Jenison Esqr or to his Assignes the sum of Seven hundred pounds without Acco^t : We being graciously pleased to allow the said sum

---

time immemorial. In 1735 the Lord Chamberlain, the Duke of Grafton, gave orders to the Hon. Mrs. Campbell, the then housekeeper, "to permit the neighbours to walk in the garden and to play at bowls on the green there, as in former times." In those days the grounds at Somerset House constituted a charming sylvan retreat, and were greatly appreciated by the citizens.

* It is possible this hospitality grant continued to be received by the successive Masters of the Buckhounds to the time when Swinly Lodge was pulled down in 1824. But it seems the official dog-in-the-manger would have gone mad if this simple point was allowed to be ascertained.

to him in consideration of the Extraordinary Charge he was at in furnishing himself with Horses and other necessary Equipage as Master of Our Buckhounds in and for the Year 1747. And for so doing this shall be Your Warrant. Given at our Court at St. James's the 28th day of October 1747 in the 21st year of Our Reign

By His Majesty's Command
H. PELPHAM.
G. LYTTELTON.
J. CAMPBELL.

To the Comm^{rs} of
Our Treasury.
War^t signed thereupon
29th Octr 1747. Do. Lords.
—*Treasury Records*, K. W. B., vol. xxxvii., pp. 151–537.

At any rate, we know for a positive fact that during this, his second term of office, Mr. Jenison received his stipend yearly from 1746 down to the quarter of a year ended January 5, 1757, at the rate of 2,341*l.* per annum. He retired from this office, which he had filled altogether for seventeen years, on February 5, 1757, and on relinquishing the golden couples was accorded a pension of 2,000*l.* a year, which is the only instance (so far as we are aware) of a pension having been granted to any Master of the Buckhounds under similar circumstances. It does not appear, however, that this retiring allowance, or any part of it, had ever been received by him, his heirs, or executors.

Mr. Jenison was a prominent patron of the turf, and one of the original members of the Jockey Club. He owned and bred some fairly fine horses, amongst which his bony black mare Faustina (foaled in 1725), by Hartley's blind horse out of Blossom—Pulleine's chestnut Arabian—old Vintner mare, won (in those days of little prizes and large sport) a Plate of 40 guineas at Barnard Castle in September 1729, carrying 9 stone, 3 miles; at Morpeth, September 1730, a Plate of 20*l.*, carrying 10 stone, in two heats, beating four others, 4 miles; at Preston, July 1732, a Purse of 40 guineas, 10 stone, 4 miles. At the Hambleton May meeting of this year she beat Mr. Bowe's Othello in a match for 100 guineas, 10 stone each, 4 miles. In the ensuing September she won the Gold Cup at Barnard Castle, 10 stone, 4 miles; at Leeds, May 16, 1733, a Plate of 20*l*., 10 stone, 4 miles—after three heats, in which she beat Mr. Brewster's black mare, Miss Nesham, and the Duke of Hamilton's dun mare. At Durham, on the 9th of July in this year, Faustina and five other horses ran for a Purse of 60 guineas; 10 stone each, 4 miles. The first heat was so near, that three out of the six tryers in the chair gave it in favour of one horse, and three in favour of another. It was, therefore, after some disputing, declared to be a dead heat. Four more heats followed, at the conclusion of which the prize was claimed by the representatives of four of the competing animals. One of these resigning his claim, the others proposed to the stakeholder that if he would pay it to them in conjunction, each would give him his discharge, and they would divide the prize. This proposition was accepted. On the last day of this meeting (July 13) Faustina ran and won a Plate of 50 guineas, 4 miles, 10 stone, by beating the Duke of Bolton's chestnut horse, Sweepstakes, and Mr. Pennyman's black gelding, Thumper, in the two first heats. Mr. Jenison also owned Joseph Andrews, a chestnut horse, foaled in 1743, by Roundhead, out of Hip—Hartley's blind horse—Flying Whig, upon which this Master of the Buckhounds frequently followed the Royal pack. This horse made his first appearance on the racecourse at Lincoln on September 14, 1748, in a Plate of 50*l*., for five-year-old horses which had never won; three 2-mile heats, 11 stone each, and won the race by beating the Duke of Ancaster's Scar, and four others. Joseph Andrews also won a Plate of 50*l*. for six-year-old horses, 4-mile heats, 10 stone, on the following May 2 at Epsom; His Majesty's Plate of 100 guineas, 4-mile heats, 12 stone, at York on July 31; a similar Plate at Lincoln on September 5; and ran second to Lord Portmore's Othello in His Majesty's Plate of 100 guineas in the ensuing October meeting at Newmarket. Shortly before his defeat in the last-mentioned race

Mr. Jenison gave the horse to his nephew, Captain Shafto, by whom he was sold to Messrs. Smith and Luck, in whose names he ran on this occasion.

At Barnet Races, August 5, 1756, Mr. Jenison's grey horse, Second, beat Mr. Adam's chestnut horse, Crispin, in a 50*l*. Plate. The odds at starting were 5 to 1 on Crispin, who won the first heat, " pretty hard run "; but the second and third were won by Second. "They were very fine heats, and the Knowing Ones were taken in again." During this meeting some persons " being arrived there too soon for the Diversion proposed to entertain themselves with a ride to Kirk's-End to pull down the famous Admiral Byng's home there, but a person present, who had great interest therein, persuaded the people, that his house being forfeited to the Government, was designed as a present to General Blakney, which prevented their journey, and fully satisfied the angry Populace for the present."

Mr. Ralph Jenison was the last commoner who filled the office of Master of the Royal Buckhounds. He married on November 10, 1751, Miss Suky Allen, of Durham (of whose family Sir Henry Havelock-Allan, Bart., is the present representative), by whom he had no issue. He had one sister, who was married to Robert Shafto, Esq., of Benwell, county Northumberland. Two of their sons were celebrated sportsmen, proficients in all phases of athletæ, Jenison Shafto having been famous for riding at Newmarket 50 miles in less than 1 hour and 50 minutes. To his great-grandson, Colonel A. W. Adair, of Heatherton Park, Wellington, Somerset, we are indebted for the engraving of his ancestor, Ralph Jenison, Esq., Master of the Royal Buckhounds, from the original picture by Sir Joshua Reynolds, for which that celebrated artist only charged the modest sum of 18 guineas, for the good of his pains: a unique masterpiece (from our point of view), which is now, in all probability, worth eighteen hundred times that money. It is the only portrait of a Master of the Buckhounds we know of in which the Master is represented in the official uniform of the Royal Pack. Here we see Mr. Jenison in his hunting habit as he lived. His coat is green, full skirted, with upright collar, very narrow lace round the cuffs and on the button-holes; gold-braided chevrons embellish the front, sloping on either side. The waistcoat is red, and more deeply laced. This Master is represented in a sitting posture; his bridle hand reclines upon the near side arm of the chair; his whip hand lovingly caresses the neck of a hound, which gazes on his master's face with unspeakable affection. At the moment the Master seems to have partly turned his face, as if in the act of addressing some auditor, "Love me, love my dog"—an adage we would commend to some occasional careless followers of the pack, in the modern language of venery, "'ware, hounds!" The whole *ensemble* of the picture is exquisite in conception and execution, worthy of the magic brush by which it was created; and as a faithful historical relic of the Royal Hunt in the days of George II. it is simply unique.

Mr. Jenison was M.P. for county Northumberland during several sessions of Parliament. In 1737 he had to relinquish his seat, and offer himself for re-election, in consequence of having accepted an office of profit under the Crown—*i.e.*, the Mastership of the Royal Buckhounds— on which occasion he was returned without opposition. He afterwards sat for the borough of Newport, Isle of Wight, which latter constituency he represented in the House of Commons to the time of his death. He died in London May 15, 1758, sincerely regretted by a large circle of friends, more especially by the numerous followers of the Royal Hunt.

GEORGE MONTAGU DUNK, second Earl of Halifax, succeeded Mr. Jenison on the termination of the latter's first term of office, and consequently his lordship became the thirty-ninth Master of the Royal Buckhounds, and was duly installed into that office, pursuant to the annexed Warrant, dated December 31, 1744:—

GEORGE R.

Our Will and Pleasure is, That you forthwith swear and admit, or cause to be sworn and admitted, Our Right Trusty and Right

Welbeloved Cousin, George Earl of Halifax, into the Office and Place of Master of our Buckhounds; To have, hold, and enjoy the same, during Our Pleasure, with all Rights, Fees, Salaries, Profits, Privileges and Advantages thereunto belonging, in as full and ample Manner, to all Intents and Purposes, as Ralph Jenison Esqr, or any other Person has held and enjoyed, or of Right ought to have held and enjoyed the same. And for so doing This shall be your Warrant. Given at Our Court at St. James's the 31st day of Dec^r, 1744, in the Eighteenth Year of our Reign.

To Our R^t Trusty & R^t Entirely Beloved Cousin and Councillor, Charles Duke of Grafton, Our Chamberlain of Our Household.

By His Majesty's Command
HOLLES NEWCASTLE.

—*Home Office Records.* *Warrant Book*, vol. xxiii., p. 372.

Lord Halifax received the same remuneration as his predecessors and successors holding this office during the reign of George II.—viz., 2,341*l.*, out of which sum he had to discharge all the ordinary charges incidental to the pack. His term of office was short and merry, he having resigned on June 25, 1746, when Mr. Jenison, for the second time, donned the official insignia of the pack. His Lordship—eldest son of George Montagu, first Earl of Halifax, by his wife, Lady Mary Lumley, daughter of Richard, Earl of Scarborough — was born on October 6, 1716. He was educated at Eton and Trinity College, Cambridge. On the death of his father, May 9, 1739, he succeeded to the family honours and estates; and was appointed Ranger and Keeper of Bushey Park, and Chief Steward, Keeper, and Lieutenant of Hampton Court. About this time his Lordship was a Lord of the Bedchamber to Frederick, Prince of Wales. On the resignation of his office of Master of the Buckhounds he was appointed Chief Justice in Eyre of all the Royal Forests, Parks, Chases, and Warrens, south of Trent. His Lordship subsequently held several high offices of State, and was Principal Secretary of State for the Northern Department at the time of his death, which occurred on January 22, 1771, when all his honours became extinct.

When Mr. Ralph Jenison relinquished his second term of office, early in the year 1757, LORD BATEMAN was appointed his successor; and in pursuance of the subjoined Warrant his Lordship was ordered to be sworn and admitted to the vacant post. Consequently, he became the fortieth Master of the Royal Buckhounds on July 2, 1757.

GEORGE R.

Our Will and Pleasure is That you forthwith Swear and admit, or cause to be sworn and admitted, Our Right Trusty and Welbeloved Cousin John Viscount Bateman, of Our Kingdom of Ireland, into the Office and Place of Master of Our Buckhounds; To have, hold and enjoy the Same, during Our Pleasure, with all Rights, Fees, Salaries, Profits, Privileges and Advantages thereunto belonging, in as full and ample Manner to all Intents and Purposes as Ralph Jenison Esq' or any Other Person, hath held and enjoyed, or of Right ought to have held and enjoyed the Same. And for so doing This shall be your Warrant. Given at Our Court at Kensington the Second Day of July 1757, in the Thirty First Year of Our Reign.

To Our Right Trusty and Right Entirely Beloved Cousin and Councillor, William, Duke of Devonshire, Our Chamberlain of Our Household.

By His Majesty's Command,
HOLDERNESSE.

—*Home Office Records.* *Warrant Book,* vol. xxvii., p. 392.

The first payment recorded in the Accounts of the Treasurer of the Chamber of the Household to this Master is as follows: "To Ralph Jenison Esq' and John, Lord Bateman successively Master of the Buck Hounds, at 2,341*l*. ℞ annum (for their salaries for three-quarters of a year) from January 5, 1757 to October 10, 1757, 1,755*l*. 15*s*." In the following year Lord Bateman was paid "in lieu of all other charges at 2,341*l*.

a year, for one year ended October 10, 1758, 2,341*l.*" His Lordship received the annual stipend of this post down to the year 1782 (when the office of the Treasurer of the Chamber was abolished by Act of Parliament), when what appears to be the last payment, in that series of official documents, runs as follows: "To William (*sic*) Lord Viscount Bateman and the Earl of Jersey successively Master of the Buck Hounds at 2,341*l.* per annum for three-quarters of a year ended July 5, 1782, 1,755*l.* 15*s.*"

In plodding through these accounts, we find, down to the end of the reign of George II. (1760), that the then Master is designated therein as "John, Lord Bateman"; but in the Account for the first year of the reign of George III. (1761) he is designated "William Viscount Bateman." From this year onward to 1782—when this series of documents terminated by the abolition of the Department—the Master is styled William Viscount Bateman; but whether he altered his Christian name from John to William, or whether the scribe altered it for him, we are not allowed to ascertain. If you please, gentle reader, the official dog-in-the-manger objects to having this momentous STATE SECRET divulged, as to whether the Christian name of the forty-first Master of the Royal Buckhounds, at this time, was John or William. Faugh!

CHAPTER XVII.
GEORGE III. TO VICTORIA.

The History of the Royal Buckhounds stopped by Her Majesty's Ministers.—Official Dog-in-the-Mangerism.—Red Tape.—No more Official Information permitted.—Conjectures and Speculations.—No Official Information of the Buckhounds during the Reigns of George IV., William IV., and Victoria.—The Masters and the Hunt-Servants.—And, "God Save the Queen."—Postscript.

GEORGE II. expired quite unexpectedly on October 25, 1760. The sad intelligence was immediately conveyed to his grandson, George, Prince of Wales, henceforward King George III. And it is a remarkable circumstance—especially in relation to our subject—that just as the young monarch had unknowingly passed over the threshold of the throne, he was proceeding, accompanied by Lord Bute, to a meet of the Royal Harriers in the New Park, Richmond. This good omen in the career of the Royal Hunt during his long and prosperous reign was not belied, as it is notorious the Royal Buckhounds were sustained more efficiently, showed better sport, gave the best average runs, and were better patronised by all classes during this sovereign's reign than had ever previously been known in the annals of the hunt. Yet in full view of this universally admitted fact, how tantalising is the circumstance that during the greater portion of this glorious epoch the official dog-in-the-manger effectually puts an embargo on the voyage of this "harmless historie."

Soon after his accession, George III. renewed and filled up all the patent and other offices of the Household and administrative departments, one of the first appointments being the Earl of Huntingdon as Master of the Horse. Lord Bateman retained the official insignia of the Buckhounds, and was most appropriately re-sworn into that office on the festival of his national saint—March 17, 1761 *—an office which he concurrently retained for a quarter of a century, which we believe to have been a record of unprecedented duration in the Mastership in the latter-day annals of the pack. The Princess Amelia having resigned the office of Ranger of Richmond Park, the Earl of Bute was nominated to succeed Her Royal Highness in that turbulent office. This appointment occasioned a full gale of apprehension, it having been assumed that in consequence of the strong convictions which the King and the Royal Family entertained as to their rights and privileges in that park, Lord Bute's long and trusted services at the Court would naturally lead him to second those views to the prejudice of the public. Nevertheless, the apprehension entertained on this point was promptly and emphatically allayed, for the first act of the new Ranger was to conform to the dictates of the law; and by a stroke of his pen all the objectionable notice-boards and bars were removed for ever, amid the rejoicings of the inhabitants. One result of this policy was the immediate removal of the Royal Fox and Harrier Pack from Richmond—where those hounds had been kennelled at and for some years before his time—to Windsor, where they were located down to the time when they were abolished, pursuant to the provisions of the Act of Parliament of 22 George III., chapter 82, in 1782.

Soon after the accession of George III. the House of Commons granted His Majesty, for the support of his Household and of the honour and dignity of the Crown, a yearly fund of 800,000*l*., out of which the Dowager Princess of Wales was to receive an annuity of 50,000*l*., the Duke of Cumberland 15,000*l*., and the Princess Amelia 12,000*l*., each during their lives respectively. Upon the determination of those annuities the clear yearly sum of 800,000*l*. was to be paid to the King per annum. As this income represented about one and a half million sterling in present currency, there could be no lack of funds to sustain all the departments of the Royal Household in a thorough state of efficiency. Of course we have nothing

* *Home Office Records. Warrant Book*, vol. xxix., p. 99.

to do with the then establishment of the Civil List, except so far as it related to the Royal Buckhounds.

It seems (so far as we can ascertain) that the nominal yearly cost of the Royal Buckhounds from the 1st to the 22nd regnal year of the reign of George III. was 2,341*l.*; but there must have been additional annual expenses for kennels, hound meat, and other incidental charges which we are not allowed to ascertain. However, we may take it generally that the annual cost of the pack from 1761 to 1782, when Lord Bateman went out of office, was about the same as prevailed during the reign of George II. In the latter year, the department of the Treasurer of the Chamber having been abolished, some of the duties of that office were transferred to other departments; that of the Master of the Horse taking over and administrating some functions and discharging certain liabilities incidental to the pack, which had been executed in the office of the Treasurer of the Chamber during the preceding 225 years.

Owing to a fortuitous oversight on the part of a clerk at the Public Record Office, we obtained access to the accounts of the Master of the Horse from 1783 to 1813, the outcome of that mistake having led to the withdrawal of the restrictions which had been previously placed on the official documents of that classification—viz., the Audit Office Records, Declared Accounts (Treasury Series), all of which are now open without reserve to the investigation of historical students down to the year 1821. Thus in the first of these accounts it transpires that the department of the Master of the Horse was saddled in 1783 with certain duties which previously had been executed by the defunct department of the Treasurer of the Chamber; and "according to His Majesty's Establishment, dated the 27th of August, 1783," we obtain the following payments in connection with the Royal Buckhounds for the year 1783, viz.:—

George, Earl of Jersey, and Viscount Hutchingbrook, successively Master of His Majesty's Buck Hounds, at 2,000*l.* ℔' ann., and for an allowance for breakfasts at Swinly Lodge, at 300*l.* ℔' ann., for the same time—2,300*l.*

William Kennedy, huntsman, at 100*l.* ⅌ ann., for the same time —100*l.*

James Johnstone and five other yeomen prickers, at 104*l.* each ⅌ ann. —624*l.*

William Kennedy, huntsman, for the expenses of His Majesty's Buck Hounds, for the same time, by four quarterly abstracts signed by the Master of the Buck Hounds, appears 812*l.* 5*s.* 3*d.*

More to him for sundry disbursements on account of the stables for the same time as by four like abstracts appears—275*l.* 12*s.* 10½*d.*

Richard Harrison, for saddler's work and goods delivered in September 1783—65*l.* 15*s.* 6*d.*

William Kennedy, for carting deer within the time of this account, as by an account thereof signed by the Master of the Buck Hounds—163*l.* 0*s.* 6*d.*

Thomas Cox, Esq., head keeper of Hanniken Lodge, for keeping deer within the time of this account, as by a like account, signed as aforesaid—72*l.* 4*s.* 10*d.*

William Kennedy, for stag fees for one year to Michaelmas 1783, as by a like account signed as aforesaid—129*l.*

It therefore appears from the above several sums that through this Department alone nearly 4,450*l.* had been distributed in the year 1783 on account of the Pack. It is obvious other expenses were incurred and payable through different offices which we are not permitted to investigate, and, what is more important, the details would probably be ascertained. It is, therefore, hardly necessary to give the items as they are recorded in these accounts of the Master of the Horse year by year down to 1813, when this series terminates. From 1784 onward the Master of the Buckhounds received in addition an allowance of 150*l.* a year for horses to mount the yeomen prickers. In this year, also, the huntsman's salary was raised to 125*l.* per annum. David Johnston appear to have succeeded William Kennedy as huntsman in 1785, with a salary of 125*l.* a year. From 1787 onward, what appear to have been the Kennel expenses exhibit an annual increase in maintenance. In 1795 three widows of deceased yeomen prickers received a pension of 20*l.* a year each. In 1797 Martha Grover received 63*l.*, " His Majesty's bounty, in consideration of her being maimed by one of the King's deer." Thomas Lamb, surgeon, in payment of his bill " for cutting Martha Grover of a broken leg," received 24*l.* 16*s.* In 1800 George Gorden and others received an allowance of 152*l.* 10*s.* a year " for attending the King home after hunting." This item appears in the accounts to 1812, but the amount was reduced to 31*l.* 10*s.*

The subjoined is the final account (which we have been permitted to consult) in this series, for the year ended January 5, 1813:—

	£	s.	d.
The Marquis Cornwallis, Master of the Buck Hounds, at 2,000*l.* ℔' ann., for one quarter of a year to the 5th of April, 1812, 500*l.*, and at 1,700*l.* ℔' ann. for three-quarters of a year to the 5th of January, 1813, 1,275*l.* 0*s.* 0*d.* In both	1,775	0	0
More to the same Person, at the rate of 300*l.* ℔' ann., an allowance for Breakfasts at Swinley Lodge for one quarter of a year to the 5th of April, 1812	75	0	0
One Huntsman, at 125*l.* ℔' ann., for a year to the 5th of January, 1813	125	0	0
Six Yeomen Prickers, for salary at 50*l.* ℔' ann. each, necessaries at 8*l.* ℔' ann. each, and for keeping two horses each at 46*l.* ℔' ann. each, for one quarter of a year to the 5th of April, 1812—156*l.* The same Persons at 104*l.* ℔' ann. each, and for keeping two horses each at 25*l.* ℔' ann. each, for three-quarters of a year to the 5th of January, 1813—580*l.* 10*s.* In all	736	10	0
The Marquis Cornwallis, Master of His Majesty's Buck Hounds, an allowance at the rate of 150*l.* ℔' ann. for the Horses of Yeomen Prickers for one quarter of a year to the 5th of April, 1812	37	10	0
Jane Johnstone and Mary Jewell, widdows of Yeomen Prickers, allowance at 20*l.* ℔' ann. each for one year to the 5th of January, 1813—40*l.* ; and Jane Johnstone, Huntsman's widdow, at 30*l.* ℔' ann., for one quarter and forty-three days, to the 5th of January, 1813—10*l.* 16*s.* 5¾*d.* In all	50	16	5¾

	£	s.	d.
Two Feeders, at 57l. 4s' ann. each, for three-quarters of a year to the 5th of January, 1813	85	10	0
In all Hunt Salaries and allowances	2,885	6	5¾
David Johnstone and George Sharpe, successively Huntsmen, for the expenses of His Majesty's Buck Hounds, as by four quarterly abstracts, signed by the Master of the Buck Hounds, appears	2,192	9	11½
More to the said Persons on account of the Hunters' Stables, as by the like abstracts, signed as aforesaid (including 6l. 6s., the net produce of a horse sold, and which forms an article of voluntary charge in this account)	715	1	0
G. Sharpe, Huntsman, expense of taking lame Hounds to Shoreham, signed as aforesaid	75	16	1½
David Johnstone and others, for Carting and feeding deer, as by accounts of particulars signed as aforesaid	441	11	3
David Johnstone and G. Sharpe for Stag-fees, as by certificates signed by the Master of the Buck Hounds	105	0	0
David Pollock, sadler	99	18	5
Edward Addams, bitmaster	12	2	0
Dr. R. Pope, for attending the late David Johnstone, Huntsman, as his Physician, as by Treasury Letters respectively dated 30th November, 1812, and 4th March, 1816, and the receipt of Dr. Pope, appears	22	1	0
Mr. W. Leake, apothecary, for medicines and attending the before mentioned person, as by the same authorities, and the receipt of Mr. Leake, appears	55	12	0
George Gosden and two other Yeomen Prickers, their allowance for protecting the King and the Prince Regent while hunting	31	10	0
In all Hunt-bills and other disbursements	3,751	1	9

Now, as to Masters of the Royal Buckhounds in succession to John, Viscount Bateman, with whom we closed our last chapter, we are compelled to turn from the official information, which has been hitherto derived from the Home Office Records, to imperfect printed ephemerides and cognate calendars, in order to continue the chronicle of the holders of the office down to the present time. Thus we miss all the authentic details given in the Home Office and Treasury Records relating to the Masters, the hunt-servants, the kennels, and the horses,* connected with the pack. Here, at the very outset, the printed ephemerides are at fault, as the Earl of Jersey's name, as Master of the Royal Buckhounds, does not occur in them until the year 1783, whereas he was sworn into the office by the Lord Chamberlain March 29, 1782. In 1784, Viscount Hichingbroke † is first mentioned in the "Royal Kalendar" as Master of the "Royal Hunt," with a salary of 2,300*l.* a year, under whom was one huntsman (W. Kennedy), salary 125*l.*, and six yeomen prickers, who received 129*l.* each per annum. This is likewise inaccurate, as his lordship was sworn into office by the Lord Chamberlain on May 30, 1783; he carried the official insignia of the pack until February 12, 1806, when he was succeeded by the Earl of Albemarle. The Marquis Cornwallis does not appear in the "Kalendar" list until 1808, nevertheless, if we had access to the Home Office Records we should probably find the Warrant of his appointment dated about March 1807—when the Earl of Albemarle resigned; at any rate, the marquis was sworn into office by the Lord Chamberlain on May 13, 1807, as appears by the subjoined certificate :—

Certificate of Appointment of Charles, Marquis Cornwallis.

These are to Certify that in Obedience to His Majesty's Commands I have Sworn and Admitted the Most Noble Charles Marquis Cornwallis into the Office and Place of Master of His Majesty's

---

* On March 11, 1782. George III. commanded the Lords of the Treasury to pay Viscount Bateman the sum of 700*l.* to reimburse him for "the extraordinary charges he was at in furnishing himself with horses and other necessary equipage as Master of our Buckhounds." This annual allowance probably continued to be paid to subsequent Masters; but, of course, it is impossible to say whether or no, in the absence of the Records containing the facts.

† Became Earl of Sandwich on the death of his father, April 30, 1792.

Buckhounds to have hold and enjoy the same during His Majesty's Pleasure with all Rights, Fees, Salaries, Profits, Privileges & Advantages thereunto belonging in as full & ample manner to all Intents & Purposes as William Charles Earl of Albemarle or any other Person hath held & enjoyed or of Right ought to have held and enjoyed the same. Given under my hand and Seal the 13th day of May 1807 In the forty-seventh year of His Majesty's Reign.

DARTMOUTH.*

According to the "Kalendar," his lordship's stipend was 2,000*l.* a year; the huntsman, David Johnson, had 125*l.*; and six yeomen prickers, whose names are not given, were in receipt of 104*l.* each per annum. We believe the marquis carried the golden couples of the Royal pack for seventeen years—from the 47th year of the reign of George III., during the Regency, and into the 4th year of the reign of George IV., and that he died in his hunting harness in August 1823, when he was succeeded by Lord Maryborough (afterwards third Earl of Mornington), who was ordered to be sworn into the office on August 22, 1823, pursuant to the following copy of the Royal sign manual in that behalf:—

GEORGE R.

Our Will and Pleasure is, that you forthwith Swear and Admit, or cause to be sworn and admitted, Our Right Trusty and Welbeloved Councillor William Lord Maryborough, into the Office and Place of Master of Our Buck-Hounds; to have hold and enjoy the same during Our Pleasure, with all Rights, Fees, Salaries, Profits, Privileges and Advantages, thereunto belonging in as full and ample Manner to all Intents and Purposes as Charles Marquis Cornwallis, deceased, or any other Person hath held and enjoyed, or of right ought to have held and enjoyed the same, and for so doing this shall be Your Warrant.

---

* *Lord Chamberlain's Records. Appointments,* 1793–1820, vol. cxciii., p. 104.

Given at our Court at Carlton House the Twenty-Second Day of August 1823 In the Fourth year of Our Reign.

By His Majesty's Command,

ROB. PEEL.

To Our Trusty and Right Entirely
Beloved Cousin and Councillor
James Duke of Montrose, K.G.,
Our Chamberlain of Our House-
hold.

Endorsed.—The oath administered to Lord Maryborough by the Duke of Montrose at the Office, January 13, 1824.
Appointment Book, fo. 62. Not Gazetted.*

If we can trust the "Royal Kalendar," Charles Davis, who was groom to the pack in 1816, and one of the whippers-in from 1817 to 1824, was promoted to the place of huntsman in 1825, and filled the post until 1867, when, we believe, he was succeeded by Mr. Henry King. Lord Maryborough figures as the Master of the Buckhounds in the "Kalendar," from 1824 to 1831, but there is no doubt his tenure of office terminated soon after the death of George IV., as Viscount Anson was ordered to be sworn into the office by William IV. on December 24, 1830, as appears by the subjoined Royal sign manual :—

WILLIAM R.

Our Will and Pleasure is, that you forthwith Swear and admit, or cause to be Sworn and Admitted, Our Right Trusty and Wel-beloved cousin and Councillor Thomas William Viscount Anson, into the Office and Place of Master of Our Buck-hounds; to have hold and enjoy the same during Our Pleasure, with all Rights, Fees, Salaries, Profits, Privileges and Advantages thereunto belonging in as full and ample manner to all Intents and Purposes as William Lord Maryborough, resigned, or any other Person hath held and enjoyed, or of Right ought to have held and enjoyed the same; and for so doing this shall be Your Warrant. Given at Our Court at

---

* *Lord Chamberlain's Records. Sign Manuals for Appointments*, 1804–55, vol. $\frac{78}{125}$, p. 222.

Saint James's the Fourth day of December, 1830, In the First Year of Our Reign.

By His Majesty's Command,
MELBOURNE.

To Our Right Trusty and Right Entirely Beloved Cousin & Councillor William Spencer, Duke of Devonshire, K.G., Our Chamberlain of Our Household.

(*Great seal in red wax. Embossed revenue-stamp for* 1*l.* 10*s. in margin.*)

Endorsed—Sworn by the Duke of Devonshire. Appointment Book, fo. 51. "Not Gazetted." *

On December 29, 1834, George, Earl of Chesterfield, was appointed Master of the Royal Buckhounds, *vice* "Thomas William, Viscount Anson, now Earl of Lichfield." His lordship was gazetted the following day, and sworn into the office by the Lord Chamberlain (the Earl of Jersey) on March 12, 1835; nevertheless his name does not occur in any calendar or ephemeris in his capacity of Master of the Buckhounds. It is absurd to place implicit reliance upon such obviously inaccurate works of reference; yet, in the absence of official data, we know of no other sources of information on the subject. Under these circumstances, it must here suffice to give the successive Masters of the Royal pack as their several names occur in the " Royal Kalendar "—viz., 1836, Earl of Errol; 1841, Lord Kinnard ; 1842, Earl of Rosslyn ; 1847, Earl Granville; 1849, Earl of Bessborough ; 1853, Earl of Rosslyn; 1854, Earl of Bessborough; 1859, Earl of Sandwich ; 1860, Earl of Bessborough ; 1867, Lord Colville of Culross ; 1869, Earl of Cork ; 1875, Earl of Hardwick ; 1881, Earl of Cork; 1885, Marquis of Waterford; 1886, Lord Suffield; 1887, Earl of Coventry. Mr. Francis Goodall, the present † popular huntsman of the pack, is mentioned as having filled the office since 1873.

---

* *Lord Chamberlain's Records. Sign Manuals for Appointments*, 1804-55, vol. $\frac{54}{125}$, No. 26.

† June 1887.

SWINLEY LODGE.
(*From an Engraving in the "Sporting Magazine," 1795.*)

CHAPTER XVIII.

SWINLEY LODGE.

IT is probable that a lodge and kennel had been in Swinley Walk, Windsor Forest, from time immemorial. Nevertheless, the earliest specific mention of Swinley Lodge which we have met with does not date farther back than the reign of James I., and is comprehended (*inter alia*) in John Norden's unique survey of Windsor Forest, made "by order of the King," in the year 1607. At this time Sir Henry Nevill was—like Herne the Hunter—"sometime Keeper there." According to this crude, though carefully coloured and gilded plan, drawn to scale, on a fine membrane of vellum, and spoiled by the binder through whose hands it subsequently passed, the lodge appears to be a small structure with gables at the northern and southern extremities. The front door faces south-west. A small hut (probably a kennel) stands within the enclosure toward the east in the front view of the lodge. These two buildings are enclosed by a railed-in paddock. The outer enclosure was "environeth" on all sides by a rail of high hurdles—as were all the walks in Windsor

Forest at this time. In 1607 Swinley was a red deer walk, containing 100 head, of which 30 were "antlers," 16 "stags," and the rest probably hinds.

We have not noticed any further reference to Swinley Lodge until the reign of Queen Anne. In August 1704, pursuant to commands, the Lord High Treasurer, Sidney Godolphin, signified Her Majesty's wish that the ground "within and without" Swinley Rails, in Windsor Forest, should be levelled, and the rabbits therein exterminated. From the report made thereon by the surveyor, it appears, at this time, that this part of the forest comprised about a thousand acres, and that it would cost about 450l. " to trench the burroughs, which must be at least three foot deep, fill them in again and ram them, to make ye ground fitt & safe for her Majesty's hunting."

On January 31, 1715-6, the Duke of Kent submitted a representation to the Lords of the Treasury, "that for the better preserving the deer in Swinley Walk, a new foddering pen" was absolutely necessary, which he thought ought to be enclosed within the rails, and made so as to shelter the deer from cold, with a loft over the shelter, to place hay in, for the winter's foddering. The Duke adds that there were some small repairs required at the barns, etc., " belonging to the Lodge," which might be done at the same time. His Grace further observes : " Mr. Bret the Ranger at Swinley has represented to me, that he did fodder the Deer there all the last season, at his own expense,"—Mr. Mildmay, late Ranger under the Duke of Northumberland, refusing to provide hay, or to allow any part of the 50l. per annum, appointed for that purpose; "therefore," he adds, " I hope your Lordships will direct the Surveyor of the Woods, to pay to Mr. Bret such part of the preceeding allowance, as you shall think sufficient, to reimburse him for that service." He then appeals to their Lordships to order payment to the under-keepers of their salaries and allowances, which at this time had been two years in arrear, as he was satisfied that " some of those poor men who subsist chiefly by that salary, do at this time want bread for the support of themselves and families."

On the ensuing March 15, the Surveyor submitted an estimate of the probable cost of executing these repairs, which, it was computed, would amount to 108l. 7s. 7$\frac{1}{2}d$. The repairs of Swinley Rails appear to have been executed soon after at a total expenditure of 178*l.* 4*s.*, which amount was derived from wood felled and sold in Windsor Forest.

On March 20, 1716-7, Lord Cobham sent a memorial to the Lords of the Treasury setting forth that the fences round the new planted coppices belonging to the walk called Swinley Rails were so much out of repair that the young wood was in danger of being utterly destroyed, by the deer cropping it, unless it was speedily repaired. "And," he adds, " as that is the only proper place in Windsor fforest to breed & preserve Game for his Majesty's Diversion, I think it fit to acquaint your Lordships that I conceive it necessary for the King's Service that these fences be immediately put in Order, as the only means to preserve the Game ab^t Swinly."

In the following month the Surveyor-General, in obedience to the orders of the late Lords Commissioners of the Treasury, reported that he had viewed the fences round the new planted coppices at Swinley, and found them so ruined and decayed that, unless they were repaired, the deer would prevent the young trees ever becoming a covert for His Majesty's game, and that the probable expense thereon would be 294*l.* The rails, posts, etc., necessary for making the said fences might be procured out of dotard and decayed trees, which might be felled in Windsor Forest, but he feared it would be difficult to raise the money there to defray the charge of workmanship, without some destruction to the forest.

This report was translated into French, and duly submitted to George I., but whether His Majesty ordered the work to be undertaken or not, does not transpire.

On May 4, 1722, 69*l.* 6*s.* 11*d.* was expended on Swinley Lodge. The original estimate was for 231*l.* 4*s.* 8*d.*, but the Treasury disallowed 143*l.* 17*s.* 9*d.* of it " as the necessary repairs only do require," because my Lords thought " it unnecessary to put his Mat^y to the expense of additional buildings at the Lodge for the conveniency of Inhabitants there."

In 1723, the keepers of Swinley Rails and the bailiff of Battles bailiwick collectively received 50*l.* for hay for the deer therein ; and the under-keeper of Swinley was in the enjoyment of an annual salary of 20*l.* The aggregate sum paid this year for the salaries of the officers of Windsor Forest amounts to 537*l.* 9*s.* 11½*d.*

On June 11, 1725, the Surveyor of Woods, in compliance to the order of the Lords of the Treasury, reported that he had carefully surveyed Swinley Lodge and Walk, relative to the "particular works and plantations" which His Majesty had ordered to be made there "for the increase and preservation of the game"; and found that there were many acres of land to be ploughed and sown with different sorts of grain; many hurdles and gates to be made according to the different occasions that may happen to arise; many vermin of different kinds to be destroyed; and many other changes incidental to this service which could not be precisely estimated; therefore he proposed that the Lords of the Treasury should authorise him to defray the necessary cost of the work out of any money that shall be or remain in his hands arising from wood sales or otherwise, and afterwards to lay the bill of particulars before their Lordships, with an estimate of the annual allowance reasonable to be made for the future.

The Lords of the Treasury—viz., Sir Robert Walpole, Sir William Yonge, George Dodington, and William Strickland—by a minute dated May 18, 1726, issued orders that the sum of 1,000*l.* was to be expended on Swinley Lodge and within the Walk called Swinley Walk or Rails, in Windsor Forest, for the purpose of maintaining, preserving, and increasing the game there for the King's "Royal Sport and Diversion." Trees in the Bourn Wood were to be felled and sold to defray this expenditure. The Surveyor-General of Woods was thereupon enjoined to see the work was duly and effectually executed. Without going into full details of the several items, it may be mentioned that the cost for repairs done to the house, outhouses, and ponds was 68*l.* 15*s.* 5*d.* Tilling, sowing, and planting the ground from Lady Day 1725 to Lady Day 1726, 118*l.* 9*s.* 11*d.* Beans to feed the deer, pheasants bought, corn to feed them, husbandry utensils, and traps to kill vermin, 62*l.* 14*s.* 8*d.* Servants' wages to look after the game and feed them for one year, 30*l.* Repairs about the dwelling house, outhouses, barns, granary, and stables, 167*l.* 5*s.* 2*d.* Repairing all the out fences and in fences separating the grounds, with the gates, bridges, and trunks belonging to them, and for making a new deer pen, 185*l.* 15*s.* 1*d.* Four hundred 9 × 7 feet hurdles to be moved as required to protect fresh ground of tillage and covert, 120*l.* And for a plan of the Lodge and the adjacent parts of the Walk, 30*l.*

On April 26, 1727, Colonel Francis Negus presented a memorial to the Lords of the Treasury directing attention to the state of

Swinley Lodge, and submitted that certain repairs were urgently wanted in respect of that place. It seems, however, that, probably in consequence of the death of George I., many contemplated improvements to the Lodge and Swinley Walk dropped, and we hear nothing further of those affairs for some considerable time.

On April 26, 1748, Mr. Robert Nunn was paid 138*l.* 2*s.* for his charges and expenses for feeding and carting stags and red deer, "which were catched and put into pens at Swinley Lodge and Windsor Great Park for the Royal Family to hunt," from March 1745 to December 1747, by virtue of a Certificate by the Earl of Halifax and Ralph Jenison, Esq., the late and present Masters of His Majesty's Buckhounds. On July 4, 1750, he received a further sum of 81*l.* 18*s.* "for catching and carting hinds and stags in Windsor Great Park, and for catching, carting and feeding deer at Swinley and Bagshot Lodges in the years 1748 and 1749 by right of a like Warrant. On July 30, 1760 he received a like sum for taking, feeding and carting deer from Windsor Great Park, Swinley and Bagshot Lodges " and carrying them to several places for the Royal Family to hunt from Midsummer 1759 to Midsummer 1760." These details came out in a casual search, from which we infer that a succinct investigation would show that the charges above mentioned were incurred and defrayed year by year during the reign of George II. It may also be noted here that 35*l.* per annum was allocated to buy turnips to feed the red deer in each of the Walks in Windsor Forest in the winter time.*

From 1774 to 1789 the following sums were expended on the Lodge and Walk—viz., 1774 and 1778, 881*l.*; 1782, 1,049*l.* 16*s.* 11*d.*; 1783, 672*l.* 1*s.* 6*d.* and 253*l.*; 1784, 526*l* 9*s.* 3*d*; 1786, 847*l.* 9*s.* 11*d.*; 1787, 150*l.* 15*s.*; 1788, 509*l.* 4*s.* 6*d.*; 1789, 269*l.* 12*s.* 4*d.*

In the estimate and specifications for necessary repairs required here in 1788 it transpires that the " elm water pipes " which supplied the kennels were out of order, and that it was urgently necessary they should be " repaired and cleaned " at a cost of 22*l.* 18*s.* The pale and fences of the deer paddock at Swinley, the horse paddock, and the adjoining pastures, likewise needed repairing at an estimated cost of 69*l.* 12*s.* 4*d.* Lord Hichingbrooke, Master of the Buckhounds, made pressing representations to the Lords of the Treasury and to the authorities of the Office of Woods and Forests as to the necessity

* *Treasury Records, M.S., P.R.O.*

of attending immediately to these matters. It appears that in the year 1791 one of the walls of the kennel was blown down, whereupon Lord Hichingbrooke suggested that it should be rebuilt in some other situation, "at such distance from the Lodge as to avoid the present noise and inconvenience of that kennel." This recommendation (which seems to have been rather selfish) was evidently ignored, for in the following year 2,000*l.* was expended on a "new bitch and puppy kennel at Swinly." *

In 1801 an estimate for necessary repairs at Swinley Walk amounted to 2,344*l*. 5*s*. 6½*d*. In 1805, 2,232*l*. 16*s*. 7*d*. was expended on repairs of the lodge, fences, pales, etc. In 1808 650*l*. was paid for building and fitting up, adjoining the lodge, a washhouse and laundry, with sleeping rooms over it.

In 1810 Lord Cornwallis directed attention to sundry necessaries that were required at the Lodge, and that "2 chairs and 3 sofa covers were wanted for His Majesty's room." In 1818 this Master of the Buckhounds called attention to the state of the Lodge, particularly the bedrooms, to repair which an estimate was submitted for 237*l*. 6*s*. 2*d*.

In this year the kitchen range of the Lodge was so "out of order" that Lord Hichingbrooke, Master of the Buckhounds, complained to the Lords of the Treasury that he could not cook "any victuals there in consequence." In 1792 the Duke of Gloucester, in his capacity of "Keeper and Lieutenant of H.M. Forest, Parks and Warrens of Windsor," passed the Warrant to pay the keeper of Swinley Lodge his salary at the rate of 50*l*. a year, also 20*l*. for the under-keeper there. There was also a charge of 40*l*. for feeding the deer. In 1794 an estimate was submitted for urgent repairs at the lodge amounting to 669*l*. 15*s*., including an item of 1*l*. 7*s*. 2*d*. for "repairing the cornice of the King's room." In the following year 1,620*l*. 18*s*. 5*d*. was laid out in repairs at the Lodge, the ice house, deer paddocks, kennels, stables, and out offices. In 1799 the interior of the rooms of the lodge having been newly painted and decorated, the Duke of York objected to the walls of the rooms being covered with cheap and nasty paper.

On June 24, 1824, Lord Maryborough received the King's commands to deliver the land held by him, as Master of the

* The kennels (probably the dog pack) were "upon Ascot Heath" prior to 1782.

Buckhounds at Swinley, to the Department of Woods and Forests, but the paddocks in which the deer were kept there were to continue to be occupied as heretofore. It was now proposed to let the land, called Swinley Park, containing 297 acres, 2 roods, and 4 perches, to H.R.H. Prince William Frederick, Duke of Gloucester, at an annual rent of 128*l*.

As to the lodge, it was in such a state as to be no longer habitable, incapable of being repaired unless at a very great and unwarrantable expense, consequently it was decided to pull the whole down, and dispose of the materials to the best advantage. It transpired in this affair that Lord Maryborough's predecessors, as Masters of the Royal Buckhounds, respectively enjoyed, in right of their office, the use of about 230 acres of arable, pasture, and woodland adjoining Swinley Lodge, from which must have been derived considerable advantage (of which Lord Maryborough and his successors would be dispossessed); consequently it was suggested that Lord Maryborough should not be deprived of those advantages if it could be found convenient to provide a suitable habitation for him in the neighbourhood.

About this time the lodge consisted of a ground floor, containing the King's room, parlours, entrance hall, servants' hall, kitchen, and storerooms. Over this were twelve bedrooms, closets, etc. This edifice, with the offices, stables, etc., was sold by auction, in small lots, in 1831, the materials having been estimated at the value of 220*l*.*

---

* *MS. Department of Woods*, etc., 1, Whitehall Place. S.W., by permission of Colonel Sir Nigel Kingscote, K.C.B.

CHRONOLOGICAL INDEX TO THE MASTERS, HUNTSMEN, AND HUNT-SERVANTS OF THE ROYAL BUCKHOUNDS FROM THE REIGN OF KING EDWARD III. TO THE REIGN OF H.I.M. QUEEN VICTORIA.

THE HEREDITARY, OR MANORIAL PACK.

MASTERS.	PAGES
1. Sir Bernard Brocas, 1362 to 1395	13— 14
2. Sir Bernard Brocas, 1395 to 1400	15— 17
Sir Rustin Villenove (Intervenient Master)	17
3. William Brocas, Esq., 1401 to 1456	18— 20
4. William Brocas, Esq., 1457 to 1484	21
5. John Brocas, Esq., 1484 to 1492	21— 22
6. William Brocas, Esq., 1492 to 1506	23
7. John Brocas, Esq., 1508 to 1512	23
8. George Warham, Esq., *jure* Anne Brocas, 1513 to 1514	24
9. Ralph Pexsall, Esq., *jure* Edith Brocas, 1515 to 1518	24— 27
10. Sir Richard Pexsall, 1519 to 1571	80— 81
11. Sir John Savage, 1574 to 1584	82— 86
12. Sir Pexsall Brocas, 1584 to 1630	87— 92
13. Thomas Brocas, Esq., 1630 to 1633	93— 94
14. Sir Lewis Watson, First Baron Rockingham, 1633 to 1652	203—210
15. Edward Watson, Second Baron Rockingham, 1653 to 1689	211—212
16. Lewis Watson, First Earl of Rockingham, 1689 to 1707	213—215

THE HOUSEHOLD, OR PRIVY PACK.

I. George Boleyne, Viscount Rochester, 1528 to 1536	35— 49
II. Sir Richard Long, c. 1537 to 1545	50— 51
III. Thomas, Baron Darcy, K.G., c. 1546 to Jan. 28, 1551	51— 52
IV. John Dudley, Earl of Warwick, April 5 to Nov. 10, 1551	53— 56
V. Sir Robert Dudley, Nov. 11, 1551, c. to Aug. 1553	57— 60
VI. Robert Dudley, Earl of Leicester, May 28, 1572, to Sept. 4, 1588	61— 75
VII. Sir Richard Pexsall,* May 23, 1554, to Nov. 17, 1558	81
VIII. Sir Thomas Tyringham, July 21, 1604, to March 25, 1625	95—118
IX. Sir Timothy Tyrell, March 26, 1625, to May 19, 1633	119—134

* Sir Richard Pexsall was appointed "Custodian or Master" of the Privy Buckhounds by Letters Patent, dated May 23, 1554, but he does not appear to have exercised the duties, or to have received the emoluments, of that office during the reign of Queen Mary.

THE HOUSEHOLD OR PRIVY PACK—continued.

MASTERS. PAGES
X. Sir Thomas Tyringham (ii.), May 20, 1633, to Jan. 1637   129—134
XI. Robert Tyrwhitt, Esq., May 4, 1637, to Jan. 6, 1651   . 134—148
XII. John Cary, Esq., July 7, 1661, Feb. 5, 1685   . . . 149—176
XIII. Colonel James Graham, March 25, 1685, to Sept. 29, 1688   177—183
XIV. James de Gastigny, Esq., Sept. 9, 1689, to c. July 1698   . 184—188
XV. Reinhard Vincent, Baron Van Hompesch, July 6, 1689, to March 8, 1702. . . . . 184—194

THE UNITED PACKS.

XXXII. Sir Charles Shuckburg, June 6, 1703, to Sept. 2, 1705   . 216—227
XXXIII. Walter, Viscount Chetwynd, Oct. 4, 1705, to June 7, 1711   230—232
XXXIV. Sir William Wyndham, June 8, 1711, to June 27, 1712   . 233—235
XXXV. George, Earl of Cardigan, June 28, 1712, to June 11, 1715 . . . . 236—251
XXXVI. Colonel Francis Negus, July 11, 1727, to Sept. 9, 1732   . 268—291
XXXVII. Charles, Earl of Tankerville, June 21, 1733, to June 1736. 292—293 —360
XXXVIII. Ralph Jenison, Esq., July 7, 1737, to Dec. 25, 1744 .   . 317—361
XXXIX. Earl of Halifax, Dec. 31, 1744, to June 25, 1746   .   . 336—368
XL. Ralph Jenison, Esq. (ii.), July 2, 1746, to Feb. 5, 1757   .   361
XLI. Viscount Bateman, July 2, 1757, to July 5, 1782 (?)   . 370—373
XLII. Earl of Jersey, March 29, 1782 to (?) . . . .
XLIII. Viscount Hichingbroke, Earl of Sandwich, May 30, 1783, to (?) . . . .
XLIV. Earl of Albemarle, 1806 or 1807 to (?) 374-379
XLV. Marquis Cornwallis, May 13, 1807, to 1823 (?). . .
XLVI. Lord Maryborough, Earl of Mornington, Aug. 23, 1823, to (?) . . . .
XLVII. Viscount Anson, Earl of Lichfield, Dec. 4, 1830, to (?) .   380
XLVIII. Earl of Chesterfield, Dec. 29, 1834, to (?) . .
XLIX. Earl of Errol, 1836 (?) . . . . .
L. Lord Kinnard, 1841 (?) . . . . .
LI. Earl of Rosslyn, 1842 (?) . . . . .
LII. Earl of Granville, 1847 (?) . . . .
LIII. Earl of Bessborough, 1849 (?) . . . .
LIV. Earl of Rosslyn (ii.), 1853 (?) . . . .
LV. Earl of Bessborough (ii.), 1854 (?) . . .
LVI. Earl of Sandwich, 1859 (?) 381
LVII. Earl of Bessborough (iii.), 1860 (?) . . .
LVIII. Lord Colville of Culross, 1867 . . . .
LIX. Earl of Cork, 1869 . . . . . .
LX. Earl of Hardwick, 1875 . . . . .
LXI. Earl of Cork (ii.), 1881 . . . . .
LXII. Marquis of Waterford, 1885 . . . .
LXIII. Lord Suffield, 1886 . . . . . .
LXIV. Earl of Coventry, 1887 . . . . .
LXV. Lord Ribblesdale, 1892 . . . . .

POSTSCRIPT.

A SERIES of articles, condensed from the subject matter in this work, entitled "The Royal Buckhounds and their Masters," was contributed to and published in *Baily's Monthly Magazine of Sports and Pastimes*, from July 1886 to June 1887. Want of space necessarily excluded all the interesting details relating to the *personnel* and to the maintenance of the Pack which now appear in this volume, from the time when the Royal Buckhounds were instituted in the reign of Edward III. to soon after the accession of George III. Within that period of four hundred years all the official records relating to the subject are open to the public for consultation without reserve. But from the reign of George III. onwards to the present time the official records cannot be consulted without permission of the departments to which the several sets of documents respectively appertain.

In order to continue the subject on the same lines as had hitherto been followed, and to carry it on from the reign of George III. down to date, it became necessary at this chronological epoch to apply to the administrators of the different departments for permission to consult their archives, so far as they might contain information relating to the work in hand. Accordingly, on February 28, 1887, the Compiler wrote to the Secretary of State for the Home Department to inquire if he would accord him (the Compiler) permission to consult the State papers of his department from the year 1760 to (say) 1860, relating to the Royal Buckhounds, which were deposited in the Public Record Office, for the purpose of continuing and bringing this work to a conclusion. In this and a subsequent letter (March 8, 1887), the Compiler referred to the circumstance that when the office of the Treasurer of the Chamber had been abolished, on July 5, 1782, pursuant to the Act of the 22 George III. c. 82, the duties which had been administered by that department (under the Lord Chamberlain) seemed to have been transferred to the Home Office during the interval pending the re-organisation of the Royal Buckhounds under the department of the Master of the Horse.* But, as to what had actually taken place on this point the Compiler is unable to say in the absence of the departmental records which he has not been permitted to consult. At any rate (as shall presently appear), there is no doubt whatever that the Home Office continued to be the channel through which certain official correspondence passed in connection with the Royal Buckhounds down to 1782.

On March 21, 1887, the Secretary of State for the Home Department wrote to the Compiler (B. 1036/3) acquainting him "that the Public Record Office report on enquiry that there is no series of Home Office papers in that department which relate to the Royal Buckhounds."

On March 22, 1887, the Compiler wrote, in reply, to the Secretary of State, asserting that the report he mentioned was false; and, in order to prove that the alleged report was inaccurate, he gave eight specific references taken from the series of Home Office Records known as "Warrant Books" and "Domestick Books" from the time of William III. to George III., and renewed his application for permission to consult the "after date" records of the department for the purpose specified in his application of the 28th ultimo. The reply to that letter is subjoined:—

[*Copy.*]

"WHITEHALL,
"*April* 6, 1887.

"B. 1036/6.

"SIR,

"With reference to previous correspondence, and particularly to your letter of the 22nd ultimo, I am directed by the Secretary of State to acquaint you that the authorities of the Public Record Office positively assure him that there are no such papers in their custody as you suppose relative to the Mastership of the Royal Buckhounds.

"I am, Sir,
"Your obedient Servant,
"(*Signed*) E. LEIGH PEMBERTON.

"J. P. HORE, Esq."

* See p. 374.

Assuming the assertions made in these two letters, dated March 21 and April 6, 1887, of the Secretary of State for the Home Department to be correct, it follows, as a matter of course, that the eight specific references submitted by the Compiler in support of his application of March 22, 1887, must have been fictitious. It would therefore ensue that all the references, and the copies and extracts derived from the Home Office Records relating to the Royal Buckhounds, and inserted in this volume, must have been not only spurious, they must have been concocted by the Compiler with an intention to deliberately mislead. Fortunately all the documents which purport to have been derived from the series of Home Office Records deposited in the Public Record Office, as quoted in this book, from the time of William III. down to 1760, are open to the inspection of any one, consequently the Compiler can safely rely on their verification; and, notwithstanding the allegations of "the Authorities of the Public Record Office" to the Secretary of State for the Home Department, the Compiler had recourse to the only means at his disposal to refute, under the hand and seal of the representative of the Master of the Rolls, the gross calumny which had been imposed on him. His vindication was accomplished by means of what is technically known as "an office copy" of the document contained in the "Home Office Records Warrant Book," vol. xi., page 47, as printed in this volume, p. 231. It was transcribed by the officials at the Public Record Office, and certified correct under the hand and seal of Peter Turner, Esq., an Assistant Keeper of that Department, on April 14, 1887, at a cost of 3s., as appears by receipt of same date, No. 140.* Apart from independent evidence, it is clear that by virtue of this certified copy there must be documents relating to the Royal Buckhounds in the Home Office Records now deposited in the Public Record Office. It is really beyond dispute and evident to every one down to 1760. And if the index volumes are correct, there are also documents in the Home Office series relating to Lord Bateman as Master of the Buckhounds in 1782 and 1783, the reference thereto being thus indicated: "Home Office Records: Warrant Book, vol. xxvi.B, page 205; *Ibid.*, vol. xxvii., page 1." The Compiler having applied

---

* An office or certified copy of any official document is, under the Judicature Acts, received as irrefutable evidence in the courts of law. If we were obliged to obtain certified copies of all the original records used in this work it would probably entail an expenditure of 6,000l. or 7,000l.

for certified copies of the two last-mentioned entries, was informed, on April 19, 1887, that it was not the practice of the Record Office to supply certified copies of any portions of index or catalogue of documents preserved there except when the Records themselves are wanting.

On May 7, 1887, the Compiler wrote to the Secretary of State, Home Department, Whitehall, directing his attention to the certified copy of the document contained in the "Home Office Records: Warrant Book," vol. xi., p. 47, and the communication of April 19 from the Record Office, pointing out that the latter was tantamount to an admission that the documents referred to were in the custody of that department notwithstanding the report to the contrary, as alleged in the letter of the Secretary of State to the Compiler of the 6th ultimo (B. 1036/6). Both of those original papers were enclosed on that occasion; and on the strength of that evidence the Compiler again reiterated his application for the usual "permit," as he was much pressed for time, and requested, in a postscript, that the enclosures should be returned to him.

On the ensuing June 13 the Compiler finally wrote to the Secretary of State, Home Department, Whitehall, requesting attention to his (the Compiler's) letter of the 7th inst., and the favour of a reply at his earliest convenience, and that the Secretary of State would be good enough to return the enclosures contained therein. That letter was registered by the Compiler, who holds the receipt given by the Post Office for its safe delivery. No acknowledgment or answer has yet been received by the Compiler to that letter, nor have the enclosures been returned to him.

Such are the pleasures incidental to original historical researches, particularly in the "after date" period. Fortunately the Compiler can stand aside. The imputation on his veracity is untenable. But it is a public duty that this singular incident should be cleared up. It rests between the two Public Departments to decide which is the ———. If the Record Office reported to the Home Office that no such documents as those in question are in their custody, the certified copy, e.g., supplied to the Compiler must have been spurious, and consequently he was defrauded of the fees demanded and paid thereon. He knows, as a matter of fact, that such a contingency, under the circumstances, cannot be entertained. Likewise he knows nothing of the report alleged to be made by the Record Office to the Home Office. That document is too interesting to remain buried in obscurity. It must be exhumed, and before its translation to a worthy sepulchre we shall see what we shall see.

As to the Treasury Records relating to the affairs of the Royal Buckhounds from the reign of George III. onward to the present time, the Lords Commissioners of that department graciously permitted the Compiler to consult their archives down to the year 1793, but in reply to his application, dated April 2, 1887, their Lordships were not prepared to extend the permission which they had already granted to him. In so doing that department was quite within their rights, but at the same time there is certain information preserved in those papers which cannot be obtained from any other source. Take, for instance, the subjects which transpire in the subjoined note,* and then draw an inference of

---

* Danl Parker Esqr resp^g ⎰S^r,
a letter from Lord ⎱ Upon reading to the Lords Comm^{rs} of His Maj'ty's
Hichingbrook Master of ⎰ Try., a letter from Lord Hichingbroke Master of the
the Buck Hounds. ⎱ Buck Hounds stating that he is of opinion that it may
be proper to make an Addition of £25 ℔ Añn. to the salary of Willm Kennedy
the Master Huntsman, and that the additional allowance of £25 ℔ Añn., which
their Lordships have directed to be made to each of the Six Yeomen Prickers of his
Majesty's Hunt, should be paid into the Hands of the Master of the Buck Hounds
to be by him paid to such Yeomen Prickers who are in possession of two horses
fit to do the duty; I am commanded by their Lordships to desire that you will
move the Duke of Montagu to insert on the Establishment of the Master of the
Horse the sum of £25 ℔ Añn. to the Master Huntsman to commence from the
5th Ap^l 1783. And I am further commanded to desire that you will move His
Grace to insert on the said Establishment the Sum of £150 ℔ Añn. to the
Master of the Buck Hounds (in addition to his former Allowances), to commence
from the said 5th Ap^l 1783, to be by him applied for the purposes aforesaid, in
lieu of the additional allowance of £25 ℔ Añn. directed to be made to the Six
Yeomen Prickers from the 10th Octr 1783, by Mr. Sheridan's letter of the
3rd December last.

I am, &c., 12th May 1784,
GEORGE ROSE.

—*Vide Treasury Records: Letter Book*, $\frac{\text{Feb.}}{\text{Nov.}}$ 1784, vol. xxx., p. 205.

similar information relating to the pack, which no doubt run on on a similar line throughout the whole series, and are presumably embodied in the annual accounts of the Master of the Horse. And if we are deprived of the foundation, how is it possible to compile the super-structure? It is simply impossible to do justice to this subject except one has access to all the records of the different departments relating to the official annals of the Pack.

The interesting archives of the Lord Chamberlain's Department, which are deposited in the Public Record Office, having been placed, without reserve, at the perusal of the Compiler for purpose of this work, he takes this opportunity to again acknowledge, with thanks, the favour accorded to him by the Lord Chamberlain, per the Hon. Sir S. Ponsonby Fane, and for which he is very much obliged.

The Compiler has likewise to return his best thanks to Colonel Sir Nigel Kingscote, for allowing him to consult the official papers and plans which are preserved in the Department of Woods, etc., relating to the History of the Royal Buckhounds.

With reference to the agitation instigated last year under the auspices of the now defunct "Humanitarian League" on the subject of alleged cruelty perpetrated by and incidental to the Royal Buckhounds hunting "tame deer," it will be sufficient here merely to mention that not one of those allegations has been substantiated or proved in point of fact. On the other hand we have the evidence of Mr. Tattersall as a follower of the Royal Hunt going back to some fifty years, and the tradition of his family for three generations, to prove, beyond controversion, that no such "cruelty" was known to have occurred in those days. And Mr. Bowen May, the *doyen* of the Pack—a gentleman of irreproachable veracity, who has actually hunted with the Royal Buckhounds for sixty consecutive seasons—solemnly asserts in the public press that he had never seen a single instance of cruelty to stag or hind in the hunting field. As the positive statements of these gentlemen, and of other followers of the Pack, have not been challenged or contradicted, the unsubstantiated allegations of the late Humanitarian Leaguers (who probably could not tell a hound from a hunter) necessarily fall to the ground—let us hope, to rise no more. There is no doubt, however, that in former times it was customary to "hunt and kill" the quarry, an obsolete custom which was induced in order to blood the hounds and to entitle the Hunt servants to certain fees or (in lieu of fees) to certain joints of venison for pot and pasty: the latter varying and passing from time to time through curious chops and changes according to the local custom observed at the time being in the several forests, until this custom was eventually abolished. Yet, even in those days, that now obsolete custom was by no means the general rule, as we have frequent incidents showing that when the hunted stag or hind had given good runs of forty or fifty miles the hounds were stopped and the quarry "taken," by royal will and favour, to hunt another day, or was accorded a silver collar, and was never to be hunted again. It is probably a true tradition that the custom of killing the quarry terminated in "the Bishop's * year"; and that from about that season to the present time the stag or hind was "taken" instead of being killed. If we had access to the certificates of the Masters of the Buckhounds this reform would be, in all probability, proved on official authority. Thus the protest of the Humanitarians, even if it were *bond fide*, has been made a century too late. In our opinion the only persons who have any *locus standi* or right to object to the continuance of the Royal Buckhounds are the farmers and land-owners over whose "country" the Pack hunts; and they are, to a man, in favour of the hunt.

There are nevertheless certain faddists, who, in attacking stag-hunting in general, and the Royal Buckhounds in particular, on the plea of cruelty to animals, know that if they were successful in this

* We believe it was in 1783-4 that the Bishop of Osnaburg hunted five days a week during that season. The Buckhounds used to meet on Tuesdays and Saturdays, and the Harriers on Mondays and Thursdays. The alternate Wednesdays and Fridays were bye-days with both packs. It is said the Bishop stipulated that the stag or hind was to be "taken" and not killed. This having received the approbation of the King and the Prince of Wales, the Hunt servants were forbidden, for the future, to allow the hounds to pull down, worry, or kill the quarry. Prince Frederick (second son of George III.) was by his father nominated Bishop of Osnaburg in 1765, when His Royal Highness was in the second year of his age, and was created Duke of York and Albany in November 1784. In 1785 he went to Osnaburg and remained in Hanover for some years. By the Treaty of Westphalia, in 1648, it was agreed that every alternative Bishop of Osnaburg should be a Catholic and a Lutheran: the former to be elected by the Chapter; the latter (usually a young Prince) to be nominated by the head of the House of Hanover.

respect it would become impossible to defend all other branches of the chase and many of our manly rural sports. If stag-hunting is stopped there must be an end to fox, hare, and otter-hunting. There would be no more coursing. Instead of shooting we must stalk grouse, partridge, and pheasant with a pinch of salt, and, by simply sprinkling it on the tail of the bird, thus "grass" it without the aid of "villainous saltpetre." Hunters and hacks would soon become extinct animals. The multifarious benefits which hunting confers on the British farmer would cease; and the enormous sum of money now circulated at home on our national sports and pastimes would be diverted into other channels, to the utter loss of Her Majesty's liege subjects. When asked what alternative or substitute he would apply in the event of hunting and shooting being "utterly suppressed, abolished, and taken away," by Act of Parliament, the faddist replied, "Lawn Tennis and Croquet!" Fancy Lawn Tennis and Croquet in a wintry southerly wind and a cloudy sky, with the going fetlock-deep, and the players attired in waterproof garments! That answer is characteristic of the faddist, as he must have been ignorant of the rudiments of his own alternative exercise; nevertheless he has the audacity to bring unfounded charges against the followers of the Royal Buckhounds, concerning whom his theoretical and practical knowledge is absolutely *nil*! Fortunately the future of stag-hunting was never so promising as at the present time. It is extending, obtaining new adherents, and attracting votaries in every part of the civilised globe. And, even if the Royal Buckhounds were to be suppressed—as an adjunct associated for successive centuries with the "honour and dignity" of the Throne—to please the faddist, it is probable that atrabilarious individual would not be satisfied until he suppressed every institution of the State, and finally abrogated every institution of the Crown and Constitution.

Before concluding this Postscript, the compiler must openly confess to a sin of omission for neglecting to carry on the annals of Ascot Races down to the period when the Plates which had been run for by the followers of the Royal Buckhounds and by the Hunt servants dropped out of the programme. As we have seen, this truly national race meeting was instituted in 1711, chiefly for the purpose of celebrating these two Plates, in connection with the Royal Hunt, as an exhibition of speed and stamina by the horses, and a display of jockeyship by the riders, who had been in the first flight, during each successive season, with the Royal Buckhounds in the hunting field. The early history of this race meeting is, therefore, closely affiliated with our leading subject, and we believe our compilation of those races during the pre-calendar period will be found novel and interesting. After 1760 the results of the sport at Ascot come out year by year in Weatherby's *Racing Calendar*, from which it appears that the last Plate run for there by the Royal Hunt servants took place in 1784, and the Plate for hunters belonging to the followers of the Pack who had taken "tickets" in that season, was run for the last time in 1817. And it is a singular circumstance that in April 1817, by the award of the Commissioners, and in compliance with the directions of the Acts of Parliament,* "the Race-Course at Ascot Heath, and the proper avenues thereto," were directed "to be kept and continued as a race-course for the public use at all times, as it had usually been." It therefore appears that Ascot has the honour to be the only racecourse in this country which is dedicated to the public for ever by Act of Parliament. "The Royal Hunt Cup" perpetuates the old association of the race meeting with the Buckhounds, and we pray it may continue so "for ever and a day."

The liberal patronage conferred on the meeting by the Royal Family and the Public, in the opinion of the Compiler, is not sufficiently appreciated by the executive. The "management," in view of modern requirements, is defective in almost every detail. Take, for instance, the last reunion: the old popular fee for admission to the public stand was doubled. At the extremity of this stand, what appears to be a huge gasometer has been erected, effectually obstructing the view of the races run on the T. Y. C. and the Straight Mile courses. Except to the fortunate few in the immediate front row, nothing can be seen of the finish of the races run on the Cup and other courses, from the bend in, particularly when the horses incline to the near side. The parentage of the two-year-old colts and fillies (many of which are maidens) should be inserted and it is desirable that the colours of the jockeys should be given correctly on the card. With a proper public stand, " replete with all modern improvements," popular prices, and an efficient C. C., there is no reason why the surplus revenue of the Ascot Race Meeting might not be allocated

---

* See Statutes 53 George III., c. 158—55 George III., c. 122—56 George III. c. 132. Also, 2, 3, and 4, Reports of the Commissioners of Woods, etc., March 1816 and June 1819; and the Award of the Commissioners, April 1817.

to the support of the Royal Buckhounds without entailing any charge on the Civil List.

On the plea of "put yourself in his place," the Compiler craves indulgence for the minor blemishes that meet the eye of the critical reader. As to the major blemish, incidental to every unfinished work, that, in this case, is beyond the Compiler's control. "Finis Coronat Opus." Exactly. And if the end crowns the work, it behoves the Ministers of the Crown to explain why this work was not allowed to be brought to an end.

J. P. HORE,

22, DALBERG ROAD, BRIXTON, S.W.,
June 1893.

FINIS. NON FINIS.

Printed by Hazell, Watson, & Viney, Ld., London and Aylesbury.

www.ingramcontent.com/pod-product-compliance
Lightning Source LLC
Chambersburg PA
CBHW030602300426
44111CB00009B/1072